D1154740

APPROPRIATING THE
LONERGAN IDEA

Frederick E. Crowe, S.J.

APPROPRIATING THE LONERGAN IDEA

Edited by Michael Vertin

The Catholic University of America Press
Washington, D.C.

Copyright © 1989 Frederick E. Crowe

All rights reserved

Library of Congress Cataloging-in-Publication Data
Crowe, Frederick E.
  Appropriating the Lonergan idea.

  Bibliography: p.
  Includes index.
  1. Lonergan, Bernard J. F.   2. Theology.
  I. Vertin, Michael, 1939–   .   II. Title.
  BX4705.L7133C76   1989   230'.2'0924   87-33855
  ISBN 0-8132-0668-5

Contents

Editor's Introduction

Frederick Ernest Crowe was born on 5 July 1915 in Jeffries Corner, a hamlet in the eastern Canadian province of New Brunswick, third of the six children of Jeremiah and Margaret Crowe. He received his primary education in the local one-room schoolhouse; he attended high school in nearby Sussex, New Brunswick; and he spent a good many of his after-school hours measuring out sugar and flour, wrapping packages, and listening intently to stories in the general store that was run by his parents. At the end of high school he did extremely well in the province-wide exams—so well, in fact, that he received a Beaverbrook scholarship to the University of New Brunswick. He spent his college years in the study of electrical engineering and graduated with a Bachelor of Science degree in 1934, at the advanced age of eighteen.

In the months following graduation, two things conspired to move the young Fred Crowe toward a crucial, life-shaping decision: his efforts to find a job in the engineering field proved unsuccessful; and he found himself again hearing a call that he had originally experienced in his early teens, a call to the religious life. Thus in 1936 he joined the Upper Canada Province of the Society of Jesus. For the next seventeen years his life was to follow the lines of the standard Jesuit order of studies. He spent four years in the Jesuit novitiate and juniorate at Guelph, Ontario, three years studying philosophy at Christ the King Seminary in Toronto, three years teaching languages, physics, and philosophy in Halifax, four years studying theology in Toronto—during which time he was ordained to the priesthood—and, after a year of tertianship in Connecticut, another two years in advanced theological studies in Rome. And it was during his philosophy studies that he first met the teacher and confrere, eleven years his senior, who was to join Thomas Aquinas, Ignatius of Loyola, and John Henry Newman as major influences on his adult life and work: Bernard Lonergan.

In 1953 Crowe successfully defended his doctoral dissertation, *Conflict and Unification in Man: The Data in the Writings of St. Thomas Aquinas*. Returning to Toronto, he was assigned to Christ the King Seminary— subsequently Regis College—as a professor of theology. He carried out that assignment with high distinction for the next twenty-seven years, also accepting a variety of pastoral and administrative jobs along the way. Professor Emeritus since 1980, he has continued—and, indeed, intensified—his research and writing; and he serves at present as Director of the Lonergan Research Institute of Regis College.

The scholarly reputation Fr. Crowe has built during the past thirty-five years rests upon two different kinds of work. First, there is the enormous labor that has gone into fostering study of the work of Bernard Lonergan: authoring numerous expositions of Lonergan's ideas and reconstructions of his intellectual biography; conducting several courses and overseeing many dissertations and group research projects on Lonergan; collecting and cataloging all of Lonergan's manifold writings and editing many of them for publication or republication, an effort presently culminating in the editing (with Robert Doran) of the twenty-two volume *Collected Works*; establishing the Lonergan Research Institute of Regis College, and guiding other Lonergan study centers in places so diverse as Melbourne and Dublin, Naples and Montreal, Boston and Manila, Sydney and Santa Clara and Rome. In addition to this, however, Crowe has shown himself to be an eminently erudite, highly creative, and remarkably balanced theologian in his own right. His more than one hundred publications include a number of detailed and penetrating studies of Aquinas; he has done truly groundbreaking work on the development of doctrine, the human psychology of Jesus, and the missions of the Trinity; and in recent years he has elaborated a rich, nuanced, and timely account of the actual process of individual and ecclesial learning. Although, with typical modesty, he is wont to dismiss his own writings as "merely highlighting and embroidering ideas of Lonergan," his professional colleagues have judged otherwise: he has received four honorary doctorates, and in 1977 he was honored with the John Courtney Murray Award for outstanding theological scholarship by the Catholic Theological Society of America.

The relative unavailability of many of Crowe's writings, excellent though they are, was the immediate occasion of the present volume. Thus far a good number of his published essays have appeared only in small journals, conference proceedings, and *Festschriften* or other small-run books. His aforementioned modesty has made him slow to seek a wider audience for them; but this has meant that only with great difficulty are they accessible to many of the students, teachers, and other scholars already eager to read more of Crowe on Lonergan or other topics, let alone the still broader group of readers not yet familiar with Crowe who might benefit from making his acquaintance. Aware of this difficulty from my own experience as a graduate student and later as a teacher, I thought of an obvious remedy; and after refining the idea through consultation with colleagues at several schools, I approached

Fr. Crowe for permission to assemble and publish a collection of his most important essays. After only a few moments of being entreated, he agreed; and this volume is the result.

The title of the volume, *Appropriating the Lonergan Idea,* is intended to suggest two different processes, each with two complementary moments. First, it is meant to suggest the process in which Crowe himself "makes his own" the set of claims distinctive of Lonergan's work. In one moment of the process, Crowe is *exploring* that set of claims by carefully investigating various aspects of its meaning and evolution in Lonergan's own writings. This moment is represented by the nine essays (chapters 1–9) that constitute the first main part of the book, essays treating Lonergan's academic formation and the first part of his scholarly career, the main features of his work on cognitional structure, his emerging notion of value, the evolution of his notion of God, some similarities between his work and that of the liberation theologians, the underlying pastoral orientation of all his scholarly efforts, and the requirements and challenges of coming to grips with his writings.

In another moment of his process of appropriation, Crowe is *expanding* the set of distinctive Lonerganian claims by creatively developing and applying it in his own scholarly endeavors. This moment is represented by the thirteen essays (chapters 10–22) that constitute the second main part of the book, essays dealing with the dynamic of ecclesial learning, the conservative and creative dimensions of the theological task, certain ontological, psychological, and cultural features of Jesus' humanity, the missions of the Trinity, some recurrent factors in human and Christian development, and a framework for thinking about the life of the unborn.

Besides alluding to Crowe's activities, however, the title of this book is meant to suggest the twofold process in which you, the reader, could come to "make your own" the claims that are characteristic of the Lonergan enterprise. That is to say, it is intended to raise the possibility of your own engagement in *exploring* those claims by carefully investigating what Crowe writes here (and, at some point, what Lonergan himself writes, as Crowe recommends—see his preface below); and even in *expanding* them by creatively developing and applying them in your own particular work, whatever it may be.

There are several further things I should point out about the volume's contents. The essays included here were selected on the basis of their individual importance, collective diversity, and relative unavailability; and their order within each of the book's two main parts is roughly chronological. Fr. Crowe's homily at Fr. Lonergan's funeral is included both because of its intrinsic importance and because it seemed that it would be a fitting epilogue. Save for occasional minor changes, and prescinding from chapter 21 (which appears for the first time here), the text of each selection unless otherwise indicated appears as it did in the original; and thus you should be prepared to make appropriate adjustments, especially in matters of temporal perspective. The notes are likewise as they appeared originally, except in two respects: citations of Lonergan's writings refer to them in their most recently published form; and notes are sometimes added or expanded in order to draw attention to some subsequent development in Lonergan or in Crowe on Lonergan, or to highlight certain relations among the essays of this volume itself. Save for four quotations (including the two from the Hebrew scriptures) in chapter 3, for which the *Chicago Bible* was used, all scriptural quotations are from the *New English Bible*. Finally, the comprehensive list of the author's writings will serve as a handy guide for anyone wishing to study more of Crowe.

I wish to thank the following for permission to reprint material that previously appeared in the form indicated by the respective introductory notes to each chapter: the trustees of the Lonergan estate, for chapter 1; the editor of *Science et esprit*, for chapters 2, 4, 13, 14, 15, and 17; the editor of *Philippine Studies*, for chapter 3; the editor of *Lonergan Workshop*, for chapters 4, 13, 17, 20, and 22; the editor of *Ultimate Reality and Meaning*, for chapters 5 and 6; the editor of *Gregorianum*, for chapter 8; the editor of *The Maroon and White*, for chapter 10; the editor of *The Villanova University Theology Institute Proceedings*, for chapter 12; the Manila Lonergan Center, for chapter 7; the State University of New York Press, for chapter 9; the Fordham University Press, for chapter 11; Campion College, for chapter 16; and Joseph Armenti, for chapter 18.

For helpful advice regarding the conception of this volume and timely encouragement regarding its merit, I would like to express my appreciation to Walter Conn, Robert Doran, Charles Hefling, Matthew Lamb, Jean-Marc Laporte, Fred Lawrence, Philip McShane, and Margaret O'Gara; and for astute and effective help in actually getting it under way, my special thanks to Doran and Laporte.

My final remark regards the volume's author. By his judicious suggestions and his generous assistance to me on this project, Fr. Crowe greatly reduced the magnitude of my editorial task. Far more broadly, in both his writing and his living he has long constituted for me an inspiring model of wonderfully integrated scholarly excellence, personal goodness, and Christian zeal. For the latter gift, as for the former, I am profoundly grateful to him.

St. Michael's College   MICHAEL VERTIN
University of Toronto
31 July 1987

Preface

Readers of this volume should be told at once that it is a collection of various papers written over a period of thirty years. If the editor and the publisher judge that the contents are nevertheless unified enough to make a book, their reason is possibly discernible in their happy choice of a title; for all the book's essays center on the work of Bernard Lonergan, either to interpret his ideas, or to try to develop and apply them in particular areas.

The essays are a selection from my writings, which are in turn only part of the work I have done on Lonergan since I began to study him forty years ago. That is a way of stating that these four hundred pages do not say all I want to say, so one may wonder what I can hope to add in a two-page preface. At least I can try to locate my work in the wider context of Lonergan studies and of what is being called the Lonergan movement.

This century, by and large, has not known what to do with Lonergan. He appeared on the academic scene in the 1940s with his Thomist studies, but Thomists had trouble coping with interpretations of their master that deviated so widely from the tradition. He was catapulted onto a larger stage in the 1950s with his *Insight*, a book that looked like a philosophy but studied a mental activity that many philosophers judged nonexistent. After some delay his *Method in Theology* finally arrived in the 1970s, and it was the theologians' turn to be puzzled: here was a book whose title included the word "theology" but whose contents showed hardly any theology at all. Still, the works produced were in every case too formidable to be totally ignored—monumental was a favorite term of description; so people tended to walk around them as they do around monuments, keeping generally a respectful distance, referring cautiously to this idea or that, but by and large leaving Lonergan alone.

For some of us that cautious approach is impossible. We have been stirred by a profundity we have dimly glimpsed in Lonergan's work; we have a sense of an enormous potential to be developed. We cannot leave it alone. That does not mean, however, that we know what to do with him either. The history of the Lonergan movement, now that its lines have emerged after some decades, is seen to be less that of a steadily unfolding system than that of a twofold to-and-fro movement. One of these is the more familiar to-and-fro of the hermeneutic circle: the details of Lonergan's thought cannot be understood without a clear grasp of the whole, and it is impossible to grasp the whole without an accurate idea of the details. The other is the to-and-fro of mastering an organon and applying it: the depth and power of a principle are discovered in its application, but the effort to apply it sends us back to the source with new questions on its meaning.

That makes for essays that approximate to three types: the two general types of exploring and expanding-applying (I borrow some terms from the Lonergan Workshop of Boston College), with the former subdividing into general and special studies. All three will be found here in more or less typical form. If I may express an opinion on the relative value of my own contributions, I would give a certain priority to the special studies I have made of Lonergan's own ideas. Applications of his thought have to suppose a general knowledge which may be lacking: in any case they are legion, and none of them will appeal to all readers. General studies themselves necessarily use general terms which reveal little of the author's understanding and may contribute as little to that of the reader. But I hope that my studies of detail will illustrate, in a few samples out of the hundreds waiting to be done, the range and versatility of Lonergan's thought, and perhaps provide a manageable access through particular questions to a worthwhile overview.

It is the fate of all thinkers who are ahead of their time to be misunderstood by their readers and inadequately presented by their students. There is no immediate way for us who try to present Lonergan to avoid doing him this injury, but there is an immediate way for the reader to avoid the consequences of our inadequate presentation: to go to the original. May that be the means taken by any readers I have.

Let me end with a word of thanks and one of apology: of thanks to Prof. Michael Vertin for the labor and care he has devoted to the tedious task of editing this volume (personal experience makes me an authority on the tedium of editorial tasks); and of apology to the female half of our race—it was only around 1984 that I abandoned the pretense that God and the whole human race were male, so only a few of these essays reflect the change that decision necessitated in my writing style.

Lonergan Research Institute
of Regis College
Toronto School of Theology
1 June 1987

FREDERICK E. CROWE, S.J.

Abbreviated Titles of Certain Works of Bernard Lonergan

The footnotes to the essays in this volume make frequent reference to certain works of Bernard Lonergan. In any given essay, the first reference to one of these works gives the full title (and page numbers) but no additional information, and subsequent references give just an abbreviated title (and page numbers). The standardized abbreviations, together with complete bibliographical information on each of the works, are as follows:

Insight	*Insight: A Study of Human Understanding.* London: Longmans, Green; New York: Philosophical Library, 1957. 2nd ed., 1958. 3rd ed., 1970. 4th ed., San Francisco: Harper & Row, 1978. (The pagination remains the same for all the editions, except that in the 4th edition the pagination of the preface is changed from ix–xv to x–xvi but with no corresponding change in the index.)
Verbum	*Verbum: Word and Idea in Aquinas,* ed. D. B. Burrell. Notre Dame: University of Notre Dame, 1967.
Collection	*Collection: Papers by Bernard Lonergan, S.J.,* ed. F. E. Crowe. New York: Herder and Herder; London: Darton, Longman & Todd, 1967.
Grace and Freedom	*Grace and Freedom: Operative Grace in the Thought of St. Thomas Aquinas,* ed. J. P. Burns. London: Darton, Longman & Todd; New York: Herder and Herder, 1971.
Method	*Method in Theology.* London: Darton, Longman & Todd; New York: Herder and Herder, 1972.
Philosophy of God	*Philosophy of God, and Theology: The Relationship between Philosophy of God and the Functional Speciality, Systematics.* London: Darton, Longman & Todd, 1973.
Second Collection	*A Second Collection: Papers by Bernard J. F. Lonergan, S.J.,* ed. W. F. J. Ryan & B. J. Tyrrell. London: Darton, Longman & Todd; Philadelphia: Westminster, 1974.

Understanding and Being — *Understanding and Being: An Introduction and Companion to "Insight,"* ed. E. A. Morelli & M. D. Morelli. New York and Toronto: Edwin Mellen, 1980.

Third Collection — *A Third Collection: Papers by Bernard J. F. Lonergan, S.J.,* ed. F. E. Crowe. New York: Paulist Press; London: Geoffrey Chapman, 1985.

I

EXPLORING

I

The Growing Idea*

The formation of the young Lonergan from his birth at Buckingham, Quebec, on 17 December 1904, to the end of his sophomore year at Loyola College, Montreal, was probably not significantly different from that of thousands of other Canadian boys of his time. But in the summer of 1922 he entered the Jesuit Novitiate at Guelph, Ontario, and began to encounter more distinctive influences. His two years of ascetical training finished, he returned to his interrupted study of the classics in an atmosphere of somewhat more concentrated attention than would be normal in a secular college. It was a particular piece of good fortune to have as professor then the late J. I. Bergin, a Latinist of quite outstanding ability, whose influence is to be seen forty years later in the mature Latin style of his pupil's *De deo trino*. In 1926, Lonergan went from Guelph to Heythrop College, Oxfordshire, for three years of scholastic philosophy, to which a year was added for a degree at the University of London. The thousand-year tradition of the "English way" made an immediate appeal in its own hardly definable fashion. Academically, the result might be symbolized by the very title "general degree," which the University of London granted him (the last year, incidentally, the degree was issued), and by the courses he took there: Latin, Greek, French, and mathematics. More impalpably it appears in such little details as his affection for Lewis Carroll and Gilbert Keith Chesterton, or, more generally, in a whole way of living and thinking and doing. But if, as he later asserted, this period was the setting for a decisive commitment to the intellectual life, the reason does not seem to lie in the standards which prevailed rather generally in the Heythrop philosophy courses of the time. He does speak with deep gratitude of the tutoring he received in mathematics from Fr. Charles O'Hara, a man who "understood" (high praise, this, from Lonergan!) what mathematics was about. And then there was Newman,

---

*Previously published as pp. viii–xix of "Introduction," in *Collection: Papers by Bernard Lonergan, S.J.*, ed. F. E. Crowe (New York: Herder and Herder; London: Darton, Longman & Todd, 1967), pp. vii–xxxv. The rest of the introduction, dealing as it does with the several chapters of *Collection*, is omitted here.

3

whose works were available in any land but could be read with so much more sympathetic insight almost within view of the Oxford spires he loved; at any rate, *An Essay in Aid of a Grammar of Assent* had a profound influence on Lonergan's developing epistemology.

The three years that Jesuit scholastics traditionally spend teaching before they begin theology may well be omitted from an account that describes academic formation. Instructing college students in the classics enabled Lonergan to "keep his hand in" but almost certainly did not greatly extend his intellectual range or powers. In 1933, however, he went with four other Canadian Jesuits to start theology at the Gregorian University in Rome. The scholastic residence where he lived as undergraduate was in those days the "Bellarmino" in the Campo Marzio. This plain, the old Campus Martius, stretches westward from the Quirinal to fill the oxbow made by the Tiber as it turns right towards Vatican Hill and then bends back to resume its southerly course to the sea; in the maze of twisting streets and narrow alleys and sudden bustling piazzas that now make the Campo a tourist's delight, the via del Seminario runs a short two hundred yards to terminate at the Pantheon in the very heart of the Campo; and midway on the via stands the Bellarmino. A residence for doctorate students since the last great war, it is familiar in its present form to Jesuits from every land. Repeated remodeling within has not changed the forbidding exterior; the old "cortile" is still there, the courtyard where the scholastics played volleyball, Roman-style, in their cassocks, "frothing at the sides."[1] The quaint elliptical refectory is the same, and the gallery-height pulpit where a Canadian scholastic preached his practice sermon in Ojibway, surely a stringent test for the *ex opere operato* effect claimed for the sacrament of the word.

The Gregorian itself in its brand-new building under the Quirinal (it had been opened only three years earlier) was coming to the close of a splendid phase in its four-century history. Two famous professors, Louis Billot and Maurice de la Taille, had just died, leaving great names and disputed doctrines behind; Francis Ehrle would follow them in another year. The two new faculties of Church History and Missiology had just been started. There was a little galaxy of ranking scholars on the staff: E. Hocedez, L. Keeler, H. Lennerz, J. de Guibert, A. Vermeersch, P. Hoenen, F. Pelster, P. Galtier, P. de Leturia, to mention only some of those now dead. Under such men and in the closing years of an age, Lonergan did his undergraduate and doctorate studies in

1. The locale of these cassocked struggles is now uncertain; it may have been the Frascati villa where scholastics went on holidays.

theology (periods of four and two years, separated by a final year of religious formation—the Jesuit second novitiate—at Amiens), and prepared his dissertation on the Thomist theory of grace.

The rapid spread of the war in the spring of 1940 marked his transition from formation to teaching, as it marked also the end of an era in Gregorian history. It was not just the special difficulty such an "international" university had then in recruiting professors; it was much more the coincidence of that crisis with the turning of theology into new ways. Yves Congar had already published his book *Chrétiens désunis* (1937); Karl Rahner had written articles on grace for both *Gregorianum* (1937) and *Zeitschrift für katholische Theologie* (1938). In those years few could even have guessed what was developing, and Angelo Roncalli was only an obscure apostolic delegate in the Middle East, but the revolution in theology was to be as world-shaking in its genus as the war had been in international politics. The gathering of professors at the Gregorian in the thirties represented the fine flowering of the old "classical" culture and from them Lonergan imbibed much that was best in the patrimony they had inherited and built up and handed on, but the future belonged to other men: new ways of thinking, new attitudes to fellow Christians, new programs in theology were taking over.

To those new trends Lonergan was to make his own contribution as his ideas slowly matured. In the nature of the case, with a crisis at hand that was making all things new, his contribution could not be merely a function of his formal training. Anyway, quite apart from the crisis, he was not one to follow the well-trodden paths, and it would be hard to estimate the comparative influence of standard curricula and sideline pursuits of his own. Already in the pre-war years he was making his personal intellectual pilgrimage: first it was from Newman to Augustine to Plato; then he imbibed Maréchal "by osmosis" from a fellow scholastic at the Gregorian; and in his doctorate work he came to a personal confrontation with St. Thomas and Aristotle that would lead him far from the established "schools" and be a powerful fertilizing influence for further evolution and new creative thinking. For St. Thomas, even the genuine St. Thomas, was now so obviously not enough. So much had happened in seven centuries, so much was happening in the present generation; the challenge could not be declined except under pain of being ranked with the "mean-spirited knights" of whom St. Ignatius speaks in the *Spiritual Exercises*. The quarter-century of Lonergan's teaching career, thirteen years in Montreal and Toronto of his native Canada, from 1953 on at his Gregorian alma mater, has been occupied with a relentless struggle to bring the new ideas into relation with the old. It is not easy to pin down in words the contribution he has made to the new theology, but the lines his thinking has followed can be indicated at least superficially by a summary glance at his writings and lectures during this period.

His doctoral dissertation, of which the main part was published in four articles in *Theological Studies* (1941–42), was a study of the concept of *gratia operans* in St. Thomas. It was an old question on which two sides had long ago planted their flags on a bitter battleground, but the debate could not continue forever as it had been conducted in the past; as one of the papers in this collection says in reference to it, the flourishing state of medieval studies involves "not only the discredit of baroque procedures but also an unexpectedly quiet funeral for a once celebrated and very passionate debate."[2] Whether we are right who think Lonergan's own work delivered the *coup de grâce* is not now the relevant question. More important are the long-term effects of this first encounter with St. Thomas, of this vigorous wrestling with the ideas of an overwhelmingly powerful thinker. As happens with many leaders of thought in our day who begin with a dissertation on one of the greats of the past, the chief benefit is not any collection of ideas they gather in files or brain-cells but the personal development involved in reaching up to the mind of a genius. This held for Lonergan's work on grace and it holds still more for his next full-length work, also on St. Thomas but dealing now with cognitional theory. It too was first published in *Theological Studies* (five articles from 1946 to 1949), but it has been translated into French by *Archives de philosophie,* and a new edition of the English has been prepared at the University of Notre Dame.[3] Again an unremitting struggle with the most fundamental Thomist ideas, it dealt this time with an area more directly relevant to the very idea of developing thought, involving profound questions on the nature of thought itself, and of understanding and reflection and judgment. At the same time its relative freedom from the passionate debates that had characterized the grace question allowed Lonergan to concentrate more on growing personally in the mind of St. Thomas, and I should say that this work marked the term of his dependence on the great Medieval theologian.

The next step in the evolution of his thought was quite personal, moving from study of a historical figure to independent affirmation. *Insight: A Study of Human Understanding* was a Thomist work, if you like, in its fundamental metaphysics and epistemology, but references to St. Thomas are fewer in number than those to Kant or Newton, and

2. *Collection: Papers by Bernard Lonergan, S. J.,* p. 67.
3. *La notion de verbe dans les écrits de saint Thomas d'Aquin* (Paris: Beauchesne, 1966); *Verbum: Word and Idea in Aquinas* (Notre Dame: University of Notre Dame, 1967).

scarcely more than those to Descartes, Galileo, or Einstein. The book is, in fact, a profound rethinking of cognitional theory on the basis of seven centuries of mathematics, physics, chemistry, biology, depth psychology, the social and human sciences, and modern philosophy. The net result was a transformation of the transcendental method as developed by Maréchal in correction and complement of Kant: a critical appropriation of human cognitional structure as a basis for a methodical science and philosophy.

But, despite all its wealth and fertility, *Insight* was really only preliminary and preparatory; it had not yet come to the heart of the matter in regard to goals and objectives. It was a necessary foundation, solid ground for either the methodical promotion of the sciences or that integration of differentiated cultures and ways of knowing and doing that poses such a problem today. But it dealt mainly with the subject, and the subject was irrevocably oriented to the object in an *intentio entis intendens*. The object is always being in its totality. Still, different periods of history emphasize different regions of being, or divide being in different hierarchies, or conceive the totality under different aspects. In that sense the object today is no longer the object of olden times: the material world with its grades of minerals, plants, animals and men. It is not even the "modern" world with its hierarchy of physical, chemical, biological, anthropological areas of study. It is a world transformed by human and divine meaning. And this is the object now for Lonergan. His lectures in graduate courses at the Gregorian and in summer expeditions to the United States and Canada have moved since *Insight* through the implementation of methods founded on that book, to the question of the meaning that constitutes human institutions and, because meaning develops in history, of the new historical consciousness of man. Symbolic of this preoccupation is the title of a recent talk at Marquette University in the Distinguished Lecture Series there: "Dimensions of Meaning."

If social and cultural changes are, at root, changes in the meanings that are grasped and accepted, changes in the control of meaning mark off the great epochs in human history. . . . The classical mediation of meaning has broken down. It is being replaced by a modern mediation that interprets our dreams and our symbols, that thematizes our wan smiles and limp gestures, that analyzes our minds and charts our souls, that takes the whole of human history for its kingdom to compare and relate languages and literatures, art-forms and religions, family arrangements and customary morals, political, legal, educational, economic systems, sciences, philosophies, theologies, and histories. . . . But the vast modern effort to understand meaning in all its manifestations has not been matched by a comparable effort in judging meaning.[4]

4. *Collection*, pp. 255–56, 265–66.

In this area the greatest expectations may be entertained, but we are handicapped in discussing it at present by lack of published materials.

A paragraph must be added now on Lonergan's theology manuals and opuscula, lest I seem to do an injustice to his everyday tasks in the classroom. Since his transfer to the Gregorian University output under this heading has become more organized, with four volumes now available on the theology of the Trinity, incarnation, and redemption. Those volumes are a curiosity, to be sure. Written in a language that hardly anyone uses nowadays outside seminaries, and in a thesis style that repels the free-wheeling dialoguers of our time, they have all they need in language, style, structure, and content to discourage the prospective reader; one can hardly imagine an independent researcher sitting down to plow through those 1,400 pages of theses presented in an antique tongue. Yet they abound with the profoundest reflections on such topics as theological method, the human condition, the nature of love, the structure of the graced universe. And the reflections occur in the most unexpected places; one might naturally look for a discursus on theological method at the beginning of the volume, but who would expect to find those brilliant pages on the human subject and his temporality in a chapter with the heading "*De personis divinis inter se comparatis*"? Besides the works available in print, there is an accumulation of opuscula put out in mimeographed form, *ad usum auditorum*, at various stages of his teaching career; some of them are extremely short, some are almost a small book; altogether they would make a good-sized volume, but Lonergan has steadily resisted the pressure put on him to publish them. Finally, besides these routine products of classroom work, there are the recordings or *reportationes* of many lecture series, a number of reviews and writings of a more popular kind, and the lean scattering of published scientific articles collected in this volume.

The output altogether is not enormous, if one measures bulk; rather less than that of many contemporaries, certainly small compared to his own potentiality as judged by pupil and auditor. There may be a degree of perfectionism in his unwillingness to publish before he has quite exhausted the topic under study. But, on the other hand, there is certainly a partial explanation in the notions I will take up now, his special theoretical interests and his "style" of thinking, so much influenced by that theory.

In regard to the first point, his interests have regularly gone behind products of mind to the performance that produced them. Whatever the objective question on which he happened to be working, be it geometry, or logic, or marriage, or the consciousness of Christ, or the communication of the divine nature to creatures, it was apt to be treated mainly as supplying materials for another, underlying question, one that had to do, not with the particular object, but with the field of method, of the operations of the subject, of what since Kant's time has been known as transcendental philosophy (and theology). Lonergan has been transcendental with a vengeance, and this fact exercised a twofold limitation on his literary output: first, his interest in publishing his views on objective questions was reduced to second rank, and then the transcendental interest, just as it is harder to grasp, is also necessarily more meager in material results. The latter point may be illustrated by the difference between a mathematical series, the members of which might fill more books than the world could contain, and the rule of the series, which can be expressed in a one-line formula; similarly, the study of objects could go on forever, but the rule of that study, the rule discoverable in the operations of the human subject—that is a much less garrulous matter.

In regard to the second point, study of the subject results in a "style" of thinking. Human operations have a built-in normative; to study them is to become aware of the standards intrinsic to their nature, and this awareness is almost certain to be reflected in one's further operations and ways of studying and thinking and writing. This has definitely been a factor in Lonergan's style of thinking, and consequently in regard to his material output. When I wrote the biographical introduction to a volume of studies honoring him on his sixtieth birthday, I called it "The Exigent Mind."[5] Despite the rather harsh sound of the title, I do not know a better way to describe in one word the quality of his work; it is imperiously exigent, the normative which was so long the object of his study having come to be more and more the decisive factor in his subjective operations of thinking and writing.

This point seems to me so much a key to understanding Lonergan that I will delay on it for a few paragraphs. The instance of interior exigence familiar to everyone is the *dictamen conscientiae*, the force of moral judgment impelling us to action, what Fr. Lonergan's own *Insight* describes in chapter 18 as the rigorous demand for self-consistency, or agreement between our knowing and our doing. But, as readers of *Insight* know, this familiar instance appears there as just the final manifestation of an exigence that directs all properly human activity. Human spirit is constituted as exigence, the exigence unfolds in a series of structured steps, and the moral exigence is merely the final element of the integral structure. The series begins with the desire for understanding: not content with the stream of internal or external experience that belongs to animal consciousness and the merely biological subject, man

5. "The Exigent Mind: Bernard Lonergan's Intellectualism," *Continuum* 2 (1964), pp. 316–33.

is impelled by the dynamism of his intellect (the spirit of inquiry—
Aristotle's agent intellect) to seek and discover a form in materials, an
idea in images, an explanation in data; and this first phase comes to a
term only in the articulation and formulation of the idea: that is, there
is a demand not only for the idea in the particular instance but also for
the disengagement of the idea so that it can be set forth in universal
concepts. Further, the basic exigence does not allow us to rest compla-
cently in the idea even when it is universalized, or to settle easily for
the first idea that springs to mind: there is a demand for critical reflection, the idea has to be verified, there must be a grasp of the evidence
sufficient for its assertion; and this second phase, like the first, comes
to a term only with the formulation of a judgment in which one passes
from subjective actuation to objective statement in the absolute sense
of objectivity. Though it may be difficult to cast the grounds for judgment in full and ordered sequence (see Newman's efforts to discover
the grounds for what he knew very well, that Great Britain is an island),
one comes in judgment to "possession" of an item of knowledge. Then,
if the judgment be in the field of the not-yet that is subject to my
intervention, there may emerge the final exigence, the most familiar in
everyday life, that for action and conduct suited to my possessed convictions.

What I have described is an *integral structure* of the exigence built
into human spirit.[6] There is a series of plateaus with the possibility of
getting off the cable-car at many points and, in fact, an extremely high
incidence of dropouts at the earlier stages. If the metaphor is challenged
on the ground that dropouts earlier would make the final step of decision impossible, when in fact everyone makes decisions, I answer that
everyone makes decisions in the field that is familiar to him where the
earlier steps are a habitual possession, but to make decisions in an
unfamiliar field is simply rash or arrogant if one does not undertake
the labor of inquiry, formulation, reflection, and judgment. Thus the
figure of plateaus is accurate enough for the structure men have for the
proper use of their powers, and brings out the high degree of courage
and perseverance required to follow the exigence to its end, to respond
to the *integral* structured demand of spirit as inquiry. Karl Rahner has
remarked that, despite all its talk and ferment, this age is not much
given to work on the really difficult problems of theology—which, I
think, adverts to a clear instance of human failure to follow to the end
the native exigence of mind. There is an interrogative spirit very evident
in the perpetual "Why?" of the child, vigorous in the student theologian

6. My "integral structure" here envisions only upward, not downward, development.
See ch. 20 below.

who pesters his professor with questions, still active in the dissertation project that pushes out hesitantly into unknown territory, faintly alive in the article that skims over the surface talking quite peacefully of "questions" but not really concerned to find answers for understanding, not sufficiently anyway to undertake the labor of attaining them; the process has come to a halt when it should be only starting. There *is* a concern for understanding in the work of the serious, creative artist; he has undoubtedly got hold of an idea, he has "constellated" the data to quicken the understanding of the viewer, he has perhaps profound insights into human nature and conduct; but, tied to the particular image, he will not hear the call for disengagement and refuses to formulate, conceptualize, and generalize. The logician works in the area of those who have taken that further step; he has disengaged the idea and, setting it before him in splendid isolation, spins out all its implications; but, though he is in perfect possession of the idea as conceived and even, perhaps, does not cut himself off from its origins in the image, he still does not as logician take the step of asking what relation his ideas have to reality, whether they are a true interpretation of the universe. The scientific mind shows that concern: it would verify its ideas by submitting them to the test of a crucial experiment; but the failure now is in stopping short of the full range of questions, there is confinement to a *region* of being.

For Fr. Lonergan, in his theory and his practice, the exigence is *total*. There is a total *structure* with regard to each increment of knowing: "Human knowing . . . puts itself together, one part summoning forth the next, till the whole is reached."[7] Also, there is a totality in the *range of questions:* "Man wants to understand completely. As the desire to understand is the opposite of total obscurantism, so the unrestricted desire to understand is the opposite of any and every partial obscurantism no matter how slight. . . . Nor is the existence of this unrestricted desire doubtful. Neither centuries of inquiry nor enormous libraries of answers have revealed any tendency for the stream of further questions to diminish."[8] Thus one is led from the particular field of one's research to ask more general questions, to become a philosopher; one is led from the philosopher's view of the world and men, of their high aspirations and their sorry performance, their dreams of immortality and the fact of death, to ask whether there is something undiscoverable by philosophy and, if so, whether it has been communicated to men in favor and grace. If one comes to faith, one is led to theology, and the theology inevitably attempts to unify the whole body of revealed and acquired knowledge.

7. *Collection*, p. 223.
8. *Insight: A Study of Human Understanding*, p. 638.

All this is relevant to the question of Fr. Lonergan's literary output, as well as helpful for understanding his underlying purpose and the status within the total plan of the articles collected here. His bent is not for "tossing off" articles on topics of the day; we really have few such contributions, and their frequency seems to be falling rather than rising. His practice is a good illustration of (and perhaps an argument for) his theory on the totality of the object of human spirit and on the rigorous requirements of the structured process that carries one by partial steps to increments that in turn accumulate and reach towards the totality. In this respect, his present work on the method of theology is as instructive as finished products like *Insight,* for here we can follow his production *in fieri.* He has labored for over a decade expressly on the question of theology, its nature, method, implications, divisions; in the course of that time, he has given courses and lectures on the topic that would make a hundred articles; but he has persistently delayed publication of a definitive statement till understanding and judgment are formed to the degree demanded in the present situation by the normative dynamism of intellect.

2

The Origin and Scope
of Bernard Lonergan's *Insight**

Fr. Lonergan's long-awaited *Insight,* a quarter of a century maturing, some five years in actual composition, and three more in reaching the bookstalls, has at last appeared in a neat and reasonably priced volume that does credit to the courage and scientific interest of the publishers.

Reviewers regularly complain about the difficulty of their task of compressing a whole volume into a few pages, but faced with a book like this they may well throw up their hands in complete despair. The wealth of ideas here is truly enormous; hardly a page but merits special attention. The depth of the author's thought calls for explanatory expansion of each step instead of a brusque summary of the whole. The range of implications of his basic theme, reaching into diverse branches of learning, requires rather a battery of specialists than a single reviewer.

In these circumstances I have thought to cover up the inadequacy with which I perform the primary task by adding a second. For those who have not read *Insight* and may wish to know in a general way what it is about, I shall attempt in a first section some sort of synopsis. But, if I am not mistaken, the reading of the book will mark for many, not the mere satisfaction of a curiosity that is only superficially intellectual, but the beginning of a new and extended intellectual experience. I think it rather likely that they will find the author has given them a new orientation, and that they will want to know what his antecedents are, what his long-range purpose, and what the place of *Insight* in the unfolding development of his thought. Although I do not pretend to any special competence in answering these questions, it is possible that a long familiarity with the work of Fr. Lonergan will enable me to throw some light on them; at least I hope to contribute something to the discussion which I expect to be raised by the publication of this re-

*Previously published as pp. 263–79 of "The Origin and Scope of Bernard Lonergan's *Insight,*" in *Sciences ecclésiastiques* [later *Science et esprit*] 9 (1957), pp. 263–95. (References to the preface of *Insight* retain the pagination of that book's first three editions.) The remaining pages of the original article are not included here, because the subsequent appearance of Lonergan's *Method in Theology* has rendered their forecast less useful.

markable book. Accordingly, I turn in a second section to the sources from which *Insight* developed and study the author's relationship to St. Thomas Aquinas; and then, because the book, though autonomous as a philosophy, represents only a step towards an ultimate theological goal, a third section will take up the relevance of *Insight* to the formation of a methodical theology.

1. The Theme of *Insight*

A simple listing of chapter headings or a catalogue of the topics touched on would indicate, perhaps, the range of the author's interests, but it may be more useful to concentrate forces at one point of attack and to present the theme of *Insight* in a series of spheres expanding from a center. To this purpose, I begin with a quasi slogan, develop it briefly by indicating the three levels on which *Insight* operates, and then try to characterize the aim and intention of the book still more precisely by enlarging the question under five headings. Fortunately, it is possible to draw freely on the preface and introduction themselves in this section.

(1) The quasi slogan which sums up *Insight* in Fr. Lonergan's own words runs as follows: "Thoroughly understand what it is to understand, and not only will you understand the broad lines of all there is to be understood but also you will possess a fixed base, an invariant pattern, opening upon all further developments of understanding" (p. xxviii).

(2) Our first expansion of this theme will be to say that the work operates on three levels: "It is a study of human understanding. It unfolds the philosophic implications of understanding. It is a campaign against the flight from understanding" (p. xii).

The goal then is "insight into insight" (p. xxvii). "Mathematicians seek insight into sets of elements. Scientists seek insight into ranges of phenomena. Men of common sense seek insight into concrete situations and practical affairs. But our concern is to reach the act of organizing intelligence that brings within a single perspective the insights of mathematicians, scientists, and men of common sense" (p. ix).

Secondly, insight into insight confers "a basic yet startling unity on the whole field of human inquiry and human opinion" (p. ix). Unifying and organizing other departments of knowledge, it provides a philosophy, a unified and organized knowing; from a unified and organized knowing we conclude to a unification and organization of the known, a metaphysics; and this philosophy and metaphysics will be verifiable in cognitional acts just as scientific insights are verifiable in colors, sounds, and other data (p. xi).

Thirdly, there is oversight and flight from insight. If the book were merely a logical development of a set of premises and readers were merely electronic computers, this third factor would require no attention. Once a way were found of causing the printed pages to produce the properly consecutive impulses in end-organs of sight or hearing, the rest would follow. Again, if readers were pure intelligences, uncomplicated by the duality of human knowing, little or nothing would need to be said here. But none of these conditions is verified, and so this third factor receives considerable attention, not only in more obvious forms such as the concern with psychoneuroses (ch. 6) or with the critique of mistaken beliefs (ch. 20), but in a more general way in the pedagogy of the whole construction and treatment.

(3) The theme of *Insight* can be exposed more fully under five headings.

Our aim regards: (1) not the fact of knowledge but a discrimination between two facts of knowledge, (2) not the details of the known but the structure of the knowing, (3) not the knowing as an object characterized by catalogues of abstract properties but the appropriation of one's own intellectual and rational self-consciousness, (4) not a sudden leap to appropriation but a slow and painstaking development, and (5) not a development indicated by appealing either to the logic of the as yet unknown goal or to a presupposed and as yet unexplained ontologically structured metaphysics, but a development that can begin in any sufficiently cultured consciousness that expands in virtue of the dynamic tendencies of that consciousness itself (p. xxviii).

The first point regards the twofold knowing of man, his animal and his human knowing. This may seem fairly simple, but some hint of its real difficulty is had from the fact that it took St. Augustine years to discover that "real" might have a different connotation from "body" (p. xx). A more precise idea derives from a study of Cartesian dualism and its subsequent history: "Cartesian dualism had been a twofold realism, and both the realisms were correct. . . . The trouble was that, unless two distinct and disparate types of knowing were recognized, the two realisms were incompatible" (p. 414). "While the two realities as realities may be coincident, the two knowings must be distinguished and kept apart; and it is failure to keep them apart that originates the component of aberration in our dialectic of philosophy" (p. 423). It may be possible to miss the point here, despite the recurrent references to the polymorphism of human consciousness and the repeated castigation of the view that intellectual knowing is merely taking an intellectual look. But it seems rather important not to miss it; I should say that there is an intellectual purification that stands to intellectual development somewhat as ascetical purification stands to advance in charity, and that intellectual purification requires a well-defined distinction between intellectual knowing and looking, between verification and imagination, between the objectivity that is based on intelligent inquiry and critical reflection and the objectivity for which animal extroversion serves as model (p. 385 and ch. 13).

Secondly, there is the structure of human cognitional activity. Schematically it rises on three levels: experience, understanding, and reflection (ch. 9). The level of experience we share in large part with animals; it is the level of data, of presentations, of the empirical, of the merely given. Understanding is properly human; here occurs insight into data, the insight whose content is an idea, whose products are hypotheses, theories, definitions, concepts, formulations, systems; this is the level of thought. Insight is a new beginning, impossible to electronic computers and a mystery to logicians who remain only logicians. Its possibility is the possibility of all that enormous development of intelligence that the human race has undergone in the course of millennia and that the individual attempts to appropriate for himself in a short lifetime. Yet thought is incomplete, it is not yet knowledge; we may think of centaurs and perform acts of understanding with regard to them but we do not know them. On the third level there is reflective understanding, the taking possession of the evidence, which issues in judgments, affirmations, the truths by which we know what is; it is the level of rationality, reasonableness, knowledge.

The operator of the ascent to successive levels, and of development on the level of understanding first and consequently on that of judgment, is the question. "When an animal has nothing to do, it goes to sleep. When a man has nothing to do, he may ask questions" (p. 10). It is a commonplace that Aristotle made wonder the beginning of all philosophy. Fr. Lonergan has taken Aristotle's two basic questions, *an sit* and *quid sit*, linked them sharply to the *duae operationes intellectus* of St. Thomas, understanding and reflection, and made them central to his account of the dynamism of cognitional activity.[1] Presented with data, man wonders, looks for meaning, asks *quid sit*? The answer is formulated in a theory, a hypothesis. But this only gives rise to a further question, "Is the theory correct?," *an sit*? The hypothesis must be tested by verifying its implications. The two questions are the operative element in the advance of knowledge.[2] Hence the references, over and over again, both to "the obscurantism that arbitrarily brushes questions

---

1. Auditors of his seminary lectures will remember remarks like, "Suntne quaestiones? Intellectus agens interdum agit, et tunc dantur quaestiones."

2. Why did Aristotle give priority to *an sit*? I believe philosophers are still discussing Aristotle's mind; Fr. Lonergan's view is that there is descriptive knowing and explanatory knowing, each with its own levels of understanding and reflection. Aristotle presupposed descriptive knowing where *an sit* receives its answer, proceeded to the *quid sit* of explan-

aside" (p. xxix), and to the pure, detached, disinterested, unrestricted desire to know, the dynamism that sets man free from lower levels of nature while animals remain locked in sensitive routines, that drives him to understand what is merely presented for understanding, and when he has understood, drives him to the further question whether his understanding is a mere bright idea or reveals the actual shape of things in this concrete world.

Thirdly, there is the reader's appropriation of this structure, not only in the simple scheme I have outlined, but in all the complexity of its details. More important, it must be an appropriation, not of mere words on a page, but of a consciousness living and dynamic within oneself. When we would appropriate for ourselves the geography of Siberia and have reasons for not visiting that country, books and maps may substitute imaginative representations for the sensitive presentations denied us. So too when we would become familiar with the history of physics without repeating experimentally the steps of its development. Here we are forced to imagine what others have experienced, and to this end books are an intrinsic element of an accurate cognitional process. That is not true, however, of self-appropriation. For that we are our own field of observation; we have only to study our own activities to become informed of what insight is; indeed, unless we practice such introspection, we shall never learn from books, for no imagination can be a substitute for insight. This book then is extrinsic to the process it would initiate; it merely asks us to open our eyes, to turn attention to possessions we may have neglected. It issues "an invitation to a personal, decisive act" (p. xix). "The aim . . . is to assist the reader in effecting a personal appropriation of the concrete, dynamic structure immanent and recurrently operative in his own cognitional activities" (p. xvii). As the original subtitle stated, and the closing paragraphs still insist, this is an "essay in aid of a personal appropriation of one's own rational self-consciousness" (p. 748).[3]

But if the appropriation is to occur through one's own cognitional activities, the activities must come first. What are they? And in what strategic order are they to be marshalled? This is a question of some

---

atory knowing, but failed to notice that a prior *quid sit* had been answered in descriptive knowing and a second *an sit* remained to be answered in explanatory knowing. "The intrinsically hypothetical character of explanation and its need of a further, verifying judgment of existence were overlooked" (*Insight: A Study of Human Understanding*, p. 366).

3. A simple proportion will indicate what one may hope for in such self-appropriation: A plethora of quiz experts have taught us what it is to have an encyclopedic memory; a thinker scorns this multiplicity in comparison with the universality of an idea; the proportion is that, as the thinker's idea stands to a multitude of items of information, so the self-appropriation of one's cognitional structure stands to the multitude of ideas of thinkers.

importance. There is no doubt that acts of insight occur by the hundreds to all of us, whether in playing bridge, driving a car, chatting with neighbors, or perhaps even in studying a railway timetable. But there is some doubt that daily acts of common sense offer any great advantages for an accurate study of what insight is; in fact, when they come up for discussion in chapters 6 and 7, it appears that our common-sense use of intelligence is so abundant in oversights, so complicated by anti-intellectual prejudices, so crippled by unconscious flights from understanding, that it can hardly offer an advantageous starting-point for the methodical determination of what happens when we understand. Accordingly, Fr. Lonergan begins with those "fields of intellectual endeavour in which the greatest care is devoted to exactitude and, in fact, the greatest exactitude is attained" (p. xx). Chapters 1 to 5 then deal with mathematical and scientific illustrations. What is relevant in them is not any clarity they may bring to the objects of those disciplines, though that may be a valuable by-product, but merely the clear illustration of insight in act and the accurate characterization of it in its complexity. The importance then of the notions of direct and inverse insight, of higher viewpoints, of heuristic structures and the scissors-action of heuristic method, of the transition from descriptive categories which relate things to our senses to explanatory concepts which relate them to one another, the differentiation of classical and statistical methods, the study of abstraction with its enriching addition to the concrete, the importance of all this lies simply in the revelation it holds of universal properties of human knowing which may be exploited for methodical cognitional activity.

Fourthly, there is the labor of development. The book is offered as an aid to that process and so it does not tell us everything at once, or even set out the premises from which everything will follow. It is written "from a moving viewpoint" (p. xxiii), beginning with a minimum, exploiting it to raise a further question that enlarges the field, and so proceeding in cycles until we reach the universal viewpoint. In chapter 1 the author is satisfied to illustrate insight by the procedures of mathematics and proceeds with complete unconcern for problems of things, objectivity, the real, and so forth. Nor does he hurry to approach those problems. The partly static view of insight resulting from the first chapter is enlarged in the next to take in its dynamic aspect by a study of the heuristic structures of empirical inquiry. Meanwhile the method of empirical inquiry has been emerging in its generality; its general canons are set forth in chapter 3; the objective here is "to reveal the intelligible unity that underlies and accounts for the diverse and apparently disconnected rules of empirical method" (p. 71). In chapter 4 the duality that has consistently appeared in what are called the classical and statistical, in the "domination of the concrete by the abstract-and-systematic" (p. 104), is studied to reveal the complementarity of the two as types of knowing and the corresponding complementarity in the known. Chapter 5 with its study of space and time provides "a concrete and familiar context for the foregoing analyses of empirical science, and . . . a natural bridge . . . to an examination of common sense" (p. 140) in the two following chapters. Chapter 8 enters a new field to consider at some length the notion of things. The notion, it is argued, is "necessary for the continuity of scientific thought and development," for "scientific thought needs, not only explanatory systems, but also descriptions that determine the data which explanations must satisfy" (p. 247), and it is the thing which unites in itself descriptive and explanatory attributes. "Description supplies, as it were, the tweezers by which we hold things while explanations are being discovered or verified" (p. 291). And still we have not determined whether things exist, for the answer to that question is not a concept based on any insight of the types we have so far considered, but a judgment based on reflective understanding, and these notions remain to be studied in chapters 9 and 10, to complete the first part of the book, "Insight As Activity."

Part II, "Insight As Knowledge," is the longer and, from a metaphysical point of view, the more basic. Moreover, I believe that in the long run it will be the subject of far more discussion than the first. Those who find that the appropriation of their own rational self-consciousness puts them in possession of a powerful method for thinking philosophically will be apt to take Part I for granted, once it is assimilated, and proceed to the fascinating pastime of implementing the method in a growing understanding of the universe. Those of an opposite view on the appropriation of rational self-consciousness will be apt to find Part I irrelevant and, setting aside the general philosophical basis of Part II, proceed to debate its particular theses. However, for present purposes we can deal more briefly with "Insight As Knowledge." The slogan ran: "Thoroughly understand what it is to understand, and . . . [you will] understand the broad lines of all there is to be understood." Here we have the broad lines of all there is to be understood, a philosophy and a metaphysics.

Already in chapter 4 an isomorphism was noted between knowing and known: "Knowing and known . . . stand in some correspondence and, as the known is reached only through knowing, structural features of the one are bound to be reflected in the other" (p. 115). Then there was question only of schemes of recurrence emerging from the primeval chaos but now there is question far more generally, on the metaphysical plane, of the correspondence of potency, form, and the act of existence, to experience, understanding, and judgment of act. "That parallel is missed by Spinoza's deductivist *ordo idearum est ordo rerum*. The correct locus of the parallel is to be found in the dynamic structure of our knowing" (p. 486; cf. pp. 499–502).[4] This correspondence guides the structuring of a metaphysics of proportionate being, that is, a metaphysics of "whatever is to be known by human experience, intelligent grasp, and reasonable affirmation" (p. 391). This "restricted metaphysics" (p. 666) is conceived as "the integral heuristic structure of proportionate being . . . [It] is the anticipatory outline of what would be known by affirming a complete explanation of experience" (p. 483).

But there are both preliminary and subsequent questions. The preliminary question is about the evidence for metaphysics. Fr. Lonergan believes, because of the manifold of disputed alternatives, that the answer can be supplied only in dynamic terms; he uses the military metaphor of "a break-through, an envelopment, and a confinement." The break-through occurs in the self-affirmation of chapter 11, the envelopment in chapter 12 with "the protean notion of being," the confinement in the following chapters "through the dialectical opposition of twofold notions of the real, of knowing, and of objectivity" (p. 484). Subsequent questions regard an ethics whose structure is parallel with that of restricted metaphysics (ch. 18), and the extension of restricted metaphysics to include transcendent reality (chs. 19 and 20). The same dynamism of mind which gave rise to mathematical higher viewpoints in chapter 1 is still operative. "Understanding is incompatible with the obscurantism that arbitrarily brushes questions aside. The issue of transcendent knowledge has to be faced" (p. xxix). And that means not only attempting to determine what we can know about God, but also envisaging his solution to the problem of evil in the universe and asking for an anticipatory outline of what generic form that solution will take (ch. 20).

Fifthly, the order of the book is governed, "not by considerations of logical or metaphysical priority, but by considerations of pedagogical efficacy" (p. xxvi). On logic it is simplest to note that it supposes formed concepts, that, on Fr. Lonergan's view, the concepts suppose an insight into data, and that, consequently, there can hardly be a logical starting-point for a study of insight that will prove universally convincing; one can only give examples of insight and list its properties, and then invite others to substitute their own acts of understanding (p. 31) and see whether the properties do not correspond. On metaphysical priority,

4. This isomorphism, as I understand Fr. Lonergan, serves two functions: it gives meaning to the metaphysical elements, and it is a premise for their affirmation. Both functions have to stand the weight of legitimate criticism, but I think it would be missing the point not to see that the main concern of the book is with the first.

something will be said in the next section in discussing the relation of *Insight* to Thomist thought.

These hints must do for our present account of the theme of *Insight*. They seem to me hopelessly inadequate to indicate the riches of the study, but perhaps something of its panoramic breadth of view has appeared; as the preface says, "In constructing a ship or a philosophy one has to go the whole way" (p. xiii). Moreover, they are certainly not a sufficient basis for evaluating the book; in any case, on this point there is not much use in trying to anticipate too exactly the decision of history. My own tentative view is that *Insight* is destined to take a place among the great books of modern thought, but it might be rash at the present time to assign it a more specific ranking. Perhaps, however, it will not be out of place here to recall for comparison two great events of our times. It is just sixty years since Freud undertook that analysis of his own unconscious in which a biographer finds the achievement at last of the task (as he understood it) set by the Delphic oracle, Know thyself,[5] and just thirty years since Heidegger published the analysis of the being of man which he intended only as a preliminary step towards a new ontology. It is no disparagement of two famous men to recognize that the one was a long way from the full perfection of self-knowledge and the other has not yet fulfilled his promise of an ontology. Neither can one establish, by mere manipulation of the number thirty, the success of the human self-knowledge and consequent ontology offered by *Insight*, but the interesting sequence will provide readers with a handy mnemonic to the author's express purpose and a frame of reference for estimating the comparative worth of his contribution.[6]

II. *Insight* and St. Thomas Aquinas

Anyone familiar with the reverence for the genius of St. Thomas Aquinas manifested in Fr. Lonergan's earlier writings will have anticipated what in fact is verified, that *Insight* is not intended as a totally new line of thought but as a development of Thomism according to the Leonine *vetera novis augere et perficere*. An account of the sources of *Insight* reduces therefore to two broad headings: the Thomism at its basis, and those features of the last seven centuries of thought which

---

5. Ernest Jones, *Sigmund Freud: Life and Work,* vol. I (New York: Basic Books, 1953), p. 351.

6. It is noticeable that *Insight* gives little attention to existentialist and personalist philosophies. It is not, apparently, that they fail to interest the author, if one may judge from his lectures and the repeated references in his writings; but it seems to be his view that they can be treated better in a theological context: *Insight*, p. 731, n.; *De constitutione Christi ontologica et psychologica*, p. 18.

have been integrated into Thomism. Moreover, such an account will emphasize the first of these two topics, for it was Fr. Lonergan's labor for a personal recovery of St. Thomas that he regards as decisive. Indeed, it seems possible to generalize here and make this *the* procedure in philosophy, both because the necessity of such a personal labor is easily overlooked by those brought up on manual digests of Thomism, and because once the labor is thoroughly done its fruits follow in never-ending abundance. Call it architectonic in relation to developments, speak of its assimilative capacity, refer to it as an upper blade in the scissors-action of heuristic method, whatever terms we use to describe it, Thomist thought has an inherent power for expansion that has not yet been superseded. Thirdly, an account of Fr. Lonergan's dependence on St. Thomas that merely listed legacies of words or even of ideas, useful as that might be, would miss the main point; beyond words and ideas is mind in its dynamism, and the closer we come to appropriating a mind the less relevant is the literal sense of the word "legacy." To set this forth, I am afraid, calls for some discussion of the very idea of intellectual dependence in its nature and conditions.

At least since John of Salisbury attributed the phrase to Bernard of Chartres,[7] it has been something of a commonplace that we are pygmies standing on the shoulders of giants. It is not quite so commonplace that the mere accident of belonging to posterity does not automatically install us on the giants' shoulders, that there remains a labor of climbing more arduous than John seems to have supposed. It is still less commonplace to endeavor to fix the nature and conditions of that climb. But Bernard's metaphor begins here to lose whatever elegance it may once have had; we had best turn to more direct language.

In plainer terms, a modern infant, if we allow for the possibility of change in biological factors which are only dispositive to intelligence, is born in no better intellectual condition than an infant of the most primitive tribe. He is *omnino in potentia in genere intelligibilium.*[8] As the material universe evolved through millions of years from primeval chaos to its present order of fairly durable species and schemes of recurrence, as the human race itself traversed in its millennia the distance that may be estimated by comparing, say, a Cardinal Newman and the Australian aborigines, so the child has to evolve through his allotted years to something like a formed intelligence.

Moreover, the basic condition of that evolution is intrinsic to the

---

7. *Metalogicus,* lib. III, c. 4 (P.L., 199, col. 900). For some notes on the history of the phrase, see G. Sarton, *Isis* 24 (1935–36), pp. 107–109, and R. Klibansky, *Isis* 26 (1936–37), pp. 147–49.

8. *De malo,* 16, 12, 4m; cf. *Summa theologiae,* I, 87, 1, etc.

child. Despite the difficulty of the question there is no need here of the attempts to make a *mystique* of communication. Educators may present the child with a graduated set of volumes leading from picture-books to the *Summa theologiae*, but basically they are doing nothing that his primitive environment does not do. Instead of the blue sky and rustling leaves and running water they are presenting him with much less interesting sets of inkmarks on paper. What they count on is the inner reaction which can be exploited to provoke a further reaction, and so on in a strategic series which does not allow reactions to be wasted in isolated futility. "Teaching is a vast acceleration of the process of learning" (p. 289).

But what is that inner reaction? It is, in the first place, wonder, the dynamism of inquiring intelligence in motion, without which we have animals with memories to be trained but not children with intelligences to be educated. It is, in the second place, the occurrence of an act of understanding. Educators shuffle the data to hasten the occurrence; the more aptly they shuffle, the more frequent by statistical laws is the occurrence. But they cannot force the act to occur; it is a new beginning dependent on agent intellect, an inner event removed from their immediate control. It is, in the third place, perseverance in wonder beyond the first act of understanding to further and further acts that bring the subject in spiralling cycles to continually greater heights. This is crucial. Wonder is only one of the elemental drives in the human subject; its demands can subside under the drugging influence of sense or be thwarted by the hard necessity of earning a living. More important in the present context, it can lose its urgency in the satisfied contemplation of heights already scaled. One such natural resting-place is the understanding of words;[9] this is less dangerous in the study of Aquinas, for his words as words have not the attraction of Shakespeare's; still it does happen even here that, where the *scientia nominum* should be only heuristic in advancing to the *scientia rerum*, it becomes instead an end in itself. Another resting-place is specialization in science; ensconced in the narrow but familiar field of our specialty, we easily brush aside the questions which would lift us to a general view in which our specialty would be but a part; in some degree, perhaps, such an attitude contributes to painstaking positive research,[10] but it is fatal to perseverance in wonder on the grand scale. Finally, beyond the reaction of individual acts of understanding and a somewhat *per accidens* persever-

9. On understanding of words, see "A Note on Geometrical Possibility," *in Collection: Papers by Bernard Lonergan, S.J.,* pp. 98–102.

10. As the great positive scholar de Ghellinck used to tell his students, "Surtout, il faut ne pas penser"; and as a wit remarked: "If you are going to specialize, you have to be narrow-minded."

ance in their pursuit, there is a grasp of the strategy of advance, not only in the conditions set by the nature of human intellect but in those determined by past human accomplishment; when that strategy is grasped, inner development has reached a self-propelling stage which *per se* assures continuance.

Now the interiority of development in the pupil is matched by the interiority of the teacher's mind. If in the pupil there is a breathless ascent from presented words to the spiritual plane of intelligibility, necessarily in the teacher's words there is a descent from mind to mere mechanical instruments of communication. Behind the words is the mind of the teacher. If we turn to his origins, the milieu in which he lived, the historical conditions of his thought, we are similarly boxed; they are material, or can be recovered in the first instance only in their materiality; his mind is beyond them.

The problem becomes acute with a mind like that of Aquinas, for, if the clarity of his expression is proverbial, his intelligence towers enormously above the average. We become familiar perforce in Catholic seminaries with his favorite expressions. Again, to gain some acquaintance with his milieu is not too hard, at least since the labors of the last century and the Thomist revival. It is quite another matter to reach the mind of Aquinas; neither the *scienta nominum* nor specialization in Medieval history can automatically effect that contact; his milieu conditioned his mind antecedently, his words express it subsequently, but hidden behind both is that mind itself, ranging and versatile, with all the power and all the elusiveness of a vast and enormously developed intelligence.

The difficulty is increased by the influence of schools which too easily suppose themselves to be already in possession of the mind of Aquinas and to need only to find texts to prove their case in particular questions. But that is not the basic difficulty; in any case, it seems likely to disappear when scientific methods of historical research become more widely adopted. The basic and at first sight insuperable difficulty is that, to reach the mind of Aquinas, one must be in possession of it already. Words mediate between two acts of understanding, but the acts are by no means equal. The words are the expression of one mind and supply data for an act of insight by another; but as expression they have their meaning measured by the intelligence of the mind that uttered them, and as material for insight they have their possibilities of meaning limited by the development of the mind that strives to understand. And so the meaning of Aquinas, or his mind, is more or less accessible to us according as our intelligences are more or less on a level with his. How does one solve this dilemma? There is no logical path leading inevitably in a series of well-defined steps to the desired goal; but, once we are free from the error that we know already, further progress is a matter of the "self-correcting process" of learning (p. 286). We read to acquire some elementary insight; the elementary insight enables us to read more intelligently a second time; and so we ascend a spiral staircase, continually returning but continually rising. A good course in St. Thomas vastly expedites the ascent, but it cannot eliminate the personal labor. Hence Fr. Lonergan, at the conclusion of his *Verbum* articles, describes his method as follows:

Only by the slow, repetitious, circular labor of going over and over the data, by catching here a little insight and there another, by following through false leads and profiting from many mistakes, by continuous adjustments and cumulative changes of one's initial assumptions and perspectives and concepts, can one hope to attain such a development of one's own understanding as to hope to understand what Aquinas understood and meant.[11]

Later in *Insight* he describes the result and essential benefit of the years he has spent "reaching up to the mind of Aquinas" as simply his own interior change (p. 748).

But this is rather generic and applicable to the works of any great thinker. I think the facts force us to recognize a special difficulty in reaching the mind of St. Thomas. Writing neither for those who hold he has already given all the answers nor for those who would write him off as an error of seven centuries' duration, but for those who know, at least obscurely, that his position is unique in the history of thought and that his *Opera omnia* form an instrument of enduring vitality even in the twentieth century, I would put two questions: Why is St. Thomas so widely disregarded outside the Church? And why has Thomism not developed in a degree proportionate to its potentialities? Neither speculative indifference nor prejudice can be alleged to account for the isolation of Thomism.[12] We may invoke the alien context of his thought, its ancient physics and its theology of revelation, but many attempts have been made to disengage his philosophic thought and present it to our times. Why, if it is unique, has it not swept the world? And the second question remains: Why within Scholasticism itself has Thomism not developed in proportion to the development of other fields of culture and in a measure consonant with what we feel to be its intrinsic resources?

---

11. *Verbum: Word and Idea in Aquinas,* p. 216.

12. As Carl Jung told a priest-student of his, Raymond Hostie, S.J., "I have tried to read Aquinas, but I could make nothing of him." The example recorded by M. J.-M. Aubert at the end of his *Le droit romain dans l'oeuvre de saint Thomas* (Paris: Vrin, 1955, p. 139, n. 1) of a thinker who came too late to realize what he had missed through ignorance of St. Thomas strikes us as authentic; moreover, we could collect others, but we cannot assert that they are abundant.

It would seem that either Thomism is not what we thought it or we have not yet found the key to unlock its treasures. To face these questions may dispose us to consider the approach finding more favor among Thomists nowadays[13] and worked out in full detail by Fr. Lonergan. It is to postpone metaphysics and take our departure from the subject, in the present case, from the dynamism and immanent laws of cognitional activity itself. It is not that Fr. Lonergan is unconcerned about metaphysics; it is the outcome finally of his method. It is not that he denies Thomist metaphysics; what he arrives at in its essential structure is the metaphysics of St. Thomas. It is merely that a new approach seems indicated by our failure so far to make fruitful contact on a wide scale with modern philosophy, that to begin on a cognitional basis offers real hope of meeting a secular mind largely concerned with methodology, and that the approach through cognitional activity seems to offer the intrinsic possibility of a basic method which will enable us and succeeding generations to do with our mediocre resources in our times what St. Thomas accomplished by genius in his.

The approach offers antecedent probability of success. If it is correct that the goal of studying St. Thomas is to reach his mind, then, although there is no doubt a way back to that mind from its metaphysical products, it is far more direct to study the very activity of that mind itself in its unfolding. That is, we may begin with the objective world of Thomist thought, organized in grades of being, distinguished into act and potency, and so on; but if there are data in the writings of St. Thomas that indicate the inner dynamism and laws of operation of his mind they offer an immediate entry.[14] Moreover, the oscillating process described above between the minds of disciple and master would be greatly expedited by such an entry, for, instead of pivoting between a world of Medieval physics and twentieth-century science, the disciple would pivot between operating mind and operating mind; and here, despite the difference of development, the basic laws of operation would seem to be discoverable in approximately the same terms.

A second consideration is this. Although for St. Thomas the proper object of human understanding[15] is the *quidditas rei materialis* whether

13. See Robert Johann, *The Meaning of Love* (Westminster, MD: Newman, 1955), p. 4, n. 1, for some references. But, by Prof. Johann's account, the trend must differ enough from Fr. Lonergan's approach; the latter would not speak of an experience of being, and his views on objectivity are quite different.

14. For an illuminating comparison of Thomist method with scientific, see "Isomorphism of Thomist and Scientific Thought," *Collection*, pp. 142–51. It illustrates briefly the possibility of such a "direct entry" and the consequent contact possible with modern thought.

15. "Proper object" here means what can be understood *per species proprias;* it does not mean the end of human intellect. A good idea of how proper understanding enters into that understanding of God and his revelation which was St. Thomas's objective may be had by working through the question, "De nominibus dei," *Summa theologiae*, I, 13.

the *res* be a stone or a philosopher, and his concern is for a unified view in which man is but a part of the *ordo universi,* still it is also true that stones and philosophers enjoy by no means equal shares of his attention. We can run through the *Summa theologiae* and find myriad instances of Aristotelian physical terms, but if we take a synoptic view we shall see that whether the question be *De deo uno,* or *De deo trino,* or the procession of creatures, or, most evidently of all, *De motu hominis in deum,* what is understood properly is man. St. Thomas will refer to the concept of stone to illustrate reasoning but what in fact he spends his time reasoning about is man.[16]

Moreover, the study of man offers unique possibilities to the thinker, not merely because man is a *minor mundus* in the sense sometimes assigned that he combines in his body all the material elements,[17] but because his own consciousness directly opens up a new world, and that new world is what man pre-eminently is. "The study of man . . . enjoys through consciousness an immediate access to man" (p. 333). Hence this study is possible in a way the physical sciences are not, it is possible in any age or at any point of material development, given only a degree of intellectual development and the scientific spirit. Both introspective science and empirical science are subject to the law of cyclic growth, but in the circuit of empirical science an essential factor is the devising of observable experiments which, as the science advances, require more and more intricate apparatus. Consciousness, on the other hand, is directly accessible to oneself, and indeed only to oneself; it is beyond the reach of instruments, though lie-detectors may have their uses, and so its study escapes in large measure the dependence on external apparatus which limits the advance of empirical science. Finally, there is no doubt that for St. Thomas it is within this area that man is pre-eminently man: *homo maxime est mens hominis.*[18]

At any rate, to come to *a posteriori* considerations, Fr. Lonergan's approach was, first, going beyond the words and milieu to attempt to reach the mind of Aquinas by a pivoting movement between his own developing rational self-consciousness and that of his master, and then on the basis of that appropriation to develop Thomism in the manner required by seven centuries of thought.

16. "Just how Aquinas reasoned out his concept of a stone, I cannot say; but in the second book of the *Contra gentiles* there is the magnificent reasoning out of the concept of the human soul; it runs through no less than forty-five chapters; and that long argument provides an excellent example of what exactly Aquinas meant by knowledge of essence" (*Verbum,* pp. 55–56).

17. *Summa theologiae,* I, 91, 1.

18. Ibid., I-II, 29, 4, c.; cf. II-II, 141, 1, 1m: "homo inquantum huiusmodi est rationalis"; I-II, 3, 5, c.: "unusquisque videtur esse id quod est optimum in eo," where the *optima potentia* in man is intellect; etc.

The first phase has its own interesting history. His technique is not to sit down and read St. Thomas through five times, but to study a particular question as it recurs in the *Opera omnia*. Any significant question will do to force that acquaintance with modern Thomist *Wissenschaft* which is a necessary material substratum for understanding his thought. But the question with which Fr. Lonergan began had more intrinsic influence on his development; the articles on *Gratia operans*[19] contain the presupposition of all methodical further study, the clear distinction between the natural and supernatural and hence between reason and faith. "For once reason is acknowledged to be distinct from faith, there is issued an invitation to reason to grow in consciousness of its native power, to claim its proper field of inquiry, to work out its departments of investigation, to determine its own methods, to operate on the basis of its own principles and precepts" (p. 527).

The *Verbum* articles[20] completed the first phase; in general, they were a movement from a conceptualism whose dreary possibilities are best measured by the achievements of electronic computers to an intellectualism that studies intellectual knowledge at its source in insight into phantasm, follows its operations in the *emanatio intelligibilis* of concepts and judgments, and ends with a grasp of cognitional process in its dynamism and the immanent conditions of its unfolding. This was not an easy task. Aquinas was concerned to present the universe from the explanatory point of view which relates things to one another; here, as was noted already, the human subject is one being among others and cognitional theory is cast explicitly in metaphysical terms. But "there is to be pieced together from Thomist writings a sufficient number of indications and suggestions to form an adequate account of wisdom in cognitional terms" (p. 407). It is this account of wisdom that, in Fr. Lonergan's view, mediates most successfully between Thomist and modern thought.

This brings us to the proper contribution of *Insight* to Thomism. I believe that contribution is basically one of method. The wealth of more particular ideas crowding its pages may offer more palpable evidence of development, and readers may be caught up by those topics which lie in the field of their own interests: myth, schemes of recurrence, consciousness, space-time, emergent probability, scotosis, etc. But these are rather the first-fruits of his method and disclose its potentialities. It is method itself that is most at stake.

Genetically a method for reaching answers presupposes that we have

19. "St. Thomas' Thought on *Gratia operans*," 1941–42, subsequently republished as *Grace and Freedom: Operative Grace in the Thought of St. Thomas Aquinas.*

20. The Concept of *Verbum* in the Writings of St. Thomas Aquinas," subsequently republished as *Verbum: Word and Idea in Aquinas.*

already reached at least some of them. Only when we have groped our way down the dark corridor and found the light-switch can we look back and see how we should have come. The illustration is rough but will serve, for the corridors of knowing show a pattern. Method then is not essential to obtaining results, but it accelerates the process, eliminates misconceptions, and where the question is that of metaphysics, frees the Thomist position from an antiquated science that risks giving it the appearance of a mummy (pp. 400–401).

Consequently everywhere in *Insight* we meet the concern for method, for an intelligent anticipation of the answers. First on the scientific level: "The scientist pins his faith, not on this or that scientific system or conclusion, but on the validity of scientific method itself " (p. xxi). Fr. Lonergan finds four methods necessary to an adequate scientific methodology:

The anticipation of a constant system to be discovered grounds classical method; the anticipation of an intelligibly related sequence of systems grounds genetic method; the anticipation that data will not conform to system grounds statistical method; and the anticipation that the relations between the successive stages of changing system will not be directly intelligible grounds dialectical method. But data must either conform or not conform to system and successive systems must be either related or not related in a directly intelligible manner. Accordingly, taken together the four methods are relevant to any field of data; they do not dictate what data must be; they are able to cope with data no matter what they may prove to be (p. 485).

But these four methods apply on the level of empirical inquiry and understanding. Above this is the critical level of reflection, and here the concern is with a method of philosophy. A first and important step is to divide clearly the fields of philosophy and science. Medieval Scholasticism discovered the distinction of reason from faith, the Renaissance exploited the distinction but without discovering the need for a similar distinction between science and philosophy (pp. 527–528). Fr. Lonergan divides the explanatory field "into science that explains and metaphysics that anticipates the general structure of proportionate being as explained" (p. 524). "Metaphysics contains virtually and structurally what the sciences are to discover formally and in detail" (p. 508). It "derives from the sciences the content and enrichment that actual activity brings to a dynamic structure" (p. 509). But the findings of science are not a basis for philosophy, for they are hypothetical and subject to constant revision. The basis for philosophy is cognitional activity itself in its unchanging structure, and "the contribution of science and of scientific method to philosophy lies in a unique ability to supply philosophy with instances of the heuristic structures which a metaphysics integrates into a single view of the universe" (p. 430). Basing philosophy on cognitional activity and its heuristic anticipations gives it permanent stability and removes it from the possibility of radical revision, for the revision could only be made by an empirical, intelligent, and rational knower, who could only attempt the revision by appealing to data to justify his positing in judgment the concept he has formed by understanding. But then he has himself supplied an instance of the unchanging structure of cognitional activity.

Now it is evident that both scientific and philosophic method owe much to the Herculean efforts of the last four centuries; this then would be the place to discuss *Insight*'s debt to modern thinkers, did not the complexity of that question put it beyond my competence to handle. It is clear that, in the Scholastic tradition, Fr. Lonergan takes resolute issue with many great names on a series of fundamental questions. It is also clear that, along with progressive Scholasticism, he refuses to present forever a merely negative attitude towards aberrant genius.[21] But if it is correct that the direct development of *Insight* from St. Thomas involved a process more complex than the common notion of intellectual dependence, we must expect an even greater complexity in fixing its dialectical relationship to the "counterpositions." Perhaps those who have read and pondered chapter 17 will agree that so delicate a task could not be undertaken in a few pages or by any other than a speculative historian of philosophy and science.

21. See *Insight*, p. 374, his remark on a positive attitude toward Hegel.

3

Neither Jew nor Greek, but One Human Nature and Operation in All*

The differences between Hebrew and Greek thought-patterns are a common-place today in the academic world, and are rapidly becoming such in popular journalism. One sees the dynamic opposed to the static, the existential to the essentialist, the concrete view to the abstract, the active surrender of faith to the cold speculation of reason. The temporal and historical are contrasted with the timeless and unchanging and permanent, and the total view, in which knowing includes loving, to the analytic tendency which distinguishes faculties, habits, and acts, categorizing the latter according to their specifically differing objects.

It is no argument against the core of truth in these contrasts to say that they have begun to be used as mere clichés, without effort to define and be precise, without sense of limits, nuances, exceptions, without urge to investigate accurately the truth of the matter. It is not even relevant in this context to remark that the clichés are sometimes uttered in the same breath with a rather haughty condemnation of the scholastic clichés they would replace, nor is it any refutation of their fundamental truth that they can be and are made to serve personal interests as well as scientific objectives. For clearly at their origin was a moment of creative insight, which responsible scholarship has been concerned to formulate with care, elaborate in detail, and verify by patient research. Whatever the exaggerations therefore in their further use, whatever the unauthenticity of the user, the differences between Hebrew and Greek are now part of our patrimony of learning, and only the most unin-structed of theologians would dispute the need of taking the distinctive character of Hebrew ways into account when he interprets the Bible.

This particular set of differences, more familiar of course to those who ply the trade of theologian, is nevertheless just an instance of the widespread phenomenon of differentiation that can be observed in mentalities, mores, institutions, civilizations and cultures, between suc-

*Previously published in *Philippine Studies* 13 (1965), pp. 546–71.

cessive ages of history, between peoples living in isolation from one another in a given age, and even between groups and social castes within a given tribe or people. Hebrew and Greek, opposing one another across the great divide between East and West, may already forecast the full possibilities of differentiation inherent in human ways, but their differences are after all minor compared to those that exist between the extremes of Oriental and Occidental cultures—differences so radical that missionaries sometimes feel forced to question the validity of our most basic philosophical principles, to ask whether it is not simply more of European imperialism when we try to impose them on the peoples of the Far East, whether we must not learn a quite different philosophy from Chinese or Indian thought, and learn to express our Christian faith in terms that bear little or no relation to the Judeo-Hellenic terms in which the early Church formulated it. Further, this difference between Far East and European–New World West is itself, perhaps, by no means the most radical phenomenon of its kind: the study of the pre-logical mentality of primitive peoples that has produced such interesting results in this century provides indications of still more fundamental differences among those we nevertheless recognize as belonging to the community of mankind.

Finally, there is the fact, with its own relevance to the present problems of theology, that, within a given culture and among those who greet one another from day to day, there are comparable differentiations. A few years ago C. P. Snow, in the Rede Lecture at Cambridge University, gave what has become almost classic expression to the alienation of scientific and literary men from each other. Working in the daytime with scientists and spending evening hours with literary colleagues, he felt he "was moving among two groups—comparable in intelligence, identical in race, not grossly different in social origin, earning about the same incomes, who had almost ceased to communicate at all."[1] Most readers will have some acquaintance with the storm of conflict the lecture caused,[2] but whatever the flaws in Snow's argument and however real the victory claimed by his opponents, the situation remained problematical enough for *Daedalus* this year to devote a special issue to the theme "Science and Culture"[3] in order "to study some

1. *The Two Cultures and the Scientific Revolution* (Cambridge: Cambridge University, 1959), p. 2. See also *The Two Cultures: And a Second Look* (New York: Mentor, 1964), which adds Snow's comments after four years.

2. One indication: the article of F. R. Leavis and the consequent flood of letters in *The Spectator:* see 9 March 1962, pp. 297–303, and 16 March 1962, pp. 329–33.

3. *Daedalus* 94/1 (Winter, 1965), with Gerald Holton as guest editor. German interest in the question can be gauged from P. K. Kurz, "Literatur und Naturwissenschaft," *Stimmen der Zeit* 176 (1965), pp. 1–20.

of the connections that exist" between the activities represented by those two headings, and "to gauge the accuracy of popular views which emphasize the supposed isolation of humanists, scientists and artists."[4]

Such phenomena as I have been sampling have not failed to excite the interest of philosopher and theologian, and to enter largely into theories of history, development, crosscultural communication, and the like. In this field Vico (1668–1744) is credited with founding the philosophy of history with his *Principii di una scienza nuova . . .*, setting forth the development of nations in the three stages of the age of the gods, the heroic age, the human age. We know the tremendous advances achieved by this science in the centuries since Vico's time, and the relevance of those achievements to the task of the theologian, whether he be engaged in the crosscultural task of transition from biblical categories to theological, or the task, likewise crosscultural, of passing from theological terms to a kerygma that is differentiated, adapted, contemporaneous, immediate, relevant to his hearers in their present concrete situation.

But the purpose of this article is not to talk about differentiations of culture—it presupposes them—but to ask about the community that is prior to the differentiations, to sketch one view of its structure and list some of its manifestations, and to suggest lines for investigating its relevance to the diversity of Jew and Greek. Is there a community that lies behind their differences and makes communication between the cultures possible, allows transition from one to another as well as integration of their goods and achievements in the realm of spirit? A rather consistent and, in my opinion, inevitable concern of students of culture has been to find something like a universal base from which to attempt a general critique of the various cultures. It is that underlying unity which is the theme here rather than the more obvious diversity. Though positivists despair of finding such a unity and resist what they would regard as philosophical imperialism in this field, the philosopher and theologian should be open to its discovery. For, if it is found, it should greatly promote the solution of the crosscultural problems that beset us today in the sacred sciences. No doubt the problem of communication generally admits an *ad hoc* solution; as Robert Oppenheimer said of the tensions that develop in modern society between men in diverse academic pursuits, there is a remedy open to us in this, that "we can have each other to dinner."[5]—An ambiguous suggestion, perhaps, should we happen to be dealing with a cannibalistic culture, but

---

4. *Daedalus* 94/1 (Winter, 1965), p. iii, from the preface by S. R. G(raubard).
5. Quoted by Gerald Holton, ibid., p. xii.

even then means of communicating could surely be worked out at some elemental human level of understanding and sympathy. But our concern is for a basic theory that might systematize the various *ad hoc* proposals and be fertile in the creation of better ones.

I

To speak of differentiations is already to suppose an original unity from which the differences developed. Moreover, that usage is justified in some fundamental sense by the fact that our problem concerns members of one human race, for there is surely some obscurely glimpsed reason for the unanimity with which we set the creature we call "man" apart from other beings in the visible world. Even those who are most vocal in their rejection of a philosophical *a priori*, in their denial of anything like an "essence" in man, take this stand for the paradoxical reason that men are such as to be clearly distinguished from the world of animals, plants, minerals, etc. Very well, that "suchness" which is the basis of their discrimination, I will refer to as "nature," for, even though that nature is simply "possibility," it is a possibility that animals do not share; and then we can say that the community of human nature that lies behind differentiation, supplies also the underlying possibility of communication and integration. One might add a further *a priori* unity from the religious side, in the will of God that all men be saved, in the universal application of redemption and the gospel, but in this article I limit discussion to more secular factors. Hence my title. Though it will seem deliberately provocative to the enemy of the secular in religious questions, it indicates quite accurately the scope of my article.

Let us begin, not with the basic community itself, but with a rather simple clue to the way we might profitably investigate our question. The clue consists in the stability of the descriptive categories used in the natural sciences, as contrasted with the extreme variety and change of the categories that pertain to the cultural side of human life.[6] Thus, colors, sounds, the feel of things, hot and cold, hard and soft, light and heavy, all these categories remain relatively constant for men across time and space. We observe other men reacting in the same way as we do to external stimuli and, though we have no access to their internal experience, we presume reasonably enough that they see the same colors in the spectrum and hear the same range of musical notes; if a person is obviously color-blind or tone-deaf, we put it down to a defect in his organic or nervous system. Similarly, we are accustomed within limits

6. See Bernard Lonergan, *De deo trino* (Rome: Gregorian University, 1964), vol. 2, pp. 42–47, for this idea and its elaboration; also vol. 1, pp. 88–91.

to common modes of operation, seeing men everywhere using their legs for locomotion, their hands for guiding tools in doing and making, their vocal apparatus for speaking. On the other hand, whatever pertains to the cultural exists in the widest variety, beginning with the very words we use to describe our common experiences: "hot," "*chaud*," etc. The music and dance of India are so different from those of Europe as barely to be included within the same category; one does not readily pass from knives and forks to chopsticks; a hockey fan can be extremely bored at a cricket game; and so forth.

What accounts for this contrast? Clearly, the sensing and performing structures of the human body are the constant factor that make the same colors distinguishable by all men, that make "hot" and "cold" categories that apply everywhere, that make all men walk about in an upright posture. But the structures are merely formal as regards the materials to be "processed," and with regard to these materials and their combinations the greatest variety is possible. All men use their eyes to see, but they see different things, they look for different things to see, and—most important of all—they can use their free imaginations to construct different objects for observation or contemplation. Similarly, all men use their legs to move about, but they go different places. All men use their hands for performing delicate operations on materials—*organum organorum,* Aristotle and Medieval thinkers called the hands—but they make different artifacts. Thus, human ingenuity plus the variety of materials result in the differences of "hot" and "*chaud,*" of Indian dance and European, of hockey and cricket, and so likewise of boomerang and rifle, of guild and labor union, of cave-dwelling and sky-scraper, of *Arabian Nights' Entertainment* and *Hamlet* or *King Lear.*

I have called the foregoing merely a clue, for our concern is not with hockey and cricket, obviously, but with more basic activities. The very fact that one man uses his eyes on his wheat-field and finds his interest there, while another is completely absorbed in looking at a set of black inkmarks on paper, suggests that there is an "internal" activity which is more properly human than merely seeing or hearing, using hands or feet, one that determines the choice of objects at which to look and the use of the body's members. But there is a clue in these more "external" activities, in that we can discern there something like a formal structure which remains relatively constant, and distinguish from it the materials that continually change, enter into different combinations, issue in extremely diversified products. And the question now is whether there is, in this more properly human activity, some counterpart of that distinction, and some analogous structure which remains as a permanent way of operating in all the changes of the *operata*. We may even ask in anticipation whether that internal structure will not be so much the more stable as it belongs to "spirit" rather than to "body" and so is removed from even the chance variations that have their possibility in the material substrate and occasionally issue in malformed human beings.

The purpose here is to go beyond generalities. Everyone who talks about "men" must concede, grudgingly perhaps, some basic community that makes us one and offers the possibility of communication. Almost any Thomist would go further and assign the basis of differentiation in a subjective element of potentiality corresponding to an objective. Objectively, there is the infinite potentiality of matter that admits of such a bewildering variety of forms in the physical, chemical, biological, zoological realms, matter that is open to development, not merely through chance variation and emergent probability, but also through the intervention of the artificer, that may be molded into tools, buildings, artifacts and institutions of boundless variety. Corresponding subjectively, there is the infinite resourcefulness of intelligence, *potens omnia facere,* capable in its wide-ranging fertility of conceiving mentally and directing the creation in reality of all the forms that the material universe offers in potency. Now I certainly do not contemn such generalities as these; in the long run they are more significant than the notion of structure to be exposed in this article. But they are even less likely to interest specialists and, as I shall explain, it is the specialists who must eventually take up the challenge if we are to see more of a community between Hebrew and Greek than we have done in the recent past. We have to be more specific therefore, and so we speak of common structures.

II

The notion of structure received a 748-page introduction in Bernard Lonergan's *Insight,* the aim of which was "to assist the reader in effecting a personal appropriation of the concrete, dynamic structure immanent and recurrently operative in his own cognitional activities."[7] His exposition, which I follow here, may be briefly outlined as follows. In the beginning is experience: I hear and taste and feel and smell and, most of all, I see. So of course does my dog; but there is the difference between me and my dog that I get ideas about my experience; more basically, there is in me a wonder, a capacity to inquire and seek the

7. *Insight: A Study of Human Understanding,* p. xvii. See also *Verbum: Word and Idea in Aquinas.*

intelligibility of experience; it is this wonder that gives rise to ideas. Sooner or later, however, in the self-correcting process of learning, I discover that my ideas are not always right, that error abounds when I accept my ideas uncritically, that ideas in general are just *possible* explanations of the data and, if I am to be rational, I must institute a further inquiry, I must reflect on the correctness of my ideas; it is this reflection that gives rise to rational truth and knowledge of the real. So there are three levels: experience (data, presentations of sense, representations of imagination), understanding (ideas, thoughts, suppositions which are possible explanations), reflection (grasp of evidence grounding judgment and knowledge). And the dynamism which operates the transition from level to level is manifested in a twofold question: the question for understanding which turns experience into something to be understood, the question for reflection which turns the idea into something to be investigated for its truth. Furthermore, within each of the two higher levels there is the extremely important element of formulation, the Thomist twofold *verbum*: on the level of understanding, ideas are formulated in concepts (transition from engagement with the particular to release from the particular in universalization); on the level of reflection, grasp of evidence is formulated in judgments (transition from subjective grounds for affirmation to objective judgment and the "public" character of knowledge, the possibility of communication).

The foregoing account was limited to the three levels of cognitional activity. If we add now the very essential further element of the affective and voluntary, we have four levels of human consciousness and activity: the empirical (experience), the intellectual (understanding), the rational (reflection), the moral (voluntary). To quote a summary account that Fr. Lonergan himself gives in a recent article:

If one wakes, one becomes present to oneself, not as moved but as moving, not as felt but as feeling, not as seen but as seeing. If one is puzzled and wonders and inquires, the empirical subject becomes an intellectual subject as well. If one reflects and considers the evidence, the empirical and intellectual subject becomes a rational subject, an incarnate reasonableness. If one deliberates and chooses, one has moved to the level of the rationally conscious, free, responsible subject that by his choices makes himself what he is to be and his world what it is to be.

Does this many-leveled subject exist? Each man has to answer that question for himself. But I do not think that the answers are in doubt. Not even behaviorists claim that they are unaware whether or not they see or hear, taste or touch. Not even positivists preface their lectures and their books with the frank avowal that never in their lives did they have the experience of understanding anything whatever. Not even relativists claim that never in their lives did they have the experience of making a rational judgment. Not even determinists claim that never in their lives did they have the experience of making a responsible choice. There exist subjects that are empirically, intellectually, rationally, morally conscious.[8]

III

The question now is of the verification of this structure in different activities of different cultural groups, for the universality of the structure remains just an idea until rational reflection on the evidence grounds its assertion. That is, just as the intrinsic dynamism of the structure, if it exists objectively, calls for verification of every idea conceived in the mind of man, so it calls for verification of our ideas about the structure itself. We have to adduce some evidence that scientist, artist, philosopher, theologian, believer, types at first sight so alien to one another, nevertheless operate in patterns that are similar in form, isomorphic. So I propose to indicate that isomorphism here in two paradigm comparisons: that of Thomist procedures with those of empirical science, that of the latter with everyday intersubjective procedures. Then, in the following section I shall go on to suggest that biblical procedures themselves follow a similar pattern. For simplicity's sake I will limit my brief considerations to cognitional structures, there being less doubt, I should think, about the fact of a moral conscience operating in all men in some manner that is relevant to their particular activities.

The first point, the isomorphism of Thomism and science in their cognitional structures, has been the object of a special study of Fr. Lonergan himself,[9] and I simply summarize his findings here. Briefly, the relation of hypothesis to verification in science is similar to the relation of definition to judgment in Thomism, the empirical character of science rendering verification necessary just as the freedom of divine providence determines the need of Thomist judgment in addition to definition. Further, with regard to origins, "just as the scientific problem leads to a scrutiny of sensible data that ultimately results in an hypothesis, so the Thomist question leads to a scrutiny of sensible data that ultimately results in a definition."[10] Again, Thomist abstraction corresponds to scientific invariance, both claiming independence "of the spatio-temporal conditions of their origins on the level of sense."[11]

---

8. "Cognitional Structure," in *Collection: Papers by Bernard Lonergan, S.J.*, p. 227. Notice that the special interest in our quotation is the human subject as subject, as conscious and present to himself; however, the four levels of consciousness are the same as the four levels of operation.

9. "Isomorphism of Thomist and Scientific Thought," *Collection*, pp. 142–51.

10. Ibid., p. 145.　　　　　　　　　　　　11. Ibid.

And, as scientific scrutiny leads only to approximate laws, so too Thomist effort to define is marked by a parallel modesty that recognizes very few essential definitions and struggles towards its goal by a reasoning process rather than by a leap of intuition. Then, scientific anticipations form a heuristic structure similar to the metaphysics that results from Thomist operations: "it is remarkable that the scientist conceives as his ideal goal knowledge of theories verified in any number of different instances and that the Thomist will add that by verification the scientist knows contingent existence, by theories he knows essences and forms, and by appealing to instances he acknowledges matter as well as form and existence. . . . Because every revision is simply a repetition of the same general process of experience, of hypothesis, and of verification, the structure of scientific knowledge is a constant and that methodical constant squares with the Thomist metaphysical constant of potency, form, and act."[12] Finally, besides the moving object of understanding (quiddity or form emergent in sensible or imagined objects), there is the end or goal that is being in its full sweep, and this, besides being explicit in Thomism, continually challenges the scientist to proceed beyond the narrow limits of his specialty, and so "contemporary science finds itself compelled to relinquish its traditional naive realism and to come to grips with philosophic issues."[13]

It should be repeated that the structural isomorphism allows full scope to differences arising from different materials, different "formal objects" of the various sciences, different sources of truth.[14] The significant point here is that the scientist deals with data, hypotheses, and verification, where the Thomist cognitional structure deals with *sensibilia, intelligibilia,* and *vera,* relating them to the corresponding elements of the ontological counterpart, potency, form, and act.[15] If the materials are so different, that very fact makes the similarity of pattern in the operations all the more remarkable, suggesting already a more universal occurrence of the pattern.

That suggestion receives strong and perhaps unexpected confirmation in the entirely different situation of everyday life and its cognitional activity. For there is little trouble in showing that cognitional activities

---

12. Ibid., pp. 146, 150.   13. Ibid., p. 150.

14. Ibid., p. 142. "Isomorphism, then, supposes different sets of terms; it neither affirms nor denies similarity between the terms of one set and those of other sets; but it does assert that the network of relations in one set of terms is similar to the networks of relations in other sets."

15. The reader will ask for documentation of this point (the relation of cognitional and ontological structures in Thomism), but here I can only refer to my article, "St. Thomas and the Isomorphism of Human Knowing and Its Proper Object," *Sciences ecclésiastiques* 13 (1961), pp. 167–90.

occur here in the very same general relationship and pattern as they do in science.[16] Both the scientist and "everyman" begin with experience. The scientist observes data: the paths of the planets, the lid of the tea-kettle puffing up and down, the more controlled experiments of the laboratory. The plain man observes data: the rattle in his car, the look of anger from his employer, the strange silence in the house when he goes home. Both the scientist and "everyman" are concerned to under-stand. "Why" is as familiar a word to one as to the other; each in his own way ponders, turns over the data in his imagination, puzzles, worries, finally gets an idea. Both the scientist and "everyman" are concerned with truth. The plain man does not rest content with his idea, at least when something he values is at stake; if, for example, there is question of investing money, the mere possibility that things may be as represented by the salesman does not move him, he wants to check and make sure, to get at the truth of the matter. Further, he can be quite adept in conversation at exposing the defects in his neighbor's view, pointing triumphantly to contradictions there, marshalling evi-dence for his own position. He might be repelled by such words as "verification," "crucial experiment," and the like, but the procedures they name are not totally unknown to him. It has even to be said that "everyman," like the scientist, is concerned in due measure to formulate his understanding, to find words to communicate it. Undoubtedly, this exigence is less demanding in everyday life where understanding so often remains in the preconceptual state, where the death of a child brings father and mother together in wordless sorrow. But even then they feel the need to talk, to put their sorrow into words; and the other children, too young for speeches, find a solace in hearing their parents give voice to the common grief of all.

Again, of course, the differences are great. The lacunae in the pro-cedures of "everyman" are more obvious than the structural elements that are present. He does not pursue understanding as a career; he easily gives up the attempt to formulate his thoughts; except in certain restricted areas, his efforts at verification are half-hearted; he does not consciously set the universe of being as his goal but recognizes mind's exigence mostly in the field of the practical and so, when his family's needs are provided for, is quite content to sit with pipe and slippers without caring to dominate the universe by knowledge. But the fact that he *sometimes* follows the same pattern as the scientist and philos-opher, that he *can* inquire into the meaning of data, formulate an idea, and investigate its truth, makes it legitimate to ask whether the more

16. For the relation of our cognitional theory and structures to "common sense" and "mythic consciousness," see *Insight* (index, under those words).

noticeable lacunae, instead of indicating a quite different procedural structure, are not rather signs of a failure to respond to the native exigence of human spirit, a failure that is perfectly understandable in the context of practical life and the pressing need of earning a living for his dependents.

There is a connected area that seems to me extremely important for this question; I add a word on it here by way of appendix to this section. We find, in modern literature, almost an obsession with the problem of meaning in interpersonal relationships. A novelist is not content, for example, to have his characters join in love as brute animals do; the relationship must be suffused with meaning, and invested with a ceremonial, and lifted to the level of the artistic. Just as eating and drinking are an artistic performance in man and their execution in a merely animal way revolting, so also the marital relationships of man and woman. This is so much the case that it provides a clear and generally applicable distinction between pornography and art, the one merely unreeling a succession of images to arouse animal passions, while the other is concerned to give meaning and dignity to those same passions and their consequents by raising the biological to the artistic.[17]

Now that concern seems relevant to our exposition of cognitional structure and even to scientific procedures. True enough, since Dilthey a whole school of thought has diligently distinguished "understanding" in the human area from "explanation" in the natural sciences: I *understand* my friend's need, but I *explain* the eclipse of the moon. However, it seems to me that both examples are concerned with the exigence for understanding in some more fundamental sense, with the need, let us call it, for *intelligibility* in the world, be it the world of man or the world of nature. To be accurate here, we should notice that the artist also *creates* meaning and intelligibility, endowing otherwise brute materials and actions with form and dignity and meaning, and so the analogy is not so much with pure science as with technology. If this evokes a still keener protest from the artist, who certainly does not want the characters of his novel compared to mousetraps and detergents, I can only reply again that this is to attend to the differences of materials, which may be enormous, but is to overlook the common structure that is my only concern in this article.

One can press the isomorphism further still and insist that even the exigence for formulation and abstract conceptual expression appears in the field of art. Not necessarily in the artist himself, who will sometimes decline to formulate the meaning of his work, but in the work of critics. What are the critics doing if not attempting to detach the meaning of

17. Ibid., p. 187.

the artistic creation from the particular image or form in which it is embodied or incarnate and universalize it, make it public intellectual property through words and concepts? However much the artist may condemn the critics as parasites on his creativity, it seems clear that the human race is not going to dispense with them; they answer to a basic need of the human cognitional structure. Finally, the exigence for truth is implicit in the moral judgment of the artist, when he asks, not whether his work has value as art, but what the morality is of his executing the work and presenting it to the public, *this* public in a particular state of development, education, etc. I think that, despite all their rebellion against the less intelligent elements in law and censorship, responsible artists do experience and submit to this exigence.

IV

We come now to the chief interest of this article: the isomorphism of Hebrew and Greek cognitional structures, to put the theme in the most unprepossessing terms. In entering this important field of debate and proposing to say something on this vexed question, I would respect the norm that always guides the responsible writer but presses on him here with a special urgency, of not pronouncing on matters that lie beyond his competence and of informing his readers as well as possible what he is trying to do. First, then, my purpose here is merely to suggest possible lines of approach. We very much need a *thorough* study of the type that is only hinted at here, even if it should come to conclusions opposed to those I anticipate—especially so, in that case. But it would have to be done by a specialist in biblical thought. As a theologian, I cannot very well undertake the detailed investigation, though I believe that a theologian has to conceive the question, set the terms of the inquiry, and propose the general procedures consonant with the question that is being investigated—I shall return to that point presently. Secondly, the biblical data which I will study in a tentative way are the question for understanding, the question for reflection, and the objective of truth. But the study will not consist in writing dictionary articles on the biblical words for question, understanding, reflection, truth; it will consist in studying the activities denoted by those words. The search is not for these ideas *in actu signato,* as themes, but *in actu exercito,* as lived and practiced. Thirdly, I make no concession to the view that creates a mystique of the Hebrew mind. I assume that the word "why" manifests similar mental operations whether it occurs in the mother of Jesus or in Aristotle. If my assumption is wrong, my error can be demonstrated, but the demonstrator will be asked to give me his views on the general community and differences of cultures, the relationship of nature and grace, the potentiality of intellect with regard to natural science and divine mysteries, and other matters that pertain to the presuppositions of such a demonstration.

My first question regards the biblical interest in questions for understanding. As stated, we will not pursue a linguistic study of the word "question"[18] or write a commentary on the "useless questions" which are a theme in the Pastoral Epistles,[19] necessary as those lines of investigation may be in the thorough study that is desired. Our few and hasty soundings have to do with the *performance* of questioning; they cannot be independent of words which are, after all, the immediate object of study on the *sacra pagina*, but they will regard words that denote the activity in its occurrence, and not as thematized. The relevant words are "what," "why," "how," and the like, rather than "question," "inquiry," "heuristic," etc. Here innumerable instances leap to mind. The occurrence of "what?" on finding food in the desert: "When the Israelites saw it, they said to one another, 'What is it?'—for they did not know what it was" (Ex 16:15); or in the wonder created by the Lord's first miracle as recorded by Mark: "They were dumbfounded and began to ask one another, 'What is this?'" (Mk 1:27). The occurrence of "why?" in Mary's "Why have you treated us like this?" (Lk 2:48), or in the Lord's "If I spoke well, why strike me?" (Jn 18:23). The occurrence of such words as "how?" in Mary's "How (pôs) can this be . . . when I have no husband?" (Lk 1:34), or Nathanael's "How (pothen) do you come to know me?" (Jn 1:48).

A more reflective attitude, though still occurring without thematization of the questioning nature of man, is found in statements indicating the inner tension of inquiry, the dynamism of the search for understanding. Luke tells us that "Mary treasured up all these things and pondered over them" (Lk 2:19), where the word "pondered" is the same one he uses for the "discussion" of the Jewish rulers on how to handle Peter and John (Acts 4:15), and for the "debate" in which the Athenian philosophers engaged Paul (Acts 17:18). Linked with this is the occurrence of wonder in its milder forms. Generally *thaumazô* refers to the amazement of those witnessing signs and prodigies, but it can also refer to sentiments of simpler curiosity more akin to our English *wonder*, as when outside the sanctuary "the people were waiting for Zechariah, surprised (*ethaumazon*) that he was staying so long inside" (Lk 1:21). And, in general, there seems to be a wealth of relevant data in the references to the teaching process, the lack of understanding

18. See H. Greeven's article on *erôtaô* and its cognates in Kittel's *Theologisches Wörterbuch zum Neuen Testament*.

19. 1 Tim 6:4; 2 Tim 2:23; Tit 3:9.

charged as a failure,[20] the request for explanation indicating an existential need,[21] the apparent satisfaction that explanation gave.[22]

There is a second type of question: the reflection that requires evidence enough to justify a judgment on the matter. This question regards truth, it asks which side of a contradiction is right or, in the absence of contradiction, whether my idea is the right one. Again, we do not demand a thematization of the terms "reflection," "grasp of sufficient evidence," "verification," and so on, in the biblical record; we simply look for the performances that correspond, at least in a rudimentary way, to the elaborate procedures which we now denote by those terms. A paradigm will be helpful here, and a famous one exists historically in Abelard's *Sic et non*. The reader will remember that that book, so characteristic of the Middle Ages, so influential in promoting the dialectical spirit of those times, drew up with regard to some 158 propositions, the reasons for and against acceptance. It is a classic formula for the dialectical way to truth.

Now the Bible seems to give many instances, in its own way, of that sort of thing. A story of the legendary wisdom of Solomon supplies one perfect instance, when the two prostitutes stood before the king and argued: "'The child of this woman died in the night. . . . Then she arose . . . and took my child. . . .' 'No; but the living child is mine and the dead child is your child,' the other said" (1 Kgs 3:19 ff.); an open contradiction, if ever there was one, no more to be admitted by the Hebrew mind than by the Greek, as Solomon's judgment brought out in dramatic fashion. Or one could take an instance of a pattern that is recurrent in John: "There was much whispering about him in the crowds. 'He is a good man,' said some. 'No,' said others, 'he is leading the people astray'" (Jn 7:12). Later, we have the significant statement: "Thus he caused a split (*schisma*) among the people" (Jn 7:43).

In the light of this practically explicit admission of the principle of non-contradiction, one might examine more closely other episodes in the Bible. There is the test to which the Pharisees put Jesus on the marriage law: "'Why then,' they objected, 'did Moses lay it down that a man might divorce his wife by note of dismissal?'" (Mt 19:7). The objection, it seems to me, has as implicit presupposition the principle of non-contradiction: "You are saying one thing, Moses said the opposite, how do you get out of that?" Likewise, there is the question of the Lord's own disciples later in the chapter: "'Then who can be saved?' they asked" (Mt 19:25). God was certainly savior, and their Bible seemed to make prosperity a sign of his favor; but against that is a statement

20. See, e.g., Mk 6:52; Lk 2:50; Acts 7:25.
21. See, e.g., Mt 13:36.
22. See, e.g., Mt 13:51; 16:12; 17:13; Lk 24:45.

that seems to make salvation impossible to the wealthy—explain the contradiction. Clearer still is the Lord's own cross-questioning of the Pharisees on the Messiah: "'Whose son is he?' 'The son of David,' they replied. . . . 'If David calls him "Lord," how can he be David's son?'" (Mt 22:42–45).[23]

Questions for reflection lead naturally to their complement of truth, the judgment that answers "yes" or "no" and gives us knowledge. For the third time I insist on my procedure here: my appeal will not be to the biblical use of the word "truth"[24] but to the performance of asserting the truth. In that context, a very significant word is the simple copula, "is." When he wrote that the signs in his book "have been recorded in order that you may hold the faith that Jesus *is* the Christ, the Son of God . . ." (Jn 20:31), John is a witness for my case that the biblical writers are concerned with truth in the Scholastic sense of the word. Of course, the special interest of those writers appears in the very next line: "and that through this faith you may possess eternal life by his name." But no amount of insistence on this aspect ought to dilute the force of that "is." Such instances are legion, as when the centurion in Mark said, "Truly this man *was* a son of God" (Mk 15:39), or when the high priest challenged Jesus: "By the living God I charge you to tell us: *Are* you the Messiah, the Son of God?" (Mt 26:63).[25]

23. The questions which, following *Insight* (cf. index), I divide into types, may be introduced by the same interrogative and show the same grammatical form; so it is the *intention* of the questioner that determines the type of question. Does he intend to put an objection as one contradicting, as one concerned with the truth? Or does he intend to ask for explanation as one puzzled and desiring understanding? I would assign Mary's question in Luke 1:34 to the latter type, the Lord's in Matthew 22:45 to the former, but this is a point for exegesis to decide.

Generally, I should think, questions put in sarcasm (Jn 1:46) or hostility (Jn 6:42, 52) intend to contradict and regard the level of truth, whereas a more neutral attitude such as that shown by the Jerusalem delegation to the Baptist (Jn 1:25) could pertain to either level. In fact, the average man freely mingles both levels in confusion, and there is no reason for insisting that a given question must be a pure case of one or the other type.

Add one final note: many questions are implicitly statements, and then they pertain to our next paragraph.

24. The stock specialist account has been that the Hebrew meant by truth, not the "Greek" *adaequatio intellectus ad rem,* but something like fidelity. But that great debunker, James Barr, an Old Testament specialist himself, has recently produced a mass of evidence to show a common usage of the word in Greek and Hebrew writers; see his *The Semantics of Biblical Language* (Oxford: Oxford University, 1961), especially pp. 187–200. Our procedure avoids this controversy.

25. It is remarkable that little two-letter words should have such a profound philosophical and theological significance. "Is" is a prime example, but "yes" is equally pregnant; and so is "no" corresponding to "is not." Not only that, but a language may dispense with the copula, as Hebrew sometimes does, and then the same effect is gained without words, by the juxtaposition of subject and predicate or by other means. The answer of Jesus to the high priest was clearly an assertion, but may have been in an Aramaic form that would hardly be recognized as an assertion by a Westerner; so Mark translates very simply, "I am" (Mk 14:62).

What I have been trying to point out is an isomorphism of structure, a similarity in relation between cognitional acts, a formal likeness of biblical performance in this field to Greek and modern. If the reader wishes to judge the truth of my idea, he should attend rather exactly to the data I have presented, and not to some other data illustrating the more familiar differences between Hebrew and Greek. It is quite easy to be misled here by the vast difference in materials, or by the subtler difference between performance and thematization of the performance. Certainly the Hebrew "What is it?" is exercised on other materials than Aristotle's "Let us state what . . . substance should be said to be,"[26] and is much farther from thematization of performance; but is the performance itself similar in the two cases? Does each question manifest the same need of understanding, the same dynamism of intellect seeking explanation? Certainly the Hebrew "No; but the living child is mine and the dead child is your child" is very different from the Aristotelian "They do not all agree as to the number and the nature of these principles [of things]. Thales . . . says the principle is water. . . . Anaximenes and Diogenes make air prior to water. . . . Anaxagoras . . . says the principles are infinite in number,"[27] but is there a similarity in the dialectical form in which the argument is carried out and the truth pursued? Certainly the Hebrew "If David calls him 'Lord', how can he be David's son?" is a long way from the explicit and thematic formulation "The most certain principle of all is . . . that the same attribute cannot at the same time belong and not belong to the same subject and in the same respect . . .";[28] but would the Lord's point be valid without his implicit recognition of the principle Aristotle formulated, or would his case be cogent against the Pharisees unless they too recognized implicitly the principle involved? I believe that, if one gets hold of my point and achieves personal openness to the possibility of isomorphic structure in cognitional activity, he will have little trouble in discovering what seems so obvious to me, a basic community of mentality that underlies all the more superficial differences between Jew and Greek.

V

I have said that the thorough investigation of the topic I have merely introduced would have to be undertaken by a biblical specialist, but that the determination of the topic and of the general procedures consonant with its nature, the procedures that should be followed if *that* question is to be investigated and not some other, belongs to the more

26. *Metaphysics*, VII, 17.   27. Ibid., I, 3.
28. Ibid., IV, 3.

systematic tasks of the theologian. After all, one who reads the modern exegete will really not expect him to undertake an enthusiastic study of Aristotle's *Posterior Analytics*! Yet we can hardly have an expert knowledge of what a question in general is, if we ignore that kind of book; and not to have an expert knowledge of what a question is would be a very bad beginning for the investigation of the questioning nature of the Hebrew and the structure of his cognitional activity. It seems then that there must be place for more philosophical and theological considerations at the very outset of the study, and I should like to enlarge on that point before concluding.

It is a striking fact that almost every page of the New Testament is crowded with questions, and yet the *theme* of the question hardly occurs at all in the biblical dictionaries, commentaries, and manuals. But perhaps the oddity of that will disappear if we look at a few parallel cases in the history of theology. It is probable that the first treatise we know to have been called *De trinitate* was written by Novatian around 250 AD, but afterwards treatises under this title slowly became the fashion. And similarly other treatises begin at a point in time, to become later a regular occurrence: *De incarnatione* in the early fourth century, *De spiritu sancto* in the late fourth century, and so on. Not as if no one had worshipped the Father, Son, and Holy Spirit before 250 AD, but the holy three as such were not a theme; they *could* not be a theme, for, by all evidence, no one had even *counted* them before the last decades of the second century. The point is that thematization supposes a moment of creative insight; one must have the idea at least obscurely in mind first and then one attends more diligently to the data, either for conceptual formulation or for judgment on the fact. The Messiahship was a theme in the early Church and the Christian community ransacked the Old Testament for prophecies and elaborated on their fulfilment in the New. The destiny of the Jewish people became a theme for Paul in the Epistle to the Romans and he wrestled with the data to discover and explain to himself God's mysterious dealings with his chosen people.

Now the idea of human spirit as marked by its questioning character, as almost constituted by inquiry, though it has a kind of charter in Greek philosophy, became an explicit theme of philosophy only in relatively recent times—the human mind is so ponderously slow. The idea therefore could not possibly be a theme of investigation in New Testament studies before our times. This is not to claim that the idea must first occur to philosophers before it can enter biblical studies; as Gilson has long and eloquently insisted, many fundamental ideas of "Christian" philosophy were conceived under the influence of the word of God. My point is that the idea must occur somewhere and be at least obscurely formulated in someone's mind before it becomes a theme; it is most likely to occur to those who make a career of ideas; but even if it occurs in study of the New Testament itself, thematization will involve a return to the New Testament data for a thorough and proper investigation.

I have been talking of the priority of certain ideas in investigating the isomorphism of Hebrew and Greek mentalities, the need of a prior *Begrifflichkeit,* and I illustrated the need with the example of the question. This kind of program is not at all alien to the spirit of modern biblical research or of scientific investigation in general. It is another commonplace today that the interpreter brings his suppositions in every case to his task, that the ideal of presuppositionless inquiry, which prevailed when history was an emerging science, is really nonsense. The favorite example here is Bultmann, who has very definitely formulated presuppositions, uses them openly in his exegesis of the New Testament and, so far from repenting of his misdeeds, states that all other interpreters do what he does, only without acknowledging the fact. There can hardly be any doubt that Bultmann's program contains a valid point, for the only one who lives without presuppositions is the newborn babe: the infant is not much of a scholar, and neither would the adult be a competent interpreter if he tried to leave all ideas behind as he came to his task.

Nevertheless, we have to be accurate here to avoid relativism. An obvious objection might run: as your presuppositions, so your interpretation; modern science has taught us to be obedient to the facts, but the approach through presuppositions seems to determine beforehand what the facts are going to be allowed to be. The objector will supply instances of the corrupting influence of presuppositions on judgment: the decadent Scholastic insists on finding his notions of eternal procession, logical truth, substantial form, etc., in biblical terms that have a verbal resemblance, and similarly the uninstructed exegete cannot bear to find anything in the biblical record that savors of Scholastic procedures of defining terms, stating and proving a thesis, etc.

The answer to the objection consists in subjecting the cliché about presuppositions (for it too is a cliché) to precise analysis. What it seems to mean is that one's presuppositions yield a range of *possible* interpretations, they limit interpretation to a field, but within that field they do not determine which interpretation we must accept. It now becomes clear that the way to escape relativism is to adopt the universal viewpoint, to be open to all explanations and interpretations, excluding none *a priori,* admitting none *a posteriori* till rational evidence is forthcoming. The analogy here is the creative mind of God. It is filled with ideas of possible worlds and, the greater the number and variety of his ideas, the greater his freedom in creating, the less the necessity imposed on his actual choice of a world. That is, his ideas are an *a priori* on the level of possibility that eliminates any imposed *a priori* on the level of actuality. Similarly, the wider the viewpoint of the interpreter, the greater the number of possible interpretations open to him, and the greater his freedom in discovering the correct one.

But the universal viewpoint is not enough either, if we do not take possession of the operational structures which are ours. The world of objective being and the openness of subjective spirit can be completely universal, and our conversion to the universality of object and subject can be as genuine as you please; but if we have no grasp of the structure we necessarily use in guiding spirit to being, we can hardly avoid the most serious blunders. We need then a critical awareness, an appropriation and evaluation of our own powers of intelligent grasp and reasonable affirmation of the universe of being; we need also an awareness and appropriation of our power for harmonious accord with the universe, but the emphasis of this article has been on the cognitional side rather than on the affective. It was this taking possession of our operational structures that was treated in the second and third sections above.

Finally, there is knowledge of the particular differentiations that result when the structure is used on different materials and with different interests and with different degrees of correspondence to the dynamism that man is. Here the role of the specialist is to the fore. Every differentiated culture requires its own specialist, the Hebrew culture likewise requires its own, and my superficial efforts in the fourth section of this article should not be taken as a specimen of what a specialist might be able to do with the same material. But it seemed important to attempt a sketch myself, for otherwise the point of the preceding paragraphs was less likely to come through, or they might seem to be mere *a priori* reasoning without application to the biblical documents. There is indeed an *a priori* element in them, not an *a priori* that requires us to find, for example, the principle of non-contradiction in biblical writers, but the kind that enables us to see it if it is there. I think that the implicit admission of the principle is there, and that the apparent neglect of it on some occasions is explained here as it would be if found elsewhere, even among logicians—by the contradiction not being brought sharply to their attention, by the matter lying outside their present field of interest, etc. If then I were told by an exegete that Hebrew man cares nothing for my principle, I should listen, I hope, with respect, I should not label the exegete incompetent in his own specialty. But I should want to examine his presuppositions, I should regard it as within my competence to judge those presuppositions, and, if I found them faulty, I should continue to look for a specialist who is open to the universe of being, who has a view of man that does not *a priori* exclude Hebrew openness to the universe of being, and then I should put my question to him: Do you find an isomorphism in the cognitional structures of Hebrew and Greek?[29]

29. The same general attitude should be taken towards specialists in every culture, for, despite all the protests of the specialists and due regard being paid to the real dangers of imperialism on the part of general science, it can hardly be denied any longer that certain very general presuppositions guide every investigator who is worth his salt, and it is the business of general science to examine them.

This remark is made in relation to a short note of E. Bréhier, "Originalité de Lévy-Bruhl," *Revue philosophique de la France* . . . 139 (1949), pp. 385–88. Bréhier's thesis is that whereas study of primitive mentalities had formerly been dominated by the idea of genesis (that is to say, early myths are but an imperfect form of the true explanation science will discover), Lévy-Bruhl on the contrary discovered in the primitive mind irreducible structures not to be supplanted by "better" ideas; we are dealing with thinking of another nature, quite content with its achievements.

But everything here depends on how deeply one penetrates. The example given in the article is that of "causality": primitive myths are not to be reduced to a primitive idea of causality. Our notion of structure goes deeper than such comparisons, just as our notion of intelligibility goes deeper than causality; and so there is room for putting the question again: Is there an isomorphism between the primitive mentality and ours?

4

An Exploration of Lonergan's New Notion of Value*

In "*Insight* Revisited," a kind of intellectual autobiography, Fr. Lonergan describes, among other developments in his thinking, the change that took place between *Insight* and *Method* in regard to the notions of good and value:

In *Insight* the good was the intelligent and reasonable. In *Method* the good is a distinct notion. It is intended in questions for deliberation. . . . It is aspired to in the intentional response of feeling to values. It is known in judgments of value. . . . It is brought about by deciding and living up to one's decisions.[1]

This is a very concise statement of what seems to me to be an extremely important development. I propose to study it in this paper and my interest is not, I hope, foreign to that of our symposium. The notions of good and value enter explicitly as a factor in the functional specialty of dialectic, and it seemed to me that a study of Lonergan's advance under this heading, and an exploration or at least indication of a few of the questions it raises, could have some utility for our discussions.

We should not, of course, lose perspective in this exploration. First, it is possible that in some respects we are dealing, not with a development of Lonergan's thought, but with a further stage of its manifestation; we know that theological method was his goal when he began work on *Insight* and it is not always easy to decide whether later developments were overlooked at the time of *Insight* or simply postponed as a tactical measure to a later occasion. Next, even when there is development in his thought, the task remains of studying his work again to see whether there is an underlying unity between earlier and later stages that modifies the impact of the development. Thirdly, we should

*A paper presented at the first annual Lonergan Workshop, Boston College, 17–21 June 1974, where the general theme was "Faith and the Crisis of Our Culture." Previously published in *Science et esprit* 29 (1977), pp. 123–43, and *Lonergan Workshop* 3 (1982), pp. 1–24.

1. *A Second Collection: Papers by Bernard J. F. Lonergan, S.J.*, p. 277.

51

remember that what happened once may do so again; if the three levels of consciousness expanded to four, the four may expand to five, and the five to six. But one thing at a time, and I am content at the moment to study the difference between *Insight* and *Method* which is indicated in the brief, not to say cryptic, remark which I quoted at the beginning of this paper.

There is no grand strategy in my approach, nor do I hope to wrap up the entire question in this paper. Quite the contrary. Early in *Insight* Fr. Lonergan refers with evident approval to a point in Descartes' method: "Great problems are solved by being broken down into little problems."[2] The bulk of my paper will deal with just such a succession of little problems, and the best I can hope for is that the succession will prove to be a series leading towards a helpful conclusion.

I would like to begin with a few pointers that may indicate in a preliminary way the extent and character of the change we are investigating. The first is supplied by Lonergan's use of two quotations that may stand as symbols of his changing interest, one for that period in which he was preoccupied with *Insight* and the other for the period in which he was preparing *Method*. I have examined six larger works Lonergan wrote between 1953 and 1959 and in every one of them, as well as in *Insight* itself, there is a reference to the *Summa theologiae* of St. Thomas, part I-II, question 3, article 8. That article deals with the desire of the human mind for understanding, a desire that will not be satisfied until there is understanding of what God is, when man will enjoy perfect bliss. I find the recurring reference to this text[3] a clear and useful index to the predominantly intellectual interest that was Lonergan's at this time. But then I examined five of his writings in the years between 1968 and 1972, just before the appearance of *Method*, and found that in these, as well as in *Method*, the predilection for the Thomist natural desire to see God has been replaced by another; now the text that is regularly quoted is from St. Paul's letter to the Romans, and the passage speaks of God's love flooding our hearts through the Holy Spirit who is given to us.[4] Interest centers now on love, or on the affective, or on values.

2. *Insight: A Study of Human Understanding*, p. 3.

3. Works and references as follows: *De ratione convenientiae . . .* (Rome: St. Francis Xavier College, 1953–54), p. 9; *De sanctissima trinitate . . .* (Rome: Gregorian University, 1955), p. 34; *De constitutione Christi . . .* (Rome: Gregorian University, 1956), pp. 17, 19; *Divinarum personarum conceptio analogica* (Rome: Gregorian University, 1957), pp. 76, 265; "*Insight:* Preface to a Discussion," in *Collection: Papers by Bernard Lonergan, S.J.,* p. 157; "Christ as Subject: A Reply," in *Collection,* p. 191. In *Insight* itself the reference is on p. 369.

4. Works and references as follows, all in *Second Collection:* "The Natural Knowledge

A second pointer is similar, though not so clear-cut. Far back in the *Verbum* articles, Lonergan remarked: "For Augustine our hearts are restless until they rest in God; for Aquinas, not our hearts, but first and most our minds are restless until they rest in seeing Him."[5] I think it is fair to detect in this remark, especially when it is seen in the total context of the study, a clear leaning towards the Thomist attitude rather than to the Augustinian. And yet in *Method*, while this reference to Augustine does not occur, I think it fair to say that the thrust of the work is more in resonance with the Augustinian phrase than with the Thomist.

A third is found in the place and role that Fr. Lonergan assigns to feelings in relation to values. In *Insight*'s account of a possible ethics, feelings are of little relevance except as a likely source of bias. Lonergan therefore explicitly sets them aside:

[I]t will not be amiss to assert emphatically that the identification of being and the good by-passes human feelings and sentiments to take its stand exclusively upon intelligible order and rational value.

Feelings and sentiments are by-passed for, though one begins from objects of desire, one finds the potential good not in them alone but in the total manifold of the universe.[6]

Method, on the contrary, takes up feelings in its second chapter and develops a rather detailed view of them before moving on to incorporate this view into a theory of values.

A fourth pointer comes from an observation on the index I made for *Insight*. I notice that in drawing it up I first wrote a mini–essay (the only one, I think, in the index) on "Experience–Understanding–Reflection" as three levels of cognitional activity, and then gave 27 references to the text. The next entry in the index is "Experience–Understanding–Reflection–Will"; there is no essay, and there are only two references to the text. Clearly the three-level structure is dominant in *Insight*. But just as clearly a four-level structure has taken over in *Method*; we meet it already in the first chapter under the heading "The Basic Pattern of Operations," the levels are identified as empirical, intellectual, rational, and responsible,[7] and probably no idea in the whole book recurs so often.

---

of God," p. 129; "Theology and Man's Future," p. 145; "The Future of Christianity," p. 153; "The Response of the Jesuit as Priest and Apostle in the Modern World," p. 171; and "Philosophy and Theology," p. 204. For references in *Method*, see the index, *s.v.*, Romans.

5. *Verbum: Word and Idea in Aquinas*, p. 90. The reference to Augustine occurs again in "Theology and Man's Future," *Second Collection*, p. 146.

6. *Insight*, p. 606.

7. *Method*, p. 9. The first three names in this listing are not new—all occurred repeatedly in *Insight*.

It is to be noted, however, in regard to this fourth pointer that the difference is not just in the frequency with which the idea of responsibility occurs. Responsibility now belongs to a new level, as distinct from that of reflection as the intellectual is from the empirical and the rational from the intellectual. That was not the case in *Insight*. There, deliberation, decision, and the like, do not constitute a new and distinct level, but a continuation or extension of cognitional activity: "[T]he goodness of being comes to light only by considering the extension of intellectual activity that we name deliberation and decision, choice and will."[8] The accent is so much on the cognitional that the criterion of the good is seen as self-consistency in the knower between his knowing and his doing,[9] and value is defined as the "possible object of rational choice."[10]

The general lines of the contrast under this heading between *Insight* and *Method* are therefore fairly clear. There has been a shift from the cognitional to the affective, from the dynamism of "mind" intent on knowing God to the dynamism of "heart" oriented to him in love and bent on union with him, from a three-level structure of conscious intentionality to one with four levels, from an emphasis on what is reasonable in conduct to an emphasis on what is responsible.

I think we can say also that the outline of the chronological stages in the shift are fairly familiar to all of us. The turn to the subject which was already accomplished in *Insight* has led to an emphasis on the existential subject, and then to a locating of the criterion for judgments of value in the authenticity of the subject. There are milestones of progress in the Boston College lectures of 1957,[11] with their attention to the horizon of the subject and his existential concerns; in the Latin treatises of this period with their work on the consciousness of Christ and the theology of the three divine subjects;[12] in the concluding section of the 1964 paper "Cognitional Structure,"[13] with its brief but important linking of subjectivity to objectivity; most of all, in the Aquinas Lecture of 1968, *The Subject*: here we have the explicit abandonment of faculty psychology, the addition of deliberation as a distinct level of the existential subject, the doctrine of the sublation of lower levels by

---

8. *Insight*, p. 596.

9. Ibid.; see the index, *s.v.,* Self-consistency.

10. Ibid., p. 601.

11. Unpublished typescript, mimeographed at the Thomas More Institute, Montreal, in 1957, under the title *Notes on Existentialism*.

12. *De verbo incarnato,* 3rd edition (Rome: Gregorian University, 1964). See esp. thesis 10a, "De conscientia Christi." See also *De deo trino,* 3rd edition (Rome: Gregorian University, 1964), esp. vol. 2, c. 5, "De divinis personis inter se comparatis."

13. *Collection,* pp. 221–39; see pp. 236–39.

the higher, and other elements that prepare us for the transition brought to completion in *Method*.[14]

The general lines of the contrast and the milestones on the course of development are surely an invitation to further investigation. They tantalize us with a desire for the enrichment that we feel a thorough study of the materials would provide. But I leave that further study to some young and energetic doctoral candidate. My own purpose has been merely to set up a context for the questions that have occurred to me in my attempts to understand Fr. Lonergan's new position. I turn now to my own series of questions.

My first question is this: Has Lonergan abandoned the strongly intellectual cast of mind that characterized *Insight*? Does *Method* lack intellectual rigor? The question might arise in two ways: on Lonergan's position, or on the consistency of that position. Those who may not have noticed the explicit stand Lonergan takes in *Method* for the intellectual might ask the simple question what his position is; but even those who have noticed his defense of intellectual rigor may feel compelled to ask whether that position is consistent with the rest of *Method*. In one form or the other this question has given very real difficulty to a number of Lonergan's students, and I think it useful to be precise in dealing with it. Let us then postpone the nuanced form of the question to third place in our series, and deal with the simple form, however rhetorical and superfluous the question may seem. Luckily we can handle it with dispatch. *Method* is clear and unequivocal; the intellectual factor is not abandoned, it is sublated, which not only means the retention of the intellectual on the higher level, but also confers on it a new value and purpose:

> [W]hat sublates goes beyond what is sublated, introduces something new and distinct, puts everything on a new basis, yet so far from interfering with the sublated or destroying it, on the contrary needs it, includes it, preserves all its proper features and properties, and carries them forward to a fuller realization within a richer context.[15]

This principle is then expressly applied to the retention of truth with its proper intellectual character on the higher level of decision and love:

> [T]his in no way interferes with or weakens his devotion to truth. He still needs truth. . . . The truth he needs is still the truth attained in accord with the exigences of rational consciousness.[16]

14. *Second Collection*, pp. 69–86. See also "Theology in Its New Context," pp. 55–67 of the same volume.

15. *Method*, p. 241.

16. Ibid., p. 242, and see pp. 316, 340.

But a second question arises immediately: a sublation, our quotation tells us, "introduces something new and distinct." What is this "new and distinct" element on the fourth level of values? Already in a preliminary outline of the contrast between *Insight* and *Method* I have anticipated the answer, but it is time to collect the data more thoroughly and analyze them more deeply.[17]

The data from *Method*, we find, turn into a little cascade of terms. The first listing of the four levels refers to the fourth as the "responsible" level.[18] Later it is called "existential."[19] Later still, it is the level "of freedom and responsibility, of moral self-transcendence and in that sense of existence, of self-direction and self-control."[20] It is also the level for the exercise of vertical liberty.[21] Again, it is the level of "authenticity" (or unauthenticity),[22] and "the level on which consciousness becomes conscience."[23] We are likewise told that "as we mount from level to level, it is a fuller self of which we are aware,"[24] that on the fourth level "we emerge as persons,"[25] that "a man is his true self inasmuch as he is self-transcending,"[26] but there is a self-transcendence that is "only cognitive,"[27] and "knowledge alone is not enough" to determine values on the fourth level.[28]

One could go on in the direction of complexity to develop the wealth revealed in this set of terms, or one could go back in the direction of analysis and try to discover an underlying unity. My option is for the second, but first let me delimit carefully the field of inquiry. There is a distinction between the way the operations of conscious intentionality go forward "ordinarily,"[29] that is, from the empirical through the intellectual and rational to the responsible level, and an exception to this "ordinary" process which occurs in God's gift of his love in religion.[30] In this exceptional case, deliberation and intellectual activity are not prior to the fourth level; they are subsequent.[31]

17. As I enter more deeply into this question, I should acknowledge the help I have received from prolonged discussion with the following philosophers and students of Lonergan: Ney Affonso de Sá Earp, Giovanni Sala, Jesus Vergara.

18. *Method*, p. 9.

19. Ibid., p. 35.

20. Ibid., p. 121.

21. Ibid., p. 40.

22. Ibid., p. 35.

23. Ibid., p. 268.

24. Ibid., p. 9.

25. Ibid., p. 10.

26. Ibid., p. 357.

27. Ibid., p. 104.

28. Ibid., p. 38.

29. Ibid., p. 122.

30. Ibid. I omit the question of human love, which *Method* seems to leave unsettled; p. 122 makes it an exception, along with God's gift of love, to the ordinary process, but pp. 278 and 283 do not make it an exception. See also "Bernard Lonergan Responds," in *Foundations of Theology*, ed. P. McShane (Dublin: Gill & Macmillan, 1971), p. 227. (At the time of this lecture, 1974, I did not know of Lonergan's two ways of development—for which see ch. 20 below.)

31. *Method*, p. 283; and see pp. 340–41. The same point is made repeatedly in *Philosophy of God, and Theology: The Relationship between Philosophy of God and the Functional Specialty, Systematics;* see pp. 10, 50, 51, 52, 53–55, 58, 67.

I think it would be a mistake for me to try to handle this exceptional case simultaneously with the "ordinary" case of the fourth level. First of all, Fr. Lonergan himself has begun to talk about the level of love as a fifth level distinct from the fourth.[32] If he is serious about that, we must anticipate a further advance that will take us as far beyond *Method* as that book took us beyond *Insight*. With that prospect before us we may be pardoned for judging that we have task enough to deal with at the moment. In the second place, my preliminary study indicates that a solution to the present problem is operative analogously on the level of love also. In any case I intend to be faithful to my purpose of breaking big problems down as much as possible into little ones, so I set aside a study of love and values.

The task then is to determine whether there is a way of unifying the rich diversity of terms discovered in descriptions of the fourth level. I find a valuable clue in the source of the shift from third level to fourth. Lonergan's general term in *Insight* for the force that moves us from level to level was "operator," and the operator in the cognitional field was the "detached and disinterested desire to know"[33] expressing itself in questions.[34] Although *Method* shows a tendency to think in terms more of the whole subject than of the dynamism as the operator,[35] there does not seem to be any change in the role of the question: the operator of the shift from first level to second is the question for understanding, the operator of the shift from second level to third is the question for reflection, and the operator of the shift to the fourth level is the question for deliberation.[36] There may be a semantic problem connected with the use of "question" on this last level, but the dynamism is clear enough.[37]

When we ask therefore what is the new and distinct element added on the fourth level we come finally to the structured dynamism of human spirit that is given. It is the openness of human spirit to the intelligible, the reasonable, the good, an openness that reveals itself in successive steps as conscious intentionality, as demand for fulfillment. It seems unnecessary here to seek beyond that given structure for a further foundation and explanation of the content of the fourth level.

32. In an interview of 7 May 1973 for the CBC radio program, *Concern,* broadcast on 24 October 1973.

33. *Insight,* p. 532.

34. Ibid., p. 469.   35. *Method,* p. 7.

36. Ibid.; see pp. 34–35, also pp. 10, 11, 12, and passim.

37. My difficulty is that the term "questions for deliberation" puts the emphasis on the cognitional factor in fourth-level operations, whereas the fundamental drive comes from a force that moves us beyond the cognitional. One can get round the difficulty by understanding "question" analogously, as indeed it must already be understood analogously in "questions for understanding" and "questions for reflection," but commonly people will not think of the analogous use.

It is time now to go back to the question postponed earlier: Is Fr. Lonergan consistent in his claim that intellectual rigor is retained in *Method*? The book may assert that truth and intellectual rigor are sublated, not abandoned, but can this position be maintained in the face of all we read elsewhere in the volume on the influence of subjectivity on value-judgments? Is the rational element in values and conduct really included, preserved, and carried forward, when the truth or falsity of value-judgments "has its criterion in the authenticity or the lack of authenticity of the subject's being"?[38] This is the really difficult question. I have struggled long with it, and I must ask leave to deal with it slowly. Let me therefore subdivide again. We can consider the question either as an objection charging involvement in a vicious circle, or as a more positive request to give a critical grounding to the position of *Method*. The two aspects are intertwined, but I find it helpful to take them separately. So I turn to the question whether there is a vicious circle involved in Lonergan's view of value-judgments, and take it up as the third in my series.

The principle at issue here has an ancient history, going back as far at least as Aristotle's *Nicomachean Ethics*. Books II to V of that work deal with the moral virtues and, in the general account which precedes consideration of the particular virtues, Aristotle talks about the conditions of responsibility for action. Here a basic principle is that the end, that is, the good or the apparent good, is what we wish for, and the means are what we deliberate about and choose. But an objection arises at once; in the excellent English provided for him by Ross, Aristotle says: "Now some one may say that all men desire the apparent good, but have no control over the appearance, but the end appears to each man in a form answering to his character."[39] The last part of that quotation came into Medieval Latin in the form, "Qualis unusquisque est, talis et finis videtur ei," and is used over and over by St. Thomas.[40]

Aristotle's answer to the objection is that, if each man is somehow responsible for his state of mind, he will also be somehow responsible for the way the good appears to him; in other words, he made himself what he is. Aquinas refines considerably; in his *Commentary* on the *Ethics* and elsewhere, he distinguishes a universal and speculative knowledge from one that is immediate and practical, and subdistinguishes the latter according to whether it is under the influence of habit or of the impulse of the moment.[41] But he agrees with Aristotle on the basic

38. *Method*, p. 36.
39. *Nicomachean Ethics*, Bk. III, ch. 5, 1114a 30 f.
40. For St. Thomas on Aristotle, see *In III Ethic.*, lect 13; some references in the *Summa theologiae:* I, 83, 1, obj. 5a; I–II, 10, 3, obj. 2a.
41. *Loc. cit.*, nos. 518–20.

point that a man is responsible insofar as he made himself what he is; neither of them, as far as I know, denies the premise of the objection; the end *does* appear to each man in a form answering to his character.

The similarity of the problem raised by *Method* to the one faced by Aristotle and Aquinas is surely obvious. Lonergan, as far as I can judge, would not question Aristotle's principle any more than Aquinas did. In fact, he extends its application till it comes to bear on all that lies within a man's horizon. When horizons are opposed dialectically, he says, "What in one is found intelligible, in another is unintelligible. What for one is true, for another is false. What for one is good, for another is evil."[42] He not only seems to accept and widen the application of the principle, he makes it a positive element in his position rather than an objection to be answered; he glories in it, one might say: "Genuine objectivity is the fruit of authentic subjectivity."[43] At the same time he keeps using phrases like "what truly is good,"[44] "when the values . . . really are values."[45]

And that puts the problem squarely before us in a new form: How escape the vicious circle of judging our judgment of the values we choose as good for us? How do we go beyond the good for me or the good for us, to what is truly good, to what transcends the self? Our problem has transposed that of Aristotle and Aquinas; they were concerned with liberty and responsibility; our problem is epistemological, it concerns the objectivity of our judgments.[46] The need for an answer becomes acute when "we" who are right undertake to tell others they are wrong, and they in turn, convinced of their own rightness, reply in similar vein. And why should they not do so? All of us are victims of our past and enclosed within our present horizons, we as well as they, those who are right as well as those who are wrong. Is the whole business just too complex? Should we simply chuck it and go back to saying "God wills it and the Bible tells me so"?

I refuse to be so faint-hearted, and I think there is an Ariadne thread to lead us out of the labyrinth. It is Newman's view, developed by Lonergan, on "the true way of learning." Directly it deals with escape from a vicious circle that apparently encloses our cognitional efforts, but I believe this way of escape will prove very illuminating for escape

---

42. *Method,* p. 236.   43. Ibid., p. 292; see also pp. 265–338.
44. Ibid., p. 35.
45. In "Bernard Lonergan Responds," *Foundations of Theology,* p. 230.
46. There are many differences. Aristotle's approach was negative by way of an objection against his basic principle; ours is positive by way of establishing grounds of true objectivity. His context was that of liberty; ours is that of horizons that determine all judgments and choices. His problem was how to impute responsibility; ours is how to break out of an epistemological circle. His area of study was habits; ours is all that constitutes us existentially.

from the vicious circle that seems to imprison us in our efforts to ground our value-judgments. Let us turn then to Newman and "the true way of learning."

Newman's *Grammar of Assent* sets forth his opposition to Descartes' way of advancing in knowledge. Where Descartes would begin with a universal doubt and go on to establish all knowledge on this secure basis, Newman would begin from a universal credulity, with the prospect of eliminating error in due course as the truth developed and occupied the mind.

Of the two, I would rather have to maintain that we ought to begin with believing everything that is offered to our acceptance, than that it is our duty to doubt of everything. The former, indeed, seems the true way of learning. In that case, we soon discover and discard what is contradictory to itself; and error having always some portion of truth in it, and the truth having a reality which error has not, we may expect, that when there is an honest purpose and fair talents, we shall somehow make our way forward, the error falling off from the mind, and the truth developing and occupying it.[47]

The exercise of a certain amount of hindsight enables us now to analyze Newman's statement and find in it an assumption and an explicit program. There is an assumption of what we may call in Lonergan's terms the dynamism of a spontaneously operative cognitional structure; it lies behind such a statement as "[W]e may expect, that when there is an honest purpose and fair talents, we shall somehow make our way forward. . . ." There is a program which we may relate to Lonergan's self-correcting process of human learning; it appears in phrases like "begin with believing . . . ," "discover and discard what is contradictory to itself. . . ."

But, whether or not I am correct in finding anticipations in Newman of these two elements of Lonergan's cognitional theory, they are certainly key notions in *Insight*. There is little need to delay on the first, the spontaneously operative cognitional structure. Let us simply note that it appears as the ultimate bulwark in our defense against the ravages of the critical problem. That problem is not solved "by demonstrating that one can know." Even to seek such a foundation "involves a vicious circle." More positively, what is the solution? It is "pragmatic engagement" in the process of knowing. There are

natural inevitabilities and spontaneities that constitute the possibility of knowing . . . by engaging one in the process . . . The ultimate basis of our knowing is not necessity but contingent fact, and the fact is established, not prior to our engagement in knowing, but simultaneously with it.[48]

47. John Henry Newman, *An Essay in Aid of a Grammar of Assent* (London: Longmans, Green, 1930 [1870]), p. 377.

48. *Insight*, p. 332.

This, I would say, makes explicit the assumption behind Newman's program for learning.

To this fundamental dynamism of human spirit we have now to add a modality of its functioning, Lonergan's extremely important and widely neglected notion of the self-correcting process of human learning. The notion is recurrent in *Insight,* but what is perhaps the fullest exposition is given in the context of discussing men of good judgment. Good judgment requires a happy balance between rashness and indecision. But how does one strike that balance? "How is one to know when it is reached? Were there some simple formula or recipe in answer to such questions, then men of good judgment could be produced at will. . . ."[49] So what does one do? One gives the further questions a chance to arise. One builds on the previous acquisition of correct insights. But this amounts to a vicious circle: we become men of good judgment by being already men of good judgment! It is here that the process of learning becomes relevant:

So it is the process of learning that breaks the vicious circle. Judgment on the correctness of insights supposes the prior acquisition of a large number of correct insights. But the prior insights are not correct because we judge them to be correct. They occur within a self-correcting process in which the shortcomings of each insight provoke further questions to yield complementary insights. Moreover, this self-correcting process tends to a limit. We become familiar with concrete situations . . . and we can recognize when . . . that self-correcting process reaches its limit in familiarity with the concrete situation and in easy mastery of it.[50]

Few ideas in *Insight* are at once so innocent in appearance and so momentous in their consequences. I do not think we will ever get hold of either *Insight* or *Method* unless we give serious attention to the role of this self-correcting process. Lonergan's use of it is most fully acknowledged in the areas of concrete judgments of fact,[51] of the critique of beliefs,[52] and of the hermeneutic circle,[53] but it seems to have a much wider application. Further, it seems to have as competitor only a fixed and indubitable starting-point, a premise which is somehow self-validating and really involved in a vicious circle. In any case, as we turn now to *Method* and ask how we break the vicious circle enclosing our value-judgments within the confines of our own subjectivity, I think we find there an answer analogous to the one we have discovered in *Insight* for the cognitional problem.

Method does not take up the problem of epistemology as directly as *Insight* does, and we may have to read a bit between the lines to find a

---

49. Ibid., p. 285.
51. Ibid.
50. Ibid., pp. 286–87.
52. Ibid., pp. 713–18.
53. *Method,* pp. 159, 208–209. See also "Merging Horizons: Systems, Common Sense, Scholarship," *Cultural Hermeneutics* [Boston College] 1 (1973), pp. 92–93, 94, 95.

parallel answer. However, it is not difficult to do so in the lines I am about to quote. The context is that of conversion as the foundation for the second phase of theology, and deliberate decision as the human side of conversion. Lonergan says of this conversion:

It is a fully conscious decision about one's horizon, one's outlook, one's world-view. It deliberately selects the frame-work, in which doctrines have their meaning, in which systematics reconcile, in which communications are effective.

Such a deliberate decision is anything but arbitrary. Arbitrariness is just unauthenticity, while conversion is from unauthenticity to authenticity. It is total surrender to the demands of the human spirit: be attentive, be intelligent, be reasonable, be responsible, be in love.[54]

That is, it is still the dynamism of human spirit that is operative, not to "prove" the validity of our deliberations and value-judgments, but to engage us pragmatically in the decision-making process. As *Insight* takes its epistemological stand on the "natural inevitabilities and spontaneities" of the mind, so *Method* takes its corresponding "epistemological" stand on "the demands of the human spirit," demands that now include one for responsibility.

Furthermore, these demands do not achieve results with anything like mechanical efficiency; rather they are effective by promoting our growth towards maturity in moral judgment—a process analogous to that of the self-correcting process of human learning. I can show this most expeditiously by simply quoting a paragraph in *Method*, and adding my own emphases to bring out the analogy; the paragraph proceeds in two parts, first speaking of the growing that precedes conversion:

As our knowledge . . . *increases,* our responses . . . *are strengthened* . . . our freedom may exercise its *ever advancing thrust* toward authenticity. So we *move* to the existential moment. . . . Then is the time for the exercise of vertical freedom. . . .

The next part speaks of the growing that follows conversion:

Such conversion . . . falls far short of moral perfection. . . . One has *yet to uncover and root out* . . . bias. One has to *keep developing* one's knowledge. . . . One has to *keep scrutinizing* one's intentional responses. . . . One has to *listen to criticism* and to protest. One has to *remain ready to learn* from others. For moral knowledge is the proper possession only of morally good men and, until one has merited that title, one has still to *advance* and to *learn.*[55]

54. *Method*, p. 268.

55. Ibid., p. 240. Note that the contrast I made between Descartes and Newman derives from Lonergan. It likely lies behind his critique of mistaken beliefs in *Insight* (see the references to Descartes on p. 716), it becomes explicit in his course *De intellectu et methodo,* at the Gregorian University in 1959 (see pp. 44–45 of the *reportatio* made by his students), and it returns with a nuance in the article I quoted above (n. 53), "Merging Horizons. . . ." The nuance lies in a distinction between system and common sense. Lonergan does not

The parallels then between *Insight* and *Method* are striking. In each case there is a spontaneously operative dynamism that engages us pragmatically in a process—of knowing in one case, of responsible action in the other. In each case it is fundamentally what we are that determines what we can do, cognitionally or responsibly. In each case we become what we are by growing, and that growing is a remedial process, the self-correcting process of learning on the cognitional level, and the ever advancing thrust towards authenticity on the level of responsibility. In each case it is this growth that breaks the vicious circle in which we are doomed to remain enclosed as long as the rules of static system govern us. One might adapt an old proverb here and say, *Solvitur ambulando*: the problem of walking is solved by walking. Adaptation is required, however, because we are at the moment incapable of walking, present resources not being sufficient; but present resources are sufficient for learning to walk, and that possibility is the possibility likewise of escape from the vicious circle.[56]

Our fourth question asks whether the position just taken is critical. It seems to me that this is little more than a modality of the previous question, the positive counterpart of what had been put in the form of an objection. Nevertheless, it will be helpful to consider it separately, asking what "critical" means, how criticism operates in *Insight*, how it operates in *Method*, whether there is an analogy of criticism to be conceived and worked out.

First then our third and fourth questions are closely linked. Antecedently, the very notion of self-correcting process implies criticism, and criticism implies the possibility of correction. Or, one might examine the section entitled "The Critique of Beliefs" in *Insight*[57] and observe that throughout this section it is the self-correcting process that is operative. Surely it is superfluous to dwell on so obvious a point. It will be more profitable to examine closely the meaning and role of criticism.

---

make it clear what his view is on the application of the Cartesian method to the field of system, but he leaves no doubt in regard to common sense: "We have no choice but to follow the advice of John Henry Newman—to accept ourselves as we are and by dint of constant and persevering attention, intelligence, reasonableness, responsibility, strive to expand what is true and force out what is mistaken in views that we have inherited or spontaneously developed" (p. 98).

56. In fundamental differences of opinion, therefore, the effective procedure can hardly be the simple one of showing your adversary that you are right and he is wrong; by hypothesis, he is likely to be incapable of seeing that. The strategy then will be to ask yourself why he is incapable of seeing what is so clear to you, and then proposing to him considerations that may help him grow out of his dwarfed condition (always keeping an open mind to the possibility that you yourself are the dwarf, that you yourself may need to grow in order to be able to learn from your adversary).

57. *Insight*, pp. 713–18.

Generally and technically, Lonergan contrasts "critical" with "inquiring," and links them respectively with the two types of questions that occur in cognitional process. The "question," he says, means two things:

The attitude of the inquiring mind that effects the transition from the first level to the second and, again, the attitude of the critical mind that effects the transition from the second level to the third.[58]

In this sense criticism seems intrinsic to the very process of forming a judgment. As such it should be as versatile as the capacity itself for judgment, and have as wide an application. We have seen some of these applications in *Insight,* and there are others.[59] But the exercise *par excellence* of criticism is in judging our judging, not in the old sense of an attempt to demonstrate that we can and do know, but in Lonergan's sense of understanding and judging the nature of our knowing. From criticism in this sense there results both a position on knowing, objectivity, and reality, one that is consonant with the spontaneously operative structure in man, and as well a rejection of counterpositions, those not consonant with the inevitabilities of that structure. Thus, where commonsense eclecticism cannot be critical and so fails to reach the proper meaning of knowing, objectivity, and reality,[60] orientation to the objective of the unrestricted desire to know effects the antithesis of positions and counterpositions, and enables one to achieve a critical philosophy or metaphysics.[61]

My last paragraph left a loophole. It said criticism *seems* intrinsic to the process of judging and *should be* as versatile as the capacity for judgment. In fact, there is a nuance to add. There is one exception to the far-ranging object of criticism and that is rational consciousness itself:

Still, if rational consciousness can criticize the achievement of science, it cannot criticize itself. The critical spirit can weigh all else in the balance, only on condition that it does not criticize itself. It is a self-assertive spontaneity that demands sufficient reason for all else but offers no justification for its demanding.[62]

When we turn to *Method* we find a remarkable parallel between this position on the self-justification of rational consciousness and the self-justification of the love of God experienced as a result of religious

---

58. Ibid., p. 274; see also p. 348.
59. E.g., the critical distinction of "things" and "bodies," *Insight,* p. 253; and judgment on the existence of God, ibid., pp. 685–86.
60. Ibid., pp. 420–21. 61. Ibid., p. 514.
62. Ibid., p. 332.

conversion. Lonergan affirms that being in love in an unrestricted manner (that is, in love with God)

is the religious conversion that grounds both moral and intellectual conversion; it provides the real criterion by which all else is to be judged; and consequently one has only to experience it in oneself or witness it in others, to find in it its own justification.

He goes on, "Accordingly . . . there is no need to justify critically the charity described by St. Paul in . . . Corinthians."[63] The parallel is indeed remarkable but unfortunately I cannot use it in the context of my paper. I have set aside the question of love of God in order to concentrate on the "ordinary" process from the rational to the responsible level, so I have to look further for the position of *Method* on my question.

The place to look is obviously the chapter on dialectic, since dialectic occupies the role in the shift to the fourth level that questions for reflection occupied in the shift from second to third. Central to our purpose in this chapter are four short sections entitled respectively "Dialectic: The Issue," "Dialectic: The Problem," "Dialectic: The Structure," and "Dialectic as Method." As in *Insight* the basic strategy is to allow the spontaneously operative structure inherent in human spirit to unfold, but Lonergan gives more prominence now to the role of encounter with others.[64] The specifically critical strategy is expressed as in the earlier book by the two precepts: "[D]evelop positions; reverse counterpositions."[65] But again the perspective is that of encounter: differences in horizon which lead to different views on what the positions are will be handled by dialogue, by the mutual aid investigators offer one another when one understands others by overcoming his own conflicts and evaluates himself through knowledge and appreciation of others. Of this method Lonergan says:

While it will not be automatically efficacious, it will provide the open-minded, the serious, the sincere with the occasion to ask themselves some basic questions, first, about others but eventually, even about themselves. It will make conversion a topic and thereby promote it. Results will not be sudden or startling, for conversion commonly is a slow process of maturation. It is finding out for oneself and in oneself what it is to be intelligent, to be reasonable, to be responsible, to love. Dialectic contributes to that end by pointing out ultimate differences, by offering the example of others that differ radically from oneself, by providing the occasion for a reflection, a self-scrutiny, that can lead to a new understanding of oneself and one's destiny.[66]

63. *Method*, pp. 283–84; see also p. 123: "the gift itself is self-justifying," and p. 290, on love as "unassailable fact."

64. Ibid., p. 247.   65. Ibid., p. 249.
66. Ibid., p. 253.

The rest of the chapter on dialectic deals with philosophies that would subvert this program; in other words, the preceding quotation is a kind of final positive word on the way dialectic functions critically.

Is this critical? The question was put expressly by Prof. David Tracy at the Lonergan Congress of 1970,[67] and Fr. Lonergan takes up the question in his response to the first volume of the Congress papers. His answer appeals to *Insight* as an aid to self-appropriation and the consequent option for the positions on knowledge, objectivity, and reality. But in theology we prolong these procedures, for now we have the further problem of values. We cannot evade that problem; neither can we simply assert our own values as the true ones. However:

There exists . . . a third way. One can allow all-comers to participate in research, interpretation, history, and dialectic. One can encourage positions and counter-positions to come to light concretely and to manifest to all their suppositions and their consequences. One can expect some to mistake counter-positions for positions and, inversely, positions for counter-positions. One can hope that such mistakes will not be universal, that the positions will be duly represented, that they will reveal themselves as positions to men of good will.[68]

This response deals with theology, where the prior quotation from *Method* seemed to have a wider application to the areas touched by dialectic. But they are very similar in their thrust, and I thought it useful to set them side by side with one another.

Let me add some reflections. One factor in Prof. Tracy's position was the contention that, whereas *Insight* had a critical foundation for intellectual conversion, *Method* had no parallel foundation for religious conversion and theology (or, presumably, for the ethical field).[69] Perhaps I have done something to meet that point in drawing out the parallel between the two volumes. But I note again that the parallel does not lie in premises available for the philosophical and the theological enterprises, by which we might validate our judgment on our judgments in one case and our evaluation of our evaluations in the other; rather it lies in the fact that each book rejects the demand for such validation and takes its stand on the spontaneous dynamism of human spirit working itself out in time by correction and growth.

Next, have we not to recognize an analogous use of "critical" and "critically founded," so that the critical enterprise on the fourth level

---

67. In his paper "Lonergan's Foundational Theology: An Interpretation and a Critique," *Foundations of Theology*, pp. 198, 210, 214–20. Note that Prof. Tracy's objection is meant to apply in the field of theology, and that I am taking liberties with his thought when I extend it to the ethical. By my principles the extension is legitimate, since I regard the situation as sufficiently similar in ethics and theology; but Prof. Tracy may have his own views on that.

68. "Bernard Lonergan Responds," in *Foundations of Theology*, p. 231.

69. *Foundations of Theology*, p. 210.

of intentionality is not simply univocal with that on the third?[70] I have already pointed out the need for analogous understanding of "question" in "questions for understanding, for reflection, for deliberation."[71] We have adjectives that do good service for two of the levels when we speak of the "inquiring and critical" spirit of man; we can add to the list and speak of the "inquiring, critical, and evaluating (or deliberating)" spirit of man. But if we are going to use "critical" on the fourth level we need to take account of the analogy.

There is a parallel development in regard to the use of "objectivity." Ten years ago, in his lecture at Gallarate in Italy on the notion of structure, Fr. Lonergan outlined the familiar isomorphism of cognitional operations with the ontological constitution of reality, and extended it to the epistemology of the human spirit, that is, to the structure of objectivity.[72] There is the objectivity of the experiential, of the normative, of the absolute levels; and these three correspond to experience-understanding-reflection in cognitional operation, as well as to potency-form-act in ontological constitution. Now, after *Method,* when we speak of the objectivity that is the fruit of genuine subjectivity, we have to recognize that this use too is analogous.

My topic reduces almost entirely to examining the question of judging our judging and evaluating our evaluating. Perhaps it is time to put that question to my own contribution to this workshop. I have called it an "exploration" of Fr. Lonergan's new notion of value. If you accept the image of a continent to be explored, then you might say that I have been mapping some details of inland geography. If you prefer more literal language, then I have been trying to understand Lonergan on his own terms and in his own perspective. Further, I have assumed, though I hope I am ready to let the assumption yield to fact, that his thought hangs together, that there is an inner consistency which I must discover under pain of missing his point altogether. The result is the foregoing series of groping questions, reflections, and tentative conclusions.

Two limitations of the paper then are the very personal character of my study, which may make it less helpful to those in a different situation from mine, and its confinement to the writings of Fr. Lonergan himself, and a consequent failure to help locate him in the stream of ongoing

70. For example, see the usage of *Method,* p. 84: "There is to human deliberation a criterion that criticizes every finite good."

71. See above, n. 37.

72. *De notione structurae,* a lecture at the Collegium Aloisianum, Gallarate, 7 March 1964. Published under the same title in the student journal *Apertura,* May, 1964, pp. 117–23.

thought. I would like therefore in concluding, if I may return to my metaphor, to emerge from my lonely geographical expedition to the inland, to stand upon the shoreline, and to look around me a little more widely. May I suggest two directions that further question might take? One pertains to metaphysics and I would put this question to both Fr. Lonergan and ourselves; the other pertains to dialectic and my question is directed to those of us who consider *Method* a seminal work and would implement it in a new theology.

The metaphysical question is this: What becomes of the isomorphism of intending subject and intended object in the four-level structure of *Method*? In *Insight* the ontological structure of reality, potency-form-act, has as its counterpart in the knowing subject the three-leveled structure of cognitional activity, experience-understanding-reflection. And this isomorphism has its roots solidly in the doctrines and views of St. Thomas Aquinas.[73] At that stage the good presented no special problem; it is structured, as reality is, on three levels, so that the section entitled "The Ontology of the Good" speaks of potential, formal, and actual good.[74]

Now, however, we have a problem. Value is not just an extension of the object of cognitional activity. It is a new notion; it adds a new level to intentional consciousness. So we have to ask: Does it correspondingly add a new level to reality? If so, what could that level be? And the difficulty becomes more pressing if we regard love as a fifth level of intentionality.

One can displace the question and ask why we speak of "levels" at all in our analysis of intentional activity. After all, introspection reveals ten thousand activities of mind and heart; we group them on levels, so that understanding and conception are said to belong on one level but reflection and judgment on another. Why? We can try to answer in terms of operators, and say that the operator in one case is the question for understanding, in the other the question for reflection. But that only displaces the problem once again: Why do we assign levels to the *operators*? After all, even questions for understanding take different forms; for example, "What?" "Why?" "How often?" all are questions for understanding.

I know of no better answer to this puzzle than to recognize the "selectivity of intelligence" in the way described by *Insight*:

Properly, to abstract is to grasp the essential and to disregard the incidental, to see what is significant and set aside the irrelevant, to recognize the important

73. See my article "St. Thomas and the Isomorphism of Human Knowing and Its Proper Object," *Sciences ecclésiastiques* 13 (1961), pp. 167–90.
74. *Insight*, ch. 18, sect. 1.5; see especially p. 605.

as important and the negligible as negligible. Moreover, when it is asked what is essential or significant or important and what is incidental, irrelevant, negligible, the answer must be twofold. For abstraction is the selectivity of intelligence, and intelligence may be considered either in some given stage of development or at the term of development when some science or group of sciences has been mastered completely.[75]

To return then to the original question: If isomorphism is still to be affirmed, or even if it is only to serve as a useful model for thought, what metaphysical element are we going to assign to the fourth level of reality?

My second question takes us in a quite different direction: it looks towards our own self-involvement. After all, the whole thrust of the fourth level is towards such an engagement. Research, interpretation, history, we have done a bit of them all, and they sum up as leading to an encounter and a consequent challenge.

We have to be dead serious about this. We have, all of us, insisted over and over that *Insight* is to be regarded more as an invitation to self-appropriation than as a thesaurus of ideas. It is not the objects of thought that are important in that book, however brilliantly they may be conceived and explained; it is the subject who is reading the book that matters, the subject and his activity which may regard quite different objects from those of *Insight*. As Philip McShane said in his introduction to three essays of Lonergan he recently edited, "What then is Lonergan getting at? The uncomfortable answer is that Lonergan is getting at you and me."[76] I once made a similar point when I instituted a comparison between Kierkegaard and Lonergan. Perhaps I am old enough now to quote myself:

Kierkegaard's message was inwardness as opposed to knowledge. . . . [Yet] the last ignominy, for Kierkegaard, would be for someone to say [of him], "This author represents inwardness." As an abstract, everything would be said in this one word; but in effect nothing would be said, since the question was not what the author represented but what the reader would do.[77]

I do not think I can say any better now in 1974 than I did then in 1964 what is needed by the student of Lonergan. The one thing to be added is that we now have a further level of inwardness, and that this level puts the matter of self-involvement even more squarely before us.

But if the challenge is more squarely before us, the way to meet it is also indicated more extensively: it is the way of collaboration that *Method* so directly takes up; one might say that the thesis of the book

75. Ibid., p. 30; see also pp. 355–56.

76. *Introducing the Thought of Bernard Lonergan*, three papers from *Collection* with an introduction by Philip McShane (London: Darton, Longman & Todd, 1973), p. 7.

77. *Continuum* 2 (1964), p. 328.

is method and the corollary is collaboration. It so happens that this workshop was conceived as one in a series that might constitute on-going collaboration, so it seems especially appropriate to end my paper on this topic.

My own suggestion of a strategy is to plunge at once into an area of theology in which the method will be tested. No doubt we still have a great deal to learn at one remove from theology about the functional specialties and method itself; but no doubt also we will never finish talking about the latter in our lifetime. We cannot wait so long. What we need is a continual exchange between theological method that prescinds from questions of theology proper, and the theological questions in which the method is tested. I suggest further that it may be easier to get started on that testing than we imagine. For one thing, we do not have to face at the very beginning an enormous task of research; there is already research galore in the dictionaries and tools of scholarship put out by our European confreres. In general they do this sort of work much better than we do; why should we try to compete with them? The trick is to learn to use their research in implementing method. The same applies in its own measure to interpretation; we have theologies galore on a multitude of topics, many of which function as interpretations in Lonergan's sense; the trick again is to learn how to use them methodically.

With history the question is different. Still I think many of us have already worked a good deal on various areas of theology, following the lead given us by Lonergan's *via analytica*. It should not be too hard to adapt that work and use it in the functional specialty of history.

It is in dialectic that the real work begins. Most of us have little experience at such an exercise, at least in the academic world. Moreover it is bound to be painful. Already *Insight* forced us to a laborious work of intellectual conversion, and the giving up of positions long cherished. Still there was never the deeply personal involvement to which *Method* calls us. We are called by that book to examine ourselves existentially, either to be converted or to reappraise our conversion, to examine our values and ourselves in relation to them, to resolve the conflicts that may lead us to differing interpretations of the same gospel message and to different accounts of what is going on in the world.

At the same time the directions for strategy and tactics are set forth in chapter 10 of *Method* and I have quoted some of them above. I think that, if we are serious about this book—and our very presence here is surely witness to that—then we may not evade the responsibility that is ours in the *kairos* that is given to us.

5

Bernard Lonergan's Thought on Ultimate Reality and Meaning*

1. Introduction

Bernard J. F. Lonergan was born of Irish-English stock in the Province of Quebec in 1904. From sophomore year at Loyola College in Montreal he joined the Society of Jesus at Guelph, Ontario, in 1922. For the next eighteen years his life followed a normal Jesuit course as he moved through the Guelph Novitiate, Heythrop College (England), London University and the Gregorian University (Rome); the objectives: training in the religious life, in languages, philosophy, and theology, with bits and pieces of science and the humanities thrown in and some specialization in mathematics. The long period of study was broken in the usual way by three years of teaching (Loyola College again) and a further year of spiritual formation ("tertianship," at Amiens), and ended with the completion of his doctoral work in Rome in 1940.

His teaching for the next twenty-five years also followed a normal pattern: various treatises in systematic theology at the Jesuit Seminaries, first of Montreal and then of Toronto (a thirteen-year stay in Canada divided quite evenly between the two), and twelve years on the faculty of the Gregorian University, where he was able to concentrate on Christology and trinitarian theology in the basic degree courses, and work out his thought on method in the advanced degree courses for philosophers and theologians. From the summer of 1965, when he underwent grave surgery and suffered the loss of a lung, he was back at Regis College, Toronto, where he remained a decade with teaching greatly curtailed, except for a year as Stillman Professor, Harvard University (1971–72). Since 1975, however, he has been at Boston College, again carrying a considerable teaching load, but concentrating his energies on economics and a work on circulation analysis which remained from over thirty years ago as unfinished business.

*Previously published in *Ultimate Reality and Meaning* 4 (1981), pp. 58–89.

71

His major writings during these forty years began with two studies of Thomas Aquinas, one his doctoral dissertation on operative grace (*Gratia operans: A Study of the Speculative Development in the Writings of St. Thomas of Aquin*, 1940), the other on Thomist cognitional theory ("The Concept of *Verbum* in the Writings of St. Thomas Aquinas," 1946–49). There followed in 1957 the work which many consider Lonergan's masterpiece, *Insight: A Study of Human Understanding*; here, without abandoning Aquinas, he set forth his own independent ideas on human cognitional process and sketched the resulting epistemology, metaphysics, ethics, and natural theology. Between 1965 and 1971, while slowly recovering from his surgery, he produced what had been the goal of his lifework (*Insight* was only preparatory) and published it a year later as *Method in Theology*.

Meanwhile there had been a steady stream of unpublished (or "semi-published") notes for his students, almost all in Latin and many of them serving as testing-ground for his slowly developing ideas on method. Three theology manuals issued from this activity: *De constitutione Christi ontologica et psychologica* (1956), *De verbo incarnato* (1964), and *De deo trino* (1964), the latter in two volumes, with part of the first volume now in English.[1] There was likewise a steady little stream of articles, interviews, and lectures, which resulted in *Collection* (1967), *A Second Collection* (1974)—*A Third Collection* is contemplated[2]—*Philosophy of God, and Theology* (1973), and other publications. Finally, there is a considerable accumulation of mimeographed notes, and several hundred hours of tape-recorded lectures. The latter are available at the Lonergan Center of Regis College,[3] along with transcripts for many of them; the Halifax lectures of 1958 in *Insight* are just being published (*Understanding and Being*, 1980); the Cincinnati lectures on the philosophy of education (1959) have been readied for publication,[4] and the Thomas More Institute of Montreal has begun to publish some of its rich store of Lonergania.[5]

The published output has thus been considerable but not extraordinary, according well enough with the direction of his whole lifework which, as I have argued elsewhere,[6] was not toward encyclopedic schol-

---

1. *The Way to Nicea: The Dialectical Development of Trinitarian Theology*, tr. C. O'Donovan (Philadelphia: Westminster, 1976).

2. Now published: *A Third Collection: Papers by Bernard J. F. Lonergan, S.J.*, ed. F. E. Crowe, New York: Paulist Press, 1985.

3. Now the Lonergan Research Institute of Regis College, Toronto.

4. To be published as Volume 10: *Education*, in *Collected Works of Bernard Lonergan*, by University of Toronto Press.

5. E.g., *3 Lectures* (1975), including Lonergan's "Healing and Creating in History," itself also published in *Third Collection*.

6. *The Lonergan Enterprise* (Cambridge, MA: Cowley, 1980).

arship but toward creation of a new *organon* for our time, somewhat on the analogy of Aristotelian logic and the Baconian *novum organum* for natural science. It is in that context that his contribution is to be evaluated. Not primarily on the basis of his pre-1965 theology, which will have to be put through the crucible of his own method before it can be called properly Lonerganian. And not primarily on the basis of the theology that will result from the application of his method, which will be the work of his followers. But on the basis of the instrument that, with rare self-sacrificing withdrawal from the hunt, he has labored all his life to create and put into the hands of his fellow-theologians. In that precise sense an old phrase has been adapted and fittingly applied to him: a theologian's theologian. For the same reason he is not the author of many theological bestsellers. Yet there is a good index of his wide influence at a deeper level: the fact that over 150 students from round the globe have chosen his thought for their doctoral dissertations. The fascination of his difficult ideas promises to be perennial; he is, as one title has it, "A Man to Be Wrestled With."[7]

Ideally, this account of his goals should be complemented by a parallel account of his sources; practically, that is not feasible: the sources are too diverse and the documentation too sketchy. He once wrote of Aquinas that his program "was to lay under tribute Greek and Arab, Jew and Christian, in an ever renewed effort to obtain for Catholic culture" that most fruitful understanding which is theology's business.[8] Something analogous must be said of his own effort to lay under tribute, not only Aquinas and Thomist sources, but also the subsequent seven hundred years of developing thought and expanding contacts for the West. Such a comprehensive work of assimilation cannot be described in a paragraph. Worgul's dissertation[9] makes a beginning with a long introduction on Lonergan's debt to five sources: Newman, Maréchal, Thomas Aquinas, Kant and Hegel (taken together under the heading "The World of Interiority"), and modern science; but this good beginning needs to be taken up in detail under a hundred headings.

If, then, as we turn from general biographical data to the present topic, I say that Lonergan's views on ultimate reality and meaning derived from his theistic, Christian, Roman Catholic background, that will not enlighten us on specific influences but provides only a broad context. We will learn without surprise that the focus of his views is

7. Colin Brown, "A Man to be Wrestled with: Lonergan and the Question of Knowledge," *The Churchman: A Quarterly Journal of Anglican Theology* 88 (1974) pp. 47–53.

8. *Grace and Freedom: Operative Grace in the Thought of St. Thomas Aquinas,* p. 139.

9. George S. Worgul, Jr., doctoral dissertation: *Man Standing Open to Revelation: Lonergan's Theology of Revelation* (Louvain: Catholic University of Louvain, 1974, unpublished), 247pp.

God as transcendent mystery, and that the basic questions are the traditional ones: God's revelation and human reason, God's will and human freedom, God's action in the created world, and so on. But we will have no inkling of the interlocking of his thought on God with his analysis of human consciousness and human history—in short, of what is distinctive in his approach; I must present that here with little reference to its sources.

Two more preliminary remarks. First, the unity of Lonergan's theology with his study of the human situation makes it impractical to treat reality and meaning separately: the way ultimate reality is conceived already establishes it as ultimate meaning. The other remark is that, just as Lonergan's development was long and slow, so any attempt to see it whole, which is the scope of the present article, has to be historical. This will take us through four periods of his life, characterized by the thinking of his dissertation work on Aquinas, that of *Insight*, that of *Method*, and that of the post-*Method* period.

11. Ultimate Reality in the Context of the *Gratia operans* Work

The inaugural work of Lonergan's career, his dissertation on St. Thomas Aquinas, is now available in book form as *Grace and Freedom* and my references will be to that source. It is an historical study, directly therefore on the ideas of Aquinas, ideas however that Lonergan certainly made his own. He does indeed here and there translate Aquinas into the twentieth century, and iron out wrinkles in Thomist thought,[10] but that only underlines how much he himself subscribes to the ideas he sets forth here.

It is a study of divine grace, involving a doctrine of man under ramifying headings: freedom, sin, habits, conversion, perseverance, and so on. A doctrine of God is involved in God's permission of human sin, his bestowal of grace, his use of human beings as his instruments, his knowledge of contingent events and especially of those free human acts which are still in the future for us, the efficacy of his operation, and of course the transcendence and mystery of his own divine being and operation. One could construct a little treatise on God from this study but, when the topic is God as ultimate reality, it will be enough to write notes on the following points: (1) the universal operation of God in all created activity; (2) the divine transcendence of our cate-

---

10. Gerald M. Fagin has studied some details of this process in his doctoral dissertation: *The Notion of Divine Transcendence in the Early Lonergan and Some Contemporary Representatives of the Theology of Hope* (Toronto: University of St. Michael's College, 1974, unpublished), 269pp.

gories of "free" and "necessary"; and (3) the character of mystery which marks the divine and affects all our discourse on God.

The universal operation of God in all created activity, making that activity instrumental to his, is straightforward Scholastic doctrine. The general concept may be derived from an ordinary action like a writer's use of a pen. A series may be conceived, as of the force of gravity directing the flow of water, the water turning the millstone, the millstone grinding the grain; here there is a first agent and a series of instruments. This is applied to God to make him absolutely first Agent and all secondary causes his instruments, with "Agent" conceived analogously to "agents" just as God is Being in relation to created beings. The proof of such universal instrumentality is not a major concern for Aquinas or Lonergan; the latter merely notes that everything that happens is "at least in the category of being" and God alone is "proportionate to the production of being."[11]

There are complications, of course; I take space for two. One derives from the complete universality of the theorem on divine use of instruments: it is true, therefore, of free human acts, God being more a cause of these than men themselves are.[12] Here the complication arises in regard to sin, for which God cannot be made responsible. Is sin then an exception to the rule? Not with regard to anything *positive* in the sinful sequence. Thus God operates in and governs the rise of human passion in the murderer, the aiming of the gun, the propulsion of the bullet, and its penetration of the victim's body. But sin is not located in any of these; it is located in the failure of the murderer to use reason, grace, and freedom to control his passion. That failure is a gap in being, an enormity in creation, an "absolute objective falsity'" in a universe where being and the true are interchangeable.[13] Of course, this involves one in a theology of the divine "permission" of sin, and a theology of a world order in which that permission is justified, but that has to be omitted here.[14]

A second complication arises from a kind of picture-thinking on the causal series, for we are apt to imagine A pushing B, B pushing C, and so on. Then one wonders who pushed A, what kind of entity each push is, and how immediately A acts on C. Lonergan's position is worth noting, for it has far-reaching consequences: "[T]he reality of efficient causality is the relativity of the effect *qua* effect."[15] As for the causal

---

11. *Grace and Freedom,* pp. 80–81.

12. Ibid., pp. 97–98.   13. Ibid., pp. 111–13.

14. Ibid., pp. 110–15; also *De ente supernaturali,* ed. F. E. Crowe, C. O'Donovan, & G. Sala (Toronto: Regis College, 1973 [1946], unpublished), pp. 59–64; and *De scientia atque voluntate dei,* ed. F. E. Crowe, C. O'Donovan, & G. Sala (Toronto: Regis College, 1973 [1950], unpublished), pp. 37–50.

15. *Collection: Papers by Bernard Lonergan, S.J.,* p. 55.

series he distinguishes such a series "properly so called and the merely accidental series: the latter is illustrated by Abraham begetting Isaac, and Isaac, Jacob, where evidently Abraham does not beget Jacob; the former is illustrated by my moving the keys of my typewriter, and my typewriter typing out these paragraphs, where evidently I am more a cause of the typed paragraphs than the typewriter is." In the accidental series the relation of C to A is that of conditioned to condition, but in the properly causal series, "B depends on A, C depends on B, and C depends on A even more than on B."[16] Further, there is no need to imagine either a little entity running from A to B and then to C, or A receiving a push of its own. Nor is there any need to imagine A reaching around B to give an immediate push to C.

But the real complication, and its solution in Lonergan's early views on divine transcendence, bring us to the next subheading. It is the problem of reconciling God's activity, which must be understood as omnipotent and universally efficacious, with the freedom and responsibility that must be affirmed of human activity. A useful point of departure, a context that joins Aquinas, Lonergan, and a cascade of recent literature, is Aristotle's famous question of the sea-battle at Salamis: Is it true today that there will be a sea-battle tomorrow? Or, on the supposition that the battle will not take place, is it false today that there will be such a battle tomorrow? It seems the proposition must be either true or false, but, if it is determinately true or false today, then the contingency of the event on the morrow is destroyed: it has to occur in the way that is predetermined.

To curtail somewhat the otherwise endless discussion, I leave aside the complexities of the Aristotelian question and position. The answer, for Aquinas and Lonergan, can be put in four steps, with the first two of them quite Aristotelian. First, there either will or will not be a seabattle tomorrow; that follows from the principle of excluded middle. Secondly, neither of the two propositions (There will be . . . , There will not be . . .) is determinately true today; this follows from the event's contingency which cannot be co-posited with its predetermination in time.

But now difficulties arise in the context of divine providence which take the theologian beyond the philosopher. Aquinas puts them succinctly under two headings. One difficulty derives from the doctrine of a divine knowledge which is infallible, so that what God knows, has to happen; in other words, the event seems predetermined, since God knows it eternally. The other derives from the doctrine of the divine

16. Ibid., p. 56.

will which cannot be frustrated (*inefficax esse non potest*); so that what God wills, has to happen, and contingency again vanishes.[17]

The answer to the first difficulty, in Lonergan's rewrite of Aquinas, puts God outside time to exist in an eternal "now." It thus rules the whole objection out of court. The difficulty is simply that of Aristotle transferred from its abstract objectivity (the truth of a proposition) to the concreteness of the divine mind where the truth has the further endowment of infallibility; contingency disappears under an inexorable juggernaut, the predetermination consequent on divine foreknowledge. Lonergan does not doubt that, given infallible foreknowledge, the event has to occur;[18] the solution is to remove the "fore" from divine knowledge. God's knowledge is indeed infallible, as his will is irresistible and his action efficacious, but all this "in the logico-metaphysical simultaneity of the atemporal present."[19]

With that answer, however, the root problem remains. Even in this present moment of our temporal "now" and God's eternal "now" we have to reconcile divine efficacity with human freedom. The Thomist solution is that the divine will lies outside the order of beings as a cause from which proceeds all being, and from which proceed likewise all the differences of being such as "possible" and "necessary." It is by God's will, then, that there are proximate causes operating necessarily to produce necessary effects, and by his will too that there are proximate causes operating contingently to produce contingent effects. But all effects, be they necessary or contingent, depend on the divine will as a first cause which transcends the order of necessity and contingency (*quae transcendit ordinem necessitatis et contingentiae*).[20]

As an aid to understanding this position, one might think of the animal kingdom as divided into laughing and non-laughing categories, and then think of a pure spirit which would lie outside, transcend, the order in which that division finds its place. As a further aid, which transfers the analogy to the field of action, one might think of the geometer "who not only makes triangles but also makes them equilateral or isosceles at his pleasure."[21] But finally one must come to a more abstract statement, and here Lonergan seems to go beyond Aquinas in generalizing the latter's solution; he also makes the doctrine a more

17. Thomas Aquinas, *In Aristotelis libros peri hermeneias et posteriorum analyticorum expositio* ed. R M. Spiazzi (Torino: Marietti, 1955), p. 73, no. 192.

18. *Grace and Freedom,* p. 105.

19. Ibid., p. 116. The notion of simultaneity is developed in *De scientia atque voluntate dei,* pp. 3–4, 10–11.

20. Aquinas, p. 74, no. 197.

21. *Grace and Freedom,* p. 108, with a reference to the source of the example in Aquinas.

positive one, removing it from its status as merely an answer to an objection:

Such a positive statement is the affirmation that God knows with equal infallibility, He wills with equal irresistibility, He effects with equal efficacy, both the necessary and the contingent. For however infallible the knowledge, however irresistible the will, however efficacious the action, what is known, willed, effected, is no more than hypothetically necessary. And what hypothetically is necessary, absolutely may be necessary or contingent.[22]

The reference here to negative and positive factors in the solution brings us to our third subheading, for we have now to ask how far a positive solution can go, and our response has to acknowledge the presence of mystery: "The truths of faith have the apex of their intelligibility hidden in the transcendence of God."[23] To demand adequate understanding of divine transcendence can result only in frustration, if one insists on such an answer; or heresy, if one thinks to have discovered it; or unbelief, if one gives up the truths that pose the problem. But enormous relief, and no inconsiderable light, can result from an intelligent use of the combined *via affirmationis* and *via negationis*. Lonergan's second study of St. Thomas, where there is question of our "understanding" of the Trinity through use of the psychological analogy, can help us here. There is, first of all, the assertion of our hunger for understanding: "For the spirit of inquiry within us never calls a halt, never can be satisfied, until our intellects, united to God as body to soul, know *ipsum intelligere* and through that vision, though then knowing aught else is a trifle, contemplate the universe as well."[24] There is also the assertion of some limited understanding through the analogy: the way of analogy "does not renounce all thought of synthesis to settle down to teaching catechism; for it knows that there is such a thing as imperfect understanding."[25] But limiting the whole effort with the sign of human impotence is the blindness of human beings before mystery like the blindness of owls in the sunlight. The way of St. Thomas "knows just what the human mind can attain and it attains it. It does not attempt to discover a synthetic principle whence all else follows. It knows that that principle is the divine essence and that, in this life, we cannot properly know it."[26] The psychological analogy, then, "is just the side-door through which we enter for an imperfect

---

22. *Grace and Freedom*, pp. 107–108. Aquinas is credited with a "first very incomplete appearance" of this positive conception, ibid., p. 141. For its definition in Latin clarity, see *De scientia atque voluntate dei*, p. 10. On Lonergan's generalization of the Thomist idea, see Fagin, *The Notion of Divine Transcendence . . ,* pp. 58, 61, 66, 68.

23. Ibid., p. 8.

24. *Verbum: Word and Idea in Aquinas*, p. 53.

25. Ibid., p. 213. 26. Ibid.

look." The Thomist way develops key concepts but, once they reach their term, the analogy is transcended;[27] then this way "shifts to a higher level, [and] consciously confronts mystery as mystery."[28]

So much for this early stage of Lonergan's thought on ultimate reality. I leave it reluctantly with this sketch, for I believe he has much to contribute to the current debate on the topic, and yet his work has hardly been noticed.[29] Very likely the Thomist context of his published work puts the modern reader off; surely the inaccessibility and Latin language of his independent writings are barriers. Is the factor of mystery which he introduces also a barrier for some? Quite possibly. On the other side, of course, he is accused, along with the tribe of theologians in general, of destroying mystery. So I am not sorry to have had occasion to introduce that topic early in my article. Of course, one's religious attitude before mystery is adoration, and theologians are or ought to be religious. But religion cries out for a measure of imperfect understanding, and to achieve this we have to think and talk in the way theologians do. One acknowledges the mystery, but then there is not much left to say about that aspect and one goes on to speak as best one can about the ineffable.

III. Ultimate Reality in *Insight*

Some difficult procedural decisions are needed when we turn to Lonergan's *Insight*. First, we must simply omit chapter 17 with its discussion of the "known unknown," chapter 18 with its problem of evil and need of a solution, and chapter 20 with its heuristic notion of a divine solution, in order to concentrate on chapter 19, "General Transcendent Knowledge." Next, we must omit a study of the relevant secondary literature: scores and scores of articles, book chapters, book reviews, and dissertations have made this the most widely discussed and sharply controverted chapter in *Insight*; the situation is just the opposite of the neglect we noted in regard to *Grace and Freedom,* and it becomes quite impossible to handle this rain-forest growth.[30] In confirmation, add that

---

27. Ibid., pp. 208, 209.   28. Ibid., pp. 213.

29. Exceptions include William J. Hill, "Does God Know the Future? Aquinas and Some Moderns," *Theological Studies* 36 (1975), pp. 3–18; Bernard McGinn, "Development of the Thought of Aquinas on the Reconciliation of Divine Providence and Contingent Action," *The Thomist* 39 (1975), pp. 741–52; Roland J. Teske, "Omniscience, Omnipotence, and Divine Transcendence," *The New Scholasticism* 53 (1979), pp. 277–94.

30. Let me list the dissertations that have come to my attention: except for a very few later published, they are less easily discovered by the reader. Four doctoral dissertations, and one of doctoral calibre and length, are directly on ch. 19. Ronald L. DiSanto, doctoral dissertation: *Complete Intelligibility: A Study of Bernard Lonergan's Argument for the Existence of God* (Hamilton, Ont.: McMaster University, 1975, unpublished), 326pp.; Ney

in this chapter 19 we are dealing with the most difficult chapter of the most difficult book of a very difficult thinker, and my decision to use all allotted space for my own positive exposition of Lonergan becomes understandable.

A further note: Lonergan's argument in chapter 19 is of a piece with his whole cognitional theory, and the dissertations mentioned in my first group (as well as some of the others) regularly devoted several chapters to that question. But that again is a very long story, and the luxury of narrating it is denied me. These decisions are reinforced by a final point, the much discussed relationship of *Insight* to *Method in Theology*: Has the argument of *Insight* in this matter now been super-

---

Affonso de Sá Earp, doctoral dissertation: *Love and Transcendent Knowledge: A Critical Study of Chapter XIX of "Insight" in the Light of Lonergan's Later Ideas about Love and Natural Theology* (Rome: Gregorian University, 1974, unpublished), 422pp.; Joseph Martos, doctoral dissertation: *Bernard Lonergan's Theory of Transcendent Knowledge* (Chicago: De Paul University, 1972, unpublished), 348pp.; Bernard Tyrrell, doctoral dissertation: *Bernard Lonergan's Philosophy of God* (New York: Fordham University, 1972; published, with revisions, Dublin: Gill and Macmillan, 1974); Timothy Gorringe, master's thesis: *The Ground of Knowledge and the Knowledge of God: A Study of Bernard Lonergan's Insight* (Leeds: Leeds University, 1975, unpublished), 235pp. At least a dozen other doctoral dissertations deal with it expressly, often in a major part or chapter of the thesis: Bernard A. Bommarito, *The Meaning of Methodical Reorientation of Science and Common Sense in the Thought of Bernard Lonergan* (New York: Fordham University, 1972, unpublished), 260pp.; Edward K. Braxton, *Images of Mystery: A Study of the Place of Myth and Symbol in the Theological Method of Bernard Lonergan* (Louvain: Catholic University of Louvain, 1975, unpublished), 635pp.; Anne M. M. Brennan, *Bernard Lonergan's World View: Emergent Probability and the God-World Relation* (New York: Columbia University, 1973, unpublished), 265pp.; Rocco Cacopardo, *A Study of Ongoing Social Processes* (Uxbridge, Middlesex: Brunel University, 1974, unpublished), 241pp.; Jon Nilson, *Hegel's "Phenomenology" and Lonergan's "Insight": A Comparison of Two Ways to Christianity* (Notre Dame: University of Notre Dame, 1975, published, Meisenheim am Glan: Verlag Anton Hain, 1979); William James O'Brien, *The Role of Judgment in Lonergan's "Insight"* (Chicago: University of Chicago Divinity School, 1972, unpublished), 198pp.; Emil James Piscitelli, *Language and Method in the Philosophy of Religion: A Critical Study of the Development of the Philosophy of Bernard Lonergan* (Washington, D.C.: Georgetown University, 1977, unpublished), 1021pp.; Richard R. Roach, *Fidelity: The Faith of Responsible Love* (New Haven: Yale University, 1974, unpublished), 718pp.; James C. Schultz, *From Insight to Metaphysics: The Metaphysics of Bernard J. F. Lonergan's "Insight"* (Notre Dame: University of Notre Dame, 1972, unpublished), 289pp.; Marc E. Smith, *Subjectivity, Experience and the Knowledge of God in Bernard Lonergan, S.J.* (Rome: Gregorian University, 1977; partially published, Rome: Tipografia Patrizio Graziani, 1977); David W. Tracy, *The Development of the Notion of Theological Methodology in the Works of Bernard J. Lonergan, S.J.* (Rome: Gregorian University, 1969; incorporated to large extent in *The Achievement of Bernard Lonergan*, New York: Herder and Herder, 1970); George S. Worgul, Jr., *Man Standing Open to Revelation: Lonergan's Theology of Revelation* (Louvain: Catholic University of Louvain, 1974, unpublished), 274pp. One, in an interesting variation, uses Lonergan's ideas to discuss the doctrine of God of two other philosophers: William M. Shea, *Intelligence, Intelligibility, and God: An Horizon Analysis of the American Naturalist Philosophies of Frederick J. E. Woodbridge and John R. Randall, Jr.* (New York: Columbia University, 1973; published as *The Naturalists and the Supernatural: Studies in Horizon and an American Philosophy of Religion*, Macon, GA: Mercer University, 1984). For regular updatings of this list, consult the quarterly *Lonergan Studies Newsletter*.

seded? This is a major question in Lonergan's own history, and I must reserve space for it, as well as for discussion of his more recent writings which clarify the question and its answer.

Insight was written between 1949 and 1953, with a new preface and some touching up here and there in the four years preceding publication in 1957. A second edition, with a few revisions (none significantly affects our material) and correction of misprints, followed in 1958, and a third and fourth in 1970 and 1978 respectively, with a number of reprints intervening. It continues to be printed without a list of *errata*, of which several more have been noted since the second edition; in fact, the latest edition adds to them, having changed the pagination of the preface without corresponding changes in the index. But the only serious *erratum* I know of in chapter 19 is the omission of a "not" on page 659, lines 5–6 of the paragraph "Tenthly," which should read: "[T]he intelligibles identical with restricted acts of understanding would *not* be primary beings." This was noticed by Giovanni Sala, and confirmed by him in conversation with Fr. Lonergan;[31] it may be verified now by consulting the original typescript of *Insight* in the Lonergan Center, Toronto, where the missing "not" is indeed to be found.[32] There is no doubt a measure of the chapter's difficulty in the fact that so many of us could read and reread it without noticing the omission.

It is not the traditional doctrines of chapter 19 that are in question here. Most of these occur: God is the primary being, without any imperfection, the primary good, necessary, one, simple, eternal, etc.;[33] but they are included not so much for their own sake as to show that Lonergan's approach, though innovative, does not lead to a new and alien God. It is this innovative approach that has occasioned controversy and will claim our attention. The summary statement is given positively as follows: "[T]he transition to the transcendent is effected by proceeding from the contingent subject's unrestricted act of understanding."[34] In the Halifax lectures of 1958 we are told that the movement is not from limited act to pure act (the standard approach) but from limited insight to an unlimited understanding. This, however, does not pit the two against one another; Lonergan goes on to assert their equivalence, for being and intelligence are correlative, and to say that his choice was made to eliminate the ambiguities of the meaning of being.[35] *Insight* had already said as much: one can try to state what

31. Interview: *Conversazioni*, with Giovanni Sala (Toronto: Regis College, 1970, unpublished).

32. *Insight: A Study of Human Understanding*, author's original typescript (Toronto: Regis College, 1953), p. 43 of the typescript for this chapter.

33. *Insight*, pp. 657–69, "The Notion of God."

34. Ibid., p. 679.

35. *Understanding and Being: An Introduction and Companion to "Insight"*, p. 296.

being is "by proceeding on the side of the subject from restricted to unrestricted understanding and on the side of the object from the structure of proportionate being to the transcendent idea of being";[36] in each case we arrive at the same God. But clearly the focus is going to be on the subject. As far as I remember Lonergan has not given a distinctive name to his approach. It has been put in the class of cosmological arguments, but Lonergan's use of causality is quite different from the standard cosmological use. Better, I think, if we are to name it, to speak of the "transcendental" approach to the transcendent. But better still to get hold of its distinctive character.

Several factors contribute to the choice of this new orientation. One seems to be the young Lonergan's impatience with his own formation in philosophy and theology, where endless disputed questions bedeviled epistemology and metaphysics. The introduction to *Insight* refers casually to these,[37] but Lonergan's lectures attest their more than casual importance.[38] A more general factor is that "turn to the subject" which marks all, Lonergan included, who practice transcendental method. Thus, on beginning the *Verbum* articles back in 1946, he makes the revealing remark: "I have begun, not from the metaphysical framework, but from the psychological content of Thomist theory of intellect: logic might favor the opposite procedure but, after attempting it in a variety of ways, I found it unmanageable."[39] Possibly the new turn had received a latent impetus from Lonergan's early attraction to Newman's *Grammar of Assent*; demonstrably, his immersion from the time of the *Verbum* articles in what he later knew as transcendental method made it natural for him to argue the existence of God on the same basis.

A quite specific factor requires more attention: the collapse, with a new notion of science, of the old way of using causality in the argument for God. This can be studied, with caution, from statements of the post-*Insight* Lonergan. I say "with caution" for we lack a thorough history of the development in Lonergan's views on science. It is clear that already in *Insight* the business of empirical science is to study immanent intelligibility, hence correlations rather than external causality; it is clear too that this already affects the use of causality in arguing to God; but it is not clear how much Lonergan's later reflection clarified for him what he had earlier been doing in *Insight,* for there seem to be significant developments in the Marquette University Lecture of 1958.[40] With this caution in mind we may turn to the very clear statements

---

36. *Insight*, p. 644. 37. Ibid., p. xxvii.
38. See also *Method in Theology*, pp. 20–21.
39. *Verbum*, pp. 45–46.
40. *The Nature of Knowledge in the Natural Sciences* (Milwaukee: Marquette University, 1958, unpublished).

made ten years after that lecture: "While it [modern science] still speaks of causes, what it means is not end, agent, matter, form, but correlation." And that, Lonergan holds, creates a problem in knowledge of God for, where Aristotle's physics made no logical break between knowledge of this world and knowledge of ultimate causes, modern science introduces just such a break: "It is knowledge of this world and only of this world. It proceeds from data and to data it adds only verifiable hypotheses. But God is not a datum. . . . Again, between this world and God there is no relationship that can be verified."[41]

The quotation brings out the need for a history of Lonergan's thought and usage and possible development on the question, for in *Insight* he had said that "some elements in the transcendent idea will be verifiable."[42] Is there a significant change in the post-*Insight* statement? While awaiting the historical study we lack, I incline to answer no. For the context in *Insight* is his discussion of extrapolation, the illustration is from mathematics, and the full clause reads, "the extrapolation to the transcendent, though conceptual, operates from the real basis of proportionate being, so that some elements in the transcendent idea will be verifiable just as some of the positive integers are verifiable." And later in the chapter we read "what is grasped is not the unrestricted act but the extrapolation that proceeds from the properties of a restricted act to the properties of the unrestricted act."[43] The sense could, therefore, be: as we can verify the integer "two" and the integer "one hundred" and can extrapolate from "two" to the hundredth power of "two" without, however, being able to verify the result, so analogously (but only analogously) we can extrapolate to the transcendent idea from verifiable elements, again without being able to verify the result. If that is the case, then the Lonergan of 1957 would have no difficulty with the Lonergan of 1968 who says that modern science has forced a new state of the question, and obliged us to ask what kind of knowledge our knowledge of God is: "It is not a question that could be asked about knowledge at any time or place; on the contrary it is a question that arises only after modern science has been developed." The answer, in his view, should appear from the argument itself: "Now I believe that question can be answered and I attempted to do so in a book, *Insight*."[44]

To the argument then. Many discussions begin with the much-quoted proof: "If the real is completely intelligible, God exists. But the real is completely intelligible. Therefore, God exists."[45] To begin there is legitimate, but it is not where Lonergan himself begins; rather, it is

41. *A Second Collection: Papers by Bernard J. F. Lonergan, S.J.*, pp. 94–95; see also p. 107.

42. *Insight*, p. 642. 43. Ibid., p. 670.
44. *Second Collection*, p. 95. 45. *Insight*, p. 672.

where he ends after nearly forty pages of tightly packed argument, and the proof is intelligible only with the developed understanding those pages try to promote. (We may recall here the uses Lonergan sees in logic for bringing clarity, coherence, and rigor to one's developed understanding, along with the sterility of logic in the actual process of that development—another topic on which we need a thorough study of his position.) There are different ways to unpack the argument, but for purposes of my own I choose the following. There are two affirmations, Lonergan says, the affirmation of some existent reality, and the affirmation of a link between that existence and God's; the second affirmation is a process which in three steps

identifies the real with being, then identifies being with complete intelligibility, and finally identifies complete intelligibility with the unrestricted act of understanding that possesses the properties of God and accounts for everything else. In this process the expansive moment is the first. . . .[46]

I chose this passage deliberately for the sake of that last short sentence, "the expansive moment is the first." It seems a quite preposterous claim and we should assure ourselves that Lonergan is serious about it. In fact, he is dead serious: the expansive moment lies in identifying the real with being. One could demonstrate this, but at some length, from *Insight*; it is simpler to quote his own lapidary remark from the Halifax lectures a year after *Insight* came out. Here he asks whether the principle of extrinsic causality can carry us beyond this world, and answers:

That is a very fundamental question. The answer depends, first of all, upon one's notion of reality. If one does not mean being by the word "reality," I do not know of any way to prove that extrinsic causality expresses principles that are universally valid and relevant.[47]

Nine years later, in a lecture at the University of Chicago, he says that to identify the real with being is to recapitulate the Greek breakthrough from *mythos* to *logos*, that to fail to do so is to find ourselves without any valid proof for the existence of God.[48] It is critical to an understanding of chapter 19 to realize that Lonergan, with eyes wide open, is locating the expansive moment of his argument in an epistemological position established long before the question of God arises in *Insight*; otherwise we will not engage him where he stands, but will argue with an imaginary Lonergan somewhere else.

Yet his position seems, literally, preposterous. The expansive moment ought to be located in a leap from contingent to necessary being, from

46. Ibid., pp. 675–76.

47. *Understanding and Being,* p. 300.

48. Lecture: *The General Character of the Natural Theology Contained in . . . "Insight"* (Chicago: University of Chicago, 1967, unpublished), "The General Character," no. 6.

limited to unlimited act, from the realm of data to a realm beyond data, in short, from this world to another that transcends it. For Lonergan, however, the key step is to identify the real with being, and this identity is established back in chapter 16, well before he comes to the God-question, specifically in part 3.2, "Cognitional or Ontological Elements?" The point there is simply one of cognitional theory and epistemology. One may "claim that the real is a subdivision in the 'already out there now' or, if one pleases, in the 'already in here now.'"[49] But for Lonergan the real is what is known by intelligent grasp and reasonable affirmation; it is therefore to be identified with being, for being is "the objective of the pure desire to know, the goal of intelligent inquiry and critical reflection, the object of intelligent grasp and reasonable affirmation."[50] This claim was itself established a hundred pages earlier when Lonergan set up the positions and counterpositions on knowing, objectivity, and the real,[51] and so we are led inexorably back to his basis in cognitional theory. One begins to understand why those who write dissertations on chapter 19 feel obliged to spend one or two hundred pages in explanation of Lonergan's foundation. I can only repeat here that, to engage the real Lonergan, one must see how he understands the alternatives: Is the real "what is known unquestioningly because it is known before any questions are asked?"[52] Or is knowledge of the real consequent on questioning, is the real known then by intelligent grasp and reasonable affirmation, is it identical with being? Lonergan's strategy is one of *breakthrough,* when the subject recognizes that "he has a positive and effective inclination both to inquire intelligently and reflect reasonably," of *encirclement,* when he realizes that the objective of this inclination, no matter how it is defined, is being, a notion that in this sense "cannot be controverted . . . [one] assumed in all inquiry and reflection, in all thought and doubt," and, thirdly, of *confinement,* "once the subject grasps that, unless he identifies the real with being, his statements are bound to be counter-positions that eventually are due for reversal."[53]

If it is clear what the basic step is, we can turn to the second element in the process, the one that "identifies being with complete intelligibility." It is here that standard interpretation would be inclined to locate the expansive moment; for this step, linked with the affirmation of some existent reality, carries us beyond this world of incomplete intelligibility, to the existence, therefore, of complete intelligibility. If, for Lonergan, it is not the crux of the matter, it still demands careful exposition. The realities of this world, then, are not of themselves completely intelligible.

49. *Insight,* p. 499. 50. Ibid.
51. Ibid., pp. 387–88. 52. Ibid., p. 522.
53. Ibid.

So far, a quite traditional position. One item in this world can be accounted for by appealing to another in the same world. But there is no way of accounting within this world for the world itself. Must one account for it? With that question we come to the very point of the demand for complete intelligibility of being. The point is not at all that we understand complete intelligibility, or understand the idea of being in Lonergan's precise sense of "idea" and "being." The point is rather that we cannot continue to exercise our minds in intelligent grasp and reasonable affirmation without supposing the complete intelligibility of being, so we have either to accept the supposition or cease the full exercise of intelligence and reason.

What the point is *not* is clear enough; in an already quoted statement, "what is grasped is not the unrestricted act but the extrapolation that proceeds from the properties of a restricted act to the properties of the unrestricted act."[54] We may concentrate then on what the point *is*. As follows. Being is known by the exercise of our intelligence, that is, by intelligent grasp and reasonable affirmation, and the exercise has an unrestricted scope. It is the "encirclement" we saw earlier, modified now by recognition of the unlimited scope of the "break-through." The images begin to clash, as happens when we push images beyond their original purpose, but that very clash can be illuminating. That is, in the military figure we think of a limited campaign for a limited objective to be encircled; now we recognize that both the campaign and the objective are unlimited, so we might well abandon the metaphor. The supposition, then, of the continued exercise of our intelligence, "continued" in the sense that we impose no obscurantist limits, is that its objective is completely intelligible. It is quite possible to say of a particular question, "That's beyond me"; but that is a judgment on my present capacity to understand, not on the intelligibility the question would seek. It is possible too to say of a particular question that it is illegitimate, because it contains a false statement, or because it would destroy itself by destroying the dynamism that produced it. But there is no way to allow the dynamism its full exercise, that is, commit ourselves in questioning to the exercise of intelligence, and at the same time say that what we seek is unintelligible. The only recourse is to block the dynamism that, "immanent and recurrently operative" within us,[55] would continue to ask every question that comes to mind. We have to block the dynamism, or, if questions arise willy-nilly, suppress them, get rid of them, and then effect some kind of cover-up in the court of intellectual consciousness. That is the point of Lonergan's ever repeated affirmation of the unrestricted objective of our questioning

54. Ibid., p. 670.　　　　　　　　　55. Ibid., p. xvii.

and his ever repeated condemnation of obscurantism. We can protest, yet the protest contains its own refutation:

Might not my desire to understand correctly suffer from some immanent and hidden restriction and bias, so that there could be real things that lay quite beyond its utmost horizon? . . . Yet if I ask the question, it is in virtue of my desire to know; and as the question itself reveals, my desire to know concerns itself with what lies quite beyond a suspected limited horizon.[56]

It is in the context of this presupposition, and only in this context, that one understands Lonergan's actual transition from this world to the transcendent and his very personal use of the argument from causality to effect the transition:

For one misses the real point to efficient causality if one supposes that it consists simply in the necessity that conditioned being becomes virtually unconditioned only if its conditions are fulfilled. On that formulation, efficient causality would be satisfied by an infinite regress in which each conditioned has its conditions fulfilled by a prior conditioned or, perhaps more realistically, by a circle illustrated by the scheme of recurrence. However, the real requirement is that, if conditioned being is being, it has to be intelligible; it cannot be or exist or occur merely as a matter of fact for which no explanation is to be asked or expected, for the non-intelligible is apart from being.[57]

As Lonergan will say in *Method*, "implicitly we grant that the universe is intelligible."[58] I should say that the whole force of this second step we have been considering lies in making explicit that which we implicitly grant when we allow our questioning dynamism its full range. With that achieved, it is an easy task to conclude from a universe that is not completely intelligible in itself to the only ground of its intelligibility, namely, what is completely intelligible.

There remains the third step in the process, that which "identifies complete intelligibility with the unrestricted act of understanding that possesses the properties of God and accounts for everything else."[59] On the properties of God, Lonergan provides an extensive exposition; one remembers the famous line, "In the twenty-sixth place, God is personal."[60] We may be brief, since he deals here with more familiar concepts; we omit therefore not only the twenty-sixth but the preceding twenty-five points too. What is important is to note the continuity of reasoning. There is the intelligible that is immanent in the act of understanding, and there is the intelligible that is or can be understood; further, the former is the "ground or root or key" for the latter;[61] it is therefore the ultimate that we are seeking. But such an intelligibility

56. Ibid., p. 639.
57. Ibid., pp. 655–56.
58. *Method*, p. 101.
59. *Insight*, p. 675.
60. Ibid., p. 668.
61. Ibid., p. 647.

primarily understands itself, and since it is complete intelligibility it understands everything else as well. It is the unrestricted act of understanding, the idea of being that has the properties of God and accounts for all else, for all "beings" in the ordinary sense of the word. I believe this is a fair statement in brief of what Lonergan develops at length in some of his most complex reasoning. I reduce it to a few lines, well aware that some readers take issue with this step. But in a limited exposition of this difficult chapter, I must emphasize, as must anyone else, what seem to be the key points in the argument.

One may well ask, after struggling through the preceding pages, whether any philosopher on earth will be brought to God by this reasoning, and what hope there is for the non-philosopher. But for the non-philosopher at least there are encouraging words from Lonergan himself who, at both earlier and later stages of his career, continued to maintain that it is not difficult to know that God exists. For example, in *Insight:*

[B]ecause it is difficult to know what our knowing is, it also is difficult to know what our knowledge of God is. But just as our knowing is prior to an analysis of knowledge and far easier than it, so too our knowledge of God is both earlier and easier than any attempt to give it formal expression.[62]

And, again, in *Philosophy of God, and Theology,* twenty years later:

I do not think it difficult to establish God's existence. I do think it a life-long labor to analyze and refute all the objections that philosophers have thought up against the existence of God. But I see no pressing need for every student of religion to penetrate into that labyrinth and then work his way out.[63]

But philosophers too have their needs, one of them a need to render an account of the knowledge that is within them, by whatever route it was acquired. To meet that need they may be willing to undertake the labor that could use up a good part of a lifetime. It is for them, I suggest, that chapter 19 was written.

I feel a need of my own, arising out of the very labor of my exposition of Lonergan's argument, to restate and underline what I conceive to be the real issues in all the discussion that swirls around this famous chapter 19. I would do so in terms of his two presuppositions, one general, one specific to this chapter. The general supposition is the native and basic endowment of the human mind to reach truth in the sense of coming to know through intelligent grasp and reasonable af-

---

62. Ibid., p. 683.
63. *Philosophy of God, and Theology: The Relationship between Philosophy of God and the Functional Specialty, Systematics,* pp. 55–56.

firmation. There is no way to prove such a supposition, for the alleged proof would necessarily involve the use of the human mind and thus suppose what it was trying to establish. There is, then, "an immanent Anagke" to which we bow;[64] there are "natural inevitabilities and spontaneities that constitute the possibility of knowing, not by demonstrating that one can know, but pragmatically by engaging one in the process. . . . [To seek a deeper foundation for this] involves a vicious circle." Thus there are limits to criticism. "The critical spirit can weigh all else in the balance, only on condition that it does not criticize itself."[65]

Such is Lonergan's position in epistemology. To be noted: the one question that is fundamentally and on principle disallowed is the question that is self-destructive. He can speak of questioning our questioning, as we shall see presently. But that is not to question the validity of our knowing or of the questioning dynamism that leads to knowledge; it rather supposes that and asks what we must affirm if the activity is to be completely intelligible. Lonergan's position in epistemology is not therefore one that can establish its foundation in a positive way; we cannot lift ourselves by our epistemological bootstraps. Still, the position is lethal against its opponents. No one can challenge it, unless he assumes the native orientation of his mind to know and exercises his mind in intelligent grasp and reasonable affirmation: that is, he cannot challenge it without supposing it. It is this utterly lethal weapon, lethal to one's own doubts as well as to an opponent's arguments, that sets this position poles apart from a mere fideism.

The other presupposition that I would underline is specifically needed for the argument of chapter 19; it is that unrestricted character of our questioning which involves the correlative of complete intelligibility. This unrestricted character is also in its own way given; it is part of the immanent Anagke, not to be established therefore by any proof superior to the actual occurrence of further and further and yet further questions. But again, if the position cannot be established *a priori*, it too is lethal against opponents. Anyone can stop questioning at any point; at least we can avoid expressing our questions, and do much to suppress their secret occurrence by immersing ourselves in thoughtless activity. But to say that in principle certain questions are not to be allowed, that certain areas of what is or is not, what may be or may not be, are taboo to inquiry, this is simply to put oneself out of the court of intelligence and reason. One is resorting to obscurantism, and obscurantism is not a good basis for refusing the proof of

64. *Insight*, p. 331.   65. Ibid., p. 332.

God's existence. But to reject obscurantism is to allow the further and further questions to arise; to allow the questions to arise is to open the mind to ask, "Is it?," and to ask whether it is, is to admit that particular item of possible being and knowledge as part of the mind's objective.

IV. The *Method* Period

Between *Insight* and *Method* there intervened in Lonergan's career the Roman period of his teaching: twelve years at the Gregorian University. The coincidence in time is quite exact, for he went to Rome in 1953, hardly two months after finishing *Insight,* and he returned to Toronto in 1965, the year in which he began the formal drafting of *Method,* just a few months, in fact, after conceiving the key idea for structuring it: the two phases of theology, each with its four tasks based on the four levels of consciousness.

It is an oddly puzzling period to the historian of Lonergan's thought. His work during those twelve years is fairly well documented in courses, notes, lectures, tape-recordings, theology manuals; further, it was a period of enormous expansion of his student followers, who can therefore come to our aid as his interpreters. Yet in comparison with the preceding period, characterized in relative simplicity by the Thomist studies and *Insight,* and with the subsequent decade, characterized even more simply by *Method* and related productions, these twelve years abound in questions. Some obvious ones: How much did it further his own creative thinking to be professor in a Roman University? And how much was it an obstacle? In so far as it helped, was this due to his concentration on trinitarian and Christological questions? Or to his involvement with the students of Europe in their number and variety? How much of his Latin theology at that time was simply dotting the i's and crossing the t's in Scholastic theology, to be replaced therefore once *Method* made a better theology possible? And how much was it already an anticipation of what might be done through adequate method?

These and similar questions are important for the study of Lonergan's overall development, but I feel justified in omitting them here. For one thing, the answers are still obscure; despite good beginnings by some interpreters, the period needs much more study in detail. More decisive for me is the fact that the productions of those twelve years do not offer much that is directly relevant to Lonergan's views on ultimate reality. For this, *Insight* and *Method* remain fixed points, though the latter, as we shall see, does not so much set forth a doctrine of God as indicate how such a doctrine might be attained. But we can approximate through those two books to a view of Lonergan's later history on ultimate reality, and so omit a detailed study of the Roman period.

Two points only, therefore. One is the quite explicit conception of the divine nature as understanding (the Thomist *ipsum intelligere*). A question comes up in trinitarian theology of the manner in which God may be said to generate a Son, and this becomes a question of the divine nature, since parents generate offspring of the same nature as themselves. Lonergan's answer: although in God nothing is before or after, we have so to order our concepts of God that we put one first and the others in derivation from that. Lonergan's way is to put the divine understanding first, and derive from it our concepts of God's infinity, aseity, simplicity, and so forth.[66]

Secondly, there is the relation of God to his created universe. Lonergan has never abandoned the Thomist position on this, but develops it in his analysis of contingent predications about God. Let it be a true proposition, then, which we know either naturally or through revelation, that God created the world and did so freely. How can the contingent predicate "creates" be said of the necessary being "God"? Analysis reveals that God is "constituted" creator by his own infinite (and necessary) perfection, but that the truth we know (without understanding it) requires as a consequent condition (not a prior and determining one) the existence of creation as an intrinsic term of the divine operation.[67]

We turn almost directly, then, from the Lonergan of *Insight* to the Lonergan of *Method*, an experience that has been disconcerting for many of his readers. The first chapter of the latter book (on transcendental method) is obviously continuous with *Insight* and offers no special difficulty. The next two chapters (on the human good and on meaning) at least treat topics that *Insight* also handled, though there are quite significant developments. But in the fourth chapter, on religion and religious experience, we are brought up short by ideas almost totally absent from *Insight*. Not only that, but it is just those ideas that will decisively influence the crucial chapters on dialectic and foundations, and hence the three final chapters on doctrines, systematics, and communications. Since the chapter on religion and that on systematics are the best sources we have in *Method* for Lonergan's new approach to God, we must be prepared for a considerable change.

Not that *Method* provides us with a doctrine of God, or treats the topic expressly in the manner of chapter 19 of *Insight*. It is, after all, just a method for doctrines (and the other tasks of theology), and not

---

66. *De deo trino,* vol. 2, pp. 98–100.   67. Ibid., pp. 217–19.

the exercise of that specialty on any particular doctrine at all.[68] So we do not expect a detailed study of God, but only of that further element in the human subject which allows us to think of God in the new context of religion. Still, hints of a doctrine inevitably appear; one can piece them together for a view on Lonergan's new conception, in sufficient clarity to allow a comparison of the highest interest between the God of *Insight* and the God of *Method*. That comparison will be central in our next section; for the moment, the question is what *Method* says about God.

Chapter 4 then, on religion, opens with the *question* of God. This is a quite deliberate move, if we may judge from Lonergan's subsequent explanations. In the Dublin lectures of 1971, when the text of *Method* had just gone to the publisher, he remarked that now he puts in the form of a question what chapter 19 of *Insight* had put in the form of a syllogism.[69] Responding to his audience two years later in the St. Michael's Lectures, he is quoted as saying that "the question about God is much more important than the proof of God, because at the present time people deny that the question exists."[70] Not as if the question had been overlooked in *Insight*, where chapter 19 had been introduced by the notion of transcendence, and transcendence was said to be "the elementary matter of raising further questions,"[71] but that there the question led at once into a prolonged struggle to formulate an answer, whereas now it is seen as offering a common ground even when the answers do not agree.

Further, the question is put differently now: it is the question "that questions the significance of its own questioning,"[72] and this one basic question divides into three forms and a fourth. I put it that way to underline the special character of the fourth, which is the religious form and so is formulated only late in chapter 4 after Lonergan has set forth his views on religion. A year later, in *Philosophy of God, and Theology,* the four are listed in one continuous sequence.[73] The first three forms of the question, then, are these: whether the intelligibility we assume in the universe could be, unless it had an intelligible ground (a question already familiar from chapter 19 of *Insight*); whether the conditional character of contingent being requires an absolute unconditioned; and whether our moral values are valid without a transcendent moral ground.[74] Succinctly, later in the book:

---

68. *Method,* pp. xii, 131, 149, 253–54, 282, 291, 297–98, 312, 323–24, 355.

69. Lectures: *"Method in Theology"* (Dublin: Milltown Park, 1971, unpublished), p. 49.

70. *Philosophy of God,* p. 16; see also *Second Collection,* p. 277, and workshop: *Question Sessions* (Chestnut Hill, MA: Boston College, 1974, unpublished), "Fifth Discussion," p. 12.

71. *Insight,* p.635.　　　　　　　　　　72. *Method,* p. 103.

73. *Philosophy of God,* pp. 52–55.　　　74. *Method,* pp. 101–102.

Could the world be mediated by questions for intelligence if it did not have an intelligent ground? Could the world's facticity be reconciled with its intelligibility, if it did not have a necessary ground? Is it with man that morality emerges in the universe so that the universe is amoral and alien to man, or is the ground of the universe a moral being?[75]

And these forms are still later designated as "epistemological," "philosophic," and "moral."[76] But the source of the division remains as it was given in *Method:* questions for intelligence, questions for reflection, questions for deliberation, corresponding to the three higher levels of human consciousness.[77]

Thus, though *Insight* is more concerned than *Method* is with answers, the two are at one in their attitude toward questions and the dynamism that generates them. The impatient rejection, in the former book, of any and all obscurantism, appears again in the latter, stated with the same conviction, if not with the same passion: "Man's transcendental subjectivity is mutilated or abolished, unless he is stretching forth towards the intelligible, the unconditioned, the good of value." And this "orientation to the divine" is established prior to the introduction of religion: "The question of God, then, lies within man's horizon. . . . The reach, not of his attainment, but of his intending is unrestricted. There lies within his horizon a region for the divine, a shrine for ultimate holiness."[78]

But there is a fourth question and it arises with the introduction of religion. The first three questions constitute our *capacity* for self-transcendence. "That capacity becomes an actuality when one falls in love,"[79] and "religion is the . . . word God speaks to us by flooding our hearts with his love."[80] There follows faith, "the knowledge born of religious love," the kind Pascal spoke of "when he remarked that the heart has reasons which reason does not know."[81] There is "an apprehension of transcendent value" which "consists in the experienced fulfilment of our unrestricted thrust to self-transcendence, in our actuated orientation towards the mystery of love and awe," a fulfillment which "may be objectified as a clouded revelation of absolute intelligence and intelligibility, absolute truth and reality, absolute goodness and holiness."[82]

At this point Lonergan introduces for the first time in *Method* his fourth question: "With that objectification there recurs the question of God in a new form. For now it is primarily a question of decision. Will

75. Ibid., p. 342.   76. *Philosophy of God,* pp. 54–55.
77. *Method,* pp. 101–103; *Philosophy of God,* pp. 52–54.
78. *Method,* p. 103.   79. Ibid., p. 105.
80. Ibid., p. 112.   81. Ibid., p. 115.
82. Ibid., pp. 115–16.

I love him in return, or will I refuse?"[83] Further, this seems the primary question on the religious level: "Only secondarily do there arise the questions of God's existence and nature, and they are the questions either of the lover seeking to know him or of the unbeliever seeking to escape him. Such is the basic option of the existential subject once called by God."[84]

The questions that Lonergan here calls secondary are perhaps more central in an article such as mine, and so merit a further word. It is a matter of knowledge following love rather than preceding it: "[W]e are in the dynamic state of being in love. But who it is we love, is neither given nor as yet understood."[85] The "orientation to transcendent mystery . . . provides the origin for inquiry about God, for seeking assurance of his existence. . . . [In] a religion that is shared by many, that enters into and transforms cultures, that extends down the ages, God will be named, questions about him will be asked, answers will be forthcoming."[86] To be noted: In *Philosophy of God, and Theology,* the existential question recedes into the background and the "secondary" questions come to the fore;[87] they do the same in the chapter on systematics in *Method,* the existential question and our response being now presumed. To be noted also in *Philosophy:* the "majority of mankind have been religious. One cannot claim that their religion has been based on some philosophy of God. One can easily argue that their religious concern arose out of their religious experience. In that case the basic question of God is the fourth question that arises out of religious experience."[88] This point will concern us again presently.

Lonergan's approach to God in *Method* is the very heart of the matter for this article, so it will be useful to put the various aspects (many of them already noticed in preceding paragraphs) into some order. To that end I propose three headings: (1) the strategy of the approach through self-transcendence of the subject; (2) the religious experience itself as subjective and as objectified; and (3) the "object" to which the experience points and leads us.

The strategy sketched in *Method* takes us to God through the self-transcendence of the subject and its various stages. Thus, Lonergan sees a cognitional self-transcendence in the virtually unconditioned character of judgment (the absolute objectivity of *Insight*), a moral self-transcendence in moving beyond satisfactions to what is truly worthwhile as a criterion for choices, and affective self-transcendence in the event or occurrence of falling in love. Again, there are different kinds of love:

---

83. Ibid., p. 116.
85. Ibid., p. 122.
87. *Philosophy of God*, pp. 52–55.

84. Ibid.
86. Ibid., pp. 341–42.
88. Ibid., p. 55.

the love of intimacy in the family, "the love of mankind devoted to the pursuit of human welfare locally or nationally or globally," and the love of God with one's whole heart and soul and mind and strength. This last admits "no conditions or qualifications or restrictions or reservations"—that is, it is other-worldly, it is religious love.[89]

If we ask why Lonergan takes this route, we are carried back to his lifelong concern with method, and so to that turn to the subject and to interiority which is the basis of his method. It is quite in keeping, then, with his general strategy to approach God through the subject and so, since the subject is intentional in its dynamism and operations, through the self-transcendence that the subject intends. Finally, since subjective consciousness is many-leveled, we have the stages of cognitional, moral, affective, and religious self-transcendence.

Our second heading is the subjective experience itself and its expression or objectification. Love of God is experienced: it is conscious and can be described in itself and in its effects. In itself, first, and briefly for the moment: "Being in love with God, as experienced, is being in love in an unrestricted fashion. All love is self-surrender, but being in love with God is being in love without limits or qualifications or conditions or reservations";[90] more on this under our third heading. As for its effects, the following lines are typical:

[B]eing in love with God is the basic fulfilment of our conscious intentionality. That fulfilment brings a deep-set joy that can remain despite humiliation, failure, privation, pain, betrayal, desertion. That fulfilment brings a radical peace, the peace that the world cannot give. That fulfilment bears fruit in a love of one's neighbor that strives mightily to bring about the kingdom of God on this earth. On the other hand, the absence of that fulfilment opens the way to the trivialization of human life in the pursuit of fun, to the harshness of human life arising from the ruthless exercise of power, to despair about human welfare springing from the conviction that the universe is absurd.[91]

It is a clarifying exercise to compare this description with that of the act of insight fifteen years earlier.[92] There we are beginning with a very fundamental step in self-appropriation, with the act that carries us beyond mere animal routine; the rest of the book pursues the further steps and implications of the whole cognitional structure. Here in *Method* we are also beginning with a very fundamental occurrence, with the event and state that will provide the chief basis for the second phase of theology. But insight is a first step in the way of achievement, love of God is a first event in the way of gift—a difference that will concern us in the last section of this article.

---

89. *Method*, p. 289; see also p. 105.
91. Ibid., p. 105.

90. Ibid., pp. 105–106.
92. *Insight*, pp. 3–6.

Let us note here, in a digression, but a necessary one if we are to avoid misunderstandings, that in describing the experience of being in love with God, we are going beyond the experience. In fact, there is no way to talk about the experience without going beyond it. The experience itself is without words; although Lonergan calls God's gift an "inner word," he does so to set it in contrast with the "outer word," that is, with articulated language, words in the ordinary sense.[93] Further, once we resort to "words" to describe experience, we necessarily operate within a given culture, in which the speaker lives and moves and has his or her linguistic background. Lonergan's background is Christian; his description of religious experience is in Pauline terms: the love of God flooding our hearts (Rom. 5:5); but that does not mean there is question here of an experience that is Christian alone.

Return now to the topic. Two questions, among dozens, may be selected to illuminate further this objectification of religious experience. One regards the process from the nonverbal experience to articulated description. Schematically put, it is the process from love through faith to beliefs. Love is the inner word which is not a human word at all in the linguistic sense. Faith is the eye of that love, "another kind of knowledge reached through the discernment of value and the judgments of value of a person in love."[94] Beliefs are the articulated judgments of fact and of value that a religion proposes.[95] If we ask, however, for more concrete descriptions of stages nearer the psyche, we find statements like the following: "So it is by associating religious experience with its outward occasion that the experience becomes expressed and thereby something determinate and distinct for human consciousness." That is, in early stages of human development we are tied to sensible presentations and representations: "There easily is pointed out the spatial but not the temporal, the specific but not the generic, the external but not the internal, the human but not the divine."[96] So the second member in each of these pairs comes to expression only by association with the first.

The other question regards the reduction of our description to something approaching an ultimate form. Is this possible? Views vary but at least, I should say, we can try to avoid the extremes of naive confidence and wooden defeatism. It would be naive not to realize that we are using our own terms which may be quite foreign to others; but it would be defeatist to renounce all effort to speak for those beyond our circle—after all, even those who maintain there is no universal element in religious experience still speak of "all religions." Lonergan's position is sketched shortly after *Method* in this quotation:

93. *Method*, p. 119; see pp. 112–15.   94. Ibid., p. 115.
95. Ibid., p. 118.   96. Ibid., p. 108.

No doubt . . . [religious] experience takes many forms. No doubt, it suffers many aberrations. But it keeps recurring. Its many forms can be explained by the many varieties of human culture. Its many aberrations can be accounted for by the precariousness of the human achievement of authenticity. Underneath the many forms and prior to the many aberrations some have found that there exists an unrestricted being in love, a mystery of love and awe, a being grasped by ultimate concern, a happiness that has a determinate content but no intellectually apprehended object.[97]

I found it convenient to turn to a later work for this concise statement, but I do not think it in any way departs from, or goes beyond, what can be found in *Method*.

Our third topic has been cropping up throughout discussion of the second; it regards the "object" of all this religious activity and concern, surely a central concern of an article on ultimate reality. The word "object" is, however, weighted, affect-laden, something of a shibboleth. We are told that God is the Subject who is never an object, and theologians are faulted for ignoring that proscription and defiantly trying to turn God into an object. Lonergan's procedure will be to distinguish quite different senses of "object." Of that in a moment; meanwhile we may come at the question indirectly.

Probably the key term for Lonergan in speaking about God is "mystery." We recall the "known unknown" of chapter 17 of *Insight* where, however, the context was more intellectually oriented. In the context of *Method,* to be in love with God "is an experience of mystery . . . an experience of the holy, of Rudolf Otto's *mysterium fascinans et tremendum*." Further, "Because it is an unmeasured love, the mystery evokes awe."[98] Later in the same volume we read that "the orientation reveals its goal by its absoluteness: it is with all one's heart and all one's soul. . . . It is, then, an orientation to what is transcendent in lovableness and, when that is unknown, it is an orientation to transcendent mystery."[99] Now from this "experience of love focused on mystery there wells forth a longing for knowledge, while love itself is a longing for union."[100]

Is the God of such religious activity an object? Not in the naive realist sense of what is already there, out there or up there, or in here, now. If one turns to empiricism, naturalism, positivism, or idealism, one does not even speak of a God who is (so I interpret Lonergan here), and so does not make him an object in this case either. But what if one avoids these isms to take one's stand on the intelligent grasp and reasonable affirmation that provide the answers intended in questions? Then Lonergan would distinguish. One can be drawn into the cloud of unknow-

---

97. *Philosophy of God*, p. 54.
99. Ibid., p. 341.

98. *Method*, p. 106.
100. Ibid., p. 109.

ing through orientation to mystery, and in this state God is not an object. Withdrawal, however, is for return and, when people return, "they objectify in images and concepts and words both what they have been doing and the God that has been their concern"[101] and then God has become an object. This can be put in another way: "Man's response to transcendent mystery is adoration. But adoration does not exclude words."[102] And the words sooner or later generate the problems which theologians add to mystery, thereby making the mystery an object of thought.

How central all this is to Lonergan's views on ultimate reality is clear from a statement, deceivingly simple in appearance, which says that "orientation to transcendent mystery . . . provides the primary and fundamental meaning of the name, God."[103] This could well form the motto of an article that purports to give Lonergan's views on ultimate reality and meaning.

v. The Puzzle of *Insight* and *Method*

One year after the publication of *Method*, Lonergan gave the St. Michael's Lectures at Gonzaga University, Spokane; the topic: the relationship between philosophy of God and the seventh functional specialty of *Method in Theology*, systematics. The lectures illuminate several points already made, but are especially important for the intriguing question of the relationship between *Insight* and *Method* in this matter. One could adapt Pascal's phrase and ask, "Is the God of *Insight*'s philosopher the God also of *Method*'s believer?"

There are, then, illuminating remarks on the object of religious experience as not intellectually apprehended,[104] on the love of God as leading to inquiry about God,[105] on the universality of the gift of God's love,[106] and especially on the relation between philosophy and theology on the God-question; Lonergan sharply opposes Pascal's separation of the God of Abraham, Isaac, and Jacob from the God of the philosophers.[107]

This latter point leads directly to the present question; let us develop it briefly. The basis for Lonergan's position is an analytic comparison of the static and the dynamic: on a static view, philosophy and theology must be separate, for, having different premises, they cannot be united in one deductive system; but on a dynamic view this does not apply,

101. Ibid., pp. 341–42. 102. Ibid., p. 344.
103. Ibid., p. 341.
104. *Philosophy of God*, pp. 10, 38, 39, 50–51, 54.
105. Ibid., pp. 10, 11, 50–55. 106. Ibid., pp. 10, 50.
107. Ibid., pp. 11, 52.

for they may have something in common in their origin and goal and join in "the unity of a single collaborative process."[108]

The argument is developed through three headings. Philosophy of God and the corresponding theology have a common origin in the religious experience of the love of God, which leads us in both cases to ask what we are in love with. "When we find it out in the context of a philosophy, there results a philosophy of God. When we find it out in the context of a functionally differentiated theology, there results a functional specialty, systematics. So it turns out that one and the same God has unknowingly been found and is differently being sought by both philosopher and theologian."[109] Secondly, philosophy and theology complement one another here. Philosophy needs theology, for the four forms of the God-question (epistemological, philosophic, moral, religious) are cumulative and belong together. Further, the fourth form is basic for it is the universally operative one, influencing also the first three; they belong, true enough, to a philosophy of God, but that philosophy flourishes only in a climate of religious experience. On the other side theology gains from union with philosophy, for it is concerned with the significance and value of a religion within a given culture; it needs general categories to pursue this end, and the same general categories are used also in philosophy, the sciences, hermeneutics, and history. Thirdly, the union of philosophy of God and systematics is suggested by their common goal in the development of persons. For persons result from community, community is strongest when it is based on love, and the religious experience of love is at the root of both philosophy of God and systematics.[110]

We may add, as a footnote to the preceding paragraph, that Lonergan does not argue that philosophers should give up proving the existence of God. Some readers interpreted his position in that way, but several oral responses to questions both then and in later years make the point that his concern in bringing philosophy and theology together was mainly pedagogical and applied to theology students: Why should they do a certain part of theology twice, once on the basis of reason and again on the basis of revelation?[111] The transposition, then, of chapter 19 of *Insight* into a theological context does not mean that those who

108. Ibid., p. 46; note that Lonergan regularly speaks of the functional specialty, systematics, where I use the less accurate term, theology, for short.

109. Ibid., p. 51. The phrases "has been found" and "is being sought" are not a lapse in logic: they refer to Pascal's remark that we would not seek God unless we had already found him, pp. 10, 20.

110. Ibid., pp. 50–59.

111. Ibid., p. 19; workshop: *Question Sessions* (Chestnut Hill, MA: Boston College, 1977, unpublished), "First Discussion," p. 2.

do not study theology should not do philosophy of God; of course, they should.[112]

So we come to one of the difficult questions of Lonergan's historical development, the relation between chapter 19 of *Insight* and the approach to God that characterizes his later writings. There are data bearing directly on the question from Lonergan's own voice and pen, but they do not altogether solve it; one might say rather that they simply point it up. There are, however, other and later data which I believe we can use to clarify his own position for him in a way he has not done himself, data found in a distinction he has recently been using between a human development that moves upward in the way of achievement and one that moves downward under the influence of gift. The puzzle, I think, yields to analysis.

As for the data bearing directly on the problem, we can begin with an address entitled "Natural Knowledge of God" given in 1968, early therefore in the *Method* period. Here he reiterates the position of *Insight*: "[I]f human knowing consists in asking and answering questions, if ever further questions arise, if the further questions are given honest answers then, as I have argued elsewhere at some length, we can and do arrive at knowledge of God."[113] This reiterated position is, however, put in newer perspective by the added remark: "I do not think that in this life people arrive at natural knowledge of God without God's grace, but what I do not doubt is that the knowledge they so attain is natural."[114]

Then, at the 1970 congress on his work, pressed on the same point, Lonergan expanded a bit. Chapter 19, he says, was written in a different context, "prior to my concern with the existentialists" and with others; the context, he suggests, was more that of the First Vatican Council.[115] In *Method* itself there does not seem to be any reference to chapter 19, but there is a pertinent and very helpful remark: God's gift of his love, we read, "could be the finding that grounds our seeking God through natural reason and through positive religion. It could be the touchstone by which we judge whether it is really God that natural reason reaches or positive religion preaches," and a note to this passage refers us to his 1968 lecture (our preceding paragraph) for "the transition from the context of Vatican I to the contemporary context on natural knowledge of God."[116]

Only in *Philosophy of God, and Theology*, however, does Lonergan

---

112. Workshop: *Question Sessions* (1977), "First Discussion," p. 9; see also *Question Sessions* (1974), "Fifth Discussion," p. 13.

113. *Second Collection*, p. 127, with a footnote reference to ch. 19 of *Insight*.

114. *Second Collection*, p. 133.   115. Ibid., pp. 224–25.

116. *Method*, p. 278.

come to a thematic treatment of our question. He now calls chapter 19 an outline of a philosophy of God, reports the unfavorable discussion of the 1970 congress, and refers to his "brief and noncommittal" answer at the time. But then he goes on to speak of the "incongruity" of basing his cognitional theory on a methodical appeal to experience and failing to appeal to religious experience for his account of God, and adds that *Insight* did not deal with moral and religious conversion, hence could not take sufficient account of the horizon of the subject.[117] He concludes this last point with what seems a trenchant criticism of his earlier work:

The trouble with chapter nineteen in *Insight* was that it did not depart from the traditional line. It treated God's existence and attributes in a purely objective fashion. It made no effort to deal with the subject's religious horizon. It failed to acknowledge that the traditional viewpoint made sense only if one accepted first principles on the ground that they were intrinsically necessary and if one added the assumption that there is one right culture so that differences in subjectivity are irrelevant.[118]

The same substantive criticisms are repeated next spring in the paper "*Insight* Revisited," with the remark added: "In *Method* the question of God is considered more important than the precise manner in which an answer is formulated."[119]

If we take all this as an outright repudiation of the famous argument of chapter 19, we discover on further investigation that we are badly mistaken. The same St. Michael's Lectures of 1972 are quite categorical in denying that repudiation: "There are proofs for the existence of God. I formulated them as best I could in chapter nineteen in *Insight* and I'm not repudiating that at all."[120] A similarly categorical statement was made in the discussion at a 1977 workshop, where Lonergan roundly affirmed that he had never had any reason for doubting the validity of chapter 19 of *Insight*.[121]

Is there evidence here of a contradiction? The reader unfamiliar with Lonergan could easily suspect that there is. Not so easily, however, one who like myself has spent over thirty years trying to understand Lonergan and has repeatedly discovered that a seeming contradiction yields on investigation to a deeper understanding. It is not a position of advocacy, therefore, but of simple interest in learning, to look for an explanation that would turn the apparent contradiction into a solvable puzzle.

In fact, there does seem to be a valid explanation, not formulated by

117. *Philosophy of God*, pp. 11–12. 118. Ibid., p. 13.
119. *Second Collection*, p. 277. 120. *Philosophy of God*, p. 41.
121. *Question Sessions* (1977), "First Discussion," p. 21.

Lonergan himself, but grounded in a distinction he made in a lecture of 1975, "Healing and Creating in History":

> For human development is of two quite different kinds. There is development from below upwards, from experience to growing understanding, from growing understanding to balanced judgement, from balanced judgement to fruitful courses of action, and from fruitful courses of action to the new situations that call forth further understanding, profounder judgement, richer courses of action.
>
> But there also is development from above downwards. There is the transformation of falling in love. . . .[122]

This twofold scheme is new, though it stands in continuity with *Method*; it has an application to *Insight* and *Method* in their relation to one another, and will be found, I think, to shed considerable light on chapter 19 and its position in the historical development of Lonergan's thought.

The scheme, then, is certainly in continuity with *Method*, for it derives directly from the contrast between the two phases of theology,[123] and almost comes to explicit formulation at one point.[124] One could even find anticipations of the idea in the trinitarian theology of Lonergan's middle period,[125] and in the distinction between openness as achievement and openness as gift.[126] But there are signs that it is also a strikingly new development. There is the fact that, suddenly, within a couple of years of its first appearance, it is found in six other articles or lectures.[127] This proliferation suggests recent emergence from a latent state to clarity. There is a hint that it had not emerged in 1972 in the fact that *Method* still speaks so habitually of knowledge following love by way of *exception*.[128] After the 1975 development, when the two ways are both accepted as normal, one would be less likely to speak of the second as an exception.[129] Finally, there is the fact that, while the upward process is well worked out and the transitional agents differentiated,[130] the process is very little developed for the second phase of theology.

---

122. *Third Collection*, p. 106. 123. *Method*, ch. 5.

124. Ibid, p. 142.

125. *De deo trino*, vol. 2, pp. 179–80, on ways of believing that are really the way up and the way down.

126. *Collection*, pp. 198–201.

127. For documentation, see Crowe, *The Lonergan Enterprise*, p. 115, n. 37. Though the last two items listed there are dated 1978 and 1979, both were produced by Lonergan in 1976.

128. *Method*, pp. 122, 340; see also pp. 278, 283.

129. "Christology Today: Methodological Reflections," *Third Collection*, pp. 76–77, still speaks in such terms, but that was almost certainly written before "Healing and Creating in History" and perhaps retains an older usage that is now less appropriate.

130. See, for example, the question as operator in *Insight*, p. 479 and elsewhere: relevant passages may be found listed in the index under the two key words.

The tasks are clearly set forth, and the correspondence with the appropriate level of consciousness is not in doubt, but the "operator" of the transition from task to task is not a theme at all. The general and all-pervasive agent is certainly love, but is there a differentiation of minor agents as we go from one task to another, something analogous to the questions for intelligence, questions for reflection, questions for deliberation that are so basic for the upward process? Or, are the same three questions still operative, but now in reverse order? And, if so, how do they function in reverse order? These are questions that call for an answer once the twofold way of development comes into focus, but I surmise that they had not yet arisen for Lonergan in 1972.

It happens, however, that this downward process begins after 1975 to be articulated a little; it is exceptionally pertinent to the subject's approach to God; so I will offer some quotations.

The structure of individual development is twofold. The chronologically-prior phase [hardly an exception now] is from above downwards. Children are born into a cradling environment of love. By a long and slow process of socialization, acculturation, education they are transferred from their initial world of immediacy into the local variety of the world mediated by meaning and motivated by values. Basically this process rests on trust and belief. But as it proceeds more and more there develops the capacity to raise questions and to be satisfied or dissatisfied with answers. Such is the spontaneous and fundamental process of teaching and learning common to all. It is at once intelligent and reasonable and responsible.[131]

Another quotation, from another paper of the same year:

[T]he handing on of development . . . works from above downwards; it begins in the affectivity of the infant, the child, the son, the pupil, the follower. On affectivity rests the apprehension of values; on the apprehension of values rests belief; on belief follows the growth in understanding of one who has found a genuine teacher and has been initiated into the study of the masters of the past. Then, to confirm one's growth in understanding, comes experience made mature and perceptive by one's developed understanding and with experiential confirmation the inverse process may set in.[132]

The clarifying power of this distinction for a general comparison of *Insight* and *Method* is perhaps evident. The way up is the way of achievement, perfectly represented by *Insight* which is through and through a personal exercise in the appropriation of insight and judgment, with a resulting epistemology, metaphysics, ethics, and natural theology. But the way down is the result of gift (need we go through the eight centuries between Augustine and Aquinas again, to distinguish the gift of grace from the "gift" of creation?), represented by the second phase of theology, where the initiating act is God's grace effecting our con-

131. *Third Collection*, pp. 196–97.   132. Ibid., p. 181.

version, which is then objectified to provide foundations for the doctrines, systematics, and communications of the last three tasks of theology.

Similarly, the application of the same distinction to our particular question is not too difficult. Chapter 19, like the whole of *Insight*, is an exercise in upward development, the way of human achievement. As such, it has its own criteria of validity, independent of the influence of grace on the very exercise itself. DiSanto[133] offers the useful analogy of one who has weakened vision due to years in a dark room, but then receives medication, is fitted with corrective lenses, and takes up new work in the daylight. Are we to say his improved vision is not really vision because it is due to causes of a higher order? By the same token it is irrelevant to the argument of chapter 19 that the "philosopher" might not have undertaken it and might have no interest in appropriating it except through the stimulus of grace and God's gift; Lonergan then, may be clear of contradiction in arguing for its validity (in principle) even after taking the position he does take in *Method*. But, and this is the strength of his own criticism of *Insight*, there is also the way down, which is supplied by the second phase of the theology described in *Method*, where God is seen as the transcendent mystery to which we are oriented in love. If *Insight* does not acknowledge that second way, does not even recognize the influence of that second way in its own genesis (an influence that Aquinas might have named *quoad exercitium* but not *quoad specificationem*), then it does not give the whole picture; but to argue that it therefore gives a false picture is a *non sequitur,* and to argue that it contradicts *Method* not only seems to lack cogency but also threatens to deprive the one so arguing of an extremely fruitful insight.

I can hardly forbear, in concluding this already long article, to express once again my envy of those who, in the happy youth of their academic careers, can take three hundred pages to study a single chapter 19 of *Insight*. Why should they not, indeed? If Lonergan himself needed over fifty pages to set out his reasoning, the rest of us are not likely to do it more compactly. But one presumes readers of sufficient intelligence and interest to leave expositors behind and go to the primary source; this article may at least promote that good result. I permit myself, however, to remind such readers that they are embarking on a long voyage, much longer than they may suspect. The force of the reminder lies in the wide range of the interlocking ideas one must investigate in a thorough study of Lonergan's thought on ultimate reality. For some of them he has himself provided a thematic study as an entry point;

133. *Complete Intelligibility,* pp. 271–72.

for example, the natural desire to see God[134] or the new context of theology.[135] For others we have to collect the data from scattered loca in his writings; for example: the universality of religious experience, the relation of inner and outer word, the relevance of negative theology and its relation to affirmative, the order of knowing and loving, and so on. To write on Lonergan is thus a continual exercise in the art of omission as well as in the science of exposition. There is not likely to be full agreement on what to omit and what to include; I suspect one's emphases will fall on what one has most recently learned—and that means perhaps that this article points more directly to what I have learned in writing it than to Lonergan's own difficult thought.

134. *Collection*, pp. 84–95.   135. *Second Collection*, pp. 55–67.

6

The Human Mind and Ultimate Reality*

The invitation to discuss, in the context of Bernard Lonergan's thought, the questions raised by Dr. Leahy is most welcome—doubly so, for it gives me the opportunity to pursue an argument I first set forth in this journal three years ago.[1] But forced to be extremely brief, I will offer only isolated remarks under only three headings: (1) cognitional theory, (2) theories of being formulated in terms of cognitional theory, and (3) the question of ultimate reality, raised as a question, in terms of knowing and being.

Let me, however, in preface to these remarks, put our discussion in the wider perspective of life. I am not trying, in these three sections, to validate what would otherwise be invalid, as if the common man or woman were not previously able to know at all, or to know the things that are, or to know that God is, and we came along to supply the means for them to do all that. Average people, if asked, will quite legitimately say, "Yes, I am, Yes, you are. No, I am not you." But, if challenged on their spontaneous judgments, they easily become confused, and may well require a few years of psychology, epistemology, even metaphysics, to think their way out of the corner into which we, with our more practiced techniques of argument, may have driven them. This applies also to knowing that God is. In Lonergan's view, which I quoted also three years ago:

[B]ecause it is difficult to know what our knowing is, it also is difficult to know what our knowledge of God is. But just as our knowing is prior to an analysis of knowledge and far easier than it, so too our knowledge of God is both earlier and easier than any attempt to give it formal expression.[2]

Some years later, Lonergan restated this with more pointed reference to objections raised by philosophers:

---

*Previously published in *Ultimate Reality and Meaning* 7 (1984), pp. 67–74, as a comment on "Human Mind as a Way to God . . . ," by Louis Leahy, pp. 62–67 of the same number.

1. See above, ch. 5.
2. *Insight: A Study of Human Understanding*, p. 683.

106

I do not think it difficult to establish God's existence. I do think it a life-long labor to analyze and refute all the objections that philosophers have thought up against the existence of God. But I see no pressing need for every student of religion to penetrate into that labyrinth and then work his way out.[3]

We are engaged, then, Dr. Leahy and I, in that life-long labor which the common man and woman have no need to undertake. No doubt he would agree, but it is good to have this simple supposition out on the table.

1. Cognitional Theory

In the few pages available I will concentrate on the source of knowledge and the starting point of a cognitional theory. This is not any stated principles, or propositions, or concepts; it is not even understanding and ideas; though only those who have busied themselves with principles, propositions, concepts, ideas and understanding, will know that this is not the place to begin. The place to begin is the dynamism of cognitional intentionality, for that is the fertile source of all stated principles, propositions, etc. (It is itself, of course, a principle; but an operative, not a stated one.)

This dynamism is experienced; it is empirical, in the sense in which Lonergan speaks of generalized empirical method.[4] I have no space to deal with those who exclude half their experience—and the better half too—in rejecting the data of consciousness. I can only list some manifestations, to be seen generally in the outward signs we observe in others, but available for deeper and far more profitable study in our own interiority. There is, then, the unformulated wonder of the child, later formulated in his or her perpetual "Why?" There is the structured pair of Thomist questions: *Quid sit? An sit?*[5] There is the dominance of wonder, of scientific curiosity, in the dedicated investigator:

Deep within us all, emergent when the noise of other appetites is stilled, there is a drive to know, to understand, to see why, to discover the reason, to find the cause, to explain. . . . It can absorb a man. It can keep him for hours, day after day, year after year, in the narrow prison of his study or his laboratory. It can withdraw him from other interests. . . . It can fill his waking thoughts. . . . It can demand endless sacrifices. . . .[6]

The dynamism is experienced, then, as a need, a drive, a spontaneous

3. *Philosophy of God, and Theology: The Relationship between Philosophy of God and the Functional Specialty, Systematics*, pp. 55–56.

4. *Insight*, pp. 72, 243.

5. *Verbum: Word and Idea in Aquinas*, pp. 12–13; *Collection: Papers by Bernard Lonergan, S.J.*, p. 84.

6. *Insight*, p. 4.

quest, an intentionality, lying behind our cognitional activity. It is too often overlooked or not given the attention it deserves, but I believe that, once it is given that attention, the rest of a cognitional theory will follow more easily.

Why is it often overlooked or neglected? In some of us, perhaps, because our early teachers did not appeal to it, invoking rather the rod: Learn this lesson, or else. In those teachers, as in all of as, animal extroversion is always more "natural" than study of interiority. Even in those who have advanced some distance in the business of learning, there is the prompt, easy, and agreeable use of knowledge habitually in our possession (the Aristotelian and Thomist view of habits[7]) and therefore a ready forgetting of the force that originally drove us to attain it. There are various reasons, which are not to the present purpose.

What *is* to the purpose, though I can but state it, is the structured unfolding of the dynamism, the linked series of levels we mount in yielding to its pressure: from empirical to intellectual, from intellectual to rational, from rational to responsible. Restricting discussion to cognitional operations, we may say that the structure is determined by the pair of Thomist questions already mentioned. To put them in Lonergan's terms, there are questions for intelligence that seek understanding, explanation, the idea: "What is it?" "How do you understand it?" And there are questions for reflection that seek the verification (or falsification) of the idea: "Is that so?" "Is that really the case?" In mounting the first step from the empirical we are just *thinking,* thinking in order to know, of course, but still just thinking; it is the second step that brings us to *knowing.* Now, if the first quest is characterized by words like "what," "why," "how," and so on, the second and culminating (cognitional) step is characterized by the word "is": God *is.* I *am.* Or, in general, this *is* the case. It is in the positing of this two-letter word as an act of intelligent grasp and reasonable affirmation that we come to know, or reach the truth (perhaps only probable truth), or attain reality. On this simple, homespun basis, philosophers come to talk of *being,* a word that hardly occurs in common speech, though it derives from a word that occurs in almost every sentence: *is,* or a cognate form.

11. Theories of Being

The proposal here is to schematize a theory of being ("theory" is a usage to be explained presently). It will be based on our cognitional theory, and since cognitional operations are a structured and complex

---

7. *Grace and Freedom: Operative Grace in the Thought of St. Thomas Aquinas,* pp. 41–46.

whole with many self-assembling components,[8] we can distinguish various elements in our theory of being, according to the various relations between cognitional process and being. Here is one list that Lonergan drew up in chapter 19 (that famous chapter) of his *Insight:* (1) the pure notion of being; (2) the heuristic notion of being; (3) restricted acts of understanding, conceiving, and affirming being; and (4) the unrestricted act of understanding being.[9] I will say a word on each of these terms.

The pure notion of being is the dynamism itself, that notion of being which was our chief concern in the preceding section. It is not a concept of being, or an affirmation of being, or an idea of being. It is only an anticipation of being, a conscious drive to know what is, "a positive and effective inclination both to inquire intelligently and reflect reasonably";[10] most briefly and inclusively, an "intention of being."[11] "Notion" is therefore given a special meaning to denote the special reference to being we find in the cognitional dynamism. That dynamism is not a determinate component of knowledge in the way an idea or a concept or a judgment is, but it does rate a cognitional term, for it is a conscious orientation to being, not simply the orientation of a foetal eye toward seeing; and it is intelligently and rationally conscious, not just empirically conscious like the orientation of hunger toward food and eating. This is what Lonergan would convey by his special term "notion of being."[12]

We may be briefer on the other three terms. The "heuristic notion of being" corresponds to the pure notion as the mental formulation of an objective corresponds to an orientation to that objective. That is, the pure notion is the orientation itself, but an orientation is toward something, and that something can be given a name and a heuristic formulation even when it is not yet determinate. Lonergan's formulation: "whatever is to be grasped intelligently and affirmed reasonably."[13] If the pure notion is characterized by the spontaneous inquiry, the heuristic notion is characterized by the answer to the inquiry, when that answer is not yet determinate, but only "whatever. . . ."

The third element in Lonergan's list might be said to describe our human way of coping. That is, we cannot now or ever know everything about everything. If, then, we are to be intelligent and reasonable about our own practice as well as about the objective universe, we must be content to ask one question at a time and advance step by step through

---

8. *Collection,* pp. 222–24.
9. *Insight,* p. 642.   10. Ibid., p. 522.
11. Ibid., p. 355; the whole of ch. 12, pp. 348–74; or, more succinctly, *Collection,* pp. 228–31.
12. *Insight,* pp. 354–55.   13. Ibid., p. 642.

particular answers, that is, through judgments about "particular beings and particular domains of being."[14] The fourth term, finally, the unrestricted act of understanding being, is God or the idea of being.

The list of four headings does not exhaust the possibilities. I noted that the various relations of complex cognitional operations to being give various elements in a theory of being. It is important to get hold of this, to which end we may examine another list provided by Lonergan. It appeared for the first time in a footnote added to the French translation of the *Verbum* articles.[15] Curiously, it is not found in the book that collected the original English articles twenty years after they began to appear,[16] so I have to translate the French back into English and we are at two removes from Lonergan's own wording. Let me therefore give the basic line as we find it in French: "Je distinguerais maintenant: (1) notion, (2) concept implicite, (3) connaissance, (4) idée et (5) théorie de l'être."[17] Using some freedom in regard to articles, number, etc., I would render the list as the notion of being, the implicit concept of being, knowledge of being, the idea of being, and theories of being.

The notion of being is the same as it was in *Insight*; no need to delay here. But the implicit concept of being, Lonergan explains, is any concept whatever heading for a prospective judgment (where we are thinking, therefore, in order to be able to state what is). Knowledge of being is subdivided: there is knowledge of *a* being in any true judgment and there is knowledge of being (I am curious to know what the English had been for "l'être") in the totality of true judgments. The idea of being is that by which God knows everything about everything, that is, the divine essence considered as principle of divine knowledge. Finally, theories of being are those that render an account of such a cascade of terms as we have listed here—and so I called this section of my own article "theories of being."

The reader, I fear, grows impatient. But it is quite useless to talk of Lonergan on ultimate reality till we understand Lonergan on cognitional process and being (Dr. Leahy would, I think, say as much about Joseph Maréchal and Karl Rahner). Two corollaries, however, will bring us a little nearer the original context of this discussion. The first is that all the thinking in the world does not constitute an act of knowing. Or, the most brilliant act of understanding falls short of saying that any being is. Or, no collection of concepts, however vast and intricate, can of itself ground a judgment. As Newman said in an analagous case,

14. Ibid.
15. *La notion de verbe dans les écrits de saint Thomas d'Aquin* (Paris: Beauchesne, 1966).
16. *Verbum*.   17. *La notion de verbe*, p. 44, n. 196.

"Ten thousand difficulties do not make one doubt;"[18] similarly, ten thousand concepts, or any acts of thinking, do not make one judgment. It would be superfluous to insist on this were we not so prone to take the "is" of a logical proposition as an affirmation of reality. But the copula of a proposition is not the posited "is" of an existential judgment (existential in the Thomist sense). An analytic proposition is not a judgment about reality, not anyway about the reality of the object named in the proposition.[19] "A centaur is half man, half horse," says nothing of the reality of centaurs; it can be taken as an affirmation of a reality in my mind, but then a better formula would be, "What I mean by the word 'centaur' is. . . ." And so, to come to the real point of this corollary, no human concept of God, no conceptual extrapolation from, say, contingent to necessary being, so long as it is merely conceptual, can give knowledge of God's existence. Unable to argue that in this short article, I can only refer to Lonergan's answer to the "ontological argument."[20]

Our second corollary regards the subject-object relation. Nowhere in our account of cognitional process, or in our account of being, did this relation enter as a topic, still less as a foundation for any position taken. The question of that relation occurs, it is legitimate, but it is secondary. What is primary is the intention of being, realized in particular judgments of what is. After that, we may ask about those things that we are (subjects), about ourselves in relation to what we have come to know (objects, or, if subjects, then subjects as objects), and so come to the subject-object relation. This was Lonergan's position early on:

[T]he critical problem . . . is not a problem of moving from within outwards, of moving from a subject to an object outside the subject. It is a problem of moving from above downwards, of moving from an infinite potentiality commensurate with the universe towards a rational apprehension that seizes the difference of subject and object in essentially the same way that it seizes any other real distinction.[21]

On this basis the question of whether we are inside or outside the mind loses much of its interest and all of its bewilderment. It remains acute only for those who imagine they start inside and must make their way out. But suppose we start within the universe of being, remain always within it, and make our way within it propelled by the intention of being. Then getting outside the mind is no more a problem than getting inside; and getting inside is as much a problem, if it is a problem, as getting outside. That is, we are not inside till we restrict our domain

18. John Henry Newman, *Apologia pro vita sua* (London: Longmans, Green, 1900 [1864]), p. 239.

19. *Insight,* pp. 304–306, 340, 671–72.

20. Ibid., p. 670.   21. *Verbum,* p. 88.

of being to the inside, and equally we are not outside till we restrict our domain of being to the outside. But this happens in both cases within the larger universe of being. Consequently, Lonergan takes up the question of objectivity only in chapter 13 of *Insight,* following his chapter on the notion of being.

III. The Question of God

If I am not mistaken in my understanding of Dr. Leahy's article, he would be in sympathy with the approach taken in my first two sections, and maybe in agreement with most of my positions. It is here in my third section that I believe we would part company. For he holds that the intelligible totality of being is "co-affirmed in every affirmation," and on this basis can maintain that the affirmation of God is implicitly made in every affirmation: "[W]herever we affirm that something exists, we implicitly affirm the existence of this totality, of this absolute Being. . . . This absolute, infinite Being is what we call God. . . ."22 True, this co-affirmation is not formulated; it is lived, exercised, *signata.*23 Still, even in this *signata* form, I believe it differs significantly from Lonergan's position. In the latter, as the intention of being is one thing, and its affirmation in any particular case is another, so the intention of God is one thing, and the affirmation of God is another; further, the affirmation of a particular being, though it can give rise, and this in various ways, to the *question* of God, does not in itself contain the *answer* to that question; the answer will be a distinct, further step beyond the question, and consequently beyond the affirmation of the particular existent reality. There is no space here to debate the relative merits of these contrasting positions, but prior to debate is the need for clear understanding; so let me devote this third section to achieving a little more clarity on one point only, how the *question* of God arises in Lonergan's position.

My first observation: it is by means of our questioning that Lonergan introduced chapter 19 of *Insight.* The chapter is entitled "General Transcendent Knowledge," the first section is on the notion of transcendence, and the explanation is basically very simple: "Clearly, despite the imposing name, transcendence is the elementary matter of raising further questions."24 So, building upon the questions and answers of the preceding chapters, Lonergan now asks "whether human knowledge is confined to the universe of proportionate being or goes beyond it to the realm of transcendent being."25 The procedure will follow the fa-

22. "Human Mind as a Way to God . . . ," p. 66.
23. Ibid., p. 63.   24. *Insight,* p. 635.
25. Ibid.

miliar pattern of the Thomist questions (*Quid sit? An sit?*), that is, work out your concept of transcendent being, and then ask the question of existence. Hence, Lonergan first elaborates his notion of God,[26] and only then asks whether God, so understood, exists.[27]

My second observation is that interposing the question of God as a distinct operation between our ordinary cognitional activity and the affirmation of God's existence, is not omitted in Lonergan's later work; on the contrary, it acquires new importance. Thus, chapter 4 of his *Method in Theology,* entitled "Religion," begins with a section on the question of God, and offers us the following pertinent sequence. There is indeed an assumption in our everyday mental operations: "implicitly we grant that the universe is intelligible."[28] But Lonergan does not go on to say we thereby implicitly or *signate* affirm the existence of the intelligible totality, the absolute Being. Rather he goes on to say: "once that is granted [that the universe is intelligible], there arises the question whether the universe could be intelligible without having an intelligent ground."[29] A year later the matter is dealt with even more extensively, with four aspects of the question of God set forth, but even the religious aspect leaves the question of God still a question:

Now if the question of God arises on four different levels, it does not follow that there are four distinct and separate questions. The questions are distinct but they also are cumulative. The question of God is epistemological, when we ask how the universe can be intelligible. It is philosophic when we ask why we should bow to the principle of sufficient reason, when there is no sufficient reason for the existence of contingent things. It is moral when we ask whether the universe has a moral ground and so a moral goal. It finally is religious when we ask whether there is anyone for us to love with all our heart and all our soul and all our mind and all our strength.[30]

It does not seem to me that this extensive wrestling with the question of God is compatible with a co-affirmation of God, even an implicit one, in every affirmation of a particular being.

Still, I do not wish to exaggerate the differences between the Rahner-Leahy position and that of Lonergan. There is a ready admission by the latter of implicit suppositions in our cognitional activity, and they bear some resemblance to the co-affirmation of the former. But there are differences, it is important to pin them down, and to that end I venture the following statements. First, it is not the same thing in general to co-affirm one statement with another, and to lay bare the supposition of a statement and then affirm that supposition. Secondly, what is implicit for Dr. Leahy in regard specifically to God is not the

26. Ibid., pp. 657–69.
28. *Method in Theology,* p. 101.
30. *Philosophy of God,* pp. 54–55.

27. Ibid., pp. 669–77.
29. Ibid.

same as what is implicit for Fr. Lonergan. Let me expand these two points a little, referring to what I wrote in this journal three years ago.

At that time, I maintained that for Lonergan the supposition of the continued exercise of our intelligence is that its objective is completely intelligible, that to make this explicit is the major step on our way to God, but that a second step still remains, even though it is relatively easy. That is, we have to labor to make "explicit that which we implicitly grant when we allow our questioning dynamism its full range." But there is a second step: "With that achieved [explicitation of the implicit], it is an easy task to conclude from a universe that is not completely intelligible in itself to the only ground of its intelligibility, namely, what is completely intelligible."[31] Now these two steps seem to me to correspond quite exactly to the two I set forth above as pertaining to Lonergan's argument: "implicitly we grant that the universe is intelligible"; but then, "once that is granted, there arises the question whether the universe could be intelligible without having an intelligent ground."[32]

There is then a pattern, and it is as much the pattern in the *Insight* of 1957 as in the *Method in Theology* of 1972 and the *Philosophy of God, and Theology* of 1973. There is, however, a statement of 1964 which does not altogether square with these three works:

Implicit in human inquiry is a natural desire to know God by his essence; implicit in human judgment about contingent things there is the formally unconditioned that is God; implicit in human choice of values is the absolute good that is God.[33]

This text was transcribed from a tape-recording of a talk given by Fr. Lonergan, and there may be a problem of accuracy in the text; but, assuming that it is substantially faithful to his lecture, we have to ask: Does it bring Lonergan's "implicit" closer to the Rahner-Leahy "implicit," or is it rather to be interpreted as an abbreviation of the steps spelled out in his regular way of arguing? We have surely to incline to the latter, with the weight of three carefully written books against that of a transcription of a lecture.[34]

In any case there would still remain the question of the difference

---

31. "Bernard Lonergan's Thought on Ultimate Reality and Meaning," *Ultimate Reality and Meaning* 4 (1981), pp. 70–71 (ch. 5 above, pp. 000–00).

32. *Method,* p. 101.　　　　　　　33. *Collection,* p. 249.

34. After a lecture of his on 14 September 1964, I asked Lonergan, "Is the existence of God implicit in every judgment?" His answer: "No, the *question* of God's existence is implicit." This agrees with his responses at the Boston College summer institute, 1968 (ch. 6, p. 2, in transcription made by W. Mathews); and it parallels his position that realism is immediate in questions, mediate in answers (ibid., p. 4; cf. *Collection,* p. 236; *Method,* pp. 262–63). On the other side is Aquinas, *De veritate,* 22, 2 ad 1m: "Omnia cognoscentia cognoscunt implicite deum in quolibet cognito."

between co-affirming one statement with another and laying bare the supposition of a statement. This would involve, on the side of Lonergan studies, a full and thorough investigation of his use of presuppositions, of his understanding of logical implication, of the relation he sees between suppositions and logical implications, of his dialectic of explicit content and what is implicit in performance, of his study of theological conclusions, of his long concern with the development of doctrine, of the bearing on such development of the shift from a predominantly logical to a basically methodical viewpoint in theology—a nest of questions, on which there is a wealth of data that cannot possibly be investigated here. I have to be content to shed some light on some of the questions raised by Dr. Leahy. In particular, since the thought of Bernard Lonergan is so often lumped indiscriminately with that of Joseph Maréchal and that of Karl Rahner (a mistake, incidentally, that Dr. Leahy does not make), I hope my contribution will help eliminate a too facile identification of the thought of these three great thinkers.

7

Bernard Lonergan and Liberation Theology*

This article, to judge from its title, may seem to appear, somewhat like Melchisedech, without contextual father or mother, so perhaps I should take a moment to introduce it. The general context is that of the turn in our times from the abstract to the concrete, from speculation to involvement, from the merely academic and cerebral to commitment and action, from mere contemplation of history (as a famous phrase has it) to the changing of history. In this general context much modern theology, and liberation theology in particular, finds a natural home. Thus, Paulo Freire writes that we must "get rid of any illusory dream of trying to change man without touching the world he lives in. . . . The true humanization of man cannot be brought about in the interiority of our minds; it has to take place in external history."[1]

Further, to narrow the context, a particular critique is often leveled, on the ground of alleged remoteness from real life, against the current emphasis on method in theology. Thus, at a congress held in 1975, though the topic was described as the method of theology in Latin America, in fact method itself was one of the chief targets of liberation theologians present at the congress. Luis Alberto Gómez de Sousa, for example, remarked that the great masters of political thought, such as Marx and Lenin, did not write books on methodology; rather, they did analysis of concrete situations.[2] Very naturally, the work of Bernard Lonergan on method came under sharp attack at the congress.[3] The suspicion was voiced even that his thought was made to order for the ideology of the military regimes of Latin America![4]

---

*Previously published in *The Third World and Bernard Lonergan: A Tribute to a Concerned Thinker*, ed. W. Ysaac (Manila: Cardinal Bea Institute, 1986), pp. 1–15. Spanish translation, "Bernard Lonergan y la teología de la liberación," in *Humanidades Anuario* 8 (1984–85), pp. 11–23.

1. "Letter to a Young Theology Student," *LADOC* 2/29b (April, 1972), p. 1. The original source is given as *Perspectivas de diálogo* (Montevideo), December, 1970.

2. *Liberación y cautiverio: Debates en torno al método de la teología en América Latina* (Universidad Iberoamericana) (Mexico City: Comité Organizador, 1975), p. 516. An extensive account of the congress is given in *Christus: Revista mensual de teología* 40/479, (October, 1975).

3. See the indices to *Liberación y cautiverio, s.v.,* Lonergan.

4. Thus, José Comblin; see *Liberación y cautiverio,* pp. 517, 519.

It is in this context that I take up here the question of Lonergan's relation to the concerns of liberation theology. If I seem a decade late on the scene, there may be some justification for that too. Lonergan himself was busy, during much of that decade, with the study of economics, to which he turned on the completion of his work on method. The questions dealt with in that study were so relevant to liberation theology that he might well have gone on eventually to take up personally the specific concerns of that movement. But the decline of his health in later years and his eventual death made that impossible, so it may be in place for his students to reopen the debate of ten years ago.

I would note, however, that my purpose is not to offer an exposition of Lonergan's political theology—that is beyond my competence. Neither is it to discuss his methodology, or to continue the defense of his views that was undertaken ten years ago by many participants at the congress itself.[5] My purpose is much simpler, but also in a sense more fundamental. It seems fair to say that his views did not win a hearing among his opponents at the congress, because they judged that his interests diverged so widely from theirs. My purpose, then, is quite simply to win a hearing for his views, and my strategy is to set forth, in a kind of biographical sketch, the lifelong interest Lonergan has shown in the very questions that are the concern of liberation theology itself. That theology, of course, must stand or fall on its own merits, but its legitimate aspirations are the concern of us all and would find strong support in Lonergan's work. To show that, I will offer data, first from his earliest writings, then from *Insight*,[6] thirdly from *Method*,[7] and finally from his most recent studies.

It is indeed remarkable that the concerns of the liberation theologians are the very concerns of the young Lonergan at the beginning of his career. Among his earliest writings is a batch of short articles and book reviews contributed to the Catholic weekly newspaper of Montreal, when he was teaching theology there from 1940 to 1946–47. Many readers of *Insight* and *Method* would be surprised to find him writing then on such topics as Quebec's opportunity (some years before Quebec's quiet revolution!), on the Antigonish movement to help depressed fishermen, on the needed rebirth of rural living. There are, of course,

5. See Francisco Quijano, "El método trascendental en teología, " ibid., pp. 375, 408, the paper that seems to have set off the debate on Lonergan. Other favorable views: pp. 520, 531–32, 533–34, 534–35, 537–38, etc.

It puzzles me that Alfred T. Hennelly could report "divergences" in regard to Lonergan's *Method* (*Theological Studies* 38 [1977], pp. 127–28, n. 8), and quote only the extremely negative parts of critiques by Comblin and Hugo Assmann, omitting references to rejoinders by others, and even the modifying phrases of these two themselves.

6. *Insight: A Study of Human Understanding*.

7. *Method in Theology*.

the war topics: the economics of war savings certificates and, at quite the opposite pole, a moving recall of chapter 25 of Matthew in relation to feeding the hungry children evacuated from the bombed cities of England. And there is a wide humanist interest, for example, lament on the state of Western culture, or on the way foreign affairs are bungled through ignorance of the culture and history of other countries.

There is no space here or need to examine these writings in detail. But they acquire considerable importance in view of later developments, and a few brief questions on matters economic and political will highlight that importance.[8] The question is put, "Why is the control of industry in the hands of fewer and fewer?" (2 May 1941). We are told, "Unless the masses achieve economic independence, then [democracy] will be a noble experiment that failed" (2 May 1941). There is reference to "the great materialist trinity" of capitalism, communism, and nazism, and to the experiments they are performing "on the quivering body of humanity" (19 Sept. 1942), and to the way "governmental functions . . . have been multiplying and accumulating for a century under the evil influence of a mistaken economic system," so that there is little use working out "an elaborate palliative for a monstrous disease" (10 April 1943). Hardly remarks, these, of one preparing an ideology for the military regimes of Latin America! On the contrary, there is in these brief occasional writings an extraordinary anticipation of many themes of liberation theology. Were they *merely* occasional? One discovers with surprise years later that Lonergan was working at this early time on an analysis of the economic situation. Further, that the analysis was not an ivory-tower project, due to an academic interest in a *quid est?* Rather, it rose directly out of the searing experience of the thirties, the long decade of ruinous economic depression brought to an end not by the economists, who were completely buffaloed, but by the Second World War.

The same themes continue and find almost systematic expression in *Insight,* chapter 7 of which is an essay on human affairs that could well be named a liberation philosophy. For it deals, among other topics, with the emergence, rise, and functioning of technology, capital formation, economic and political systems, and cultures; with the emergence of classes and their conflicts; with the options of liberalism, capitalism, and totalitarianism; with the demand for a creative human

8. When Lonergan first wrote for it (references for 1941), the newspaper was called *The Montreal Beacon*; then it became *The Canadian Register: Quebec Edition* (references for 1942 and later). Since it will be quite inaccessible to my readers, it may be sufficient to give the date of each quotation in my text. Copies of these writings may be obtained from the Lonergan Research Institute, Toronto.

role in the making of history. Professional philosophers may incline to overlook this chapter in their hurry to discuss the great questions of epistemology and metaphysics that follow. But, if our brief glance at the Montreal writings have alerted us to the "liberation" dimension in Lonergan's thinking, we may wish now to go back and, undeterred by the odd title, "Common Sense as Object," study this chapter again.

Let us begin with the notion of social classes. As always, Lonergan sets the question in a wider context, a kind of philosophy of human living: the dynamism that powers each of us; the intersubjectivity that functions primordially long before the great structures of technological, economic, and political systems are erected, and that survives even under them "in the family . . . in customs and folk-ways, in basic arts and crafts. . . ." But intersubjectivity involves human cooperation, hence a division of labor and specialization of tasks, the emergence of a social order, and sooner or later the great systems that dominate us now.[9]

So social groups form and class conflicts arise. For progress is powered by intelligence, but intelligence rarely responds to a situation in a pure and disinterested way. "In fact, the responses are made by intelligences that are coupled with the ethos and the interests of groups," and groups have notable blind spots in self-evaluation. Thus, "Society becomes stratified. . . . Classes become distinguished . . . and the new differentiation finds expression . . . in deep feelings of frustration, resentment, bitterness, and hatred." No doubt the intelligent solution is at hand but reactionary elements in the dominant group "are out to block any correction of the effects of group bias" using "whatever power they possess. . . ." And—an almost verbatim anticipation here of later liberation thinking—" . . . to a great extent the attitude of the dominant groups determines the attitude of the depressed groups."[10]

Then, there is the related topic of human direction of history. A first approximation to the historical sequence is the "wheel" of progress: ". . . one thinks of the course of social change as a succession of insights, courses of action, changed situations, and fresh insights," and this is a wheel that keeps turning. But that is only a first approximation; besides various modifications in the course, there is also the reversal of the wheel's revolution. "In each stage of the historical process, the facts are the social situation produced by the practical intelligence of the previous situation." But, if that intelligence was not pure, it disregarded or blocked the just and timely idea. If that is not corrected, there begins a cumulative deterioration: ". . . the objective situation becomes pen-

9. *Insight,* pp. 209–214; quoted text, p. 212.
10. Ibid., pp. 222–25; quoted texts, pp. 223, 224, 225, resp.

etrated with anomalies. . . . In the limit, the only discernible intelligibility . . . is an equilibrium of economic pressures and a balance of national powers."[11]

The situation worsens with "the mounting irrelevance of detached and disinterested intelligence. Culture retreats into an ivory tower. Religion becomes an inward affair of the heart. Philosophy glitters like a gem with endless facets and no practical purpose." In this developing "social surd" intelligence heads for total surrender. It becomes "radically uncritical. It possesses no standpoint from which it can distinguish between social achievement and the social surd." Here Lonergan gives his analysis of this longer cycle of decline as it has worked out concretely in our own history in the West: in the path to totalitarianism, then to counter-totalitarianisms, and so to the grim realities and horrors of the day.[12]

And what are we to do? Take refuge in other-worldly hopes? Simply accept the inhumanity of the social surd as our cross? Nothing could be further from Lonergan's view. "The challenge of history is for man progressively to restrict the realm of chance or fate or destiny and progressively to enlarge the realm of conscious grasp and deliberate choice."[13] The longer cycle of decline has itself drawn attention to a practical theory of history: in Vico, Hegel, Marx.[14] We are not therefore to "be forced into an ivory tower of ineffectualness."[15] True, we are not to indulge in a blind activism. "There is needed . . . a critique of history before there can be any intelligent direction of history,"[16] but direction is the responsible thing.

Lonergan's own positive proposals, set forth here under the heading of "Cosmopolis,"[17] are fascinating, and one omits them with real regret. But our own space is limited, and anyway Cosmopolis was only a preliminary sketch. What is of present relevance, and fascinating enough too in its own right, is the articulation here of so many themes of liberation theology fifteen years before the famous conference at Medellin.[18] And I would conclude this little study of *Insight* with a remark of permanent and universal relevance, one for reactionary and revolutionary alike, for us in the North Atlantic nations and for liberation theologians too; it is Lonergan's warning that we be "free from the nonsense that the rising star of another class or nation is going to put

---

11. Ibid., pp. 223, 228–29.
12. Ibid., pp. 229–31.
13. Ibid., p. 228.
14. Ibid., pp. 233–34.
15. Ibid., p. 237.
16. Ibid., p. 240.
17. Ibid., pp. 238–42.
18. Fifteen years, since *Insight* was written between 1949 and 1953. Acquaintance with this ch. 7 might have made Assmann somewhat less confident that Lonergan's theology does not lead to history (*Liberación y cautiverio*, p. 296).

a different human nature in the saddle."[19] The fundamental enemy is not any group whatever, but the built-in possibilities, as widely disseminated as humanity, of inattention, misuse of intelligence, betrayal of reason, and irresponsibility.

Jumping over the years now, as we must, we come to *Method in Theology*, a work turned out laboriously while Lonergan was recovering from harrowing surgery, threatened always with a recurrence of his malady. Is there, in consequence, an unfinished and too generic character in *Method*'s chapters? Some would so label the book. I would say rather that, instead of the long approaches of *Insight*, we have a precipitate of the years of reading, studying, and thinking; the result, then, is not so much unfinished as extremely compact, calling for patient interpretation.

I pause to look at chapter 2, but only briefly, and mainly to note that here the themes of *Insight*'s chapter 7 are summarized and carried forward: those of technology, economics, politics, culture—and now religion is added; those also of the individual and the community, of group formation and group bias, of progress and decline. No need now to study this, except to notice a developed notion of value. And worth quoting, because of its echoes in liberation theology, is the remark: "The process [of meeting human needs] is not merely the service of man; it is above all the making of man."[20]

Bearing as directly on our topic, and an advance over *Insight*, is chapter 14, entitled simply "Communications." One is apt to think here of preaching the gospel in a traditional sense repudiated by liberation theology, namely, the application, with a perhaps simplistic adaptation, of eternal truths to new situations. But this would not do justice to chapter 14. Preaching of the gospel there is, and adaptation too. But the preacher must proceed "from within" the culture of his listeners. Moreover, the meaning of the Church itself, to which belongs the task of communications, has to be rethought:

[T]he modern meaning, generated by empirical social studies, leads one to speak of the church as a process of self-constitution occurring within worldwide human society. The substance of that process is the Christian message conjoined with the inner gift of God's love and resulting in Christian witness, Christian fellowship, and Christian service to mankind.[21]

This view, as one will expect, rests on an elaborated notion of society, of the role of common meaning and common values in constituting a society, of the historical factors promoting such community. But the realism of chapter 2 of *Method* (and of chapter 7 of *Insight*) is not

---

19. *Insight*, p. 240.
20. *Method*, p. 52. 21. Ibid., p. 363.

forgotten, or the bias dividing community into radically opposed factions:

Groups exaggerate the magnitude and importance of their contribution to society. . . . What is good for this or that group, is mistakenly thought to be good for the country or for mankind, while what is good for the country or for mankind is postponed or mutilated. There emerge the richer classes and the poorer classes, and the richer become ever richer, while the poorer sink into misery and squalor.[22]

Finally, two points in this chapter of acute interest to liberation theology. One is found in the concluding pages on the Church as redemptive process, on the utilization of empirical human studies in that process, on the need of dialectic to control those studies, and on the making and implementing of policies. The special interest centers here on Lonergan's version of that very attention to concrete experience that liberation theologians desiderate:

Execution generates feedback. This supplies scholars and scientists with the data for studies on the wisdom of policies and the efficacy of the planning. The result of such attention to feedback will be that policy making and planning become ongoing processes that are continuously revised in the light of their consequences.[23]

Or, to quote a statement earlier in the book, "[R]esearch tabulates the data from the past . . . communications produces data in the present."[24]

The second point of interest adds to the redemptive process a constructive side which has to do with bringing science forward and making it operative. We cannot, therefore, merely think

of forming policies, planning operations, and carrying them out. There is the far more arduous task (1) of effecting an advance in scientific knowledge, (2) of persuading eminent and influential people to consider the advance both thoroughly and fairly, and (3) of having them convince practical policy makers and planners both that the advance exists and that it implies such and such revisions of current policies and planning with such and such effects.[25]

The significance of this statement is that it not only voices an abiding and deeply felt concern of Lonergan for an up-to-date science in the Church but also leads directly to his most recent work, in which he returns to the early studies of his Montreal period.

With the publication of *Method* in 1972 Lonergan was faced with a difficult personal decision on how to use his remaining years. It is characteristic of his career that it is marked by a series of major efforts—long-term projects that might take five or ten years to finish. It is not

22. Ibid., p. 360.
24. Ibid., p. 135.

23. Ibid., p. 366.
25. Ibid., pp. 366–67.

easy, as one nears the age of seventy in a state of uncertain health, to embark on another such project, and that may account for his hesitation at this time. The options (I draw on remembered conversations) eventually became two: to try to work out a Christology in accordance with his now elaborated method, or to return to the economics that had occupied him in the early years. His choice fell on the latter—an index perhaps of his judgment on the needs of the time; just then the opportunity to pursue this interest more effectively was given him by Boston College; and these two facts largely determined his work after 1975.

The results of the work still remain in typescript, but I can at least document his continuing interest in those questions which engage the liberation theologians, to whom indeed he refers as one of his sources.[26] Thus, he discusses the factors leading to recession, depression, and crash in the economy; he deals with the colonial economy, armaments, unemployment, unions, inflation; he goes beyond national boundaries to talk of spheres of influence, protectorates, and undeveloped or underdeveloped countries. There is censure of "profits . . . reaped by owners who reside elsewhere," of "a vicious circle of ever more demands for a larger money supply with no increase in real income," and of situations in which "there has emerged in fact if not in name the welfare state."[27] And there is a lengthy section on that chief target of liberation theology, the multinational corporations.[28] These and other topics are discussed in the context of his own personal contribution, what he calls "circulation analysis," and the whole work belongs in the still wider context of a dialectic of history that would move beyond the Marxist dialectic— Lonergan's counter-reformation in an area where reform (some would prefer to say "revolution") is in many ways more urgent even than was religious reform nearly five centuries ago.

This essay is conceived as an effort to promote dialogue with liberation theologians, and specifically to focus attention on the potential contribution Lonergan's thought might make to their enterprise. If I

---

26. *An Essay in Circulation Analysis,* photocopy of typescript used in a course at Boston College, 1979–80; reference to liberation theology, p. 75. The original essay was written by about 1944, and there have been various "editions"—my references will be to the 1980 version.

For helpful information on this still unpublished work, see the contributions of Michael Gibbons and Philip McShane to *Creativity and Method: Essays in Honor of Bernard Lonergan, S.J.,* ed. M. L. Lamb (Milwaukee: Marquette University, 1981). Also two books by McShane; *Wealth of Self and Wealth of Nations* (Hicksville, N.Y.: Exposition Press, 1975), and *Lonergan's Challenge to the University and the Economy* (Washington, DC: University Press of America, 1979).

27. *An Essay in Circulation Analysis,* pp. 67–73.

28. Ibid., pp. 75–103.

have seemed somewhat overly biographical, it is because I felt it to be a prerequisite of dialogue to break down the wall of opposition some liberation theologians have erected against theology that they consider excessively academic; my essay is therefore of the genus, *removens prohibens*. In this situation simple factual information was called for, and I believe I have provided that by merely pointing out those liberation themes that from beginning to end have been crucial for Lonergan: the harsh realities of the economic situation, of dominant and oppressed classes, of biases and injustices and naked power operating to prolong the misery; likewise, the responsibility of men and women to make of themselves what they can be, to direct the course of history, to exercise their dominion over this world and not simply endure for the sake of the Kingdom; the dominant role of praxis and the danger of playing the intellectual game without alteration of the facts; the menace of neo-integrism that would bottle up Christianity in its past, and the need to attend to present experience and invoke the empirical sciences for its accurate interpretation—these and a dozen other topics echo back and forth between Lonergan's thinking and that of the liberation movement.

But, if I have been moderately successful in my task, that very success will raise a further question: How, if my analysis is correct, could Lonergan manage to give at least some of his readers an impression so wide of the mark? More pointedly, how could he himself, in an inversion of the biblical exodus, luxuriate for forty years in metaphysics, epistemology, cognitional theory, interiority, and methodology, when the poor and the oppressed were wandering in the desert, with the poor becoming more impoverished and the oppressed becoming more downtrodden?

This is a large question involving many external and biographical factors, which must, however, be rigorously excluded to focus on what the French would call *l'idée*. This, I would say (simplifying, but searching for the most comprehensive phrase in brief compass), is the principle of withdrawal and return. To quote his own express statement on the matter: "The withdrawal into interiority is not an end in itself."[29] To put the question in terms of education, one could say that education, generally, is a matter of withdrawal for eventual return, and a chief task today is the education of the educators of the Church; Lonergan's own Ignatius of Loyola is surely a classic instance of withdrawal from full involvement in the apostolate to go through long years of study, a grown man, and soldier at that, among boys on the classroom benches. Or, finally, to construct a little parable, two people went out to Calcutta

29. *Method*, p. 83.

to work for the poor. One went into the streets, found the hungry, brought them food, nourished them in their sickness; the other saw the agricultural potential of the land, studied agronomy, set up experimental farms, promoted better methods of sowing and fertilizing, etc. One figure is real, and the object of world admiration; the other is hypothetical, as far as I know, but the hypothesis serves as a thought-experiment to show our differing vocations to bring different means to bear toward the same end.[30]

With these remarks, however, our account remains partial and preliminary. It would explain why Lonergan, seeing that our moral precepts were based on a hopelessly antiquated economics, was compelled by his very interest in moral theology to critique the economic system of the West.[31] It does not explain why he felt compelled to make such a drastic withdrawal into cognitional theory, epistemology, metaphysics, interiority, and methodology. About this foundational question I can offer here only the most general statements. A philosophical foundation (to be sublated then in a theological foundation) would start with a proper use of the word "ought" and a proper use of the word "is." A proper use of those words requires critical appropriation of their foundations. And centuries of quarreling, in theology as in philosophy, in history as in economics, and indeed in those paragons of objectivity that are the empirical sciences, this prolonged quarreling has taught us what ideally we might learn from a simple and sincere love of truth and goodness, namely, that we will not appropriate our foundations without study of the human subject himself or herself, the human subject who is by turns good and bad, true and false, seeking and fleeing insight, attentive and inattentive. I allow myself one last quotation:

Nor may one expect the discovery of some "objective" criterion or test or control. For that meaning of the "objective" is mere delusion. Genuine objectivity is the fruit of authentic subjectivity. It is to be attained only by attaining authentic subjectivity.[32]

30. I am not sure the liberation theologians would accept such a distinction in vocations, given their repudiation of any thinking that does not issue from commitment and involvement. The mode, however, of involvement may be granted some latitude. I have indicated the "involvement" out of which Lonergan's early thought began; I could add, since liberation theology makes much of the cultural, that few countries are more culturally dependent than Lonergan's own native land; could we add also that even the most powerful countries are now dependent economically on the multinational corporations? In any case, whatever the validity of my case for Lonergan's relevance to liberation theology, I willingly acknowledge the relevance of that theology for implementing his seminal thinking; communications here run on a two-way street.

31. One of his favorite examples is the folly of a moral theology that simply issues the precept to employers that they pay a living wage for a family, when the result of obedience to the precept is bankruptcy. Here we have a capsule of Lonergan's practical realism.

32. *Method*, p. 292.

May the sweeping character of this quotation and of my own preceding statements not be found provocative. I realize that they call for extensive exposition and critical justification, and that in such exposition and justification one would be discussing the question with the thoroughness it demands. Which is a way of saying that I am ending my essay just at the point where it might well begin. I can only plead in defense my own necessity for a withdrawal in hope of a later return—the essay, as I said, is in the genus of a *removens prohibens*.

8

Bernard Lonergan as Pastoral Theologian*

The title of this article will surprise those who have thought Bernard Lonergan to be primarily a speculative theologian isolating himself from the involvement that is so characteristic of contemporary theology. But it is largely with the purpose of correcting such a view that I have chosen this topic, and it seems appropriate that the correction should appear in the organ of that Gregorian University where Lonergan wrote most of the abstruse Latin theology which earned him the reputation of being excessively intellectual in his interests.

Still, I do not regard the mere reversal of mistaken views on this point as a very onerous task: it will be a simple matter to adduce evidence that from start to finish of his career Lonergan was oriented and guided by a deep-lying pastoral concern. The real problem is to relate his speculative work to that guiding motivation. We can invoke, for a general answer, one of his favorite phrases from Toynbee: it was a withdrawal intended for a return. But what went on during the withdrawal, what was Lonergan up to, how did he envisage his return, and—the question most immediately pressing on us, his heirs, since Lonergan never himself effected that return on the scale his own idea demands—how does one go about the task of completing his work and adding the direct involvement he always intended?

These are the questions that most concern me in this article. But all things in order. Let me first briefly document the case for the fact of his pastoral intent, then go on to ask what he was up to in the long years of his wrestling with the nature and functions of theology, to conclude, in a third part, with some reflections on the task he has left for his theological heirs to accomplish.

1. The Fact: Two Pieces of Evidence

A pastoral concern marked Lonergan's career from beginning to end: that is so clear to those who know his history that I do not propose

*Previously published in *Gregorianum* 67 (1986), pp. 451–70.

to delay on the matter. Two soundings will be enough to demonstrate it.

One of these regards his interest in economics and takes us first into a period of his life that may be relatively unknown to most readers of *Gregorianum*: the early years from the summer of 1940 to December of 1946, when he was teaching at the College of the Immaculate Conception in Montreal and regularly writing short articles and reviews for the English-language diocesan weekly in that city. (One could list articles of piety too, written during this and the subsequent Toronto period, but I confine the evidence to items of a more academic nature.) Now it is quite remarkable that, some thirty years before the famous conference at Medellin, the concerns of the young Lonergan bore close resemblance to those that would surface in other lands and other contexts among the liberation theologians. Lonergan's context at the time was Canadian, and so we find him writing on such topics as Quebec's opportunity (some years before the quiet revolution there!), on the Antigonish movement to help depressed fishermen, on the needed rebirth of rural living, and so on.

There is no need to document in detail this little batch of writings, but they do take on considerable importance in view of developments at the end of Lonergan's career, so a few brief quotations on matters economic and political will be illuminating for our overall purpose. Thus, the question is put, "Why is the control of industry in the hands of fewer and fewer?" (2 May 1941). We are told: "Unless the masses achieve economic independence, then . . . [democracy] will be a noble experiment that failed" (ibid.). There is reference to the way "governmental functions . . . have been multiplying and accumulating for a century under the evil influence of a mistaken economic system," so that there is little use working out "an elaborate palliative for a monstrous disease" (10 April 1943).[1]

The quotations themselves are but straws in a wind, the direction and force of which were then unknown and appeared in full clarity only thirty years later, when we learn that back in the 1940s Lonergan was at work on a thorough analysis of the economic situation. The situation itself was pastoral *par excellence*: we had just lived through a decade of economic depression and abject suffering for millions, and the crying need of the times came piteously to Lonergan's ears. His concern,

---

1. When Lonergan first wrote for this diocesan newspaper (in 1941), it was called *The Montreal Beacon*; then it became *The Canadian Register: Quebec Edition* (1942ff.). Researchers will be able, from the dates I have given, to find the relevant article or review in the photocopies of the Lonergan Research Institute in Toronto, or in one of the various Lonergan Centers. The newspaper itself is practically inaccessible to most of my readers.

however, found expression, not in establishing soup-kitchens—a task he would of course recognize as essential—but in striving to achieve a fundamental understanding of the economic reality. Various bizarre theories on relief of the crisis had surfaced, in Canada as elsewhere, in the 1930s; Catholic moral theology had laid down the precept that employers must pay a living wage, often with the only result that Catholic employers who obeyed the precept went bankrupt, leaving the field to their less scrupulous rivals; and Lonergan realized that the real solution could come only from a better economics. In other words, a viable moral theology in this area required a theory of economics as much as a viable systematic theology required a philosophy. It was under such influences that he began to think out in the thirties and commit to paper in the forties his own very personal theory.

The work on economics that Lonergan composed in 1944 and later entitled *An Essay in Circulation Analysis* remained a typescript stowed away in a filing cabinet for over thirty years. But the ideas kept appearing elsewhere, notably in chapter 7 of *Insight*.[2] This chapter, a study of human affairs that could well be named a liberation philosophy, deals among other topics with the emergence, rise, and functioning of technology, capital formation, economic and political systems, and the variety of cultures; with the options of liberalism, capitalism, and totalitarianism; with the demand for a creative human role in the making of history; and so on. The same themes crop up continually in the Latin theology of the next decade and, leaping over the intervening years, we find them again in chapter 2 of *Method in Theology*, where they are summarized and carried forward.[3]

It was, however, long afterward, when Lonergan returned late in life to his economics typescript, that the full evidence of the work's pastoral orientation appeared. His courses at Boston College during these declining years remain unpublished, but are well recorded, so we can document his continuing interest in those questions which engage the liberation theologians (to whom indeed he now refers as one of his sources). For the seventies, far from having found a solution to the problems of the thirties, had instead simply added a host of others. So Lonergan is led to discuss the factors involved in recession, depression, and crash in the economy; but he deals also with the colonial economy, armaments, unemployment, unions, inflation; he goes beyond national boundaries to talk of spheres of influence, protectorates, and undeveloped or underdeveloped countries. There is censure of "profits . . . reaped by owners who reside elsewhere," of "a vicious circle of ever

2. *Insight: A Study of Human Understanding*, 1957. There is evidence that chs. 6 and 7 of the book were the first to be written; this would date them around 1949.
3. *Method in Theology*, 1972.

more demands for a larger money supply with no increase in real income," and of situations in which "there has emerged in fact if not in name the welfare state." And there is a lengthy section on that chief target of liberation theology, the multinational corporation. These and other topics are discussed in the context of his personal contribution to economics, and the whole work belongs in the still wider context of his dialectic of history, one that would move beyond the Marxist dialectic to a reformation, or counter-reformation, that is even more necessary in economics today than it was in the religious sphere five centuries ago.[4]

It is extraordinarily fascinating, this lifelong concern with the realities of economics, and it demonstrates perfectly the mode of Lonergan's pastoral involvement: concern for the poor and oppressed, but action at the very roots of the problem.[5] We shall return to that mode of involvement in due course, but we have yet to present our second piece of evidence on the fact. It lies in the field of theology and theological method, which was central for Lonergan throughout his academic career: even in economics his controlling motivation was theological. So we turn to the already mentioned work he called *Method in Theology*.

This book, as is well known, deals in the programmatic part called the Foreground with eight functional specialties, knit together in a close relationship that yet allows each to contribute to theology according to its own identity and its own specific purpose. Now the present point has to do with the eighth specialty, Communications, which in Lonergan's thinking is coincident with pastoral theology and is the crown-

---

4. *An Essay in Circulation Analysis*, unpublished typescript used in a course at Boston College, 1979–1980. Note that the work exists in several forms; my quotations are from the one dated in the spring of 1980, pp. 67–73; the reference to liberation theology is on p. 75, the section on multinational corporations on pp. 75–103. For a somewhat expanded discussion of these questions see ch. 7 above.

5. Lonergan's direct exploration of economics may obscure the fact that his thought has profound implications in fields he did not explore. Let me take as an example the life of the unborn, and put together three separate passages from his writings. In *Verbum: Word and Idea in Aquinas*, we find his position on the soul as *logos*: "the denial of soul today is really the denial of the intelligible, the denial that understanding, knowing a cause, is knowing anything real" (pp. 20–21). The original of this study appeared in *Theological Studies* in 1946; it was followed by the study, in *Insight*, of finality as the immanent intelligibility of development (ch. 15, see especially "Potency and Finality," pp. 444–51, and "Human Development," pp. 469–79), which allows us to add a dynamic aspect to the otherwise static notion of *logos*. Thirdly, there is his study of the self-mediation of an organism, worked out in lectures at Gonzaga University, Spokane, and the Thomas More Institute, Montreal, in 1963: "The organism lives, it has a reality that is superior to the whole business of cells and their differentiation and specialization"; it is a *self-mediation*. See Lonergan's "The Mediation of Christ in Prayer," *Method: Journal of Lonergan Studies* 2/1 (March, 1984), pp. 1–20 (quotation, p. 7). The three ideas linked in series would be highly illuminating, it seems to me, for studies in embryology. (For an expansion of this example, see ch. 21 below.)

ing exercise of the whole unitary process. First, then, it is coincident with pastoral theology: when Lonergan would show the kinship of his specialties with divisions and procedures already operative in theology, he will say, "Thus, our divisions of the second phase—foundations, doctrines, systematics, and communications—correspond roughly to the already familiar distinctions between fundamental, dogmatic, speculative, and pastoral or practical theology."[6] And when he comes to communications itself and would illustrate it concretely, he will say, "if the reader wishes to contemplate theologians at work in our eighth functional specialty, I would refer him to the five-volume *Handbuch der Pastoraltheologie* edited by F. X. Arnold, F. Klostermann, K. Rahner, V. Schurr, and L. Weber."[7] Next, communications crowns the whole process of theology: "It is a major concern, for it is in this final stage that theological reflection bears fruit. Without the first seven stages, of course, there is no fruit to be borne. But without the last the first seven are in vain, for they fail to mature."[8] We may add that, in one of his last papers, when he was reflecting on the Second Vatican Council and on Chenu's analysis of its pastoral nature, Lonergan remarked: "Now I feel that Fr. Chenu's position is unanswerable, and in fact I include the pastoral function as the crowning specialty in my *Method of Theology*."[9]

The basic fact of Lonergan's pastoral orientation is, I think, established, but it will leave many readers with a puzzle: Why was he not more directly involved in the questions of the day that so exercised other theologians? What was he up to in that massive withdrawal that characterized the central period of his life, a withdrawal so prolonged that he lacked time at the end for the return for which it was intended? That is the real question. Absence of a clear answer accounts for much mistaken understanding of his purpose, and so I will deal with it at somewhat greater length in my next section. I confine my remarks, however, to the area of central importance: his work on theology and on theological method.

II. Lonergan's Strategy

What, then, was Lonergan doing in his years of withdrawal from the life of the marketplace and even from the pulpits of our churches? In a generic way the answer lies in the strategy of his planning and the

---

6. *Method,* p. 136.
7. Ibid., pp. 355–56.   8. Ibid., p. 355.
9. "Horizons and Transpositions," Boston College Lonergan Workshop, 1979; I quote from Lonergan's unpublished typescript (p. 17), reproducing his mistake in the title of his own book!

mode of his involvement: he would get to the bottom of things. To grant that there was a strategy in his planning need not conceal from us that he was under a kind of compulsion as well: he *had* to get to the bottom of things. Like a famous reformer, there he took his stand because he could do no other. We have seen this in his economics, where he felt compelled to get behind the precept of a living wage to the most fundamental analysis; we shall see it now in his area of special interest, the Christian message and the role of theology in teaching and preaching that message. Here the question is complicated by extensive developments in Lonergan's thinking as he wrestled with the problem, but study of that development is *de rigueur* if we are to grasp with any accuracy what he was up to. We can simplify the study, as I will now, but we cannot by-pass it. Hence the following division.

1. The Early Period

There are various ways, all somewhat arbitrary, of dividing Lonergan's career. For present purposes I find it useful to speak of three periods, beginning with his thirteen years (1940–1953) in the Jesuit theologates of Montreal and Toronto. It happens that, soon after, he published in *Gregorianum* an article that not only marks the culmination of this first period, but also begins the transition to the next. Historically, then, it is of special significance; moreover, its content provides a shortcut to the thinking of the early Lonergan on theology.

The title of the article is already luminous, for it was called "Theology and Understanding," and from start to finish of his career understanding was a focus for Lonergan.[10] In this early period, indeed, it received more than the lion's share of attention: understanding was the very business of the theologian. Even then, however, understanding was not a private reward and privilege for the exclusive enjoyment of the theologian, but was to enter into the theologian's preaching of the word of God. Here is a relevant passage in which Lonergan, speaking of the *ordo doctrinae* of Thomas Aquinas (which is almost equated here with theological understanding), writes as follows:

With some approximation to a single view it gives rise to an apprehension of the exact content and the exact implications of the many mysteries in their many aspects. That single view both simplifies and enriches one's own spiritual life and it bestows upon one's teaching the enviable combination of sureness

10. His students will remember his frequent reference to two favorite passages. One is the *Quodlibetum* in which Thomas Aquinas notes the difference between merely giving authorities for doctrine, thus sending pupils away with empty minds, and bringing to light the ground of the doctrine and sending them away with some understanding; see *Method*, p. 357. The other is the "aliquam intelligentiam, eamque fructuosissimam" of Vatican I; see again *Method*, pp. 309, 321, 323, 336.

of doctrine with versatility of expression. Finally, the single view remains, for it is fixed upon one's intellectual memory. So we find that non-Catholic clergymen, often more learned in scripture and the fathers, preach from their pulpits the ideas put forward in the latest stimulating book or article, while the Catholic priest, often burdened with sacerdotal duties and administrative tasks, spontaneously expounds the epistle or gospel of the Sunday in the light of an understanding that is common to the ages.[11]

I very much doubt that Lonergan would have wished, twenty years later, to defend all the views of this article or even of the quoted paragraph, but dated though those views may be they still witness to the ultimate pastoral purpose of his theology.

At this time, however, a development of considerable significance is beginning, as appears from this very article. For, though he still claims validity for Thomist thought in speculative theology, Lonergan is beginning to realize that the reign of that theology is over; it must step down to the level of partnership with other functions. There is now a whole new problematic, arising from post-Thomist thinking, one he sets forth under four headings: "the problem of patterns of human experience, of the *Denkformen*"; "the problem of the relations between speculative and positive theology"; "the problem of the relations between speculative theology and the empirical human sciences"; and a fourth area, not given a specific name, that raises questions ranging from epistemology to dialectic and foundations—we might, I think, call it the area of methodology.[12]

2. The Middle Years

The second period of Lonergan's career, as I divide it, coincides approximately with his professorship at the Gregorian University, 1953–1965. It was then that he worked on his solutions to the new problems listed in the 1954 article. His reading too was extended now and his horizons broadened through contact with his huge multicultural audience. His *cursus speciales* in the university's doctoral programs, along with the summer institutes and lectures he gave during these years, especially in the universities of Canada and the United States, provided a new stimulus for his thinking. It was very much, then, a time of experimenting with new ideas, though we should not forget that the arena, as it were, for testing the new ideas was still the familiar scene of traditional theological treatises.[13]

---

11. "Theology and Understanding," in *Collection: Papers by Bernard Lonergan, S.J.*, pp. 121–41; see p. 133.

12. *Collection*, pp. 135–41.

13. This is another persistent misunderstanding, to think of Lonergan elaborating his method in isolation from theology and the life of the church. In fact, his method was worked out in continual reference to the traditional theology he taught for twenty-five

This period is fairly well documented through notes issued for his students, *reportationes* or tape-recordings of his lectures, and so on, but there do remain important gaps that need to be filled for a thorough study.[14] In the present simplified study of the development relevant to Lonergan's pastoral theology, I would say that, though he was marshalling forces for a turn to the pastoral, the war was still being fought on another front over a prior question, that of transposition of the message from the sources of Christian theology to systematics.

Two quite distinct developments were involved here, and I would say that only one of them had been completed. Thus, Lonergan was vividly aware of the difference in thought-patterns between Palestinian and Scholastic manners of thinking and acting, and fully conscious of the problem of transposing from one to the other. But I do not think that he had yet taken the measure of what he would later call the classicist view of culture, or fully realized the importance for the pastoral side of the empirical notion of culture. In any case a central issue during all this period was how to effect a valid transition from Palestinian to Hellenic and then to Scholastic categories. Thus, in a course called *De intellectu et methodo,* given in the academic year, 1958–1959, he spoke of three aspects of the single problem of method: foundations, or transition from one ordering of doctrines to another; historicity, or continuity throughout the series of orderings; and estrangement or alienation, the distance intervening as systematics takes us farther and farther from our origins.[15] How he would invoke and apply the notion of transposition to the solution of these problems is too long a story to tell here. It is indeed extremely important for understanding Lonergan's thinking, not only in this middle period but throughout his career, but I can only illustrate it by an example (enlarging somewhat one of his): thus, the Matthean image of the Son of Man coming in the clouds to the Ancient of days is transposed to the Pauline formulation of the Lord seated at the right hand of the Father, which in turn is transposed

---

years, especially the theology of divine grace, of the incarnate Word, and of the Holy Trinity.

14. For example, there was a course at the Gregorian University, 1959–1960, called *De systemate et historia*; the title is revealing—the dialectic of system and history was a preoccupation of Lonergan at this time—but documentation on the course is inadequate. Again, there was an institute at Gonzaga University, Spokane, in 1963, and one at Georgetown University, Washington, 1964, just when Lonergan's thought was poising for an immense leap forward; but both of them, and especially the second, need further documentation.

15. On this work see my contribution, "Lonergan's Search for Foundations: The Early Years, 1940–1959," in *Searching for Cultural Foundations*, ed. P. McShane (Lanham, MD: University Press of America, 1984), pp. 113–39 and 187–97, esp. pp. 130–34.

to the Nicene doctrine of the Son who is consubstantial with the Father, and this again is transposed in Lonergan's use of the Athanasian doctrine that the same things are said of the Son as are said of the Father.[16]

We must remind ourselves that the three divisions in Lonergan's life are not sealed compartments. During these middle years there were breakthroughs, to use one of his favorite metaphors, all along the line, but not the encirclement and confinement that would clinch the matter. More properly put: Lonergan had not yet conceived the integral heuristic structure that would unify what he had to say on the method of theology, and provide a basis for correlating research and magisterium, system and preaching, tradition and innovation, receiving the deposit of faith and appropriating it personally. This would be achieved, in relatively stable if not completely elaborated fashion, in the third stage of his career.

3. The Period of Integration

To study pastoral aspects in the interwoven nest of ideas that constitute Lonergan's view on theological method is to be led continually to and fro between single threads and the complex whole. For economy I will concentrate on one single thread and, without justifying my choice, separate out a new notion of culture as most directly relevant to the pastoral orientation of theology.

Here we are once again involved in the complex question of Lonergan's development, so I offer the following markers to the relevant history. Early in his career Lonergan came under the strong influence of Christopher Dawson's views on culture, though it has never, so far as I know, been made the focus of special study. Anyway we have the remark made years later testifying to and dating this influence: "In the summer of 1930 . . . Christopher Dawson's *The Age of the Gods* introduced me to the anthropological notion of culture and so began the correction of my hitherto normative or classicist notion."[17] To begin the correction of an old idea is by no means to see at once all the implications of the new, and I am inclined to think that the seed planted by his reading of Dawson lay dormant in Lonergan's mind for several years. *Insight* does not seem to have been greatly concerned with correcting the old view. The trinitarian theology of 1961 recognizes that the true reality of culture ("cultura veri nominis") is to be found in

16. Bernard Lonergan, *The Way to Nicea: The Dialectical Development of Trinitarian Theology*, tr. C. O'Donovan (London: Darton, Longman & Todd, 1976), pp. 88–104. There is discussion of this point passim in Lonergan's works.

17. *A Second Collection: Papers by Bernard J. F. Lonergan, S.J.*, p. 264.

primitive tribes as well as in the great civilizations,[18] but I interpret this as a rather abstract recognition, akin to Newman's notional apprehension of a truth, for application to the practical scene is still lacking. The following year there is clear advertence to the shift from classical culture to historical consciousness, which "effects the transition from an ideal order—what the family, the state, the law, education, the economy should be—to what *de facto* is," but even now there is a certain nostalgia for the old: "classical culture is not something to be sniffed at: it ran the world from the fifth century B.C. to the French Revolution."[19] The next two years, however, saw a full acceptance of the new. In a 1964 lecture Lonergan remarks that the word *aggiornamento* "has electrified the world . . . because it seems to imply a rejection of classicism, a rejection of the view that human nature is always the same."[20] This is fully spelled out one year later:

[B]y and large, classical culture has passed away. By and large, its canons of art, its literary forms, its rules of correct speech, its norms of interpretations, its way of thought, its manner in philosophy, its notion of science, its concept of law, its moral standards, its methods of education, are no longer accepted. . . . Classical culture has given way to a modern culture, and, I would submit, the crisis of our age is in no small measure the fact that modern culture has not yet reached its maturity.[21]

From this time on the contrasts between the classicist and the empirical notions of culture is a recurring theme; it is domiciled in Lonergan's thought.[22]

This does not mean there will be at once that application to the pastoral work of the Church which we will presently find in chapter 14 of *Method*. There is a time lag to be explained here, but I would attribute it less to lack of development in the notion of culture itself, and much more to lack of a structure into which the new notion of culture could fit and find its proper application; once the structure was in place, as it was by 1965, the full riches of the new notion of culture could pour into the idea of communications. At any rate it is this notion that in my view is the key to this crowning specialty, and thus to a full and integral idea of theology. Certainly it is of major importance for Lon-

18. *De deo trino: pars analytica* (Rome: Gregorian University, 1961), p. 84.

19. Institute on the Method of Theology, Regis College, Toronto, 1962. The lectures were tape-recorded by a person or persons unknown; the tapes were transcribed by John Brezovec; and the latter's handwritten text was the basis for a typescript by Nicholas Graham (see this, pp. 112–13, for the quoted lines).

20. *Collection*, p. 248.

21. Ibid., pp. 258–59.

22. See the indices to *Second Collection* (lectures between 1966 and 1973), and *Method in Theology*.

ergan's position on inculturation, which is so closely linked with the specialty of communications. Not that Lonergan adopts the word, inculturation, so far as I remember, but that is the right name for the process he describes in communications, and the underlying supposition is always his empirical notion of culture. Consider the following passage:

The Christian message is to be communicated to all nations. Such communication presupposes that preachers and teachers enlarge their horizons to include an accurate and intimate understanding of the culture and the language of the people they address. They must grasp the virtual resources of that culture and that language, and they must use those virtual resources creatively so that the Christian message becomes, not disruptive of the culture, not an alien patch superimposed upon it, but a line of development within the culture.[23]

The classicist would preach not only the gospel but also the classicist culture and thus "confer the double benefit of both the true religion and the true culture. In contrast, the pluralist acknowledges a multiplicity of cultural traditions."[24]

This then is the main development in Lonergan's thought that forms the relevant background to his views on the pastoral task. But what that task is in itself and in relation to the original Christian message, what the roles respectively of theologians and Church authorities in regard to it, how it relates to the various specialties of research, interpretation, history and dialectic, and how one effects the transition from a critical assimilation of the past to a personal challenging of oneself and one's time, all these are further questions. Some of them find answers in Lonergan's *Method*, many of them are left to be worked out by those who would implement the method. I will conclude my article with some remarks on such problems.

III. Lonergan's *Method* and the Pastoral Task

Lonergan worked actively for nearly eleven years after the publication of *Method*. It was a period in which his powers were still creative, one in which, had he known that time would be granted him, he might have effected a massive return to theology after his long withdrawal. But he did not know that eleven years remained, had reason in fact to expect a shorter period; in any case, he felt that others could take over the unfinished theological task, while he probably felt his work in economics needed his own input still. Thus it is that, though he has given,

23. *Method in Theology,* p. 362.
24. Ibid., p. 363.

through the lectures of this period, scattered hints on a return to theology, the work of implementing his method was left to be undertaken by his theological heirs. It is with a sense of the responsibility that such a legacy imposes on us that I propose the reflections of this concluding section.

To be constantly remembered: religion and theology are here conceived as distinct areas involving distinct activities. Religion precedes theology and would remain even if theology disappeared. Theology is a reflection on religion, a reflection that might, in Newman's theory of knowledge, be considered an end in itself, but in the total context has the practical function of mediating between religion and culture. Theology is not, however, any and every reflection on religion: the mother of Jesus and Thomas Aquinas both pondered the word of God, but Thomas did so with the aid of a highly specialized method and expressed his reflections in a highly specialized language that Mary would have found incomprehensible. Now, as religion receives a tradition to hand it on, so also does theology; but in the latter's specialized methods both the receiving and the handing on divide into four functions, distinguished, related and integrated as the four levels of human consciousness are distinguished, related and integrated. That structure will provide the context for my remarks.

The first phase of theology, the reception of the Christian heritage, divides into the specialties of research, interpretation, history, and dialectic. Of these the first three are more familiar as the work of "scholarship"—in Lonergan's sense of that word, in which it refers to particular knowledge of another culture and, even more specifically, of the common sense of that other culture, though it may be combined with science or knowledge of universal laws. There are probably very few pure examples of these specialties, but Merk's *Novum Testamentum Graece et Latine,* Dodd's *The Interpretation of the Fourth Gospel,* and Grillmeier's *Christ in Christian Tradition from the Apostolic Age to Chalcedon,* three works well known to Lonergan, would exemplify quite well the relevant areas of scholarship. These areas are not, however, directly related to pastoral work: pastors do not often need to study the variants in New Testament manuscripts, or Patristic subtleties on the God-man and *Logos-sarx* patterns of thinking; if the need arises for this kind of erudition, the pastor will have recourse to the experts: the researchers, the exegetes, the historians. Conversely, the scholar-theologian will not ordinarily need to introduce his learning directly into his preaching.

The directly pastoral function comes to light and is exercised in the second phase, in which theologians have to provide a creative restatement of their faith. But the utterly essential prerequisite to that restatement is a dialectical critique of the past, or the fourth specialty of the first phase. Lonergan's own work on Patristic trinitarian theology illustrates very well, if only partially, such a critique, and happily we have, in *The Way to Nicea*,[25] an English version of the most relevant part of that work. While some historians, then, see pre-Nicene theology as strewn with the corpses of subordinationist doctrine on the Son, Lonergan finds it quite misleading to speak of subordinationism in this period. What was occurring was a dialectical self-correcting process as the community of theologians strove to bring their imperfect conception and often faulty expression into conformity with their own and the Church's underlying faith. It was work of an ongoing community, as it must be, for the individual theologian cannot, in the nature of the case, be aware of a correction that lies in the future and will often be achieved only in reference to, and through the enlarging of, the narrow horizon that was the source of the mistake. Study of horizons is the key task in this specialty, and Lonergan therefore investigates the horizons operative in Tertullian, Origen, and Athanasius, in order to account for their several theologies, and to discern, through what he calls an X-ray of history, the fundamental structure of the development taking place in them.[26]

Theology, then, even in phase one, is a learning process long before it becomes a doctrine to be taught and, insofar as the trinitarian case is an instance of a basic human process, it becomes a paradigm for all theology. That is, if what happened on the way to Nicea happened as it did, not because of the obduracy of subordinationist heretics but because of the nature of human pondering on mystery, then it will happen that way over and over again. Two questions leap at once to mind. Where is it happening today, in regard to what questions of theology? And, what can the theologian do to expedite a happy outcome of the learning process? An answer to the first is difficult without the hindsight of the next century, and an answer to the second is rendered difficult by our own involvement in the process: we are no longer spectators coolly observing the antics of a Tertullian or an Origen. Still, the effort should be made, and the strategy imposes itself: to study the horizons, including our own, of those engaged in the process, while remaining open to the broadened horizons and the conversions the times, and the Spirit, may require of us.

Besides dialectical critique there is creative reformulation. Those whom we are pleased to call "simple believers" may hand on to their

---

25. See n. 16 above; the translation covers pp. 17–112 in a book of 308 pages. The work illustrates only *partially* the specialty of dialectic because it deals almost exclusively with the cognitive aspect, and because it is a study of an ancient dialectic: we ourselves are not very directly involved.

26. *The Way to Nicea*, Lonergan's new "Foreword," p. viii.

children the faith they received, and do so without sensing the need of reformulation; so may fundamentalists, at home or on the missions. But once we recognize the diversity of cultures in the peoples of the world, and indeed the changing face of culture within our own borders and within our own generation, that procedure is seen to be inadequate. It was awareness of this inadequacy that lay behind the urgent appeal of Pope John XXIII at the time of the Second Vatican Council, when he stated that the church did not need a reiteration of ancient doctrine, but must take a leap forward and give new expression to her teaching.[27] Here too then, and even more than in phase one, theology is primarily a learning process. Lonergan's effort to transpose old dogmas into new and meaningful doctrines is, in other words, a struggle to learn.

Doctrines, however, become meaningful through personal appropriation, so the foundations for the required transposition are placed in interiority. Not that interiority grounds for us the ancient dogma—we must be clear on that; it grounds only the transposition of the ancient dogma into new expression,[28] so that the total foundation for Pope John's new expression will be a resultant, as it were, of two vector forces; one deriving from the past where we find formulations, within a certain horizon, of the Church's faith, and the other deriving from our own creativity as we express the same faith within our different horizon. To be noted again: it is not interiority as a purely private possession that is our guide, but interiority expressed in community and tested by community dialogue.

There follows on doctrines, as has been the case from time immemorial, the need for systematic understanding, the old *fides quaerens intellectum,* once thought to constitute theology *tout court,* but now reduced to but one function out of eight. So we come, finally, to the immediate pastoral task of communications, but communications carried out on the basis of our new understanding of the diversity of cultures, and of our new realization of the need, as was said, so to preach the Christian message that it becomes, "not disruptive of the culture, not an alien patch superimposed upon it, but a line of development within the culture."[29]

The assimilative power of the structure I have outlined needs testing, and a locus for the test might well be found in the questions that surfaced at the recent extraordinary synod of bishops. Let me illustrate

---

27. Two speeches of Pope John are relevant, one at the opening of the Second Vatican Council, another a few weeks after the end of the first session (it is in the latter that the expression, a leap forward—*un balzo innanzi*— occurs); see *Acta apostolicae sedis* 54 (1962), pp. 791–92, and 55 (1963), pp. 43–45. I owe the references to Lonergan's paper, "Pope John's Intention"; see *A Third Collection: Papers by Bernard J. F. Lonergan, S.J.,* pp. 224–38.

28. *Method in Theology,* p. 267.   29. Ibid., p. 362.

that through two examples. The first is the proposal of the Most Reverend Bernard Hubert, Bishop of Saint-Jean-Longeuil

that we identify the problems that the Synod wishes to deal with and bring ourselves up-to-date next year or even later. This would allow the Synod Fathers to go back and discuss the themes considered with the members of their episcopal conferences and with all the members of the people of God responsible for the mission of the church.[30]

Now this proposal is exactly in line with Lonergan's theological method and would really test his second phase. What Bishop Hubert implies in his "two-stage synodal process" is that the Church, the whole Church, is a learning Church, and that what we need to learn is not the ancient formulas, which we can find in a good catechism, and not even the erudite nuances of the ancient formulas, which we can find by consulting the scholars, but the new expression, Pope John's "leap forward," that the times and the Spirit require. In Lonergan's preferred terms, we need to learn how to transpose the old dogmas into newly formulated doctrines.

The whole effort should be seen as the intention to save what is valid and reject what is harmful in each of two extreme positions. For the reactionary is quite right in trying to save an ancient faith, but quite wrong in thinking to save it by merely repeating the formulas of Nicea, Chalcedon, and Vatican I. Equally the radical is quite right in critiquing the dogmatic formulations of the past in terms of the horizon in which they were uttered, but quite wrong in a declaration of independence from those formulations. The transpositions proposed by Lonergan would save what is valid and reject what is harmful in both positions, but would require, almost by definition, that return to God's people urged by Bishop Hubert, or what Lonergan and others would call "feedback."[31] This clarifies the role of the local bishop in what must be the primary task for the whole Church: learning before we undertake to teach; in the present case learning through research and interpretation what the manifestations of the Spirit are in the local Church. When

30. L'Osservatore Romano, Weekly Edition (English), 16 Dec. 1985, p. 12.
31. The concept of feedback, though the word may occur only occasionally, is extremely important in Lonergan; it is almost identical with the Canon of Operations of Insight—see the index under "Canon," also pp. xiv (xv in 4th ed.), 35, 100, 104, 166, 174, 223, 226, 228–29, 303, 688, etc. In Method, see pp. 88 (n. 34), 293, 361, 366, etc.; in Second Collection, pp. 191, 216; and in Third Collection, pp. 29–30, 105–106. So far as I know this concept and its role in Lonergan's thought have not been the focus of any study, though they are touched on here and there in the literature; see, for example, John A. Raymaker, "The Theory-Praxis of Social Ethics: The Complementarity Between Hermeneutical and Dialectical Foundations," in Creativity and Method: Essays in Honor of Bernard Lonergan, S.J., ed. M. L. Lamb (Milwaukee: Marquette University, 1981), pp. 339–52 (especially pp. 349–52).

Catholics try to persuade their governments to establish an embassy at the Vatican, they often make much of the latter as a "listening post." The religious and theological needs of our time suggest a parallel role for the local bishop, and much more for national conferences of bishops: that of a listening post for the voice of the Holy Spirit. Of course, what local bishops or national conferences "hear" is to be tested in dialogue with other bishops in world assembly with the Holy Father, just as individual interiority is to be tested in dialogue with the wider community.

A second example, taken from the same synod, reveals the relevance of Lonergan's structure to the teaching, as well as to the learning, Church: it is the question of a universal teaching vis-à-vis the particular cultural needs of the local Church. The two need not be seen in opposition. For, if the Church must learn before it can teach, and if it is the universal Church that learns securely, then the very expression by the bishops, uttered in world assembly, of what they have learned, automatically becomes the teaching of the universal Church.[32] But that brings us to a second major function of the local bishops or national conferences: their teaching role. For a document produced by a world assembly, and so generalized that it can be a basis for Catholic teaching anywhere, is not likely to be a thrill to read or a joy to teach, nor can it in the very nature of the case provide an adequate doctrinal content for the local Church. This must involve the local bishop and national conference, for the same bishops who brought their reports to the world assembly and made their contribution to the sixth functional specialty of doctrines are the very ones who will return to the local Church and, aware of local culture in a way the world assembly could not possibly be, so preach the universal Christian message that it becomes, "not disruptive of the culture, not an alien patch superimposed upon it, but a line of development within the culture."

What will the role of theologians be in this ongoing, never-ending work of learning and teaching? It will be as diversified as the eight functions of theology. As scholars they will provide the research, interpretation and history the Church requires to make her return to the sources academically sound. As horizon-analysts (we have no word yet

---

32. Readers of *Method in Theology* will ask me whether I have not oversimplified the question of doctrines; in that book Lonergan distinguishes primary sources, Church doctrines, theological doctrines, methodological doctrine, and the doctrines of the sixth functional specialty (p. 295). Yes, I have, but in the direction, I think, of reuniting some of what has been distinguished; that is, Lonergan surely hoped that the doctrines of his sixth specialty would contribute to Church doctrines for our times, and I would see Bishop Hubert's proposal as heading along the same lines.

for those who will exercise the fourth function),[33] they will encounter the past with a sense of the different horizons operative in different times, with the task of critiquing the horizons of antiquity but equally with the task of broadening their own horizons in encounter with both antiquity and the present. As category-creators (again we have no word for those who work in the fifth function of foundations, though we might agree on "foundational theologians"), they will attempt to bring to suitable expression the present religious experience of the people of God, and thus provide the bishops with categories for the doctrines to be formulated in their assemblies. Then there is systematic theology, once the reigning but now the dethroned sovereign of the realm. Earlier we moved in a rather facile way from the sixth function of doctrines (bishops in world assembly) to the eighth function of communications (bishops on the local scene). But what is facile in the abstract can hardly be achieved in the concrete without the wide perspective and integral view deriving from a grasp of all eight specialties in their distinction, relation and unity, and this is the task of systematics. It is illuminating to note that it is a new task: not only must systematics unify the objective content of theology (God and all things in relation to God, as Aquinas put it), but it must unify as well the functions and operations of the theologians, from positive scholars working on the past to pastors bringing the message to the present people of God.

If my reading of Lonergan is correct, he regarded the whole Church as involved in the double process of learning and teaching; in the perspective of that position it is, of course, legitimate and necessary to divide the people of God according to their roles in the teaching function. But it is also secondary, and the whole question becomes distorted if the prior learning function is not brought into the perspective. When a university excludes a branch of science, Newman held, not only is there a gap in its program but the sciences that remain are distorted. Something parallel, I would say, has happened in regard to the learning and teaching functions of the Church: we have so neglected the one and so stressed the other that we have become like a bird with one wing overdeveloped and the other atrophied. And this can happen without positive exclusion of the learning function: from the boy and then the man Jesus to the Second Vatican Council the learning function is acknowledged. What is lacking is attention to learning as a problem, study of its implications, development of its criteria, responsible assumption of the tasks involved. If Lonergan has anything to say to

---

33. I derive the term from the cognate, horizon analysis, which I first noticed in David W. Tracy, "Horizon Analysis and Eschatology," *Continuum* 6/2 (Summer, 1968), pp. 166–79, and subsequently in various studies of Lonergan.

pastors it regards their teaching, and if he has anything to say on teaching it is that if we would teach we must first be willing to learn. What, after all, was his long withdrawal but a massive effort to learn, first from Thomas Aquinas and then from the seven centuries that followed Thomas?[34] Can we, his heirs, take up the teaching task without following the same route?

34. Readers of *Insight* will remember the much-quoted line in which he speaks of "spending years reaching up to the mind of Aquinas" (p. 748); years later he remarked to me (in a letter dated 3 March 1980): "I fear that my book did not emphasize enough the importance of research: my own work in that specialty was Gratia operans and Verbum, about eleven years of my life."

As for his effort to learn from the seven centuries that followed Aquinas, one can hardly do better than read the original (discarded) preface to *Insight,* now printed in *Method: Journal of Lonergan Studies* 3/1 (March, 1985), pp. 3–7. Note especially the remark (p. 4), "But if I may borrow a phrase from Ortega y Gasset, one has to strive to mount to the level of one's time."

9

The Task of Interpreting Lonergan[*]

I am grateful for the privilege of introducing this symposium, so generously organized by the University of Santa Clara, on the significance for religion and culture of the work of Bernard Lonergan. With all of you here, I recognize the seminal promise and potential of that work, I am aware of the problems that crowd the field of religion and culture, and I hope for a creative discussion among us that will bring the power of the ideas to bear on the obstinacy of the problems. Such creative thinking is not only the permanent ulterior motive we all have for the study of Bernard Lonergan; it is also the best way by far to fulfill our immediate objective, to honor, in this his eightieth year, a teacher and friend who has labored unremittingly in the field of religion and culture, who early in life committed his whole talent and energy to the problems they raise, but has worked always on the most remote and fundamental level, and has thereby laid on us the responsibility of developing and implementing his ideas.

With that introductory platitude—for platitude it is, even though I utter it with all sincerity—I get down to business with a thesis that on first hearing will sound simply subversive. The thesis is: we are not yet ready to begin this symposium. We are not yet ready, because the long and difficult preliminary task is still unfinished, the task of interpreting Lonergan. Let me explain. The symposium would study the significance of certain ideas for certain contemporary problems. It would engage in what *Method in Theology* calls second-phase theology and what we by extension can call the second phase in general of methodical specialization. Such a purpose may be included by some thinkers under a broader view of interpretation that would include application, but in my stricter use of the term, interpretation belongs to the first phase as one of its

*A keynote lecture at the symposium on the theme "Religion and Culture," held in honor of Bernard Lonergan at the University of Santa Clara, 15–18 March 1984. Previously published in *Religion and Culture: Essays in Honor of Bernard Lonergan,* ed. T. P. Fallon & P. B. Riley (Albany: State University of New York, 1987), pp. 3–16.

four functional specialties.[1] Its specific aim then is understanding. My thesis says we do not yet understand Lonergan, and so we are not yet ready for the work of application that the symposium proposes to undertake. My basic thesis could be divided, if you wish, into two parts: I personally do not understand him after thirty-seven years of study, and I have not found anyone who so excels in understanding him as to claim my discipleship.

The conclusion is not, however, that we should all go home and study Lonergan for another thirty-seven years, and then come together again to resume our interrupted discussion. Quite the contrary. The fact is, we never will be ready for such a symposium as this till we have held a score of them. It is the nature of seminal thinking to become clarified only in the harvest, and the harvest will raise as many questions as it solves. The process, then, is a to and fro movement in which we bring our limited understanding to bear on a problem area, discover in that effort our need for a deeper understanding, return with more specific questions to our seminal source, and so advance through lesser and lesser measures of failure to greater and greater measures of success. My conclusion, therefore, is that, because we are not yet ready for this symposium, we are obliged to hold it.

My own task in this introductory talk may be seen as the "to" in the "to and fro" swing of the pendulum of interpretation and application: that is, back to Lonergan for an interpretation that may orient us a little better in the work of application, and then forward in the discussions of the next three days of the symposium. But within the task I set for myself, there is a secondary to and fro movement, the familiar hermeneutic circle: "The meaning of a text . . . is a unity that is unfolded through parts. . . . We can grasp the unity, the whole, only through the parts. At the same time the parts are determined in their meaning by the whole which each part partially reveals."[2] The parts in question are, of course, an uncountable multitude, the several million words of Lonergan's lifetime production. Yet I propose to deal with them, as well as with the unity, at least to the extent of underlining the need we have for ongoing research into the details, in all their uncountable multitude, of Lonergan's thinking. Veterans in this field, I suspect, will await with more interest my treatment of the unity, to see whether I have anything helpful to contribute under that heading; may I say, without offense, that it is to them especially that I direct the first part

---

1. *Method in Theology.* Ch. 5 outlines the two phases of theology, each with its four functional specialties.

2. Ibid., p. 159.

of my talk; they are the very ones who need to return over and over to detailed study of their one-time teacher.

I

I am to talk, then, of the details, without understanding of which we will never fully understand the unity. I am limited to samples only, and I will take three: one from non-academic life, one that regards the sources of Lonergan's thinking, and one from the rich history of his own ideas. I deliberately choose three areas that are quite disparate; that very disparity will help the samples to function better as samples.

My sample from non-academic life has to do with music, and I introduce it with a minor bit of history. A few years ago, I was attending a congress in which discussion of Lonergan's ideas played some part, and a critic, not really an unfriendly one, told me, more or less in these words: The trouble with Lonergan is that he never listened to music; if he had done so, he would have written far better theology. The remark left me speechless—almost. We have recent documenting of Lonergan's boyhood love of music, but even years ago the general lines were familiar to anyone who knew him at all. We know, for example, that during his first Toronto period, a friend gave him season tickets to the Toronto Symphony Orchestra's performances, that he went year after year to hear them, that in fact he attributed to this musical experience the capacity to undertake and complete the labor of writing *Insight*. When his health deteriorated last year, and I had the job of packing and storing his possessions, I discovered on his desk a neatly typed set of cards listing his collection of music-recordings—there was no list of his books—and a set covering several years of the music magazine, *Ovation*. I will return in a moment to the intrinsic bearing all this may have on his thinking and theology; it is enough now to say that, if we base our interpretation of Lonergan on his supposed ignorance of music, we are moving about as directly as we can from the true course.[3]

My next sample is quite different. Last year I was browsing in the Regis College copy of Husserl's *Ideas: General Introduction to Pure Phenomenology* and discovered there a piece of paper, a mere scrap, with scribbling that is quite unmistakably Lonergan's and comments on Husserl that are quite distinctively Lonerganian. I would tentatively date

3. For some information on Lonergan's love of music, see *Caring about Meaning: Patterns in the life of Bernard Lonergan*, ed. P. Lambert *et al.* (Montreal: Thomas More Institute, 1982), pp. 28, 194, 195, 236, 258.

this scrap and this scribbling in the period 1947–1953, but I do not recall a single reference to this particular work of Husserl's in any of Lonergan's writings or lectures. Now what is the point of this second bit of history, or non-history? The point is that we deceive ourselves if we think we have easy access to Lonergan's reading and all the ideas that went into the hopper of his thinking; even those interviews in which he was extensively questioned under this very heading give us mere glimpses of his reading background. We have hardly begun even to list his sources, much less to evaluate their role in his formation.[4]

My third sample is the curious history in Lonergan of the notion of wisdom. During the years of his research into St. Thomas, wisdom was a fundamental intellectual virtue, the dominant one in the hierarchic trio that began with understanding, developed into science, and culminated in wisdom. It underwent some evolution at the time of *Insight*, but continued to play a major role well into the Roman period of 1953–65. Then, very suddenly, it drops out of the foreground and almost out of the picture.[5] Is this not a matter for curiosity, calling for research and interpretation? And might we not expect study of this detail to give us new insight into the ideas of the *Method* period from 1965 on?

I have given three samples of the need for ongoing research in our preliminary task of interpreting Lonergan. In a sense they are mere samples, that is, they stand for the three hundred, or the three thousand, points of detail that call for study. But my own view is that, in such a comprehensive and systematic thinker as Lonergan is, no sample is likely to be merely a sample. Nor are they mere straws in the wind, indicating a trend whose source and power must be investigated elsewhere. Each sample has its significance for the whole picture. Take, for instance, the case of music. Lonergan once drew an extended analogy between human consciousness and "a concerto that blends many themes in endless ways."[6] Now this is remarkably similar to what he found in the *Contra gentiles* of St. Thomas: "the same arguments recurring over and over in ever slightly different forms . . . the differentiation of operations and their conjunction in ever fresh combinations."[7] It is re-

---

4. There are references to Husserl in the Halifax lectures of 1958, but the only work mentioned is *The Crisis of European Sciences and Transcendental Phenomenology*; see *Understanding and Being: An Introduction and Companion to "Insight,"* pp. 45, 238. In *Caring about Meaning* (n. 3 above), the most persistent effort we have had to draw Lonergan out on his readings, no work of Husserl is mentioned.

5. Three soundings will show the trend: Lonergan's *Verbum: Word and Idea in Aquinas* indicates the early importance of the term; see the index, *s.v.*, Wisdom. His *Insight: A Study of Human Understanding* would develop Thomist wisdom by adding a new form of it, p. 407. The index of *Method in Theology* shows only one entry, and that to the Wisdom literature of the Bible.

6. "Religious Experience," in *A Third Collection: Papers by Bernard J. F. Lonergan, S.J.*, pp. 115–28; see p. 125.

7. *Method*, p. 30.

markably similar to what we may find in Lonergan himself. Did his love of music perhaps affect his thinking in a more intrinsic way than we have yet realized? Or take Lonergan's relation to Husserl. The latter does not figure prominently in *Insight,* but some twenty years later Lonergan distinguished three meanings of the term "transcendental": the Scholastic, the Kantian, and one (obviously Lonergan's own) deriving from Husserl's intentionality analysis, in which *noêsis* and *noêma* are correlative.[8] If we recall how pervasive that pair of correlatives is in *Insight,* we might find this detail quite illuminating. My third sample was the role of wisdom in Lonergan's early "system" and its strange disappearance later. We know that his notion of theology went through a profound transformation around 1965, and that one factor in this complex question was the displacement of intellectual habits in the individual thinker by the new role given the community of collaborating specialists. Are these two bits of history not related, and must we not think of wisdom as resident now in the community, with dialectic as its guide and interdisciplinary collaboration as its expression?

I have been dealing with matters of detail, and have stated my view of their importance for the task of interpreting Lonergan. You may not agree with that view. But you cannot ignore the fact that on what is not a matter of detail, on what is so central a concern as transcendental method itself, there are diametrically opposed opinions in the interpretation of what Lonergan says, and this among those who have been long-time students of his thought. You may think, of course, that the remedy lies in dialectic and so take flight at once to that level, arguing that what one or the other side needs is a profound horizon change. And you may be right; no one regrets more than I do our failure to engage in real dialectic, as that term is understood in chapter 10 of *Method.* But I have a more modest proposal for a starting point. I remind you of a simple statement: "Not all opposition is dialectical. There are differences that will be eliminated by uncovering fresh data."[9] My starting point, then, would be to collect, in extensive and thorough research, what Lonergan has said on the matter; I wonder how many differences would be eliminated by this simple procedure on the very first level of functional specialization.[10] In any case I am convinced, and that is the gist of this first section, that in the task of interpreting Lonergan far more attention must be paid to simple research.

8. "Religious Knowing," in *Third Collection,* pp. 129–45; see p. 145, n. 8.

9. *Method,* p. 235.

10. The investigation should take account, not merely of more formal statements on what method is, but of the use of words like "recipe," of repeated references to the New Method Laundry, of contrasts with scientific method, of the transition Lonergan calls for from logic to method, etc.—As I like to insist, we need to study the details if we are to be accurate on the whole.

II

We must understand the parts in order to understand the unitary whole, but the meaning of the parts is determined by the meaning of the whole. So we come to an overall interpretation of Lonergan, a unitary view of what he has done with his life and expressed in his work in academe. The various influences, ideas, bits of personal history—the three hundred or three thousand items that cannot even be listed here—they must yield now to some comprehensive pattern, some general view, some total framework. Since Lonergan himself, so far as I know, has never given more than stray hints for constructing such a totality, we have to supply our own, and so I am going to offer you mine.

We need, of course, some means of comprehensive classification, some device, be it only a set of pegs on which to hang our ideas. When Lonergan had set forth his eight functional specialties, to take us beyond field and subject specialization, he proceeded to demonstrate their unity. Something analogous might very well be possible here, but I have a simpler suggestion: a simple set of pegs provided by a simple logical device. I'm sure Fr. Lonergan would bristle, were he present to hear me invoking logic, as it may seem, to explain his life and work, just as I suspect he was not altogether happy five years ago with my comparison of his work with the Aristotelian *organon* and the *novum organum* of Bacon.[11] You too may be apprehensive. But, audience, be not affrighted; I use logic only as an external device to classify my findings, not as a principle to derive sterile conclusions from unverified premises.

My logical device is an imitation of the Porphyrean tree.[12] I will divide Lonergan according to an existential and cognitive duality. I will divide the latter aspect into learning and teaching phases, a *discens* Lonergan and a *docens*. I will subdivide the teaching phase according to work that is realized and work that is only programmatic. I will subdivide the programmatic into the structural and the historical. And lastly I will divide the historical into the two ways of achievement and

11. *The Lonergan Enterprise* (Cambridge, MA: Cowley, 1980). See esp. ch. 1, "Lonergan's Work as an Organon for Our Time."

12. It has been remarked to me that this approach is too static to convey the wealth and dynamism of Lonergan's thinking; I quite agree, and caution my readers against taking this logical device as anything more than a means for organizing conceptually ideas that depend on a far more fertile source. Incidentally, the device was used by Lonergan himself in his lectures, *De intellectu et methodo* (Gregorian University, Rome, 1959), where he says in effect: When you would get a handle on the universe of being, and lack the idea of being, then proceed by the Porphyrean either-or dichotomies within the notion of being. (See pp. 19ff. of the student notes on those lectures, Lonergan Research Institute, Toronto.)

heritage. The divisions are imperfect, overlapping one another. The dividing principle may be hazy. So I add my own transcendental precept to the four you know so well: besides being attentive, intelligent, reasonable and responsible, be patient too.

My first division corresponds to the familiar distinction between the fourth level of consciousness and the third. But while the third is readily understood as the cognitive, it is not so easy to find a single label for the fourth. This is the level of conscience, of responsibility, of decision, of action. It is also the level on which we decide not only what to do with the next moment but what to do with our very lives, so maybe "existential" will best serve to characterize this aspect of the whole Lonergan.

It seems important for at least two reasons to put this matter up front in our study. There is an intrinsic reason. For the fourth level is that of the grounding horizon whence are determined the meanings of all our statements, the values of all our choices, the purposes of all our actions. To miss this orienting factor is to overlook what is most fundamental and thereby to distort the whole picture. There is more: fourth-level activity is not just a bringing forth of an external product, be it ever so sublime; more importantly, it is a bringing forth of oneself. It is not only a making but a doing, not only a *poiêsis* but a *praxis*, by which doing and *praxis* we make ourselves what we are to be, and thereby—since no one is an island—contribute most significantly to the universe.

My second reason is more extrinsic to the logic of my presentation: it regards the complaint that Lonergan lacks concern for common people, does not involve himself in the effort to better their conditions of life. It seems an easy way for his critics to gain an advantage, for one has only to read him to discover how difficult and demanding his thought is. Then the argument is clear: he is an intellectual, therefore he is cerebral, therefore he lacks existential involvement. *Ecce,* a sorites of sorts, very satisfying if you don't much care about either *consequens* or *consequentia.*

We have here a question of fact, to which the simple but extensive answer would be a biography; I have not the space for that now. In any case, I suspect that the chief difficulty is one of principle. Those with an activist bent simply cannot see how there can be a "preferential option for the poor" in such a lifework as that to which Lonergan dedicated himself for half a century in unremitting labor. The question of principle is one, then, of understanding, and dealing directly with it requires a Socratic art that will vary from instance to instance. But there is an indirect way that has a common appeal and is recommended by the highest authority: the way of the parable.

My parable, which I have used elsewhere for the same purpose, is of two people who went out to a third-world country to work for the poor. One went at once into the streets of a large city to search out the hungry, the sick, the homeless, and respond to the need by providing food and building hospitals and shelters; relief then was immediate and the benefits reached hundreds or thousands according to the resources at hand. The other had studied the agronomy and economy of the country, knew that the land could produce twice what it currently yielded and that better methods of distribution could bring food to millions not then being fed, so responded to the need by setting up schools for young workers on the land and forming cooperatives for a more efficient economy; benefits then were not immediate but there was a well-founded hope that in the long run the effect might be felt not just by thousands of the hungry but by millions.

Which of these two showed the greater concern for the poor? We recognize at once that the question itself is faulty. There is a valid comparison, but not in terms of greater or less concern—rather in terms of ways and means, and indeed ways and means that are complementary to, not exclusive of, one another. Not then either/or, but both/and. For in fact both people in our parable were concerned, and deeply concerned, for the poor, but they had different vocations to respond in different ways, both ways good, both ways necessary. This, I submit, is the kind of understanding we must bring to Lonergan's vocation, and I allow myself one additional note in explanation. Namely, the more fundamental the level on which we approach a problem, the less relevant is our contribution going to seem to the casual eye, but the more widespread and efficacious is the real impact going to be in the long run. Lonergan's cognitional theory, epistemology, metaphysics, transcendental method are fundamental indeed; they belong to the first moment in the rhythm of a massive withdrawal and return, but we must not expect the return to take place overnight.

Let us turn to the cognitive half of our first division. The subdivision here corresponds to the familiar two phases of theology: receiving and handing on. "If one assimilates tradition, one learns that one should pass it on. If one encounters the past, one also has to take one's stand toward the future."[13] It corresponds also to an old pair familiar from our catechetics: the *Ecclesia discens* and *docens,* the learning and the teaching Church. But that latter pair has come into some disfavor in our time, so I should explain my use of it here. There is nothing wrong, there never has been anything wrong, it seems to me, with the *discens-docens* pair as functions of the Church. The trouble occurs when we

13. *Method,* p. 133.

apply them, not to different functions but to different people, when we divide the people of God into two camps, and call one the learning Church and the other the teaching Church. If, however, we understand the pair to refer primarily to functions, we will understand also that the whole Church is a learning Church and the whole Church is in some sense a teaching Church. Then, secondarily, we may ordain, empower, delegate, certain members of the Church to speak for the whole; but on that secondary level the concept gives much less trouble.

In any case, to return to my topic, the learning I have in mind is not the learning of Church doctrine. Since the days of Henry Denzinger we have had easy access to what the Church teaches. What I have in mind is what the world teaches. Not the world simply in the scriptural sense of the enemy or even in the likewise scriptural sense of the world to be saved, though we may include both, but the world in its great enterprise of becoming human, the world in the sense of restless humanity seething with ideas and causes, advancing with incredible energy in arts and technology, developing scholarship and science, philosophies and cultures, with attention, intelligence, reasonableness, and responsibility, and just as often going astray through inattentive, obtuse, unreasonable and irresponsible conduct. It is a world from whose progress we must learn, as well as a world we must teach and redeem in its decline, but my topic now is learning, and I submit that seven centuries ago, in the person at least of Thomas Aquinas, the Church ran neck and neck with the world in the vanguard of progress, of modernity, of the level of the times. I further submit that for a hundred years now we have been waking up as a Church—waking up reluctantly, like Augustine's sluggish sleeper—waking up to find ourselves seven centuries behind the world, "in the unenviable position," to change the metaphor, "of always arriving on the scene a little breathlessly and a little late."[14]

I have said that the whole Church is a learning Church and so the whole Church must wake up and rise to the level of the times. Still, some areas and some members seem to do so faster than others—here is a context where people, and not just functions, are divided—so we have to ask what particular significance Lonergan's work of self-education has for the Church's *aggiornamento*. Possibly he has worked in some especially backward areas; possibly he has had considerable influence on others, dragging them kicking and struggling into the twentieth century. But such matters are not of world-historical significance. A full study of this question is needed, but meanwhile I would locate his importance for the Church's *aggiornamento* in the comprehensive view he has attained of modernity. We may recall his keen analyses of

14. *Insight*, p. 733.

modern scholarship, modern science, and modern philosophy, all to be laid "under tribute" to a renewed theology.[15] We are all familiar with his campaign to liberate us from a classicist world view into historical mindedness.[16] Some of us will remember his summation of five areas of modern influence on theology: "history, philosophy, religious studies, method, and communications."[17] We have read his extended study of history (the history that happens) in chapter 7 of *Insight*, and pondered his briefer but profound analysis of that history into its three moments of progress, decline, and redemption.[18] On the basis of these hints, perhaps I may say of him, due proportion being maintained, what he said of St. Thomas: "Even in this brief and rough delineation, one can perceive the magnificent sweep of genius."[19]

You realize, of course, that without giving notice of the move, I have already taken us over to the other half of our present division. Our Lonergan *discens* is already, through the power of his reflections on modernity, through the scope, the depth, the comprehensiveness of his analyses, already a Lonergan *docens*. So let us turn openly to that other half, which was subdivided between pointing the way and taking the road. More literally, it is the difference between an elaborated theology, philosophy, scholarship, science, the difference between all this on one side, and on the other the instrument of mind and heart, the organon of the incarnate subject, that he has created for our use.

It seems more natural to begin with the former, the realized work, for surely the programmatic is based on the realized as method follows achievement or procedural rules follow procedures in use. The matter, however, is not so simple. True, we have the monumental *Insight* for a sketch of a philosophy, while in theology we have some quite elaborate work on divine grace, the incarnate Word, and the Trinity, not to mention recent assaults on the economics establishment. But the philosophy has to be enlarged and completed by the work of the later Lonergan. As for his theology, we still need more study of the relation between his method and his material theology. The material theology was certainly the arena in which he worked out his method. But the method reached its term in a kind of quantum leap, and we still have

15. In his *Grace and Freedom: Operative Grace in the Thought of St. Thomas Aquinas*, p. 139, Lonergan remarks that the program of Aquinas "was to lay under tribute Greek and Arab, Jew and Christian, in an ever renewed effort to obtain for Catholic culture that [most fruitful understanding] which is the goal of theological speculation."

16. An early thematic statement is "The Transition from a Classicist World-View to Historical-Mindedness," in *A Second Collection: Papers by Bernard J. F. Lonergan, S.J.*, pp. 1–9. For further references, consult the indices in that volume and in *Method*.

17. "Theology and Man's Future," in *Second Collection*, pp. 135–48; see p. 135.

18. "*Insight* Revisited," in *Second Collection*, pp. 263–78; see pp. 271–72.

19. *Verbum*, p. 24.

to ask how a return to the theology would affect those early treatises, and what new form they would take in that total restructuring of theology his method calls for.[20]

Nevertheless, we have a number of hints and some fairly firm guidelines for that renewed theology (I will not venture to speak for the philosophy and economics). For divine grace, *Method* itself indicates the way the new theology would be structured.[21] For Christology we have such papers as "Christology Today: Methodological Reflections,"[22] too cryptic, it seems, to have received much attention from other theologians, but by the same token—in my view at least—as rich in promise as anything we have since *Method*. For the Trinity, there are scattered clues in the discussions of various workshops, with some published indications as well. And we have even a new and very important area of theology in the inner and outer word of *Method*, and the relation of this pair to the missions of Son and Spirit.[23]

That reference reminds us, of course, that we are not dealing merely with the material content of these various treatises. There are more general and formal elements which are not so likely to be affected by the quantum leap of method, elements indeed which helped greatly to ground and structure that method. I think of the place of truth in the many glories of the word of God, the notion of truth as meaning rather than formula, the transposition of meaning from context to context, the specification of contexts by differentiations of consciousness rather than by objective systems, the complementing of all this with the inner word and the eye of love, and the whole pouring into method and the functional specialties of theology. It is here, I think, that the realized work of Lonergan will have its most enduring impact. But content and program overlap in what I have been saying, and once again the first half of our division has led us inexorably into the other half—a witness to the intricate unity of the whole Lonergan we are trying to study.

So we come to the programmatic side of Lonergan's work. It was the focus of his thinking for most of his life. It is symbolized, though not exhausted, by his *Method in Theology*. It is the best known, the most distinctive, and probably the most important feature of his work. It deserves more of our time than the few minutes I can give it this evening, but some years ago I had the opportunity to devote three whole lectures to setting it forth, so I am able to refer you for a fuller

---

20. See nn. 26–27 below.   21. *Method*, pp. 288–89.

22. *Third Collection*, pp. 74–99.

23. On the Trinity: ibid., pp. 63–65, for one example. On the inner word and outer word, with a hint of their relation to Son and Spirit, see *Method*, pp. 112–15, and *Second Collection*, pp. 170–75. I myself have developed this relation a little in my "Son and Spirit: Tension in the Divine Missions?" See ch. 17 below.

account to those St. Michael's Lectures.[24] For a one-line statement I can do no better than quote Francis Bacon, whose stated purpose it was "to commence a total reconstruction of sciences, arts, and all human knowledge, raised upon the proper foundations."[25] Bacon proposed a *novum organum,* understood as replacing the Aristotelian *organon,* and I think we may call Lonergan's contribution an *organum novissimum.* I am not suggesting now, nor did I suggest it five years ago, that Bacon's plan for a *"Magna Instauratio"* of knowledge came anywhere near Lonergan's, but he did conceive with great clarity the difference between creating an instrument of mind and reconstructing on proper foundations the whole of human knowledge, and I find that illuminating for what Lonergan has been about. His precise focus may seem to limit the field, as when he speaks of "a total transformation of dogmatic theology,"[26] or again of "a complete restructuring of Catholic theology,"[27] but, if we remove the lens that served to focus his thought, we would find his instrument of mind broaden out to become a general instrument of mind and heart, of the incarnate subject; and his functional specialties would become, in his own words, "relevant to any human studies that investigated a cultural past to guide its future."[28] Such, in brief, is the programmatic side of Lonergan's work. It is programmatic, but it does not include a program. The creation of an organon does not by itself constitute a detailed plan for the new theology, the new philosophy, the new sciences and human studies. But it is a first great step; indeed, a giant step for mankind. In such matters we must say with Browning, "a man's reach should exceed his grasp."

I have been speaking in general, and all too briefly, of the programmatic work of Lonergan, but there is some compensation for the brevity in our present section. For we have now to make a further division, and can continue the same topic under two subheadings. I therefore divide the programmatic into a structural aspect and an historical, not wholly happy with those two terms, but not having a better pair at hand. By the structural I mean the invariant features of human consciousness, the levels, the framework. By the historical I mean what happens on the four levels, the various ways of filling in the framework, the differentiations of pattern and the forms of conversion that consciousness undergoes as it follows its historical course of progress, decline, redemption.

24. *The Lonergan Enterprise.*

25. Ibid., p. 11, from Bacon's *Essays, Advancement of Learning, New Atlantis, and Other Pieces,* ed. R. F. Jones (New York: Odyssey, 1937), pp. 239–40.

26. "Theology in Its New Context," in *Second Collection,* pp. 55–67; see p. 67.

27. "The Future of Christianity," in *Second Collection,* pp. 149–63; see p. 161.

28. "Bernard Lonergan Responds," in *Foundations of Theology,* ed. P. McShane (Dublin: Gill and Macmillan, 1971), pp. 223–34; see p. 233.

The structural is by far the more familiar aspect of consciousness for students of Lonergan, so much so that the pervasive but often unthematized historical treatment is regularly overlooked. That is perhaps inevitable, given that Lonergan himself focused for years on the structural levels and struggled unremittingly to distinguish and relate and exploit them.[29] There is no need to linger on this half of the dichotomy; it is enough to say that the structural is utterly fundamental, for in all we do we exercise our experience, understanding, reflection, and responsibility, and that it is in the highest degree relevant to the programmatic, for it issues in the transcendental precepts that govern all human activity: be attentive, be intelligent, be reasonable, be responsible.[30]

Let us turn to the historical. I am referring here to the history that happens, as opposed to the history that records the happenings. I am not, however, referring to objective events in the sweep of history from Adam and Eve to the Apocalypse, but to what happens in human consciousness. It is of great importance, for a grasp of Lonergan, to conceive this historical aspect in its full generality and set it off against the structural, but all I can do here is list some of the headings. First, then, there are the patterns of experience that later became the differentiations of consciousness: the differentiations that make some of us artists, others mathematicians, still others philosophers or theologians, while we all remain subject to the transcendental precepts. Derivatively, there are the realms of meaning that correspond to the differentiations. Secondly, there are the stages of meaning, which we can relate by a political analogy to the realms: the historically evolving nations of England, France, and Germany would correspond somewhat to the realms of meaning, while the various measures of democracy achieved in those nations at any given time would have some analogy to the stages of meaning. Thirdly, there are the various conversions that, through their presence or absence in different combinations, differentiate us radically from one another, and indeed differentiate my former self from the person I now fancy myself to be or hope to become.[31]

---

29. One result of Lonergan's long struggle with the structural aspect is that the rest of us can now in five minutes learn to use the words "experience," "understanding," "reflection," "value." Maybe in five years we could learn to identify and locate in our consciousness the corresponding activities, and relate them to one another. When that is done we would be ready to investigate the implications of those activities for the objects they intend in the universe. If we have not taken those three steps, we can at least conceive them with something like a notional apprehension (Newman). But we have hardly even conceived the historical side as such, in its totality and in its relation to the structural, though good work has been done on some of its elements (conversion, etc.).

30. *Method*, p. 20 and passim; see the index, *s.v.*, Transcendental.

31. The most succinct table I know, of categories pertaining to the structural and historical aspects of consciousness, is found in *Method*, pp. 286–87.

Now this historical side of consciousness is subject in its own way to law and order. For example, insofar as the stages of meaning follow something like law we have Lonergan's three plateaus for the classification of meaningful activity: the practical concerned with doing, the logical concerned with speaking, and the interiorly based and methodical, concerned with understanding.[32] We can go even further. The law discernible in historically developing consciousness grounds specific precepts of methods as well as classifications. If you go back to *Insight* and examine chapter 3, "The Canons of Empirical Method," from the present viewpoint, you will make a most interesting discovery: the first, third, and fourth canons correspond closely to the levels of experience, understanding, and judgment, and so relate directly to the structural. But the second and fifth canons relate directly to the historical side of consciousness. That is, the canon of operations, the second in Lonergan's list, has to do with the accumulation of insights, or the ongoing history of one's development; and the canon of complete explanation, the fifth in the list, has to do with perseverance toward the goal of empirical method, and not accepting to explain some data while excluding part of what is empirically given.[33]

We need one more division to complete our set: the historical side of consciousness is to be divided into two ways that we may call "the way of achievement" and "the way of heritage." They refer to the opposite directions development may take within the framework of the structural levels. There is the development that Lonergan sees as moving from below upward, from experience, through understanding and judgment, to the formation of values—the way I label "achievement." And there is development, he argues, from above downward, from values and beliefs received in trust, through critical understanding of the tradition, to more perceptive experience—the way I call that of "heritage."[34] This very fundamental division, I would say, was one of the last of his great general ideas before he turned, in the final years of his active life, to the specific field of economics, and it remains, a decade later, largely unexploited. You have noticed, no doubt, that it has a link with an earlier pair in our study: the learning-teaching, the *discens-docens*

32. "Natural Right and Historical Mindedness," in *Third Collection*, pp. 169–83; see pp. 177–79. The three plateaus correspond to the stages of meaning in *Method*, pp. 85–99.

33. *Insight*, ch. 3. The sixth canon (of statistical residues) pertains also to the historical, but in a more complex way; I have discussed this in "Transcendental Deduction: A Lonerganian Meaning and Use," *Method: Journal of Lonergan Studies* 2/1 (March, 1984), pp. 21–40; see pp. 27–29.

34. Lonergan returned over and over to this pair of complementary notions in his papers from 1974 to 1977. Two of the more accessible loca are in "Natural Right and Historical Mindedness," *Third Collection*, at pp. 180–81, and "Theology and Praxis," *Third Collection*, at pp. 196–97. Also see ch. 20 below.

division. Only now, instead of using these ideas to guide our analysis of Lonergan's life and work, we turn them on ourselves and use them to chart our own course, whether in the great plan of a life and career, or in the particular little detail of this weekend symposium.

III

My topic has been the task of interpreting Lonergan. I have gone round the hermeneutic circle from parts to whole, and will presently point to the follow-up from whole to parts. The parts, one grants, are an unmanageable multitude, but I hope my three sample details have at least shown the need for patient attention to the multitude, one by one, in ongoing research. The major difficulty is in achieving a total view, but some such view we must sooner or later adopt. We need it to research Lonergan's work as well as to interpret it; we need it to locate him in history as well as to allow him to challenge us personally. We need it too in the second-phase work of a personal stand—whatever our attitude, be it the negative one of opposing this nonsense and putting an end to this cult of method, or (an attitude some of us find more intelligent and reasonable, not to say responsible) the positive one of expanding and carrying forward his ideas, and applying his method to the problems that beset the Church on every side. So I have given you my sketch of a total view. With some such sketch of the whole one can assign the intelligibility of the parts and eliminate the misunderstanding that inevitably results from their omission or from confusing them.

One cannot insist too strongly on the importance for correct interpretation of that follow-up from whole to parts, but I can only point, and then only negatively, to the follow-up as it might regard each of the six divisions of my second section. In general, then, to overlook the existential element is to miss what has been determining for Lonergan through half a century of dedication to a distinctly conceived purpose, and thus to misread all the work of those years. The field marshal surveying an old-style battle and the recluse in an ivory tower are both high above the hurly-burly, but there is all the difference between them of involvement and non-involvement. Again, to overlook his massive engagement with modernity, with the learning process that brings one to the level of the times, is inevitably to see him as unduly concerned with documents from the past, indeed the distant past, to the neglect of present experience. In fact, that massive involvement *is* concern with present experience; only it is concern with its fundamental features, rather than with the latest Gallup poll or charismatic congress. Again, to overlook his forty-year immersion in the deepest theological problems, is inevitably to see him as working out his method in a totally *a priori* manner, decreeing from some abstract command post what theologians must do when they engage in theology. In fact, from his doctoral dissertation to his last pre-*Method* lectures of 1965—I do not recall a single exception to this—he was wrestling at one and the same time with current questions of theology and with a method that might handle them more effectively. Fourthly, to overlook the programmatic character of his work is inevitably to find him inarticulate, when we want answers, and already out-of-date on the contemporary scene; whereas, to discover his distinctive *apport,* the cutting edge of method, might alert us to the possibility that he is a generation ahead of his time, and for that reason incomprehensible to his contemporaries. Fifthly, to attend only to the structural side of consciousness and overlook the historical would be to find the programmatic devoid of the richness of life, even rigid and confining, despite its dynamism. But the historical restores the immense variety, the enormous wealth and versatility, the unlimited range of incarnate spirit. Finally, to overlook the two ways of human development is to come to confused conclusions, with regard to the Church in general and Lonergan in particular, on such stock dichotomies as those labeled the liberal-conservative and the community-individual. In fact, this pair of concepts (the two ways) enables us to see liberal and conservative, not as epithets to divide people but as functions to control heritage and achievement. Similarly, we will see the way of achievement as appealing to the individual dynamism of human consciousness, but in a community setting; and we will see the way of heritage as appealing to the community setting of love and trust, for the benefit of the individual person and individual achievement.

When Lonergan wrote *Insight* he subtitled it *A Study of Human Understanding.* It turned out that a good part of the philosophical world was not ready to acknowledge even the existence of a distinct activity of consciousness to be named understanding. But as long as we disregard that activity we are bound to be less sensitive to the need for understanding an author, most especially an author who talks a good deal about understanding. That, I think, will give a clue to the distance that separates much of academe from the very real task of interpreting Lonergan. May this essay do something to shorten the distance.

II
EXPANDING

IO

Jerusalem at the Heart of Athens:
The Christian University*

The task assigned me this afternoon is a difficult one. It could be described as the task of being wise. In ancient biblical times there was a professional class of wise men; that is, where one young man might choose fishing as his occupation, and another farming, a third would choose to be a wise man. Some such special class of men is very much needed at this time of year; a university might then draw on their members when it would deliver a last piece of wisdom to its graduates before they go out into the world in independence and self-reliance.

Personally I am going to default on my assignment. I am going to give you, not a final word of wise advice, but a question, one you may ponder as you reflect on your years at Saint Mary's University and look forward to the function you will fulfill in society. It is an obvious question, and it may seem familiar; but it is worth trying to grasp again, for it is deceptively simple in appearance. Your convocation program shows degrees or diplomas being granted in arts, science, commerce, education, and engineering. The list illustrates the role a university plays in the complex of activities that belong to civil society, and the contribution you will make to the great enterprise of building the city of man; it is a list of your title-deeds to a professional function on the team that runs the world. But at the same time, I read on page eight of your academic calendar for this year the statement that Saint Mary's "is a Christian University." It is committed therefore to building the city of God. And there, I think, we have a question. We can quite easily separate the city of man and the city of God, and set them on opposite sides of a great chasm; but to combine them, as we do when we speak of a Christian university, that presents a problem.

For what has Christianity to do with a university that is so clearly

*An address to the graduating class of Saint Mary's University, Halifax, on 10 May 1971. Also given (with slight modifications) at Newman Theological College, Edmonton, on 28 October 1971. Previously published in *The Maroon and White* [quarterly of the Saint Mary's University Alumni Association] 19/7 (June, 1971), pp. 1–3.

163

oriented toward the business of running this world: What has religious faith to do with arts and sciences and education? What has the Sermon on the Mount to do with commerce? What has the gospel to do with engineering? Is the table of logarithms any different here from the one they use at a secular university? Are the laws of micro- and macro-economics affected by the sacramental system of the Church? Is a piece of literature better literature because it is written by a good Christian? What in short has Christianity to do with a university, and how will the Christian character of a university help its graduates to function better in a world of largely secular enterprises?

The question is a real and personal one for me. If you are true graduates of Saint Mary's it will, I think, be real and personal for you. The same calendar I have already quoted states that it is the objective of Saint Mary's "to induce . . . critical thinking" in the student. To think critically is to ask questions. So you have been taught to ask questions, not surely in the irresponsible destructive manner of a child who dismantles his toy and cannot put it back together again, but in the purposeful manner in which a laboratory expert will analyze a substance, with the responsibility of one who is a warden of truth. After all, two men may ask much the same questions in regard to their wives, but there is a great difference if one asks because he wants to divorce his wife, and the other asks because he wants to establish a happier relationship. We ask about the relationship of Christianity to a university, not as men contemplating a divorce, but as men who chose Saint Mary's because they shared or at least respected her statement of purpose, and would understand the consequences of that choice for their careers in arts or science, commerce, education, or engineering.

Although the question is real and personal for us today, it is also a very old one. It was raised and put on the stage of history a long time ago. It has been there ever since like a planet that has entered our solar system and will not go away. Let me read you a few lines from a work written around the year 200 after Christ:

What has Jerusalem to do with Athens, the Church with the Academy, the Christian with the heretic? . . . After Jesus Christ we have no need of speculation, after the Gospel no need of research.[1]

The writer is Tertullian, African rhetorician, lawyer, Christian, apologist, theologian—one of the most brilliant thinkers in the early Church, the creator (it is said) of the language of Western or Latin theology.

1. "The Prescriptions against the Heretics," tr. S. L. Greenslade, in *The Library of Christian Classics* (Philadelphia: Westminster), Vol. 5 (1956): *Early Latin Theology*, no. 7, p. 36.

And he has a very simple answer to our question: he would deny there is such a thing as a Christian university in our sense of the word.

Indeed, as Tertullian asks it, the question is no question at all, but a rhetorical device. He supplies the answer before we have time to think: Jerusalem, the city of God, has nothing whatever to do with Athens, the city of man's culture and civilization. Faith has nothing to do with arts and science, the gospel has nothing to do with engineering. As for you, if you chose Saint Mary's because it is a Christian university, you cannot relate that Christian character to your degrees and diplomas in the professions of this world. It is true that Tertullian's specific target was philosophy: "It is philosophy," he says, "that supplies the heresies with their equipment. . . . A plague on Aristotle, who taught them dialectic, the art which destroys as much as it builds. . . ."[2] But the principle at stake is universal; if it is true, it applies as much to engineering in Halifax today as it did to philosophy on the Mediterranean coast of Africa nearly eighteen centuries ago.

Happily for us, Tertullian's view is just one man's opinion. Theologian he may be, and a brilliant one, but his opinion is not a dogma of faith. In fact, in the very same era of history and not too far away on the same Mediterranean seaboard, another great theologian was saying almost the exact opposite; let me quote you a few lines from his works:

The way of truth is therefore one. But into it, as into a perennial river, streams flow from all sides. . . . Man is made principally for the knowledge of God; but he also measures land, practices agriculture, and philosophizes; of which pursuits, one conduces to life, another to living well, a third to the study of the things which are capable of demonstration.[3]

The writer now is Clement of Alexandria, called the founder of Eastern or Greek theology as Tertullian was founder of Western. He too is arguing more expressly about philosophy which, in contrast to Tertullian, he calls "the clear image of truth, a divine gift to the Greeks."[4] But Clement too, and even more expressly than Tertullian, has in mind the whole patrimony of the world's culture and civilization; he would feel quite at home were he with us today attending this convocation. So here we have a question that seemed our own, real and personal to us, and it turns out to have been formulated long ago, with two great theologians taking opposite sides on the relation of Christianity to philosophy and the secular studies of a university.

At this point we may begin to find the question boring. We may

2. Ibid., p. 35.
3. "Stromata," in *The Writings of Clement of Alexandria,* tr. W. Wilson (Edinburgh: T. & T. Clark), Vol. 1 (1867), Bk. I, ch. 5, p. 366, & Vol. 2 (1869), Bk. VI, ch. 8, p. 341.
4. Ibid., Vol. I, Bk. I, ch. 2, p. 360.

wonder how so old a question can be with us still. Was I only setting up a man of straw a moment ago, in order to knock him down more easily later? Or, if it is really a hard question, how can we be expected to solve it when thinkers of many ages have failed to do so? Or, however real the question remains in theory, in practice Saint Mary's has opted for Clement's side, and we have no longer a live option in the matter.

For the moment I can only ask you to trust me. I believe the question is genuine; I have not just set up a straw man. The question may be old, but it has taken various forms in its history; I did warn you, did I not, that it is deceptively simple in appearance? You are indeed committed, as graduates of Saint Mary's, to the task Clement undertook but you are committed to more: not only to follow Clement, but to understand Tertullian, and see how each fits into the pattern of history. Finally, I expect you to contribute greatly to the solution of the problem. In fact, the opportunity is so great, the challenge so peremptory, that I envy you the exciting possibilities opening before you.

And now perhaps I can do more than merely ask questions; maybe I can pass on to you a bit of wisdom too, not my own, but the wisdom of the Church learning slowly through the ages. I suggest then that we cannot understand the phenomena of Clement and Tertullian if our camera takes only still shots. We need a movie camera. We cannot be content simply to set two polarizing forces in tension with one another, we must rather follow the movement of history and discover the changes in the situation which make both intelligible. The supposition for such a view is, of course, that the Church is a learning Church; she is a student body, not as radical as some student bodies today, though maybe not much more docile, but still slowly and painfully learning her lessons from the unfolding pages of the book of history.

What I am about to undertake then is a ten-minute survey of the history of the Church's developing attitude to this question from New Testament times to our own. The historians here will shudder at the very idea. They have had sad experience of the theologian's bent for rapid swings through vast periods of history. I can only beg their indulgence. We have had a long afternoon. The graduates are all impatient to rejoin their families and friends. I must therefore ruthlessly oversimplify and try to say in ten minutes what the Church has spent two thousand years learning.

The first thing the Christians learned under this heading was to cherish the Kingdom of God and other-worldly values above anything on earth. That much is clear. Their chief business was not in university or market place or conquering army or imperial court; it was in the Father's house, concerned with the Father's business. They were to keep minds and hearts turned toward the Lord Jesus, and wait for his coming in the clouds with power and majesty. As a result of this emphasis, they were simply not interested in this world, in its culture and civilization, its arts and sciences, its commerce and government, its loves and wars and games and amusements. There was a whole great world of humanism at their doorstep, but they had forsaken the world. They lived an idyllic existence in their own little paradise at Jerusalem; as Luke the historian reconstructs the scene: "All whose faith had drawn them together held everything in common. . . . With one mind they kept up their daily attendance at the temple, and, breaking bread in private houses, shared their meals with unaffected joy . . ." (Acts 2:44–46). Even their ethic was strongly other-worldly. Paul the apostle, writing around the year 56, is emphatic on that: "The time we live in will not last long. While it lasts, married men should be as if they had no wives; mourners should be as if they had nothing to grieve them . . . buyers must not count on keeping what they buy. . . . For the whole frame of this world is passing away" (1 Cor 7:29–31).

I called this existence idyllic. It is stretching the use of the word a bit to apply it to an urban setting, but otherwise it is a useful label; it suggests the peace and contentment, something of the withdrawal from harsh reality, that we associate with the pastoral character of an idyll. It was in fact too idyllic to last. That is not to condemn the positive values it enshrines; it is merely to recognize its deficiencies; it is one-sided; it is indeed a retreat from reality; it includes a wide measure of oversight. The early Christians were not wrong in the value they set on the Lord Jesus and on the life to come. Our faith today rests on their experience of the risen Lord as on a rock: "[I]f Christ was not raised, then our gospel is null and void, and so is your faith; and we turn out to be lying witnesses for God" (1 Cor 15:14–15). But they were so preoccupied with the life to come as to pay little attention to the life they had. They were not wrong in holding fast to their other-worldly faith, or preferring it to a humanism entirely of this world; but they had not yet learned to combine the two, to live in the world and share the world's values, while yet setting those values in their true perspective in relation to the eternal.

The next step then was for the Church to turn toward the world. The causes of this shift in attitude are complex. Partly it was the delay in the return of the Lord which taught and prepared them to settle in for a longer stay in the world than they had at first expected. Partly it may have been simply the spontaneous force of reflection on the Christian mysteries and the implications of words of the Lord recorded in their memories but not fully understood. The immediate occasion seems to have been a persecution that drove the Christians out among the gentiles and trained them to adapt themselves to gentile ways. At any rate the Church went out into the world. It was a fateful movement; it would accelerate till the next swing of the pendulum long afterward toward the close of the Middle Ages. The trend is already observable in the New Testament itself, but we have only the beginning there of over a thousand years of history as the Church moved to establish herself and assume a place in the world.

Here the opposition of Tertullian and Clement begins to make sense and fit into a moving pattern. Tertullian represents loyalty to the values of the Jerusalem community; Clement represents the dynamism of progress. Tertullian is with us still and, please God, on his positive side will be with us always; but on his negative side he is his own best refutation: the very culture he repudiated helped make him the theologian he was. In any case the swing of the pendulum was with Clement. The cumulative trend of the next twelve or thirteen centuries was simply a working out of his principles on the Church in the world of man.

Politically you could trace the story from the time of the apologists in the second century: they issued a plea to the Roman emperors for mere tolerance, just for the right really to live as second-class citizens. But a hundred and fifty years later the emperor himself joins the new religion and gives it favored status in the empire. At the end of the fourth century another emperor makes Christianity the established religion and outlaws paganism. Around the year 800 the Pope is crowning the head of the Holy Roman Empire in Rome, and in another three centuries we have the situation of the Middle Ages described by Yves Congar: Europe is one vast monastery in which the Pope rules as abbot.

The cultural trend is parallel to the political. The movement initiated by Clement began by borrowing from the culture of the Greeks; it ended with the Church pretty much in full control of all culture and civilization. Not only higher culture—literature, music, painting, sculpture, architecture, the grammar and logic and philosophy of the schools—but the various facets of everyday life, everything from forge to bakery, from commerce to war, all were subordinated to the Church and expected to serve her purpose.

To many this has seemed the perfect picture. They have slogans to proclaim it: "The thirteenth the greatest of centuries." "The Faith is Europe, Europe is the Faith." But the slogans are too facile. History does not stand still; not even the Middle Ages had said the last word on the relation of Christianity to the world of man. If we can describe the first state of the Church as idyllic, perhaps we can describe this second state as utopian. I use the word to indicate a more reflective and systematic effort to build one city of God and man, but also to suggest that the plan was too *a priori*. Again, there were great positive values embodied in the structure of the Middle Ages; there was a recognition that the Church belongs in this world, in the marketplace as well as in the imperial courts, in the home as well as in the university, in the arts as well as in the sciences. But again I think there was a grave defect; we had still a great deal to learn, and this time it was the legitimate autonomy of the human, the natural, the whole range of human institutions.

What do I mean by that? I mean that things have a value in themselves; human achievements are not merely means to a higher end. The arts do not exist simply to decorate sacred functions. The study of languages and philosophy is not undertaken solely for the exposition of scripture. Secondly, if the world has a value in itself, it also has a measure of autonomy, a limited measure to be sure, but still a measure. That is to say, the multiplication table is independent of the decrees of an ecumenical council; the problems of astronomy are not solved by looking up the Bible. Not to recognize this is theological imperialism, and no matter how paternal such imperialism is, it does not correspond to the mind and will of God for his creation.

Imperialism leads inevitably to rebellion. Where the first idyllic state at Jerusalem had been disrupted, in part at least, by persecution from without, the second utopian state of the Middle Ages was overthrown by rebellion from within. I do not mean just the religious rebellion of the Reformers, though that may be a related phenomenon. I mean rather the general movement of self-assertion and revolution all along the line. Philosophy refused to be any longer simply the handmaid of theology; the arts asserted their independence of sacred functions, to develop rather according to their own inner dynamic; nations repudiated the hegemony of a sacred rule in Rome. It is a rebellion of the whole phalanx of this world's values.

It has not been easy for us to learn the lesson of this rebellion. We were reactionary: as Tertullian was a reactionary in the Patristic age, so there has been a series of reactionaries for five or six centuries of the modern era. It is a long story and a sad one, and I need not go through it. In any case I think we have finally learned the lesson. With the Second Vatican Council we turned back to the world and took a tentative step again toward it. The longest, the most unexpected, and to my mind the most important document of that Council is called *The Pastoral Constitution on the Church in the Modern World*; it deals with society, with marriage and the family, with economic and social life, with the political community. You might say it deals by implication with arts and sciences, education, commerce and engineering. And now the attitude is not reactionary; it is positive. The Church opens her heart to the good in the world; she would join forces with it in humility.

The very beginning of the document is significant: "The joys and the hopes, the griefs and the anxieties of the men of this age, especially those who are poor or in any way afflicted, these too are the joys and hopes, the griefs and anxieties of the followers of Christ. Indeed nothing genuinely human fails to raise an echo in their hearts."[5]

This is not to say that the Church had previously despised the human; it is not to say that we now approve of all the elements in the rebellion of humanism. But I do think we have in this document a humbler attitude, a greater respect for the value of the human in God's plan, the abandonment of ecclesiastical imperialism over the human, the recognition of its limited but legitimate area of autonomy, and most of all a desire to cooperate with the world of man for his own best interests.

To desire cooperation and to implement the desire are two different things, and I would say that the implementation is your task, that of the new generation of Christian scholars and professional men and women. Vatican II did not give us a new way of life to replace the Ancient or the Medieval; it simply liberated us from undue attachment to a way that is now gone. I have not given you a blueprint on the way of the future, but simply tried to give you a better perspective on the past, to see it as movement, as the learning process in which the Church is involved. I have not therefore answered the question with which I began this talk, how to build Jerusalem at the heart of Athens. It really was a question and not just a rhetorical device; it remains a question for me; I pass it on to you of the next generation.

You yourself then will have to build the new city of God and man. It will not be a Jerusalem indifferent to the world of men. It will not be an Athens indifferent to the plan of God. It will not be the Medieval domination of all areas by the Church. Nor will it be the subsequent rebellion of the world of man against all that the Church stood for. It will be your own way, your own postmodern way, to be found with patience and reflection, maybe not without prayer and fasting. And when you have discovered what it is to be the Church in the postmodern world, you will have found also what it is to be a Christian university, and what it means to a career in arts, science, education, commerce, or engineering, to graduate from a Christian university. It is a tremendous challenge, a fascinating task, a most excellent opportunity—I run out of adjectives; let me simply say in biblical language that it is your *kairos*.

My concluding word is one of great personal hope and optimism. I think the ideas are at hand that are the tools with which to build the

5. In *The Documents of Vatican II*, ed. W. Abbott & J. Gallagher (New York: Guild, 1966), pp. 199–200.

new Christian university. We have discovered, for example, that universities are not mainly books and courses, but people; and people are existentially involved in hopes and fears, in sin and grace and forgiveness, in resolution and serenity. Besides the cold austerity of mathematics, there is the warm subjectivity of the mathematician. A proof for the existence of God is not just an exercise in philosophy, it is also a personal journey of the philosopher himself. Moreover, people live by meaning, and meaning expands enormously from level to level, as when biology is put in the context of the human, and the human in the context of a destiny to be more than human. Finally, it is fundamentally values that are the basis of meaning. Universities once tried to be value-free, but the attempt was a contradiction in itself; to choose to be value-free is to make that your value and in so doing to have chosen an inferior value. It is in the values it seeks and creates and criticizes and establishes, perhaps more in them than in any other way, that a university is Christian.

But that will be a new chapter in the history of the Christian university; it will be today's graduates, you who have today received your degrees from Saint Mary's University, you are the ones who will write it.

II

The Responsibility of the Theologian, and the Learning Church*

I

The topic on which I was invited and on which I agreed to speak was conscience, and specifically, conscience in regard to the encyclical *Humanae vitae*.[1] Nevertheless, the course of my reflections as I prepared the paper led me somewhat away from that pair of terms, and I am therefore going to take certain liberties with my assignment. I will speak regularly of responsibility rather than of conscience, and I will talk of responsibility to the ongoing Church rather than about responsibility in regard to the encyclical itself. I do intend to speak of the theologian's responsibility, but that is to retain only one of the three terms in the original assignment. So before you conclude that a theologian with so little conscience and responsibility is not to be listened to at all, I must try to explain and justify my alterations in the contract.

I prefer "responsibility," then, as pointing a little more directly to the personal involvement and intervention of the theologian. Conscience is surely the activity of the subject, it is surely personal, but it can refer to a general question on which we form a common moral judgment, though we may be called upon, as responsible persons, to take varying action. Thus, several men may be conscientious objectors to military service, but the responsibilities of a congressman and those of a drafted student are hardly the same; they differ according to the

---

*A paper given at the seventh biennial Pastoral Psychology Institute, Fordham University, 16–20 June 1969, under the title "The Conscience of the Theologian with Reference to the Encyclical." The general theme of this interdisciplinary institute was "Conscience: Its Freedom and Limitations"; the special theme of one of its eight sections was "Conscience and the Encyclical *Humanae vitae*"; and this paper was one of the five presented in that section. Previously published (under the original title, and with minor differences from the present version) in *Conscience: Its Freedom and Limitations*, ed. W. C. Bier (New York: Fordham University, 1971), pp. 312–32.

1. Paul VI, *Humanae vitae*, encyclical letter of 25 July 1968, *Acta apostolicae sedis* 60 (1968), pp. 481–503. English translation: "Human Life," *Catholic Mind* 66/9 (September, 1968), pp. 35–48.

possibilities of action afforded. To take an illustration from the topic in hand: the conscience of the 87 theologians who issued a statement on *Humanae vitae* on 30 July 1968 may have been quite the same as mine in regard to the common object, the binding force of the encyclical; but their responsibility was to take the lead in issuing a statement, while mine was the more commonplace one of subscribing to the statement.

In other words, "conscience" seems to refer more directly to *the object*, while "responsibility" seems to refer more directly to *me* and to what I should do. The difference between the two is slight; it is a matter of where the emphasis more *directly* falls; but I think it makes the change worthwhile. There is a principle of maximum concreteness involved, of what I can and ought to do within the limits of my situation. Jesus died for all men, but he could not preach to and teach all men; his responsibility for preaching and teaching was limited to the house of Israel.

The same principle of maximum concreteness is involved in my second change in the assigned topic. The situation in the Church is such today that to *talk about* responsibility is also an *exercise in* responsibility. We are not dealing with matters of merely archeological interest, but with matters of vital concern to the Church. I mean the whole Church, married or single, lay or clerical, the non-theologian as well as the theologian. For it is not really a matter any longer of what Christian married life should be; it is a matter of what the Church is to be, of how we are to exercise judgment in the Church and determine our practice. If I am to exercise my responsibility with the utmost concreteness in that situation, I must speak to the ongoing Church of today, not to the Church of last year. I will indeed say a word on the conscience and responsibility of the theologian in regard to *Humanae vitae* itself, but only to set that topic aside with all possible brevity.

The conscience of the theologian in regard to *Humanae vitae* can be simply described somewhat as follows: the encyclical is the pronouncement of the Holy Father, so the theologian will regard it with respect and study it with due care. It is not an infallible pronouncement; non-infallible pronouncements are fallible, so the theologian will not give it unconditional assent on the basis of authority alone, but is obliged to weigh the arguments provided. If his unconditional assent is not required, neither is his absolute obedience. Given sufficient reason, he may dissent; in fact, the reasons are at hand. All these headings could be expanded and, according to the makeup of the audience, ought to be expanded, but I really do not think that this audience would wish me to delay any longer on what must be obvious to all of us.

The responsibility of the theologian a year ago is a more interesting topic and I will stay a moment on that. I should say, then, that last year the pressing responsibility of the theologian was to the people of God, especially to the "poor" among them—that is, to the uninstructed, the bewildered, the heavy-burdened. A theologian, of course, has various responsibilities to different persons in regard to different values; he has a responsibility to the Holy Father, to his bishop or religious superior, to his fellow-theologians, to his students; he has a responsibility in regard to truth, in regard to understanding, in regard to communication, and so forth. But needs have an order of priority, and so have responsibilities. The need a year ago was the need of husbands and wives to know the options open to them in married life. This came out with great clarity in a meeting of the Société Canadienne de Théologie held in Montreal on 21 September 1968. In an unofficial report of the meeting,[2] requested by the theological commission of the Canadian Conference of Bishops, it is stated that the right of the poor—i.e., of those not well instructed—to know the whole truth of the matter, was one of the central concerns of the meeting. The theologians present found it unjust and monstrous that better educated persons could profit from the state of doubt in the Church, if the poor were to have a burden imposed without explanation of the whole question of morality and contraceptives.

If the articulation of the need is clear in that statement, the intervention demanded by responsibility was swiftest, most dramatic, and most widely effective in the statement of the 87 theologians issued in Washington, D.C. the day after the encyclical was published. The three final paragraphs of their statement give the Church teaching, a statement of conscience, the conclusion of the theologians about their own responsibility.

It is common teaching in the Church that Catholics may dissent from authoritative, non-infallible teachings of the magisterium when sufficient reasons for so doing exist.

Therefore, as Roman Catholic theologians, conscious of our duty and our limitations, we conclude that spouses may responsibly decide according to their conscience that artificial contraception in some circumstances is permissible and indeed necessary to preserve and foster the values and sacredness of marriage.

It is our conviction also that true commitment to the mystery of Christ and the Church requires a candid statement of mind at this time by all Catholic theologians.[3]

It is just because of such candid statements as this that the theologian's

---

2. Unpublished document: L'Encyclique 'Humanae vitae' et la théologie. Rapport . . . non officiel sur la rencontre organisée par la Société Canadienne de Théologie. . . . le 21 septembre, 1968.

3. Washington, D.C., Theologians, "Statement on the Encyclical *Humanae vitae,*" *Catholic Mind* 66/9 (September, 1968), pp. 2–4.

responsibility in regard to *Humanae vitae* can be discussed as an historical question. That is, the responsibility the time called for was discharged. In a similar way the question of conscience has been settled; it was settled within a few weeks of the encyclical's appearance, maybe even a few days. By and large the Catholic world became aware of the options open to it. Its conscience can be regarded as formed. At least, there is the possibility of forming one's conscience in peace. Too many serious believers have assumed as permissible, even obligatory, a practice contrary to that enjoined by the encyclical; too many moderate, obedient theologians have defended the right to dissent; too many episcopal conferences have spoken, respectfully but clearly, on the rights of conscience. The question is no longer a question, and ten thousand headlines in *L'Osservatore Romano* cannot change facts that are now common property.

I do not mean to overlook the continuing need of the people for instruction and support; our responsibility toward them remains. Again, I am not insensitive to the deep feelings that have been aroused in the Church; we have still to remember the saying "Blessed are the peacemakers." But the indicated responsibilities are not especially those of a pastoral psychology institute. Yet again, we do not know what suffering is in store for dissenters; it may be that things will get worse before they get better; so be it then.[4] But I refuse to be gloomy.

If this paper, then, is to be not merely *about* responsibility, but also an *exercise in* responsibility, it must regard the present situation and attempt a contribution to the ongoing Church. To my mind we are in a new situation; we are not the Church we were a year ago; there is a new spirit at work; we have a new awareness of our co-responsibility; God has taught us new ways of living as his people; he has sanctioned a new respect for pluralism, and brought more clearly to our attention the legitimacy of dissent within his Church. All this I assume as fact, and I consider it the responsibility of a theologian to try to explain that fact. Our responsibility is to go to the heart of the matter, to what was really involved in the chapter of history just concluded, to teach the deeper truths that will guide the long-range development of the Church's life. It is a matter of analyzing the new situation and of trying to indicate a style of life, a *modus vivendi,* principles of conduct, that suit our new assumption of responsibility. We have to develop a way that combines loyalty with criticism, obedience with dissent, unity with differences of opinion frankly expressed in dialogue. It is a matter really

---

4. This paper was already written when I realized my one-sided concern for fellow theologians, my failure in responsibility toward confessors disciplined by authority for their stand on the encyclical. They were the vulnerable ones; what have we theologians done in their cause? At this point I can only confess my personal negligence.

of a new self-knowledge, a knowledge of what man is and how his mind works. The theologian's responsibility is to articulate this. It is more directly theological, then, than pastoral, but perhaps it is the best way he can proceed at the moment toward pastoral goals.

A significant step in the direction of a theology of dissent has already been taken in the brief submitted by twenty professors of The Catholic University of America who were subject by the mandate of the University trustees to a faculty inquiry into their stand on the encyclical. Part One of their submission is entitled: "On the Responsible Exercise of the Role of the Theologian in the Church in General, and on a Responsible Exercise of This Role in Regard to the Encyclical *Humanae vitae* in Particular." It is a theological document of high order, calm and dispassionate, historical and systematic at the same time. It justifies dissent from non-infallible teaching in the Church with strict reliance both on historical precedent and on principles of Catholic doctrine. There is a noteworthy contribution to the analysis of the historical situation and to the lines theological understanding must take to be at the service of the Church of the future.

The document is perhaps known to many of you already.[5] I do not propose simply to repeat what has already been well done by the theologians involved. What I wish to do is proceed from one theme they introduced to further and more detailed analysis. The document again and again refers to the need of dialogue in the Church today. Why this need of dialogue? It is true that a spirit of courtesy and fellowship will suggest a degree of dialogue corresponding to the social situation and the modern facility in communications, but in my view more fundamental issues are involved than those of the ethics of democracy. We can appeal to the fact of the pluralist world in which we live and to the need we have for remaining open to one another, but that only brings up the further question why it should be a pluralist world, and I would answer that in the same way as the question "Why dialogue?"

My contention will be that the very nature of human truth and of the process by which the human mind reaches truth requires dialogue; in all but the simplest truths we simply cannot judge without dialogue. This is surely not an earth-shaking stand to take, but I think it is important to relate my contention to fairly basic ideas of cognitional theory and epistemology, and to apply those ideas to the process by which the learning Church too arrives at truth. We have passed very swiftly from practical questions of great and immediate moment to

5. This brief has now been published under the title *Dissent in and for the Church: Theologians and 'Humanae vitae,'* by Charles E. Curran, Robert E. Hunt and the "Subject Professors," with John F. Hunt and Terrence R. Connelly (New York: Sheed & Ward, 1969).

abstract questions that directly interest only philosopher-theologians. The catch, of course, is in the word "directly." I consider that these "abstract" questions underlie the immediate question and must be solved if we are to have serenity in the Church of God.

My responsibility today, as I see it, is to help you learn what learning is, and through helping you to help the learning Church learn what learning is. That is, in speaking to you I am speaking to as much of the learning Church as I can reach at the moment, and I will try to show that, just because of what our minds are and because of the one route they have to truth and being, our learning is not a matter of looking or deducing, though each has its place, but a matter of dialectical process, necessarily involving dialogue. First, I will expose the philosophical ideas we need, trusting that I have not completely misread the philosophers I will be quoting, and then I will proceed to the learning process in the Church.

II

"Dialectic" is a word with many meanings, some of them distinctly pejorative.[6] The sense that is common in philosophy today goes back to Heraclitus and his "War is the father of all," but received elaborate formulation and impetus from Hegel; it refers to "the passing over of thoughts or concepts into their opposites and the achievement of a higher unity."[7] Hegel's special contribution was the view that the dialectical process is a necessary law, and this both for mind and for reality. "The contradictions in thought, nature, and society, even though they are not contradictions in formal logic but conceptual inadequacies, were regarded by Hegel as leading by a kind of necessity, to a further phase of development."[8] In illustration: The notion of being leads to the notion of nothing, and the contradiction in turn to the notion of becoming; in nature, space completes itself in time, and space and time lead to motion and matter; in society, self-consciousness depends on acknowledgment of the other, and is first established through the master-slave relationship—but this only brings into the open the reduced self-consciousness of the slave, and both are finally superseded by the higher attitude of Stoical consciousness that disdains the master-slave distinction.[9]

Now, there is no use denying the fact that the pejorative senses of

6. R. Hall, "Dialectic," in P. Edwards, ed., *The Encyclopedia of Philosophy* (New York: Macmillan & Free Press, 1967), vol. 2, p. 385.

7. Ibid., p. 388.   8. Ibid.

9. J. N. Findlay, *Hegel: A Re-Examination* (London: Allen & Unwin, 1958), pp. 97–99, 153–59, 274–77.

dialectic are well deserved. Dialectic has been abused notably by the Sophists who developed specious reasoning for unworthy purposes. Even philosophers have exaggerated the uses of the method; we instinctively react when we see it set forth in a way that denies the principle of non-contradiction. (Incidentally, some students of Hegel absolve him from such a use of the doctrine.) We are too well aware that two contradictory statements cannot both be true; as a matter of fact even the radicals of dialectical thought are witnesses to that impossibility, maybe not in their professed principles, but certainly in their practice. You may have noticed that opponents of the principle of non-contradiction can become as annoyed as anyone else when they are contradicted; try it and see.

But the use of dialectic need not be exaggerated; we can give the term Lonergan's definition—"a concrete unfolding of linked but opposed principles of change"[10]—and find it quite acceptable. Then the word means progress by means of opposition. In the sphere of living, there is Lonergan's example of the law of the cross: Christ, by accepting in love and obedience the evil of passion and death, transformed it into good.[11] In the sphere of thought, the word means the progress of thought by means of opposition; it means thought that is dynamic, always on the go—not, however, in a logical and deductive manner, but in a way that involves alternations and antithetical statements, reconciliations, and eliminations. Dialectic, then, is opposed to deduction. In deduction we proceed from known premises, but in dialectic we do not yet know—we are only on the way to knowing.

My first proposition is that the dialectical process corresponds to the way the human mind must work to reach truth and being: in simpler terms, to know the facts. In primitive man, knowing is largely a matter of seeing and hearing, and in this stage the thinking process is limited to myth-making. A more developed stage occurs with the pre-Socratics, "those Greek thinkers from approximately 600 to 400 B.C. who attempted to find universal principles which would explain the whole of nature";[12] now myths are overcome and so is the merely practical orientation of knowledge, but the thinking process is limited to deduction. Dialectic is a third stage; we discover, with Socrates, that truth is not in our possession; it is something to be achieved. You will have noticed that the emphases of the three stages correspond roughly to Lonergan's three levels of cognitional activity: experience, understanding, and judgment.[13] Primitive man is almost confined to experience, the pre-

10. *Insight: A Study of Human Understanding*, p. 217.

11. *De verbo incarnato*, p. 556.

12. W. K. C. Guthrie, "Pre-Socratic Philosophy," in *The Encyclopedia of Philosophy*, vol. 6, p. 441.

13. *Insight*, passim.

Socratics were largely confined to the level of understanding (more accurately, to its conceptual products); modern man is concerned to verify, to reach the truth, to form a correct judgment. But he reaches truth only through a process, and the process is dialectical.

For that reason the work of Newman is now fundamental. Let us then skip over the Cartesian search for a certitude based on the indubitable fact of my thinking, the radical empiricism that then reduced ideas to sensations, and Kant's tremendous effort to certify scientific knowledge by studying the conditions of its possibility, down to John Henry Newman and *An Essay in Aid of a Grammar of Assent*. Newman has no objection to deductive processes in their place. But his concern, as he repeatedly tells us, is with judgment in "concrete matter."[14] "Inference comes short of proof in concrete matters, because it has not a full command over the objects to which it relates, but merely assumes its premisses."[15] Hence it is ". . . the main position of this Section, the Inference . . . determines neither our principles, nor our ultimate judgments,—that it is neither the test of truth, nor the adequate basis of assent."[16]

What, then, is Newman's basis for judgment?

It is plain that formal logical sequence is not in fact the method by which we are enabled to become certain of what is concrete; and it is equally plain, from what has been already suggested, what the real and necessary method is. It is the cumulation of probabilities, independent of each other, arising out of the nature and circumstances of the particular case which is under review; probabilities too fine to avail separately, too subtle and circuitous to be convertible into syllogisms, too numerous and various for such conversion, even were they convertible.[17]

Later Newman illustrates the process by the mathematical procedure of tending to a limit:

We know that a regular polygon, inscribed in a circle, its sides being continually diminished, tends to become that circle, as its limit; but it vanishes before it has coincided with the circle. . . . In like manner, the conclusion in a real or concrete question is foreseen and predicted rather than actually attained; foreseen in the number and direction of accumulated premisses, which all converge to it . . . yet do not touch it logically. . . . It is by the strength, variety, or multiplicity of premisses, which are only probable, not by invincible syllogisms,—by objections overcome, by adverse theories neutralized, by difficulties gradually clearing up, by exceptions proving the rule, by unlooked-for correlations found with received truths, by suspense and delay in the process issuing in triumphant reactions,—by all these ways, and many others, it is that the

14. *An Essay in Aid of a Grammar of Assent* (London: Longmans, Green, 1930 [1870]), pp. 7, 8, 269, 277, 284, 288, 360, 410–11, and passim.

15. Ibid., p. 269.   16. Ibid., p. 287.

17. Ibid., p. 288.

practised and experienced mind is able to make a sure divination that a conclusion is inevitable, of which his lines of reasoning do not actually put him in
possession.[18]

I am not saying that Newman gave us the last word on the question.
His very expressions are troublesome, his use of the term "probability"
obscuring his stress on the unconditional character of assent. More
fundamentally: his distinction between real and notional apprehension
is defective; what he lacks on this level is the Augustinian-Thomist
procession of concept from understanding. When he transfers his distinction to the level of judgment a still more radical defect shows up:
he has no view of being which would enable him to distinguish clearly
the object of thought from the object of judgment, and to eliminate
the confusion of his notional assent. Thus, only once in the whole
Grammar have I noticed any emphasis on the word "is."[19] What he
excelled in doing, and what by his own insistence was all he intended
to do,[20] was to describe the process that he actually found operative in
the act of assent.

Still, he was the great pioneer in a view of how the human mind
works when it is reaching out for truth—when it is learning, trying to
form a correct judgment. Others have completed his work; the fuller
view of cognitional structure, the epistemology and ontology that Newman lacked—all this has been supplied by Lonergan in his equally
pioneering work, *Insight*. The dynamism of mind oriented to truth and
being gives the basis of an epistemology; the distinction between understanding and concept shows why Newman was so concerned with images; the distinction of animal and human realism illuminates an
obscurity in the relation of Newman's image to reality, and so forth.
Some day a study should be made of Lonergan's relation to Newman,
but this is not the place for it.

We are at the very heart of epistemology here, and I have no intention
of providing a treatise on the subject. But I have to try to clarify that
characteristic of judgment which imposes the dialectical approach to
truth on the human mind—namely, that judgment is not a matter of
looking or deducing, just as being is not something sitting there to be
looked at or making itself felt by its influence; it is a matter of approaching the unconditional through conditions fulfilled, just as being
occurs contingently through a concatenation of causes.

I think the simplest device is to call your attention to your use of the
word "is," or of its equivalent in the word "yes," or if you like, in the
nod of the head that is a sign of assent. I think it will be generally

18. Ibid., pp. 320–21.   19. Ibid., p. 93.
20. Ibid., pp. 64, 160.

agreed that a dog, however "intelligent" he may be, is hardly capable of uttering "is" or "yes" or of nodding his head in affirmative response to a question for reflection—from which we may conclude that "is" is not the object of an ocular look. But we might then ask whether it is the object of any kind of look. Is there any way of pointing to its objective referent? If a child asks me what "red" is, I can point to the colors of the spectrum, naming each as I point, and he will get the idea: how I use the word "red." Later he will want to understand not only the world of human language but the physical world as well, and again I will point to charts and diagrams so that he may get the idea. But I am pointing to data that are the matrix of an idea; where do I point to demonstrate "is"? To point to a tree, a bird, a man, naming them in turn, may give the idea of tree-ness, bird-ness, man-ness, but hardly the notion of is-ness.

Have we an intellectual intuition of "is"? Some famous men have thought so, but have had difficulty convincing the philosophical world of their position. I myself would say that their position is refuted by the painstaking description Newman undertook of what actually happens when we say "yes"—or, in his words, give assent. And I would say that a view of being arises on the experience of the question for reflection "Is it so?" and the dynamism that not only will not allow "yes" and "no" together, but keeps us on the move till we are able to pronounce one or the other.

But I am not really trying at the moment to prove a position that may be settled only after a few centuries of philosophical reflection. I am maintaining that this view explains why dialectic is a necessary approach to truth, and dialogue is necessary in any community. If you are willing to accept my epistemology provisionally, I think you will see the relevance of Newman to the present question. It is true that he put at the head of his *Grammar* a quotation from St. Ambrose: "Non in dialecticâ complacuit Deo salvum facere populum suum"—but that refers to a pejorative sense of dialectic. His own process of reaching assent is remarkably like the acceptable sense of the word: "by objections overcome, by adverse theories neutralized, by difficulties gradually clearing up, by exceptions proving the rule, by unlooked-for correlations found with received truths, by suspense and delay in the process issuing in triumphant reactions. . ."[21]—what is all this but the dialectic that modern philosophers talk about? His own favorite example[22] of the truth, Great Britain is an island, supplies further evidence. How do you justify your assent to that proposition? You consider various ideas:

21. Ibid., p. 321.
22. Ibid., pp. 189, 190, 195, 198, 212–13, 294–96, 318.

island, peninsula, continental tract. You make various contrary deductions: If an island, then. . . . But, if part of the continent, then. . . . You reject certain ideas by a *reductio ad absurdum*. And so forth.

What I am saying is this: being is not there like a visible object to be looked at with the eyes, not even with the "eyes" of the mind, and truth is not a matter of letting things appear, even to intellectual intuition. Truth has to be won; it is an achievement. Further, it is not in the general case won by deduction, but by a dialectical process. Newman lists the sequential conjunctions as signs of inference: for, therefore, similarly, and so on.[23] We might list the adversatives as signs of dialectic: but, however, on the one hand . . . on the other. Finally, when the set of ideas is sufficiently clarified, we can put the question "Yes or No?" Between "Yes" and "No" with regard to a determinate question on determinate being, *non datur tertium*; that is true, but on the way, there is not only a *tertium*, but a *quartum*, and an indefinite number of possibilities. Further, when we reach "Yes," it is not because it loomed out of the darkness, letting itself appear; it is not because it clicked into place with the last movement of a logic-machine; it is because we have reached the unconditional toward which the fulfilled conditions converge much as the polygon converges with the circle.

My next proposition is that the necessity of dialogue[24] results from the dialectical process by which truth is won. Truth, in all but the most elementary instances, is not won except by the encounter of many opposing viewpoints, and many opposing viewpoints are not provided except by many persons. I do not deny the role of prophets, of what we would call "men of judgment," but even they utter their words of wisdom on the basis of many contributions. This results, I say, from the dialectical approach that Newman describes. Thus, the datum one man overlooks or forgets, another adverts to. The ideas and possible explanations that do not occur to one will occur to others. The questions that never stir a lazy mind will puzzle the alert, yet perhaps the indolent will foresee practical difficulties to which the more energetic are blind. Implications that escape the dreamer will be drawn out by the logical. Areas of application that are irrelevant to a whole group will deeply concern the stranger. Where one man's temperament inclines him to a too hasty termination of reflection, a more scrupulous type will prolong objections and doubts. And so forth.

There is an extremely simple index of this need of dialogue: the number of opinions we require in order to trust a verdict. As adversatives are the sign of dialectic, so the requirement of numbers is a sign

23. Ibid., p. 263.
24. The common root suggests an intrinsic link between dialectic and dialogue, but they have become differentiated as two functions in the cognitional process.

of the dialogic factor involved in reliable opinion. But do not reduce my statement to the easily ridiculed position that right and wrong are a matter of counting noses. Advert rather to the fact that in processes of criminal law the judgment of guilt may be committed to as many as twelve persons. What is the implication of this fact? In the U.S. Supreme Court we may have as many as nine persons sitting in judgment. Committees are formed of several members. Various speakers are invited to an institute like the one we are attending. Peter Berger remarks: "One of the fundamental propositions of the sociology of knowledge is that the plausibility, in the sense of what people actually find credible, of views of reality depends upon the social support these receive."[25] Is this a mere gregarious dependence on the crowd? I think not; I believe it rests upon a profound though inarticulate understanding of the working of the human mind. As Bernard Lonergan says: "In its judgments . . . common sense tends to be profoundly sane."[26] As a movie title had it many years ago: "Fifty Million Frenchmen Can't Be Wrong." And, to make the story a little shorter, we believe in universal suffrage, trusting that in the long run the judgment of the people will be better than that of a dictator. If it is not enough for certainty, well, at least it will provide a fairly safe working hypothesis.

Of course, that last remark brings us face to face with the fact that for a while, maybe a long while, we can all be wrong. A whole country can commit great stupidities at the polls. Fifty million Frenchmen *can* be wrong. There is also the fact that the judgment of one expert may be worth the judgment of a thousand novices. The question of numbers is not simple; there is a sliding scale. But the main point is beyond question: we judge safely in the long run when we judge together, and that accords perfectly with the nature of judgment as I have outlined it. If judgment were a matter of looking, one good looker would suffice, and certainly two or three witnesses would be quite adequate. If judgment were a matter of making deductions from premises, then one keen logician would suffice: better still, a logic-machine, especially if the moving parts are kept well-oiled. But, if judgment is the kind of process that Newman and Lonergan describe, then a wide spectrum of questions, ideas, objections, counter-objections, opinions, is necessary. It is not a matter of dividing work; often, as in a jury, the number merely multiplies the work; it is a matter of dialectic and dialogue.

We should not ignore the problem of defining what we mean by men of judgment, and of determining in the concrete case who or of what type the men of judgment are. You recognize the delicacy of the task,

25. *A Rumor of Angels: Modern Society and the Rediscovery of the Supernatural* (Garden City, NY: Doubleday, 1969), pp. 42–43.
26. *Insight*, p. 242.

given the famous proverb that everyone complains of his memory and no one of his judgment. We expect "experts" to be men of judgment in their field, yet we repeatedly find the "experts" disagreeing with one another—in our courts of law, in our civil service, and the like. We have plenty of examples too of men who exercise judgment very well in their business, and are complete fools in love or sport or politics or war. Again, the seniors of the community used to be regarded, with reason, as the men of judgment; Aristotle explained this as the result of experience, Newman[27] agreed, and common sense in general approved. But today there is a new proverb: "Don't trust anyone over thirty."

The confusion, however, is not total. The point is that judgment requires a mastery of the whole of the data; one's insight has to be invulnerable. In a developing science, the experts are ahead of the rest of us but are far from having reached mastery; their judgment consequently is insecure. In an age of transition, the old standards which the experience of years once taught have no longer the same validity; the elders must learn along with the youngers, and so judgment is not so patently on their side. But all this only illustrates more graphically the dialectical process by which we reach judgment. It does not mean that judgment is gone from the earth. There are still the basic human factors, the *existentialia,* in which common sense—that is, the judgment of men everywhere—is "profoundly sane"; a long life still gives one a wiser judgment, provided one has not arrested the learning process at thirty.

III

What I have been saying about the nature of judgment and the dialectic by which we come to know is to be applied now, *mutatis mutandis,* to the judgments we make in the Church as we gradually achieve truths we had not previously formulated. There is a basic supposition here which I notice briefly: we are an *inquiring* Church. God may have said all he is going to say on earth, but we have certainly not got all he said into our possession in the form of explicit articles of faith, and so we are in the position of Socrates who did not have truth at his disposal but had to learn. The Church is a learning Church; the *whole* Church is a learning Church. This was as clear as crystal to Origen seventeen centuries ago, when he drew up at the beginning of his *First Principles* a list of the truths given in plain terms by the apostles, and the questions they did not settle but left for us to investigate.[28] It ought to be clear

27. *Grammar,* p. 341.
28. *On First Principles,* tr. G. W. Butterworth (London: SPCK, 1936), pp. 1–6.

to all of us now, over a century after Newman's work on development. It is of very special moment just in this present period of confused stirring.

Given this learning situation, the present concern is to notice that in the Church too investigation proceeds dialectically. Certainly, truths of faith are not to be had by any act of looking, ocular or intellectual. But in the general case they are not to be had by deductions either. Deduction works when there are given terms which can function as premises. But the characteristic of *development*, of significant development as we understand it now, is just that the terms are not given; they are new; we ask questions our fathers could not understand at all. Hence deduction does not work. What does work is the antithesis of ideas, the slow clarification of the question, the gradual elimination of impossible answers—in short, the dialectical process.

The best way to see this is in a concrete example. One classic example is the development of trinitarian theology, and the finest exposition of this that I know is in Lonergan.[29] It runs through more than a hundred pages of packed Latin, some of it to be found in more readable form in the second chapter of John Courtney Murray,[30] but much of it still in the original Latin. What emerges from this study is the dialectical aspect of the two-hundred year struggle (roughly from AD 180 to 380) to formulate the basic trinitarian dogma. A deductivist mentality sees only the opposition between orthodoxy, true to its apostolic premises, and heterodoxy, in the mystery of iniquity abandoning those premises. But the dialectical mentality sees Praxeas trying to do justice to the one God of faith but unable to do justice to the data on the distinct reality of Son and Spirit; Tertullian correcting Praxeas but failing to escape a materialistic view of the three; Origen overcoming Tertullian's materialism but faltering at the idea of equality; Arius carrying Origen's trend to a logical conclusion and being rejected by the Council of Nicea; the Nicene definition itself giving rise to objections that can be met only after the patient and creative work of clarification done by Athanasius. It is a slow march toward the truth, in its gradual stages resembling the approach of the polygon to coincidence with the circle, but in its zigzag course resembling more the tacking of a ship into the wind; better still is to transpose Lonergan's image of a staircase spiraling upwards.[31]

This puts a new light on the conduct of the bishops after Nicea. It was remarked a century ago by Newman and has been repeated many times since that it was the bishops who wavered after Nicea and it was

29. *De deo trino*, vol. 1, pp. 5–112, 137–54.
30. *The Problem of God, Yesterday and Today* (New Haven: Yale University, 1964).
31. *Insight*, p. 186.

the laity who stood firm in the faith. This is not quite fair to the bishops. They were the theologians of the time, the ones who had to work out the implications of the new dogma; they could not do so except in a dialectical process where idea would be set against idea. Not till the whole new set of ideas had been fairly well worked out by Athanasius and the Cappadocians could the episcopal minds reach harmony. The laity, I suggest, had the appearance of standing firm simply because they were not moving with the times. That situation is not without parallel today, which is one reason why I make special mention of it. Vatican I and Vatican II represent arcs in the spiraling staircase of ecclesiology that has not yet come to a landing. The comparison of a dialectical process that came to a sort of term long ago with one that is going forward in our own day can be exceedingly illuminating for present questions.

My second general proposition was that dialectical progress requires dialogue, and surely it would be laboring the obvious to insist that this applies also to dialectical development of doctrine. But I think it worthwhile to delay a moment on the significance of numbers in this special area of application. Augustine, in a memorable line of one of his less memorable works, left us the slogan "Securus judicat orbis terrarum"[32]—"When the whole world agrees, you can be sure of its judgment." This stray line, almost alone and out of context, reached Newman in a roundabout way, and he tells us in his *Apologia* what a deep impression it made upon him.[33] As Newman was at once aware, the slogan was valid far beyond the original application to the Donatists. It has become, in fact, a fundamental criterion in the Church. The present point is that it accords perfectly with the dialectical approach to truth. Again, it is not simply a matter of counting noses; it is a matter of insuring that all the relevant questions, ideas, implications, applications, objections, and ramifications will be noticed and confronted with all the relevant data in the given word of God; it is our human guarantee against oversight and error in judgment.

Thus, there is a significance more fundamental than that of a traditionally "sacred" number in the fact that there were twelve apostles. St. Paul made a point of the fact that the risen Lord was seen by more than 500 Christians at once. The post-Nicene Fathers appealed constantly to the great council (as they thought it to be) of 318 bishops. It is in continuity with such instances that theologians are talking today of the community aspect of faith, that our bishops speak of the co-

---

32. *Contra epist. Parmen.*, III, 4.
33. *Apologia pro vita sua* (London: Longmans, Green, 1921 [1864]), pp. 116–17.

responsibility of the laity, that collegiality is in the air, that we think in terms of teamwork. Collegiality is in fact the teamwork of the bishops. To come for a moment to my official topic, it is not a trivial worship of numbers when we underline the fact that 87 theologians issued the statement in Washington in July, 1968, or that several hundred theologians subscribed to it, or that a good number of influential conferences of bishops sanctioned in effect the stand these theologians took. (Of course, you can count numbers on the other side too. We have not yet one voice from the *orbis terrarum*. All that I am saying is that numbers have their importance—in this case to establish a probability while we await unanimity in the Church.)

Now, I am concerned not to leave too simple a picture of judgmental activity in the church. "Securus judicat orbis terrarum" leaves many questions unanswered. Who speaks for the whole world? If we discover a consensus, have we gone far enough, or do we need an "authoritative" statement? Is the situation like Newman's accumulation of probabilities converging on assent—like it to the extent that many may voice their opinions but the truth is uttered by one? If there are specially qualified men of judgment in the Church, who are they? Are there different bodies which in different cases exercise judgment?

A generation ago, when a sharper distinction between the teaching and the learning Church was maintained, with theologians occupying a kind of no-man's land, there was indeed something like a division of labor between areas such as France and the Vatican in Rome. We would say in those days that France got the ideas, and Rome judged their orthodoxy. We were not just being facetious; there was a real validity in the arrangement. However, that was an era when the truth was more in our possession; we had not yet begun the great migration in the world of ideas; the premises were well enunciated and a fairly adequate set of terms was understood in a fairly common way. Then a board of judges, given leisure for the purpose, could examine any given idea to see whether it accorded with the premises. Then too the idea of a policeman of the faith in the Holy Office was not altogether ridiculous.

But the situation today is not one in which we study new ideas as possible conclusions from fixed starting-points in traditional premises. It is not a situation in which the main opposition is between truth and error; that will always be a question, but it is the terminal question, and we are not yet ready for it—at least, not on every front; we are engaged in the preliminary steps of the dialectical process. The situation is one in which we must form a new set of concepts, establish new premises, throw back the horizons of thought. It is not directly a matter of confronting the new ideas with the faith of our fathers, simply because the confrontation cannot be made in any easily determined way; when we do attempt the confrontation, we need to penetrate to the fundamental intention of our fathers instead of making a shibboleth of their words. Surely our new ideas must not contradict the ancient faith—in extreme radical eyes this will put me squarely among the conservatives—but today's ideas are so new that confrontation with the ancient faith is not the primary question—and that perhaps in conservative eyes will put me among the radicals.

In an age of such far-reaching transition as this is, we must allow the dialectical interplay of ideas and counter-ideas. We must talk with one another. We must openly admit that our condition is that of inquirers after truth, not possessors of the truth; we must recognize that prior to the question of truth there is an enormous problem of developing understanding. So there must be congresses and institutes, theological commissions, synods, and ecumenical councils, the whole strategy and tactics by which the people of God move toward judgment. And while definitive judgment is delayed, we can trust the people of God to judge what concerns them immediately in practical matters, just as we can trust them to change their judgment later if the weight of evidence shows them to be in the wrong.

However, I asked the question "Who judges in the Church of God?" We must face this question, but let me begin my answer with a more general remark. I would say then that this question must be inserted in the larger one of the degree of human participation in divine providence that God wills for his people. Now, it seems clear that God intends an ever-increasing degree of participation in his work. Dietrich Bonhoeffer made the famous remark from his Berlin prison that God is teaching us that we can get along very well without him. I would say that the Catholic counterpart, and perhaps corrective, is the statement that God wants us to take over more and more of the government of the world, according to our degree of maturity. As St. Thomas would say, the progressive actuation of our potencies calls for a corresponding exercise.

This increasing participation by man in the work of providence can be traced in the very matter of divine teaching. The early prophets were esctatics; not only were they singled out as individuals, but they hardly knew what they were doing—they were "seized" by the Spirit.[34] The later prophets were inspired—surely, the word of the Lord came to them—and they still act very much as individuals; nevertheless, they

34. C. H. Dodd, *The Authority of the Bible,* rev. ed. (London: Collins [Fontana], 1960), chs. 2, 3.

are much more rational: there is a greater degree of human participation. An evangelist like Luke was also inspired in his own way, but his way was to consult the traditions, the written accounts, perhaps even the eyewitnesses. The Church in her councils is not inspired but, as we say in scholastic theology, she has the negative assistance of the Spirit. The pattern is clear; it is toward assignment to men of a larger degree of participation in the divine management of the world; and fuller participation by men means a greater involvement of the multitudes. When one man speaks for God, divine intervention must in the nature of the case occur continually; when the people speak, God can trust them a little more.

I am not forgetting that we are judging in the field of mystery. The originally given word of God is not a philosophical discovery to be developed by mere human ingenuity. We cannot get along without the Holy Spirit. But the question is "Where is the voice of the Spirit to be heard?" The old question was "Who has authority to teach in the Church?" I think a much better perspective is given if we ask "Who are the authorized spokesmen of the Church?" Materially we may come to the same answer, but the perspective is different. To talk of authority puts the emphasis on the individual who has authority, but to call him a spokesman for the Church puts a needed emphasis on the fact that the Spirit is given primarily to the Church, and that it is the judgment of the Church that God intends to guide and protect. Meanwhile the adjective "authorized" retains whatever elements of authority belong by nature in a divinely founded institution.

When we view the matter from this perspective, the question becomes one of analyzing the various factors that determine who, by God's will, should act as spokesman for his Church. It is clear that there has been a certain historical variety in the matter of spokesmen. I wonder if the answer will not vary more or less as human society develops. In the early Church, individual congregations under an apostle were spokesmen to a greater degree. In the Patristic age, periodic gatherings of bishops were spokesmen for the Church. Then throughout a long period the head of the college of bishops exercised to a much greater degree the role of a spokesman. But perhaps in our more highly organized society, with a possibility of communication that our fathers could not even dream of, the people are much closer to being their own spokesmen. We do talk today of the infallibility of the Church in believing, of the *sensus fidelium*, of co-responsibility of the laity. I am not able to form a judgment on how far this trend will go, but I have been concerned to get to the heart of the matter, and to remain open to development in whatever way God is leading us.

IV

At the end of this long analysis of the learning Church and its situation today, an analysis aimed at helping you form your conscience on some of the urgent questions that agitate us, I should say a word on the general responsibility of the theologian to his Church, the Church that nourished him and made him what he is, the Church without which all his lucubrations would have no more substance than the fantasies of alchemist or astrologer. Of course, the question becomes finally quite concrete, but I can merely indicate the general factors that come into play to determine a theologian's responsibility.

Obviously, he has a responsibility for the truth, for maintaining the truth that has been given, for seeking the truth that is not yet given. The corollary that I would draw attention to is his responsibility for exposing our failure to be true to the light—our bad faith and inauthenticity. I say this, fully conscious of the ill-mannered and neurotic tirades to which it leaves us open, of the injustices done daily to our leaders, of ultraconservative reactions thereby provoked; it still remains our task. I think especially of our failure after four and a half centuries to do justice to the challenge of the Reformers. Our attitude toward them is still too much a matter of polarization, not one of dialectic. There is, or was, a school among them of dialectical theology which would resign itself to an insoluble contradiction in the object of theology—between God and man, eternity and time, and so on. But I am not referring to that theology as an ideal. The dialectical movement I have tried to expose would not rest in such a static tension, and neither should it rest in the polarization that has characterized Western Christians all these years. The theologian has a special responsibility here in that he owes so much to his Protestant colleagues.

A theologian has a responsibility for ideas, for understanding the truth that God has given and is still communicating to his people. This too is obvious, and so are the immediate corollaries—that ideas must have freedom to occur, that the theologian must be able, without being hailed into the court of orthodoxy, to expose his ideas for the criticism of the public. Naturally this means allowing expression to some rather wild ideas of some rather wild men, but the alternative is the suppression of all ideas, given that the truth, the correct idea, is achieved only dialectically. In any case, today it simply wins unmerited sympathy for wild ideas if we are too eager to forbid them, whereas they would wilt under ridicule if allowed into the open. But these matters do not directly concern the theologian's responsibility. His responsibility is to have the courage and humility to express his own ideas, to speak when he thinks he is right even though he may turn out to be wrong.

A theologian has a responsibility for communicating truth and understanding to others. He is at the service of the Church—of the Holy Father, of the bishops, of the universities, of the people. Corollaries are legion; I limit myself to one. The theologian must remember that there is a style of doing theology—sober, scientific, even pedestrian. He may not responsibly seek the notoriety of headlines or aim at creating a sensation when his job is to help people to understand. I do not wish to belittle the invaluable service being done the Church by journalists today; the cause I have advocated would be lost without them. I am not against theologians' turning to journalism; Church reporting cannot get along without them. I am merely saying that theology is one thing, and journalism is another, and a theologian should decide which is to be his vocation.

When a theologian communicates, he communicates with people, and so we have to take up the delicate question of what people are involved in the area of his responsibility. We could consider classes of people like conservatives and angry young men. Conservatives are people; angry young men are people; the Church is full of people, and people have feelings and rights which a theologian may not ignore. But the real question is more delicate still: What should the responsible theologian's attitude be toward those people who are the Holy Father and the Roman Curia? In general, he may not abdicate his responsibility to stand up and speak out when that is his indicated task. If the Holy Father speaks without adequate knowledge of the question in hand, as I think Pope Honorius did centuries ago, it devolves upon the theologians, naturally after due deliberation and with all humility, to speak their minds, however painful the duty.

Let me insist again that the present question is not one of marital ethics. Fundamentally, the question is one of the *modus vivendi* of the Church today. And the chief difficulty lies in the governing style of the Vatican. I say this with full awareness of the enormous superiority of Vatican political sagacity over ours: We are simply novices in comparison. If I consider that a theologian has still a responsibility to speak up, it is not because I impugn the real desires of the Holy Father to achieve *aggiornamento,* or am insensitive to the suffering he has undergone, or have forgotten that criticism is cheap and difficulties enormous. It is simply that I consider the measures taken as far to be too much a matter of mending fences; the desired change must be more radical.

I began this paper with reference to the need for dialogue, I moved at once to the role of dialectic, and I seem to be ending now with a state of dissent. May I say, as I conclude, that this state is not terminal. It is merely the conflict that is implicit in all dialectic, the conflict of opinions that is an essential element in reaching the truth, a built-in necessity of the human way of learning—that is, it is only a stage in the process toward the terminal position in which we are not only of one heart but of one mind as well.[35]

35. For a more recent treatment of several of these themes, see chs. 16 and 22 below.

12

Eschaton and Worldly Mission in the Mind and Heart of Jesus*

I am conscious of taking on a difficult job when I offer to talk to you about the eschaton in the mind and heart of Jesus and to relate it to his mission on earth. Every word in the title raises a host of problems. To make it worse, the problems do not stand still; there will be different problems for different persons, or different problems for the same person depending on whether he is investigating as a historian or praying as a believer. Maybe then the best beginning would be to sort out some of the problems and indicate the questions I mean to deal with and the limits of the study I propose to make.

For historians concerned with the documents, which in this case are mainly the four gospels of the New Testament, mention of the mind and heart of Jesus will suggest that I am trying to do once more what every scholar now recognizes to be a futile task, discover and delineate the features of the historical Jesus. This was the effort of the liberal theologians of the 1800's and proved abortive. After Martin Kähler showed in 1892 that the gospel records are not biographies of Jesus but expressions of the faith of the evangelists,[1] and Albert Schweitzer followed with a classic work showing the nugatory results of the quest of the historical Jesus,[2] New Testament experts reconciled themselves to the fact that we do not know what Jesus said and did in the sense those

---

*A paper presented at the fifth Villanova University Theology Institute, 19–23 June 1972, where the general theme was "The Eschaton: A Community of Love." Previously published in *The Eschaton: A Community of Love,* ed. J. Papin (Villanova, PA: Villanova University, 1974 [c. 1971]), pp. 105–144. The argument of this paper is summarized and carried forward a bit in "The Mind of Jesus," *Communio: International Catholic Review* 1 (1974), pp. 365–84.

1. Martin Kähler, *The So-Called Historical Jesus and the Historic, Biblical Christ,* tr. C. E. Braaten (Philadelphia: Fortress Press, 1964). This Seminar Edition translates the first and second essays in the 1896 edition of the original German book.

2. Albert Schweitzer, *The Quest of the Historical Jesus. A Critical Study of Its Progress from Reimarus to Wrede,* tr. W. Montgomery (London: Adam and Charles Black, 1910). The German original appeared in 1906; a new English edition was published by Macmillan (New York) in 1968.

words bear for historians today. Notice, we do not even know what he said and did, and here I propose to go farther than that: to penetrate beyond his words and actions to his mind and heart. It sounds like fundamentalism or maybe just fantasy.

Besides historians there are believers, and sometimes historical science and faith meet in the same person. I am sure that this is verified here, that those in my audience who are historians are also believers. As believers we may not forget that in talking about Jesus we are talking of one whom our fathers taught us to worship as lord and savior, the only name given to us by which we may be saved. And this further complicates the problem. When the words and deeds of Jesus disappeared, the loss was not just that of a bit of history, even of very sacred history, it was the loss of him who is our way, our truth, and our life. With Mary we have to say: "They have taken away my Lord, and I do not know where they have laid him." We no longer have the simple rule of conduct we once had, of looking up the gospels to see how the Lord acted, and transposing his pattern of life to our situation.

Of course, a thorough-going historian will tell us that a fully accurate biography of Jesus would not solve that problem anyway. He would say that the same historical cast of mind which has taught us so much about the gospels has also taught us a great deal about the relativity of language, ethics, culture, and all things human. In a sense then it does not matter so much that we do not know the words and deeds of Jesus; even if we did know his way of acting and his doctrine, we might find it so permeated with time-conditioned ideas and standards as to render it obsolete now as a model. We are a new generation, and we have to take seriously the question asked by Dietrich Bonhoeffer from his Berlin prison: "What is Christianity, and indeed what is Christ, for us today?"[3] We cannot repeat, parrot-like, the words and actions of anyone, not even those of Christ the Lord, when they belong in a different situation, occurred in response to different demands, and were guided by different cultural values from ours.

All this comes home to us in a special way and with peculiar force in the very area that is the concern of this Villanova Institute, the eschaton. For the mind and heart of Jesus, so far as we are able to conjecture it from careful, educated historical guesses, had quite a different view and estimate of the world and the eschaton from that we take for granted today. Nearly a century ago now, Johannes Weiss disturbed the liberal theology of his time with a book that showed how

---

3. Dietrich Bonhoeffer, *Letters and Papers from Prison* (London: Fontana Books, 1953), p. 91: "The thing that keeps coming back to me is, what *is* Christianity, and indeed what *is* Christ, for us to-day?" There are many editions of Bonhoeffer's Letters, so the most helpful reference is to say that this question is in his letter of 30 April 1944.

overwhelmingly the mind and heart of the Lord were oriented to the future kingdom and not, as the liberals believed, to the present kingdom of righteousness in the interior of every man's heart.[4] But, if Weiss is correct, then Jesus seems to live in another world than ours. Once more, it was Albert Schweitzer who made this thesis popular and gave us a classic passage to sum up the new view:

The study of the Life of Jesus has had a curious history. It set out in quest of the historical Jesus, believing that when it had found Him it could bring Him straight into our time as a Teacher and Saviour. It loosed the bands by which He had been riveted for centuries to the stony rocks of ecclesiastical doctrine, and rejoined to see life and movement coming into the figure once more, and the historical Jesus advancing, as it seemed, to meet it. But He does not stay; He passes by our time and returns to His own.[5]

The difference Schweitzer found so alienating was especially in this very area of eschatological thinking. The mind of Jesus, he thought, was exclusively set on the coming Kingdom, with the expectation that the day was near at hand. And we too, without the aid of Schweitzer, have noticed that the gospels do not present him as concerned with culture and art, science and civilization, sports or politics, the use of leisure, or the women's lib movement. His mission in the world seems to have been rather to save man from this wicked world than to promote the world's values. And this, especially since Vatican II and *The Pastoral Constitution on the Church in the Modern World,* makes the Lord seem less and less relevant to our age.

Add to this list of shattering blows the final irreverence that much of modern scholarship does not accept the word of Jesus as infallible. Schweitzer himself regarded Jesus as simply mistaken in his hopes, forcing the wheel of history to bring up his destiny as Son of Man, only to have it roll forward and break him in the process.[6] On the very day that I am writing this paragraph I find it said of a recent book that the author's

treatment of Jesus's moral authority appears to rest on an almost fundamentalist idea of Our Lord's teaching as "direct from God", so to say, without seeing

---

4. Johannes Weiss, *Jesus' Proclamation of the Kingdom of God,* tr. R. H. Hiers and D. L. Holland (Philadelphia: Fortress Press, 1971). The German original appeared in 1892.

5. Schweitzer, p. 397.

6. Schweitzer, pp. 368–69, where we read the following: "The Baptist appears, and cries: 'Repent, for the Kingdom of Heaven is at hand.' Soon after that comes Jesus, and in the knowledge that He is the coming Son of Man lays hold of the wheel of the world to set it moving on that last revolution which is to bring all ordinary history to a close. It refuses to turn, and He throws Himself upon it. Then it does turn; and crushes Him. Instead of bringing in the eschatological conditions, He has destroyed them." Jürgen Moltmann, *The Theology of Hope* (London: SCM, 1967), informs us (p. 39, n. 1) that this passage was deleted from later German editions of Schweitzer's book.

that Jesus's teaching, like everything else about the humanity of him whom as a Christian one believes to be the place and point of special divine activity in human history, can only rightly be understood in terms of the times, the background, and the conditions in which Jesus lived and spoke during "the days of his flesh". Nowadays oracular infallibility will not do, even in the incarnate Lord.[7]

In dealing with this complex problem I wish to take account of the fact that I am speaking to those who combine scholarship with faith, and I would do justice to both areas of life. I consider that I owe it to you as scholars to delimit my study and pursue it with accepted standards of critical research and honest regard for the facts and probabilities, but I consider that I owe it to you as believers to state my dogmatic position that you may know on what basis I carry out my study, to what I am committed and in what degree my mind is free. To this end the briefest possible statement would be that I wish to take modern criticism seriously, but I mean also to retain the faith of my forefathers. However that is an enterprise that many today find almost self-contradictory, and so I must take a moment to explain my position.

First then I wish to take the modern criticism and mentality seriously. I accept the force of Bonhoeffer's question as applying to us with peculiar urgency. They have indeed taken away my Lord and we must search for him again. I accept the fact that the gospels are not biographies, that we really do not know exactly what the Lord said and did in the way we would like to know. I accept as quite probable the view that Jesus did not claim to be Messiah or Son of God, that possibly he did not even claim to be Son of Man, that he did not particularly concern himself with the features of the true Messiah or with purifying the Jewish idea of the Messiah. To put the main point in the succinct phrase current today: The proclaimer became the proclaimed. That is, Jesus proclaimed the Kingdom; we, on the other hand, proclaim Jesus. In all this I am not eliminating history with the gnostics, but merely acknowledging with the realists developments in the content of our faith and great areas of ignorance about its origins.

Further, I accept the fact that we cannot live in the same mental world as our forefathers did. It was easy for them—in fact, it was easy for us in childhood—to live with the "powers and principalities" of Paul all around them in the atmosphere. Copernicus had somehow not got through to popular piety. God was still "up there" above the clouds, and guardian angels hovered nearby in the air. The other world, though invisible, was close at hand—literally close at hand, in the spatial sense. So we had image to pit against image; against the world that is so much

7. From an anonymous review of a book by J. N. D. Anderson *(Morality, Law and Grace)* in *The Times Literary Supplement* (London), 24 March 1972, p. 342.

with us, displaying its tempting wares, we could set another world, that was almost as vividly present, to counteract temptation. We may still find it useful to picture such a world when we pray, and we may still find it helpful to our piety to read the gospels as if it were 972 instead of 1972; many of the "Jesus people" seem to do so and, if they insist on withdrawing from the stream of culture, I have no wish to disturb their peace of mind. But I am saying that we must know what we are doing; and, if we wish to live with a good conscience and inspire credibility in the academic sphere, we have to realize that the mental world of our forefathers has vanished, and along with it the picture-story world of the gospels.

Also I think I see the point of those philosophers who talk about man as the creator of his values. In a world where all things change and develop, the human good also develops. In a human world where meaning is constitutive of man and his institutions, developing meaning puts new values before one. In men who are not definable by genus and specific difference except at the level of the lowest common denominator, the level of mere potency, the significant element is in what is added, the differentiations that make one a Newman instead of a moron. It belongs to the intelligence of man to discover the possibilities of his becoming and to work out the means to realize them. In all this we recognize a factor that we can call the creation of values, and it is conceivable and probable that Jesus in his human life on earth was an instance of such creativity. But this means that in the quite different world of the 1970's the values that Jesus worked out for himself may not be exactly the values that we must by God's will work out for ourselves.

All this I can say with a peaceful conscience because I do not find that the results of modern historical investigation of the gospels really threaten my understanding of our faith in Jesus Christ, the Son of God. The faith of my fathers remains intact, and my understanding of it is in fact enriched by the critical work of the last two centuries. The ground of my peace is not just that critical history is itself very fallible and therefore not to be swallowed whole or made the criterion of what we may believe about Christ. It is rather that our articles of faith and the doctrinal explanations approved by the Church, rightly understood, do not in fact conflict with history. The key word here is "understand"—I said that the findings of history do not conflict with my *understanding* of our faith. This sounds quite a lot like some esoteric knowledge granted to me by special divine privilege, so I want to say at once that the fundamental understanding of our faith that I am talking about was given seven centuries ago by Thomas Aquinas, for whom I feel no need to apologize.

I would ask you here to remember that understanding as such is hypothetical. What I am putting forward is a hypothesis. Whether it can ever be verified is another question. But a theologian's job must begin with the sort of task I am attempting. He comes to the faith of his forefathers and to the source-documents much as a medical doctor might come to the scriptural accounts of an illness. The medical doctor brings with him a "science" of medicine, a whole set of concepts which is a powerful instrument of explanation. Nevertheless, when he studies the symptoms related by a Luke, his particular role is to ask, "Might it be such and such a disease that we find described here?" He is not competent to perform the exercise of textual and other criticism needed to determine the real state of affairs. He does not even know whether the man X, described as having such and such an affliction, ever existed. Similarly, the theologian brings to the gospel accounts of Jesus and to the faith of his forefathers, a set of concepts that enables him to ask, that gives him the duty of asking, "Could this be the way it happened?" His job is to supply a principle of possible explanation. He does not try therefore to say what actually happened or to write a biography of Jesus; but perhaps he supplies a necessary preliminary to asking the question of fact and, if the facts can never be determined, he at least has the intellectual peace that comes from grasping and conceiving a possible explanation.

What I wish to do then in this paper is address myself to the Thomist understanding of Christ's human knowledge, and (going beyond St. Thomas now) to show on that basis by what process the eschaton in the mind of Jesus might be linked with his observation and growing understanding of earthly realities. Secondly, I will try to provide a similar and parallel account of the eschaton in the heart of Jesus and to show by what process it might be linked with his discovery and acceptance of earthly values. Thirdly and finally, I will indicate how these two accounts could be brought to bear on the question of his earthly mission.

1. Eschaton and Finite Knowledge in the Mind of Jesus

I begin with Catholic dogma and doctrine on Christ and his human knowledge. It has a very long and very involved history, but we can cover it in short order with the seven-league boots of a systematic theologian. Nicea affirmed in 325 that the Son is God in the same sense as the Father is God.[8] We should neither maximize nor minimize this;

---

8. In the Nicene phrase, the Son is *homoousios* or consubstantial with the Father. But this was turned into the plain English I have used by G. L. Prestige, *God in Patristic Thought* (London: S.P.C.K., 1952), p. 213.

the Nicene fathers did not say anything that went beyond the thrust of the New Testament, but they did say more than the New Testament says. Scripture, as St. Thomas remarks, often contains the articles of our faith "spread out . . . expressed in various ways, and sometimes lacking in clarity."[9] We need what the creeds give: a boiling down, a crystallizing, a clarification. And the resulting clarification at Nicea at once released other questions till then unformulated. With his divinity clearly affirmed, attention had to turn to his human state. It was established 126 years later at Chalcedon that he was also man like ourselves; as he is God in the same sense as the Father is God, so he is man in the same sense in which we are men. What follows from that in regard to human endowments? The question was answered after another 230 years in regard to the particular question of the human will: the God-man has a human will such as we have.

The particular question of the human knowledge of Jesus never received the attention in the Patristic councils that his will did. Different ages have different preoccupations; our preoccupation today would be more with Christ's mind than with his will, I should think, but we do not have councils running round defining dogmas the way an earlier age did. However, the conclusion was clear from Chalcedon: there is a human cognitional activity and knowledge in Christ. The further ramifications of that conclusion were worked out clearly only in St. Thomas' time, and then only slowly. But towards the end of his life, he had begun to get things straightened out. There was in the human mind of Christ a knowledge that is there by divine gift; most important under this heading is the vision of God, immediate knowledge of the divine essence. There was also in the mind of Christ what St. Thomas called acquired knowledge, knowledge based on experience and on ideas formed according to the cognitional process normal in a human being.

It was not this experiential knowledge that the Scholastics studied most diligently. It was rather the divinely given knowledge and especially the vision of God that we term beatific. The question most to the fore dealt with the extent of this knowledge. Faced with Mark 13:32, "But about that day . . . no one knows, not even . . . the Son; only the Father," they could not avoid the question. But with their strong sense of Christ as their teacher, as him on whose word our faith depends, they were extremely reluctant to admit any area of ignorance even into his human mind.[10] Thus, St. Thomas expressly asks the question

9. *Summa theologiae*, II-II, 1, 9, ad 1m: "diffuse . . . et variis modis, et in quibusdam obscure."

10. The Scholastic supposition—a perfectly valid one, in due course formulated—was that anything Christ said as man to men, he said out of the only knowledge he had at his human disposal, the knowledge in his human mind. There is a widespread and almost

whether there was ignorance in Christ and answers no that there was not.[11]

We are now beyond the borders of Catholic dogma and there is no point pursuing the question further in that direction. For our Protestant brothers the question, I would say, has ceased to be of interest; they long ago abandoned the Scholastic doctrine of Christ's immediate vision of God and have devoted themselves to his "acquired" knowledge; our introduction of the present question in Medieval language must seem to them strangely artificial, academic, remote, old-fashioned—a relic of a bygone age with which they need not concern themselves.

For Catholics the problem is more complex. We do not wish lightly to abandon a doctrine our fathers worked out rather carefully and on good grounds. At the same time we must be aware of the age we live in and awake to the need of critical examination of our history. We know that the dogma of Nicea gave an emphasis to the divinity of Christ that has made it difficult for us to think of him as man; the very difficulty we have in speaking of "Jesus" rather than of "Christ" or "the Lord" is an indication of the deep influence conciliar dogma has had on our psyche and piety. But, even if we do not abandon our dogmas or the conclusions that seem to follow directly from the dogmas, we still have to retrace the path by which we came, to see in every case what the intention of the Church was, to discern the core affirmation and not be mesmerized by the particular language used, to discover and validate the grounds on which the Church based her dogma or her view.

What I am saying is that the addition of history to dogma gives us a new problematic. We may not simply quote the words our fathers used to express their faith and consider the matter settled. We must rather observe the situation in each case and take account of the differences in expression as the situation changes from age to age. A very pertinent illustration occurs in the difference between Mark and John. The Patristic and Scholastic age based its Christology largely on John's gospel and found Mark's gospel, where ignorance is attributed to Jesus, an embarrassment. But a later age based its account of the human Jesus more on Mark and finds John's gospel an embarrassment, for in John

---

ineradicable error among those who believe in the divinity of Christ, that he had at his disposal, when he opened his lips to speak, the fullness of divine knowledge. But the divinity no more put divine knowledge at his human disposal than the divine infinity gave him a bodily weight of an infinite number of pounds, or the divine eternity made him an infinite number of years old.

11. *Summa theologiae*, III, 15, 3; see also 10, 2, where the question is whether the soul of Christ knew all things *in verbo*—the answer is yes.

all knowledge belongs to Jesus and he does not need to ask questions of anyone.

Now it is possible to reconcile Mark and John by means of distinctions, but it is more important from the historical point of view to discover the context in which each evangelist wrote, and thus to arrive at a concrete understanding which makes the distinctions valid. Thus, Mark thinks of Jesus as the strong, the mighty Son of God, wresting victory from the forces of Satan; he does not think of him as the God-man in the sense of Chalcedon, with human nature and divine nature; he would be utterly mystified by such terminology, and so he does not put the question we put: If he is God, how come he doesn't know the date of the great judgment? Mark does not even expressly see him entering the world from heaven, so he escapes a multitude of problems. John, however, does explicitly think of him as entering this world from heaven; moreover, he thinks of him as being one with the Father, as having all that the Father has, including the Father's knowledge. Hence, he attributes to him the widest possible knowledge of events on earth, past, present, and future. But John did not have the Chalcedonian distinction of natures in the back of his mind as he wrote; he did not therefore ask, "Is this knowledge human or divine?" And not thinking of the question, he does not take the precautions that a modern theologian must take. He speaks as if Jesus the man had a ready supply of divine knowledge available; but this I take to be his way of expressing the divinity of Christ, it is his Christology. I do not see it as necessarily an account, a biographical narrative, of events in the human life of Jesus.

But what becomes now of our "proofs" of the immediate vision of God in Jesus? For we based them largely on texts from John, and John, as we now understand him, does not appear to support our thesis. It seems to me we must boldly assert that "proofs" always lag behind a Catholic sense of the truth, that there is a global way of conceiving a truth and an implicit way of affirming it long before we formulate propositions that require proof, that in fact it is often heresy which does the clarifying work needed to pass from such global and implicit states of belief to the defined and explicit state. For example, the Arian heresy clarified the question on the divinity of the Son of God, and the genius of Athanasius discovered the proof that clinched the matter: the same things are said of the Son as are said of the Father, except the name of Father.[12] But, before this, proofs from scripture were inade-

12. Athanasius, *Oratio III contra Arianos, #4; De synodis, #49.* See Bernard Lonergan, *De deo trinio,* vol. 1 (Rome: Gregorian University, 1964), pp. 23, 48, 54, 85, 131, 140–41, 142–43, 202.

quate, just as the conception of the divinity of Christ was global and undefined.

Similarly, I suspect there is a Catholic sense of the vision of God in Jesus' mind. We apprehend it globally, not without reference to particular texts, but we base it more on the general thrust of the texts than on the exegesis of this or that particular text; in the latter we are apt to go badly astray. If I try to articulate that faith here, I am aware of trying to do a work parallel to that of Arius and Athanasius, as well as that of their predecessors in a long line. But I would attempt it in some such form as this: What Jesus knows as a religious teacher, he knows on his own, without asking anyone, without having someone to vouch for him, without even needing, as the prophets needed, to have the word of the Lord come to him. Possibly the heretical formulation we need to bring out our faith could be found in just those words: he knows as a prophet does, surely the greatest of the prophets but still only a prophet, to whom the word of the Lord came in a special way. But I am not sure how a modern Athanasius would destroy that heresy.

At any rate I mean to retain the dogmas of my faith, and I wish to retain also the accepted doctrines until the need to abandon them is proved. When the humanity and divinity of Christ created difficulties about his unity, the Church's method was not the easy way out of denying one nature or the other, or of affirming some kind of society of two; it was rather the extremely difficult, and still ongoing, but enormously fruitful way of living with the problem and struggling to conceive anew and less inadequately the constitution of the God-man. I think that there is a parallel here in regard to the vision of God, and that we should live with the difficulty and see whether the resulting struggle does not result in a new and fruitful penetration of the mystery of revelation.

What then is the difficulty, and how did it arise? The difficulty is that the doctrine of the vision of God seems to give Jesus a complete blueprint of creation in which he can read all that was or is or will be, and this is difficult to harmonize with the synoptic evangelists and other writers, who have Jesus learning in various ways, ignorant of the last day, asking what seem like real questions, and being surprised at the discoveries he makes. Further it seems to remove Jesus from us as a model, for he becomes a kind of automaton, subject to a fate predetermined and preformulated, and not at all a man who had to make decisions, sometimes playing it a bit by ear, and learning by the things he suffered.

But how did such a view of the vision of God arise? It arose from a "picture-thinking" concept of the immediate knowledge we believe Jesus to have had of God. We think of Jesus seeing the Father "face to face"; we add the Augustinian (and Thomist) doctrine of all creation being contained *in verbo*, in the Word the Father utters; and now we have all we need for the "picture-thinking" view of Jesus' higher knowledge. Let us put this notion in all its naiveté. The notion is that Jesus could gaze upon the other world as we look upon this one. As we see hills and trees, towns and homes and animals and men, so there is another world of objects spread out before the mind's eye in Jesus; he saw his Father in majesty, the Holy Spirit was somehow visible though he has no long white beard to manifest himself, the armies of angels were hovering there, or forming fours and right-wheeling in great precision. Moreover, he also sees this world of ours in all its spatiotemporal totality; the whole of human history and its events are somehow exposed to view; the future is visible at a glance, and no questions remain to be asked. In our piety towards our dead we think of them "looking down" upon us from the home of the blessed; but Jesus could see all this while he lived on earth, by reference to some kind of blueprint which perhaps we do not very clearly image in our minds.

Such a view is perfectly natural in the sense that it is the normal view to adopt as a first approximation. It corresponds to the biblical phrase, face to face; it is a spontaneous conception of intellectual knowledge based on the mode of ocular vision with which we are so familiar and by which we are so naturally influenced in our cognitional theory; it has been given a kind of sanction by the theologians through their use of the term "vision of God."

But suppose that is not what the immediate knowledge of God is. Suppose that the phrase, face to face, is not a premise from which conclusions may be drawn in the manner of logic, but simply a metaphor which has to be translated into more technical language before conclusions are possible. Suppose, more positively, that immediate knowledge of God is not a knowledge of particular items at all, but more a global view; suppose that this "view" is more an understanding than a concept; suppose that, as understanding, it is characterized more by the power and range of activity it gives the subject than it is by the list of objects on which it bears; suppose that even with such immediate knowledge of God there remains a real, prolonged, and difficult process to empirical understanding and knowledge of the created universe, of the course of human history, and especially of distant and obscure items like the date of the last day; suppose also that St. Thomas had not integrated the vision of God with the learning process proper to men on earth,[13]—suppose all this, I say, and see how much remains of the

---

13. This failure to integrate is the more likely since only late in life did St. Thomas reverse his former position and admit experiential knowledge in Christ: see *Summa theologiae*, III, 9, 4 c.: "Et ideo, quamvis aliter alibi scripserim, dicendum est in Christo scientiam acquisitam fuisse."

problem, whether it is not possible to accept both history and doctrine and still live in intellectual peace.

My own view is that on the suppositions stated the problem of reconciling the vision Jesus had with the normal learning process found in man, largely vanishes. We can accept the thrust and intention of the traditional doctrine we received from our fathers, and still agree with Mark the evangelist and with modern history, that Jesus was a man who thought things out, asked questions, was surprised by the answers, learned day by day the details of his mission, and did not know the date of the last judgment. I wish to explore this possibility, but I hope it is clear that my main objective is not to prove a doctrine but to render an intelligible account of it, in particular so to explain it as to effect the desired reconciliation of vision and learning process in Jesus. That means two subsections in this part of my paper: explaining the vision of God, and relating the vision of God to knowledge of this finite world.

1. The Vision of God—A Thomist Understanding

When we speak of the vision of God, we are speaking of mystery. The traditional way of dealing with mystery is by analogies, and I have three: our spontaneous notion of being, the experience of the mystics, and our own profoundest knowledge in daily life. The first is probably the dullest, but it is also the most effective theologically, and I am going to spend some time on it, beginning with the Thomist view of intellectual light and developing St. Thomas's view with the help of Lonergan's ideas on the notion of being.

The fruitful approach to the Thomist doctrine of "light" is by contrast with the doctrine of first principles.[14] We are familiar, through our training in logic, with the idea of a premise, or set of premises, from which conclusions can be derived. We come to realize that the premises themselves, most of them, are already conclusions from higher premises, and so we come to the idea of first principles which are at the basis of all organized knowledge, such apparently utterly basic premises as "A thing cannot be and not be," "The good is to be done," etc. And, if we make logic the source of cognitional process, the creative agent, then we stop with these first principles as the ultimate basis of knowledge.

For St. Thomas they are not ultimate at all. Behind them lies the native endowment and power of intellect, which St. Thomas often designates as a "light." It is the source of all principles, even first principles; it makes them intelligible, it uses them as instruments for further in-

---

14. These three paragraphs summarize a section of my article, "Universal Norms and the Concrete operabile in St. Thomas Aquinas," *Sciences ecclésiastiques* 7 (1955), pp. 115–49; see esp. pp. 121–29.

tellectual process. It is an active power, operative and self-sufficient in the whole range of knowledge pertaining to natural reason. It is a participation, a created offprint, of God's intelligence; but just here we have to correct Augustine: when he speaks of judgment by reference to the eternal reasons, we have to understand this, not as a matter of looking at truths inscribed in the divine mind, but as a matter of having in our own minds an active power which is able, of itself, to pass judgment and attain truth. There is a sense then in which it is quite true to say that we have all knowledge in our minds from the beginning, for we have a light in which first terms and first principles and all knowledge based on them can become known.

Still, that is not the whole story. We are well enough aware of the pain of the learning process to realize that the natural light of intellect does not give us actual knowledge of particular objects. There are then two sources of our knowledge, one intrinsic to mind (its own light) but the other extrinsic, the *sensibilia* by which particular objects and areas of science are brought under the illumination of intellectual light. Just as corporeal light is not itself a determined color (in the Thomist conception) but is able nevertheless to make all colors visible, so intellectual light is not particular knowledge but is able to bring all particular knowledge to actuation. The relation then of intellectual light to specific ideas is that of undetermined cause to determined effect, the relation of a general power ranging over its field to particular products of that power.

This Thomist doctrine is transformed by Lonergan into a doctrine of the spontaneously operative notion of being,[15] or the pure notion of being:

The pure notion of being is the detached, disinterested, unrestricted desire to know. It is prior to understanding and affirming, but it heads to them for it is the ground of intelligent inquiry and critical reflection. Moreover, this heading towards knowing is itself a notion, for it heads not unconsciously, as the seed to the plant, nor sensitively, as hunger for food, but intelligently and reasonably, as the radical *noêsis* towards every *noêma*, the basic *pensée pensante* towards every *pensée pensée*, the initiating *intentio intendens* towards every *intentio intenta*.[16]

This notion of being is present in all conscious cognitional activity of man. It is there as "a dynamic orientation to a totally unknown."[17] It is all-pervasive: "It underpins all cognitional contents. It penetrates them all. It constitutes them as cognitional."[18] It is the principle of all inquiry and reflection, the criterion of all judgment.

---

15. *Insight: A Study of Human Understanding*, p. 352.
16. *Ibid.*, p. 642. The index *(s.v.,* Being—pure notion) wrongly gives the reference, p. 641.
17. Ibid., p. 349.   18. Ibid., p. 356.

It is conscious, and manifests itself vividly in questions, in the need and urge to know, in the malaise of an unsatisfied intellect. But it is not conscious in the manner in which a red light or an alarm-bell enters the field of consciousness. It is not obtrusive; it is not ordinarily adverted to; even philosophers may never notice it; those who do, have great difficulty formulating their notion of it; those who do formulate their notion, have great difficulty conveying it to others.[19]

It is this light of intellect or notion of being that Lonergan uses as an analogy for what Christ understood through his immediate vision of God and for the way this understanding relates to the knowledge Christ acquired and used in daily life. Christ's understanding of the divine mysteries was inexpressible; it corresponds to the words heard by St. Paul—"so secret that human lips may not repeat them" (2 Cor 12:4). Yet his communication of the divine mysteries to others was carried out in the common language whose meaning he shared with them. There had therefore to be a translation from one understanding and knowledge to the other. Now the natural light which is our native endowment, Lonergan's notion of being, is also in its own way inexpressible; yet in another way it is expressed in our daily lives, in all we know, and in the very desire we have to know God. Christ's knowledge is similarly inexpressible, much more radically so, yet it becomes manifest in his life. There is a difference in that we operate in pursuit of the goal, with a desire to see God, where Christ operated from the attained goal, communicating what he had to others. But there is a similarity in that the vision of God gave him no actual knowledge that was expressible. He had to win this slowly; he labored to express what was first given in an inexpressible form; he labored, as it were, to fill a vacuum.

There seems to be an analogy here which we can use to understand the presence in Christ of the vision of God, to understand its influence, ever active but not obtrusive, and to understand its relation to the experiential knowledge gained in daily living. How this may work out in the concrete will occupy us later.

My second analogy is the experience of the mystics. I presume that what they were given Christ was given in greater measure. If the difference from Christ is qualitative, we would proceed in two steps, from our experience to that of the mystics, from theirs to Christ's. If the

19. If I am right, this point will be important for understanding how Christ could lead a fairly normal life while still enjoying the vision of God. It would therefore be good to get hold of it, and I suggest the following analogy as useful: we are continually conscious of ourselves in all our psychological activity, yet we do not necessarily advert to ourselves or think about ourselves, for we are preoccupied with the object of our activity; in a similar way we do not advert to the notion of being even though it is present, consciously present, and continually operative.

difference is just quantitative, we seem at first glance to lack any basis for analogy; the mystics are almost as far removed from us as Christ is. But even then there is one factor that makes their experience useful to us as an analogy: they have talked extensively about it, where Christ did not do so. He was not able to do so in the vocabulary of his time; he did not think of doing so, given the particular interests of his time; he would be quite surprised if we put questions to him in the language of St. Teresa of Avila or St. John of the Cross, surprised and somewhat at a loss to know what we meant. So the mystics serve to lead us to him, whether their difference from him be qualitative or quantitative.

What I find relevant now in the mystical experience, is the inexpressible character of their knowledge, and the great efforts they make to express to us what is beyond words. Poulain's documentation and analysis are useful here. It is said of a certain blessed Hermann Joseph: "[T]he Lord revealed to him the whole beauty and glory of the firmament. . . . But afterwards . . . the Prior could get nothing more out of him than that he had received such unspeakable rapture . . . that it was beyond human understanding."[20] Poulain also quotes Teresa of Avila: "[W]e enjoy a favour without knowing what it is";[21] and says himself "[A]s the soul experiences difficulty in understanding her state, so she finds it very hard to describe it."[22] And John of the Cross says that as the knowledge in the mystic state is "general and obscure . . . " with "the intellect unable to conceive *distinctly* . . . so the will also loves generally and *indistinctly*."[23]

Poulain therefore refers to the need the mystics have to invent images in order to express what they have experienced, and we have some remarkable comments of Teresa on her efforts to find an image that does even remotest justice to her vision—I think of the four ways of watering a garden, which she used to describe states of prayer.[24] He relates also that theologians are apt to ask the mystics what images give rise to their experiences, but the mystics themselves are astounded by such a question, since their state is quite beyond images.[25] Again, he speaks of a prayer of silence, not of the suppression of all activity,[26] but

20. Augustin Poulain, *The Graces of Interior Prayer. A Treatise on Mystical Theology,* tr. L. L. Yorke Smith (London: Kegan Paul, Trench, Trubner, 1928), p. 278. The French original appeared in 1901; it has been re-edited and reprinted many times.

21. Ibid., p. 119.

22. Ibid., p. 120.   23. Ibid., p. 121.

24. *The Life of St. Teresa of Jesus . . . Written by Herself,* tr. D. Lewis (London: Thomas Baker, 1904); see ch. XI, #9 (p. 78): "I shall have to make use of a comparison; I should like to avoid it. . . . But this language of spirituality is so difficult of utterance for those who are not learned, and such am I. . . . " Teresa then proceeds to her comparison of watering a garden.

25. Poulain, pp. 122–23.   26. Ibid., pp. 127–28.

a prayer in which: "All sounds are hushed. The soul is wholly immersed in an act of possession which seems to endure without any variation."[27]

I think we have in such accounts a very powerful instrument for understanding the mind and heart of Jesus. There is an *a priori* element in that view, the presumption I mentioned that whatever the mystics had Christ had in greater degree, but that seems reasonable to suppose. There is often a state of rapture in the mystics which we cannot easily verify in Christ, but this may well be an effect in the early stages; there may be more tranquillity accompanying the later habitual possession of the mystic gifts, the sort of tranquillity we seem to find more normally in Christ.

A third analogy is found in our own ordinary faith experience. What I mean is, the most fundamental ideas we have remain preconceptual; they are not expressed in words, though they shape our lives and guide our thinking and judging and deciding. To illustrate this, we might think of our inability to say anything appropriate on the great occasions of life—disaster and death, or love and success and triumph. There is an understanding by which we react appropriately but silently. Or we might think of our proverbs, which express the profoundest wisdom of common sense, but are almost always expressed in metaphorical language, where more is meant and understood than is uttered. That is, lacking the word of rational discourse, we fall back on the preconceptual means of the artist.

This seems to me especially true of what we hold by faith. I recall here what I said earlier about the profoundest truths of our faith resting not so much on particular texts of scripture as on a global view, a "sense" of rightness that we cannot easily put into words, though we can recognize faulty formulations (and thus heresy is always easier to spot and judge than orthodoxy is to formulate). To illustrate this we must think of the way we find our own "expressions" of faith in our dreams.[28] That is, public language is still lacking and so each one finds his own private language to express to himself what is held by all of us without words. Or think of the way we vaguely sense the thrust of a biblical parable, say, the parables of crisis, even though the imagery of the gospels may have little power in the present context and we struggle to find another (just here dreams may have their role and give each believer his private set of parables).

27. Ibid., p. 131.

28. Two recent books are useful for exploring the possibility that our dreams express to us a religious understanding that is preconceptual (though I do not attribute that phrase to either author): John A. Sanford, *Dreams: God's Forgotten Language* (Philadelphia: J. B. Lippincott, 1968); Morton T. Kelsey, *Dreams: The Dark Speech of the Spirit. A Christian Interpretation* (New York: Doubleday, 1968).

2. Vision of God and Knowledge of the Finite

The structure of my idea on the eschaton and worldly mission in the mind of Jesus is as follows: I start with the notion of the vision of God as an act of understanding, an act of understanding which is global and does not include as explicit items the objects of either this world or the other but only the divine essence; I wish to proceed from that to the formation in Jesus' mind of particular items of knowledge concerned with his life on earth and his mission. In this way I hope to provide some hint of the way the Lord Jesus could know and know with authority, could be our teacher in a way the prophets could never be, and yet have to think deeply to find his message and express it to others.

The first part of my exposition—conceiving the vision of God as a global act of understanding— has been long and difficult, but I think it was essential. There is no use rejecting the vision of God in Jesus until we know with accuracy what it means, and there is no easy way to find that out. But we have still a long way to go in working out how this "eschaton" in the mind of Jesus can be related to finite knowledge; I turn now to the second task.

A fundamental condition of the search is expressed negatively: there are no words or ideas in the mind of Jesus as an immediate result of the vision of God. You have accepted, I hope, the premise that there are no images; the vision of God is not an ocular act, a gazing upon a field of visible objects. But we must go farther and say there are no words or ideas either; that is, if we wish to conceive the state of Jesus' mind prior to his human experience as a baby, we must erase every concept we meet in scripture or tradition or catechism or any other source. In this respect, his mind was like the *tabula rasa*, the clean slate, the Scholastic theologians talk of.

Let me spell this out in tedious detail. The object of the immediate knowledge Jesus had through the vision of God did not contain the word "God" or the words "divine essence," nor did it contain the word "Father," or the word "Son," or the word "Spirit," still less did it contain the word "three." It did not contain the word "creator" or the word "judge" or the word "almighty" or the word "eternal" or any of the words, "rock," "shepherd," "shield," and the others which are applied to God in what we call the Old Testament. Much less did this knowledge he had contain words or ideas for this world, or his mission in this world, or the familiar things of everyday life at Nazareth. It did not contain the words, "papa" or "mama" or "temple" or "scripture" or "knife" or "fork" or anything of the sort.

I would apply this with special emphasis to an area where I think much modern theology is on the wrong track, the self-knowledge Jesus had or the knowledge he had through what some theologians consider to be his self-consciousness. What I am saying then is that the immediate knowledge Jesus had of God did not include the word "I." I believe the efforts made to build a theology of his knowledge of God on his self-consciousness are ill-advised. I cannot go into that now; for the moment I am content to say that the ordinary child does not know the word "I" but has to learn to use it. I am told that this occurs at about four years of age, and I know that the mere use of the word at the age of four leaves us a long, long way from understanding the reality of the self. There is no privileged position to be given therefore to the "I" in the hierarchy of things understood; on the contrary, it is one of the last things we come to understand. I see no reason for asserting anything different about Jesus.[29]

Moreover, I do not see any religious reason for supposing that the Lord Jesus went around trying to understand himself, or searching the scriptures for passages that pertained to him. The scriptures were not part of the object of his immediate knowledge of God either; the ordinary sinner does not think of messianic passages as applicable to himself, and I should think that the saints are even less inclined to that kind of narcissism. I would think, then, that the Lord Jesus, if he came eventually to think of the Servant passages in connection with his own life, would first think of them in the way we might think of them, not as a divine prophecy uttered several centuries earlier and pointing to "me," singling "me" out, but rather as a guide to God's thinking about all his children and therefore to be taken seriously by "me" too.

To hammer at this point once more, I would insist that Jesus did not have ideas of the future ready at hand whenever he wished to consult them. He did not have the success or failure of the morrow's mission already affirmed in his mind before he began it. Further, he did not have the other world before his eyes as he walked to his death; there is no other world given in the vision of God, in the sense of an afterlife continuous with this life and linked to it by the gate of death. Death, for Jesus as for us, was the dark exit beyond which nothing appeared.

We could put the main point in another way by saying that every day was to Jesus a fresh experience, an encounter with newness. The notion that, coming from the heavenly world, he brought with him a full view of both this one and the other, is to be exploded; his baby eyes opened on a world as new and strange as the one we meet is to us. His growing up was an experience in novelty; his becoming ac-

---

29. It would be unfair to list opponents, reject their position, but not allow them "equal time" to expose their views. Yet it is utterly impossible to discuss the debate in a footnote. All I can do is give the source of the views underlying my own presentation: Bernard Lonergan's *De constitutione Christi ontologica et psychologica* (Rome: Gregorian University, 1956); a later exposition is given in his *De verbo incarnato,* 1964.

quainted with the scriptures was an introduction to new religious ideas; his vocation was a call from God as startling and thrilling as that of any of the saints.

But maybe by now I have made that negative point with enough emphasis. At least, if I have not done so, further repetition is not likely to help. It is time to turn to the positive side: How does the vision of God that Jesus had relate to his thinking, to the way his mind worked to understand his world and his mission there, to the way he thought out his sermons and his teaching? I ask you to notice that my question is not simply how his mind worked on empirical data—it worked the way yours does, attending to data, forming schematic images, gaining an insight into the image, etc.; you can apply your own cognitional theory here. But I am asking how his vision of God affected that process and entered into it. In such a highly speculative enterprise we need all the guidance we can get, so I propose to start rather remotely with two clues and some backing in the prestige of St. Thomas.

The first is the parallel which I see between the way God is all yet becomes man, and the way Jesus might know the all and yet have to go through a process to know this or that particular item of knowledge. The divine being, then, is the all, the infinite ocean of all substance; and yet we cannot say that God is a tree, or a horse, or, prior to a certain event two thousand years ago, a man. If he would *be* a tree, or a horse, or a man, he must *become* tree or horse or man. He did in fact will to become man, and this becoming was an event; something happened that could be truly called a *fieri*, and in that sense a process. What I am suggesting is that, with all due account being taken of the differences, a parallel can be conceived to help us understand, or at least accept as possible, a process in the mind of the Lord Jesus. If he has immediate knowledge of God, he knows the all, and that all is the infinite ocean of being. Nevertheless, this does not automatically give him knowledge of a tree, or a horse, or a man, particularly not of *this* tree, or *this* horse, or *this* man. That is, knowledge of the all, though it contains knowledge of everything "in globo," does not contain it as individuated. For that, you need a process.

Secondly, we have a clue in Thomism to serve as guide in thinking out what this process might be like. St. Thomas, with his emphasis on the universal and the abstract in human knowing, thought that the knowledge the saints derive from the vision of God is not so much knowledge of this or that particular object as it is of general reasons, causes, explanations, the *species et genera rerum, et rationes earum*.[30] Even if we lean more towards the particular and concrete today, we can still

---

30. *Summa theologiae*, I, 12, 8 ad 4m; see also 106, 1 ad 1m.

use St. Thomas as a guide. I would myself supplement his idea with Lonergan's "scissors-action" of heuristic method: there is a lower blade that rises from data and an upper blade that moves downward from general ideas.[31] I conceive therefore the mind of Jesus to operate according to this scissors-action, with the upper blade supplied by his understanding of God and by the most general preconceptual ideas that derive from that understanding, ideas on man and life and the universe and duty, and the lower blade supplied by the thousands and thousands of items of data that met his eye and ear and taste and smell and touch during his life on earth.

But now we come to the point where many of us, and the systematic theologians especially, are likely to be deficient. If we are to follow the scissors-action that operated between the data the Lord Jesus observed and the vision he had of God, we need as accurate a knowledge as possible of the data. This means having in our memories an image of the hills and lakes and rivers he saw, the towns and villages, the homes and synagogues. We should be familiar with the artifacts he knew and used, the pots and pans, the tables and chairs, the hammers and saws, etc. We should know the customs of the land and the time—in weddings, in taxation, in education, in agriculture, and the rest. We should even think in the language he used, pray the prayers he prayed, and hear the scriptures he heard, giving the same sense to the words that he would give.

That at least is the ideal, and I begin my task very far indeed from the ideal. In that situation mistakes are likely. Still, I am not particularly anxious; if I do not know what kind of axe the Lord Jesus used, I can presume from the fact that the experts use my English word "axe" to translate the original, that there is some similarity between the Lord's axe and the one I use. Again, if errors occur here, they are not apt to be pernicious—not nearly as dangerous, in my view, as errors about that I-consciousness of the Lord. And yet I feel it as a painful lack that I am so handicapped in thinking out the Lord's thinking, in moving from the more abstract level of general ideas into the concrete data of the Holy Land and description of the everyday world of Jesus.

There is an in-between area that is not the field of either systematic theologian or historian of the concrete, and it is here I really feel most painfully the lack of guidance. I mean the lack of a history of introspection, and its emergence among the biblical people in particular. When did the dream first become differentiated as a category, understood in contradistinction to waking experience? When did the notion of a question come to formulation and receive a name? I presume that

---

31. *Insight,* pp. 312–13, 522–23, etc.

for some thousands of years the human race may have asked questions by gesture or word or intonation, without knowing they were asking questions or having a word for it. When did the word "if" come into usage, and even when they began to use it, as they have done in the scriptures, did they have the category we call "supposition" clearly differentiated?

I will not delay on the ordinary experiences and intellectual growth of childhood. In my hypothesis the child Jesus would look, wide-eyed, upon his world the way any child does. There is on the face of the infant of a few months a look that distinguishes him already, in my opinion, from the kitten or pup; the kitten may look upon a ball of yarn with great interest, but his interest is pragmatic: he wants to play with it; a child can apparently just look, lost in wonder: "Children's faces looking up Holding wonder like a cup." So the child Jesus would look on the slanting beam of sunlight coming in the door, on the knife his mother was using to cut the bread or cheese (a knife which he would naturally try to get hold of and examine), on the stranger whom Joseph brought to dinner; so he would listen to the strange noises these grownups were making as they moved about their strange business. He would come to distinguish some of these strange noises, would fix in his memory the Aramaic equivalents of "Mama" and "Papa" and learn that one was linked with this person who fed him and changed his diapers, learn that the other was linked with this man who seemed so big and strong. Etc. Why should we go through what is largely fanciful and full of anachronisms? The main point for me is this: that the child Jesus, and the boy, and the young man, looked and wondered, and thought and came to understand, and did so with the ordinary ideas and concepts that belong to daily life in Palestine; he may have done so more quickly, more surely, under the influence of his vision, but without any direct influence on the actual content of the ideas formed— the content was empirically based.

When we come to religious ideas we should not think that the situation is totally different, as if the immediate knowledge of God supplied him with "religious" ideas where it was disdainful of mere secular ideas. In my view it is almost equally distant from the one and the other. We have to ask ourselves in what sense the word "God" is a religious word and how it comes to have a religious meaning for the child. There is nothing special in the three letters; they can be turned around to mean something else altogether. There is nothing special in the sound which makes it rhyme with who knows how many other words. What experience gives it a religious meaning, and by what signs are we led as children to link its use with that experience? My hypothesis says the experience which gives it meaning is the experience of coming to the limits of the human, of arriving at horizons, boundaries, of looking farther and coming up against sheer mystery—not just the mystery of what is over the next hill when we explore it as boys, but the mystery of what is beyond the grave, as when we watch them bury our grandmother. And the sign, my hypothesis says, which leads me to link the sound "God" to such an experience is found in the sudden illumination, tranquil or piercing, with which I recognize, for example, in seeing my father and mother at prayer, that those who for me were the acme of human power, the almighty beings of my world, the eternal ones who were before I came and would be as far into the future as my mind could reach—the illumination with which I recognize they are not "God" but worship one who is.

We do, however, have to recognize differences when we try to apply this to the boy Jesus, but it is important to locate the differences and determine their influence. As I see it, there is no initial difference in the stock of particular words and ideas. There is an enormous difference in the illuminating power of the interior resources available. The Scholastic would indicate this in terms of objects: the object of vision is the divine essence, the intellect of the infant has no formed object but is pure potency to any and all objects of human intellect. We cannot omit the objective but I find it more helpful to put the emphasis on the subjective and to speak of desire attained and desire still reaching out, or of a light that contains all that is visible within itself and a dark light that illuminates objects but is itself invisible. When I turn to objects I would say that in one case there is global apprehension of the all and in the other there is the pure desire to know all though nothing is yet understood or known. We may recall here how close the all and nothing are in the vocabulary of the mystics, and I venture the guess that they are so close because in neither case is there anything like a particular word or idea.

The difference then is in inner resources and not in finite objects known. St. Thomas held that even in us all knowledge is somehow given with the native light of intellect, and it seems to follow that the differences in the boy Jesus would rather accelerate his learning process than eliminate it. He would recognize so much more quickly, in the sight of Mary and Joseph at prayer, their conscious subordination of themselves to someone higher; he would identify that someone so much more easily with the object of his interior experience. But, with all this granted, and giving due reverence to the Son of God, I think he would come to use the word "God" in somewhat the same way you and I came to use it. And if he learned to use the word "God" as we did, much more would he learn to use all the other words that formed part of his human vocabulary.

11. Eschaton and the Finite Values in the Heart of Jesus

My title commits me to speak about the eschaton in the mind and heart of Jesus. To speak of "mind" is to direct our thoughts to ideas and knowledge, but to speak of "heart" is to direct our thoughts to values. The "eschaton" in the heart of Jesus would refer to the ultimate value that engaged his heart in a fulfilling way. Our problem then in this section is to study that value in an analysis that will enable us to relate it to his earthly mission. We will be dealing, in other words, with the hierarchy of values in the human heart of Jesus, with the place given there to God and man, to a transcendent world and to this transient one. Eventually we will have to ask about the relation of his values to his daily life and conduct and thus come to their influence on his vocation and work in the world, his earthly mission.

My general procedure in this section will remain the same: that is, I will assume a hypothetical view as explanatory principle; I will expose it first in abstract generality and then speculate how on this basis we may relate the eschaton to finite values of human life on earth. The main effort then is to contribute an idea, leaving the work of verification and judgment to another time or to other persons. But in all fairness I ought to warn you that the support for my hypothesis and speculation is flimsy, more so than when I talked of the human knowledge of Jesus. In that case there was, if not a dogma, at least a long tradition of thought in the church; but there does not seem to be a parallel tradition on the question of the heart of Jesus and the values that engaged it. That statement is likely to provoke instant opposition from those who think that, if Jesus taught us anything at all, it was a set of true values. I may be inviting some opposition later on, but some is quite unnecessary, and I would like to eliminate the latter by explaining the sense in which I meant my statement.

I do not mean then that there is no evidence in the New Testament of a Christian hierarchy of values. There is a very definite hierarchy of this-worldly and other-worldly values, which are so sharply contrasted as to result in outright opposition. Paul and James agree on this, the one asserting that the wisdom of the flesh is enmity to God and the other that to be the friend of this world is to be the enemy of God. The doctrine of the beatitudes spells out the idea, and the doctrine of the perfect obedience of Jesus to the will of his Father, even when his own will spontaneously recoils, gives it a concrete focus.

Neither do I mean that this idea lacks a tradition. What is more characteristic of Christian spirituality than the imitation of Christ and the efforts of the saints, one after another, to discover his way, that is, his set of values, and make it their rule of life? I naturally remember here the *Spiritual Exercises* of St. Ignatius, the founder of my own religious order, where you have the exercise of the Two Standards setting forth the sharp contrast and conflict between the values of Jesus and those of the world, and the Principle and Foundation relativizing all worldly values in the principle of indifference. Even the theology manuals take up the question in their own way with theses on the sanctity of Jesus and his confirmation in grace. And the councils went so far as to define dogmatically that there is a human will in Christ, showing an interest here that they never showed in his intellect.

What do I mean then when I say that we have little in the way of tradition to help us in the present question? I mean that the *process* by which Jesus formed his set of values never came into question. Why should it? If you imagine a mind with a view into the other world, with the clearest picture of the joys of heaven and the torments of hell, then you have no need of any process of value-formation. The situation is clear at a glance. At least the great distance, the infinite qualitative difference, between this world's values and those of the other world is clear. You may work out more subtly the steps by which you are led to choose the better or the worse, the ways Satan has of ensnaring men's hearts, but this is not really an objective determination of the values themselves.

Now, however, our understanding of the Thomist concept of the vision of God has removed this easy supposition in which values are determined independently of us and may be taken for granted. Further, modern philosophy forces upon us the consideration that man is to a large extent the creator of his own values. The two facts conspire to raise a new question about the process in the heart of Jesus. We have to ask how he formed his heart, what forces were at work, to what extent he accepted the values of his time and culture and to what extent he forged new values of his own. We have to penetrate to the basic value which held his heart and see how that can be made operative for us today. Otherwise we drift without rudder or anchor; we judge Jesus by what is superficial in his conduct and, if that seems little relevant today, we have no way of locking our hearts into something more permanent and reliable. It is fairly clear, for example, that Jesus took little interest in the arts and sciences, the culture and civilization, even of his local world, much less of the great world of the Mediterranean. The Church, however, takes a great interest in arts and science, culture and civilization. What are we to make of this? Is Jesus not our model? Or is he our model when we so will it, and not our model when we decide otherwise? You see that, unless we undertake a careful analysis of the process by which he formed his values and distinguish the universally valid from what was particular to his time or his vocation, we are without trustworthy guidelines in the Christian way of life.

Let me digress for a minute from the route of objective theology. The difficulty, as I have put it, is not just academic. I do not apologize for that. We are personally involved here, and to a high degree. When we speculated on the knowledge of Christ, we were not quite so immediately involved; there is surely a line of influence from what we hold on Christ's human knowledge to what we recognize as a personal call to ourselves, but the line is long and indirect. Not so here. What we judge Christ to have set before himself as his value, that we ourselves must take as our value, if we are to be Christian. So it has been tacitly assumed. We could speak theoretically of a simple objective study of Christ's values, with its relevance to life for us held as a second question arising in distinction from the first. But in fact we have to discover agreement between Christ's values and ours, either by converting ourselves to what we find in him, or by finding in him (setting out to find in him) what we have already adopted as our set of values. I have to recognize openly and confess to you what you know for yourselves, that my mental power even to conceive the values Christ held is drugged by the opinion of many a counter-attraction that appeals to me, and my power to assert these to be his values is treacherously influenced by those I have already taken as my own.

That little digression was necessary if we are to keep our perspective, I think. But now back to business. We will look at the New Testament set of values and subsequent tradition in a very general way and then see whether, with the help of modern thinkers and categories, we can speculate usefully on what the process of value-formation was in Jesus. We remember always that we have no direct access to what he said and did, the data that might reveal this process; we have direct access only to what the New Testament writers said, and we cannot assume that they understood their Lord perfectly.

In general then the early New Testament writings show a marked orientation to the other world. The earliest document we have is Paul's first letter to the Thessalonians and it sets the tone at once in its description of the conversion undergone by the Thessalonians; they turned from idols, Paul says, to serve the living and true God "and to wait expectantly for the appearance from heaven of his Son Jesus" (1 Th 1:10). That phrase, "to wait expectantly," is especially significant. It is the key to what has been called the interim ethic of Paul: we are not to make much of marriage, sorrow, joy, buying, wealth, and the rest, because "[t]he time we live in will not last long. . . . For the whole frame of this world is passing away" (1 Cor 7:29-31).

As time goes on, however, and Jesus does not appear, it seems to be borne in upon the Christians of the young Church that the coming of Jesus may be delayed, and delayed a very long time indeed; they had better settle in then for a longer stay than they expected. With this realization two trends develop. One is more material and concerns the use of this world's goods, the formation of institutions, and the like. This trend comes out quite clearly in the pastoral letters to Timothy and Titus, where institutions are forming and you have explicit reference to the use of marriage, foods, etc.: ". . . God created them to be enjoyed with thanksgiving by believers who have inward knowledge of the truth" (1 Tim 4:3). The other trend, more spiritual in character, is towards an understanding of our condition in the world as one of partially realized eschatology; that is, there is a sense that we are already living in enjoyment of the final state, in communion with God and his Son Jesus through their Spirit who dwells in us. This is particularly evident in John's writings: "Everyone who believes that Jesus is the Christ is a child of God . . . every child of God is victor over the godless world" (1 Jn 5:1,4). We have already arrived, you might say; indeed, this is almost explicitly said: "[E]ven in this world we are as he is" (1 Jn 4:17).

I don't wish to exaggerate, and I know that the sketch I have given is terribly "simpliste." There is community of ideas on a broad basis in the New Testament, and what is new is not wholly new. The element of "waiting expectantly" is there from beginning to end, not only in 1 Thessalonians but far on in the pastorals, as well as in 2 Peter and in John. On the other side, the element of present communion with God and his Son in the gift of the Spirit is also found from beginning to end of the New Testament writings. So is the element of the right use of this world's goods: when Paul is telling his Thessalonians to endure patiently to the expected end, he is also telling them to get busy about their daily occupations, and not to hang around waiting for someone else to feed them (1 Th 4:11-12; 2 Thess 3:10-11). And, of course, everywhere there is inculcated love for neighbor, a love that shows itself in concern and deeds and not merely in words. Nevertheless, despite the strong continuity, I think there is a fairly steady trend in the direction indicated.

What subsequent history did was accentuate the polarization without, however, adverting to it clearly or dealing with it intellectually. I hesitate to expand that point, for anything I say will be hopelessly superficial, but even a superficial view gives markers of great significance. One marker is the effective triumph of the position represented by Clement of Alexandria over that represented by Tertullian. Tertullian thought that Jerusalem, the Church, should have nothing to do with

Athens, the world of culture and especially of philosophy; Clement of Alexandria held the exactly opposite opinion and his view prevailed; despite spasmodic outbreaks of Tertullianism, I do not think that there has been any turning back on the part of the Church from the direction vindicated by Clement. But another marker is the persistence in the Church, notably in her liturgy, of Tertullianist sentiments: collect after collect in the Roman missal urges us to despise the things of this world, *mundana despicere,* and to set our heart on heavenly things, *amare caelestia.* In other words, we have developed that ambivalent attitude I mentioned earlier: we go on collecting art treasures and cultivating philosophy and the sciences, while at the same time we profess our faith in our Lord who, it seems, couldn't care less about such matters. I do not think we have taken up this question as a Church and settled for ourselves what we really believe.

Neither the New Testament, then, nor subsequent tradition has solved the problem of a Christian way of linking the values of this world to transcendent value—"Christian" being understood here in the sense of deriving from Christ's own values. Much less has either one of them investigated the question that will occupy us now, of the process by which Jesus formed his values. We may be able to get more help from modern thinkers and their categories, and in this hope I turn to Ernst Troeltsch. He does not clearly distinguish exegesis from speculation but his views have impressed me and they will serve to introduce the hypothetical ideas I wish to contribute.

What Troeltsch tries to give, I think, is a general perspective. He sees the preaching of Jesus as emphasizing the great judgment of the coming of the Kingdom of God, and the formation of a community based on the hope of the Kingdom. Jesus does not speculate on the nature of the Kingdom; it means the rule of God on earth to be followed by the end of the world and judgment. His demand is for preparation; fundamentally, it is for the sanctification of the individual for the sake of God, with an ethic emphasizing purity of intention and reverence for all moral commands. He is marked by the religious idea of the presence of God and by the thought of the infinite value of the soul, to be attained through self-renunciation for the sake of God. Here the gospel is very radical, not ascetic, but severe. It does not allow doubt on the possibility of practice. Still there is a character of joy, gentleness, readiness to forgive. It is not an asceticism that is a provision for the future, but only a severity that makes almost superhuman demands.

Troeltsch follows this with a section on the sociological characteristics of the gospel ethic, a topic most germane to his study. There is an unqualified individualism based on call to fellowship with God and the infinite value of the self. But this very individualism also contains a strong idea of fellowship with one another, based on the fact that those being purified for the sake of God meet in him. In a further section Troeltsch takes up the gospel ethic and general social values and finds no interest there in social problems which belong to this world and perish with it. There is no thought of the state; it is the rule of God that interests Jesus, not the rule of the Jewish people. Nor is there an economic policy; we are to live for the day, share with others, work for a living. There is a more detailed teaching on the family, which Jesus uses for symbols of God's highest attributes, and the idea of the family is a fundamental feature of his feeling for human life. But sex will not exist in the Kingdom, and one may have to renounce family for the Kingdom. The message of Jesus then is not a program of social reform but a summons to prepare for the coming of the Kingdom. Even the Kingdom is not a new social order founded by God. It creates a new order on earth, but not one concerned with the state, or society, or family.[32]

Against this background we can introduce the real question: how Jesus formed his mind on values and organized them hierarchically in his heart. Here again I call upon Troeltsch, in a work dating from the last days of his life, a set of lectures that he never in fact delivered, death intervening before he could do so.[33] Three of these lectures fall under the general title of "Ethics and the Philosophy of History," and the second of the three is called "The Ethics of the Cultural Values." It is towards the end of this lecture, almost in passing, that Troeltsch voices his views on the origin of systems of ethics and introduces the question in regard to Jesus.

The context of this passage is as follows. In a previous chapter Troeltsch has dealt with The Morality of the Personality and of the Conscience, which he sees as purely formal, as lying outside history, as leading to the timelessly valid. But that supplies just one thread in the fabric of ethical consciousness; a quite different one is introduced under the heading of goods and ends, ethical values. These are entirely historical creations: family, state, law, economic control of nature, science, art, and religion. These realms are not at first matters of ethics, but belong to specific and independent sciences; for example, the family is the subject of sciences of the sexual life and its sociological forms of organization. Only in the last place do these sciences look for the character which these realms *should* assume and thus merge into ethics.

How does a system of values come into being? A number of attempts

32. Ernst Troeltsch, *The Social Teaching of the Christian Churches* (New York: Harper Torchbooks, 1960), vol. I, pp. 39–69 (= ch. I, part 1).

33. *Christian Thought: Its History and Application. Lectures Written for Delivery in England During March 1923* (London: University of London, 1923).

to construct such a system proceed from a simple beginning to a simple goal. This is easier for a morality of consciousness, but harder for an ethics of cultural values. New and original attempts were made in the nineteenth century, but in the end they must admit defeat:

All these attempts at a deduction of the system of values, be they based on the nature of Reason, or on that of the Community, or on the World-process, or on the religious goal, are helpless in the face of the fullness and vigour, and also of the tensions and cross-purposes, of cultural values in real life.[34]

Still cultural values have to be welded into a homogeneous whole; however, this is done, not theoretically, but unconsciously—the system is evolved as a pure fact. In moments of crisis and in periods of greater maturity a conscious synthesis becomes necessary. It will be an *a posteriori* construction. It must assimilate the bases of its own *de facto* existence, and only then refine and evolve itself. It does this by determining the direction, by bringing out the central value and organizing the rest around it.

This last for Troeltsch is a personal act. It is also a personal act to link this system with the morality of consciousness. There is no *a priori* system available for this:

Statesmen, reformers, poets, prophets, are usually active agents in this work. In spite of all their most elaborate reflections they can at bottom adduce for themselves no other plea than that of Jesus: "He who is of the truth heareth My voice."[35]

Faith ultimately decides and justifies the decision.

I have been greatly impressed by the passages from Troeltsch but, now that we are moving from a system of values to its subjective foundations, I am going to shift my study from him to Lonergan. Possibly we could find further precious clues in Troeltsch and, in fact, I think there is much to ponder on the relationship of Lonergan's ethical views to his, in the way they both see the formal and material elements of moral consciousness, and in the way they see the person as source, through inner experience or conversion, of the values he finds in the objectively existing universe. But, as you perhaps know, my own mind has been formed profoundly—irremediably, some would say—by long study of Lonergan and I find it so much more convenient to search for clues in his writings.

As it happens, the most useful passages I have discovered are found in a paper which Lonergan delivered here at Villanova University in your symposium of one year ago, though the same passages occur in the now published *Method in Theology* and I will therefore quote them

34. Ibid. p. 92.   35. Ibid., p. 98.

from that work. The passages deal with the relationship of love, faith, and belief. Lonergan accepts the distinction between faith and belief, calls faith "the knowledge born of religious love,"[36] and makes belief refer to the word of religion, "the judgments of fact and the judgments of value that the religion proposes."[37]

There are three terms then to be explained: love, faith, and belief. The first is best understood in terms of the state of being-in-love. The state is dynamic. Being-in-love

takes over. It is the first principle. From it flow one's desires and fears, one's joys and sorrows, one's discernment of value, one's decisions and deeds.[38]

That much is generic. But there are different kinds of being-in-love of which being-in-love with God is one:

It is God's love flooding our hearts. . . . It grounds the conviction of St. Paul that "there is nothing in death or life . . . nothing in all creation that can separate us from the love of God in Christ Jesus our Lord" (Rom 8, 38f.).[39]

Being-in-love with God

is the basic fulfilment of our conscious intentionality. That fulfilment brings a deep-set joy that can remain despite humiliation, failure. . . . That fulfilment brings a radical peace . . . bears fruit in a love of one's neighbor that strives mightily to bring about the kingdom of God on this earth. On the other hand, the absence of that fulfilment opens the way to the trivialization of human life in the pursuit of fun, to the harshness of human life arising from the ruthless exercise of power, to despair about human welfare springing from the conviction that the universe is absurd.[40]

Secondly, faith is the knowledge born of this religious love. It corresponds to Pascal's reasons of the heart which reason does not know. It is an intentional[41] response to values. It is not the factual knowledge reached by experiencing, understanding and verifying, but "another kind of knowledge reached through the discernment of value and the judgments of value of a person in love." When the love is religious love, "there is added an apprehension of transcendent value" consisting "in the experienced fulfilment of our unrestricted thrust to self-transcendence, in our actuated orientation towards the mystery of love and awe."[42] And, thirdly, there is religious belief arising out of faith:

36. *Method in Theology,* p. 115.
37. Ibid., p. 118.
38. Ibid., p. 105.
39. Ibid.
40. Ibid.
41. "Intentional"—that is, directed towards an object (not "intentional" in the sense of "deliberate").
42. *Method,* p. 115.

Among the values that faith discerns is the value of believing the word of religion, of accepting the judgments of fact and the judgments of value that the religion proposes.[43]

I have quoted Lonergan at some length on the relationship of love, faith, and belief, not because I expect to use all the details of this relationship in putting forward an hypothesis on the mind and heart of Christ, but simply for one aspect of his discussion, the harmony that prevails between mind and heart in his exposition. I do not in fact think that in Christ, or in anyone who "sees" God, the first knowledge is born of love; rather, I take it that the first understanding is already knowledge and from it love proceeds on the model of Love in the holy Trinity. But the harmony is the same. The difference is that in Christ the immediate knowledge of God is the principle of his love and obedience, whereas in us the love of God and our obedience to him form the principle of our faith.[44]

What we are dealing with then is a unitary consciousness formed by the harmony of mind and heart. It is a unitary consciousness that is

43. Ibid., p. 118.

44. There is a problem here in relating the early Lonergan to the later Lonergan. The precise question regards the interrelation of mind and heart. Most of Lonergan's work in Christology was prior to 1965 when he spoke in terms of intellect and will and saw understanding in the mind of Christ as prior to love in the heart of Christ. But most of his work on values is subsequent to 1965; he does not speak now of intellect and will but of levels of consciousness and when he applies this to us in our human condition on earth he sees falling in love with God as prior to faith in the traditional sense. Would he now see this as the order that obtains in the blessed and in Jesus? I am inclined to think that he would not but, not wishing to clutter up this paper with questions that may be of much greater interest to me than to my audience, I am leaving argumentation to this footnote.

The general principle operative here is that the relationship of mind and heart is the opposite in our religious experience and faith life of what it is in the blessed and what it is conceived to be in God. That is, the order in God is Father, Son, and Holy Spirit; or, in the Thomist transformation of these biblical names, the order is Understanding, Word, and Love. And this I take to be the natural order of the rationally conscious universe, the order therefore that obtains in the blessed who understand with a fullness that elicits expressions of awe in a never ending series and results in an eternally repeated act of falling in love with God. It is also the order for "natural" man on earth who determines his responsibilities on the basis of what he knows to be the facts. But in the graced activity of our faith life the order seems to be the reverse, as Lonergan had noted some years ago in his *De constitutione Christi ontologica et psychologica*: Ordo naturalis "quodammodo invertitur cum Deus per gratias infusas magis voluntatem quam intellectum . . . movere possit et soleat" (p. 99). That is, the Holy Spirit is given to enable us to believe in the Son who will lead us to the Father. This inverse order is paralleled in the field of the virtues: charity floods our hearts and enables us to speak the truth of what is revealed; this truth we then try to understand in the painful and inadequate achievements of theology. I conclude from all this that in Jesus the immediate knowledge of God is the principle of his love and obedience, whereas in us the love of God and our obedience to him form the principle of our faith. And this, I think, would be Lonergan's position.

Additionally, one might expect that Lonergan would enrich his account of this matter by referring to "the two ways of human development": see ch. 20 below.

fundamental, that pertains to one's being, that makes one what one is. It is a basic consciousness that is operative, that overflows into one's conduct and one's life. In this the parallel is close between the consciousness of Jesus and our own. On that basis I presume to quote again from Lonergan's paper in a passage where he links transcendent value with other values:

> As other apprehensions of value, so too faith has a relative as well as an absolute aspect. It places all other values in the light and the shadow of transcendent value. In the shadow, for transcendent value is supreme and incomparable. In the light, for transcendent value links itself to all other values to transform, magnify, glorify them. Without faith the originating value is man and the terminal value is the good man brings about. But in the light of faith originating value is divine light and love, while terminal value is the whole universe. So the human good becomes absorbed in an all-encompassing good.[45]

In this context of the link between transcendent and other values my own question now emerges: How is this link established in the consciousness of Jesus? What was the process in his heart by which other values were created and placed in the light and shadow of transcendent value? I assume that the link in values is derivative from a prior link in judgments, and then my question becomes: How did he effect the transition from a judgment on transcendent value to one on temporal value, or from a judgment on temporal value to one on transcendent value? As always, we keep in mind that we do not attribute these terms to him; we do not even attribute distinct acts of judgment to his mind; we do not attribute any clear advertence on his part to what was going on in his mind. If there was a process, it was spontaneous and unreflected; if he objectified it in any way, it would probably be by means of dreams, myths, images and the like.

With all this in mind I should say that the process now in question parallels the transition from his vision of the all to knowledge of particular items of the concrete universe, that is, knowing what-is leads spontaneously, through the negating power of the mind, to conceiving what-is-not. Conceiving what-is-not leads through the creative power of the mind to conceiving what-is-not-yet-but-may-be. Conceiving what-is-not-yet-but-may-be leads through reflection on personal responsibility to the idea of what-is-not-yet-but-may-and-ought-to-be-through-my-intervention. At this point the practical judgment emerges, the notion of particular value has been implicitly introduced, and we have the path outlined from apprehension of transcendent value to apprehension of human, cultural, religious values, the sort of thing Troeltsch talks about.

---

45. *Method in Theology,* p. 116.

We can specify the course of this transition a little more concretely. The gospel commandment tells us to love God above all things and our neighbor as ourselves. The appearance in the horizon of Christ's consciousness of the-good-to-be-done is on biblical grounds to be set in the context of love for others. But this too has its abstract and philosophic counterpart, investigated these days by pioneering branches of philosophy. The good for us is the human good, and the human good is inextricably bound up with our relations to others. Just as the self appears and is conceived simultaneously with and in correlation with the other, so the need we see and the good we conceive in response to need is defined by our knowledge and love of others. A helpful parallel here is found in our doctrine of God's creative thinking. God's goodness is *diffusivum sui*, it overflows spontaneously to be shared by others; similarly, Christ's response to the goodness of God leads directly to his concern for his fellowman.[46]

We can also clarify the process in Jesus by contrast with our own. We ourselves experience a "conversion" of heart, maybe repeated conversions, as we move from lower to higher values in the course of a lifetime. Religious conversion is the shift from all values of the human universe to the transcendent value that God is. Normally we think of the order and direction as that I have indicated: from earthly to heavenly, from human to divine. We meditate on the ephemeral character of life on earth: "Your life, what is it? You are no more than a mist, seen for a little while and then dispersing" (Jas 4:14). We come from consideration of these limits to what is without limit, the boundless being and goodness of God. Whether in actual fact our hearts follow this order of development is another question; it may be that God brings us to a sense of the ephemeral through first giving us a dim anticipation of the eternal. However, when we come to reflect on the relationship, we almost necessarily see it in terms of a shift from lower to higher, simply because we can understand and are moved by the lower in a way proportionate to human nature, whereas we cannot understand the higher but live in faith, seeing through a glass darkly.

Jesus too would establish in his heart a relationship between the earthly and the transcendent, but I think there would be a reversal of the order and of the emphasis. The direction would not be so much a

---

46. When I wrote that line, I simply took its truth for granted. But it was a good lesson for me on how little we know about Jesus to read afterwards Henry J. Cadbury, *The Peril of Modernizing Jesus* (London: S. P. C. K., 1962) and discover another viewpoint: that Jesus did not think so much of my neighbor's need as of my own duty to act rightly; the altruism of the social gospel is not characteristic of his approach (see ch. 5: "Limitations of Jesus' Social Teaching," especially pp. 101–11). It is also a lesson in the slowness of communication that Cadbury's book, which I just discovered, was first published in 1937.

conversion from lower to higher as an emerging appreciation of lower means to a higher end. Thomas Aquinas saw conversions as a change in the end one sets before oneself, with the possibility remaining of choosing various means to the one end by which we are drawn. The heart of Jesus would not undergo the radical change that is conversion to another end of life, but it would experience ever new appreciations of ways and means. He would come to see the way of the suffering Servant of Isaiah as that way in which God means his chosen representatives to go. He would learn obedience by the things he suffered; that is, obedience would become a value to him as derivative from the value which is the goodness of God and the rightness of God's will.

In this way it would be easy in principle to account for the particular choices he made during life and the successive stages in his realization of the Father's will. I say, in principle, for always in actual fact we are handicapped by inaccurate knowledge of what he said and did; and what the circumstances were in which he said and did it. In principle, then, he could come to appreciate the value of being unattached to the world's wealth; it could become part of his set of values, and this in a process that would resemble the process the saints experienced, a Francis of Assisi or an Ignatius of Loyola. He could come to appreciate the value of having disciples who would extend in space and time the message he could not personally bring to everyone. Etc. At this point, we come to our last section, the worldly mission of Jesus.

III. The Worldly Mission of Jesus

Early in my paper I quoted Bonhoeffer's question, "What is Christianity, and indeed, what is Christ, for today?" That question has been nagging at me since I first read it I don't know how many years ago. In some very fundamental but not very well-defined sense (that global apprehension I keep talking about) every Christian knows what Christ means for him today and every day. We die. We want desperately to live. Jesus lives after death and because of him we too will live. So he means everything to us. No amount of realized eschatology, or new secularity, or resolution in the face of our being-toward-death, has given me the power to cope as I move towards the dark exit. Only my faith in the risen Lord is any real help here.

But theologians may not stop at faith. We would be simple cop-outs if we did. For our faith is handicapped when its meaning is undefined. The urgency of Bonhoeffer's question remains—not the urgent need of a new apologetic for our faith, but the urgency of articulating more fully and defining the meaning of what Christ is for us today, and answering the questions that arise. For they do arise. "Jesus lives after death"—the very word "after" raises a question. It was "after" Good Friday for the apostles, for Mary and those who stood by the cross on Calvary. But was it "after" for Jesus himself, and what would "after" mean for him? He "lives" but that word too raises a question on the mode of life he enjoys. A senseless question, St. Paul said as he went ahead and tried to answer it. We too have to try to answer it. We are never going to overcome the darkness of faith by any of our theology, but we have to look for the dawn and we would not be what God made us if we did not try to do so.

So it is with the question we come to now of the worldly mission of Christ. It is not enough to say that the eschaton in the mind and heart of Jesus is the understanding, the knowledge, and the love of God. This could be said of the angels, it could be said of the blessed in heaven, it could be said of some non-existent human race who never lived on earth but were created in the eschatological state. We were not so created; we are born into this world, and the Son of God was incarnate in this world. What has this world to do with the eschaton? How do we relate the understanding, knowledge, and love of God that Jesus had to this very human world of arts and science, of culture and civilization, a world that after all God created to be enjoyed with thanksgiving by believers who have inward knowledge of the truth?

I have spent a long time and taken you through some very dull thinking in order to set up an answer to that question, but I saw no alternative if we are to have anything but a superficial answer. The options were to regard Jesus merely as a prophet to whom the word of the Lord came, or as one who had in his own inner resources that out of which the word of the Lord is spoken. If we opt for the second we are dealing with a participation in the divine understanding of mystery out of which God himself speaks when he chooses. Such an eschatological understanding is not readily related to the finite words and ideas of ordinary human activity, but we had to think out that relation in some plausible explanation if we were to talk usefully of his worldly mission. Now, however, the bulk of the work is done and our task in this final section considerably lightened.

First of all, we are not going to expect Jesus to have available from the start innate ideas and ready-made blueprints of his work. As he did not have the word "God" or the word "I" written on his mind, neither did he have the words "mission," "redemption," "savior," etc. When he first heard those words he did not know their meaning, but had to learn it as we did. When he learned their meaning, he did not at once apply them to himself, as we do not. As he learned obedience by the things he suffered, so he learned by slow degrees what his vocation was.

Secondly, I would expect this learning to follow the pattern of the scissors-action we spoke of earlier. We may have models for this nearer at hand. It is said of Ignatius of Loyola that he had an experience soon after his conversion, in which he saw his future work laid out for him.[47] The strange thing is that he still had to discover the details of his work year by year and day by day, with much prayer and reflection. Yet I do not think we need distrust the tradition on that early experience of his. It is just that a great deal of thinking has to intervene between the general idea, the *species et genera rerum, et rationes earum,* which may have been given him, and the particular, concrete form the idea takes, which was not given him.

It seems to me that in a similar way the Lord Jesus went on specifying his mission step by step. By way of illustration I continue my effort to make an educated guess and speculate that an important step could have been taken at the age of twelve. I am not about to decide whether Luke was recording historical fact or constructing a story with a point, when he wrote about the child Jesus in the temple, but I have the liberty of any believer to suppose it could have happened the way he describes it. And then how would I reconstruct the Lord's thinking? I would say that at the age of twelve profound bodily and psychic changes are taking place in a boy. A new world is opening before him, and new possibilities of life. We all know how boys at a certain age despise girls, and then rather suddenly find them extremely attractive, begin to carry their books home from school, etc., etc. It's an old story and a familiar one! I see no reason to suppose that the boy Jesus didn't have experiences and feelings that correspond in large measure to our own, due weight being given to different environmental and cultural factors. But also at this very time new questions of a religious nature are coming to for-mulation in his mind: What is the purpose of life? What is man on earth for? What should he do with the sixty or seventy years that may remain to him? He has read or heard the scriptures, he knows about the boy Samuel being called by God in the sanctuary. As he and his people come up to Jerusalem reciting and singing the gradual psalms, he finds a new meaning in the holy city, in the courts of the Lord, in dwelling in the house of the Lord.

---

47. This was the vision he had beside the Cardoner river, during the year he was at Manresa. Ignatius does not himself in his "autobiography" say that he saw his future career in this vision, but the tradition seems to have begun among those who talked with him about his experience, with Nadal a main source; see Roger Cantin, "L'Illumination du Cardoner," *Sciences ecclésiastiques* 7 (1955), pp. 23–56. The validity of the tradition is debated, with a goodly literature on the matter. Hugo Rahner is strong for the view that Ignatius saw the outlines of his Company, *The Spirituality of St. Ignatius Loyola: An Account of Its Historical Development* (Westminster, MD: Newman, 1953), pp. 96–103. Paul Dudon is on the other side, *St. Ignatius of Loyola* (Milwaukee: Bruce, 1949), pp. 452–55.

So two new worlds open at once before him and, because it is not clear that their paths point in the same direction, he is faced with a decision. There is the world of the humanly good, of trades and skills, of marriage and family, of village life with its uneventful course and religious satisfaction. There is also the world of the temple, of the sort of life Samuel was called to. It is not hard to imagine the lines forming, with a strong impulse towards one and a quiet but persistent call to the other; it is possible to imagine the resolution of the conflict in the direction of the second, of his staying in the temple, convinced that his Father was calling him to a special vocation. It is possible even to conceive that he learned, after some days, and on the return of his parents, that he was not called just yet to remain in the temple as Samuel was, that a further process of maturation awaited him and must precede his definitive response in a specific way. But I wish to emphasize that the option was real: he could choose variously—there was no blueprint in heaven to look at.

In all this there would be operative the scissors-action of his knowledge of God on the one blade, a knowledge itself wholly unspecified as to categories but one from which vague and very general categories were gradually forming, and his boyhood experiences on the other blade, his memory of what Mary and Joseph said, of what he heard in the synagogues, of what he experienced at prayer. Speculation on various other steps of his career might be similarly carried out—what happened at his baptism, what went through his mind on encountering opposition from the leaders of his people, how he formed his views on going up to Jerusalem at the end of his public life, and in this way we could work out how he conceived his worldly mission in general.

I am not concerned so much to determine what his particular vocation and mission was in its detail, as to insist that he had to work it out, and to understand *how* he may have worked it out and why he seems to have done so with such indifference to earthly values. So I underline again the fact that he learned what his mission was. What I said about his knowledge, that the empirical part of it came to his mind with startling newness, and what I said about his values, that he discovered and accepted those that were not transcendent, has also to be understood of his decisions. He did not have an action kit provided by the triune God as he left the courts of heaven for his mission on earth. We have continually to remind ourselves that he did not leave the courts of heaven as man, that he had never been there as man.

So we have to try to understand how he worked out his mission on earth. My own contribution to this task has to be made in abstract, general terms, and so I would say that he would find in the fulfillment of his own human nature (for which terms he would have biblical images, or unformulated ideas or perhaps vague conceptions) the notion of what man is and what man is to be. At some point in time he would learn, for this too would be a discovery, that other men did not have the vision he had, or the clarity of his apprehension of divine value. At this point he would more clearly perceive his mission to be one of service, and perceive himself to be "the man for others," though, if Cadbury is right,[48] this modern phase is a bit anachronistic.

We can reduce the abstractness if we return to Troeltsch and adopt his more biblical terms. He specified the notion Jesus had of God as a notion of a holy will, and more particularly as a holy will directed to his creation and his people, a will issuing a divine claim on the obedience and service of Jesus.[49] In some such biblical terms, I think, would Jesus become conscious of his responsibility; in biblical terms again would he become conscious of his solidarity with his people and his responsibility to work for and with them; in biblical terms would he come to realize the shortness of life, the limits set by a divine plan to the time of human response to God, and in some such context would he conceive the sense of urgency he shows, the exhortation to seize the *kairos,* and what we call the "crisis" parables.

But how do we explain his attitude towards the values of humanism? Towards progress? Towards abolition of injustice, and the like? For in our time we have come to take a certain positive attitude towards these and to associate such an attitude with our Christian faith. Lonergan, for example, finds that "faith is linked with human progress and it has to meet the challenge of human decline." Faith and progress thus help one another. "Faith places human efforts in a friendly universe . . . Inversely, progress realizes the potentialities of man and nature. . . ."[50] And this seems thoroughly Christian and yet not to reflect the immediate interests of Jesus himself.

We should not be "simpliste" about Jesus, however. We can say that he recognized human values within a certain range. As far as we can judge from the gospels, he knew and practiced the customs of human courtesy (Lk 7:44-46). He apparently had a sense of the value of the well-spoken word, of the well-chosen illustration. He seems to have recognized the value of human trades and settled occupations. He seems to have studied the politics of the situation and not to have needlessly antagonized the men in power. He perhaps learned to sing (Mt 26:30) and took the ordinary means, that of asking the doctors, to learn the traditions of his people (Lk 2:46).

But the degree of interest in any human value is a function of the

48. See n. 46 above.   49. *The Social Teaching,* p. 53.
50. *Method,* p. 117.

particular situation. It is one thing to learn and respect and observe the ordinary rules of courtesy, and quite another to make them your life-study, either academically or practically. Christ was not called to write such a book as Emily Post wrote. And when I say that he was not "called" to do this, I mean to indicate a very central factor in the "circumstances" that help locate a value in one's hierarchy. God calls each one of us individually. General rules may provide the institutions within which we function, and guides to the validity of the interpretation we give his call. But there is a surplus element that does not fit into the general rules. Colwell, speaking of our efforts to categorize Christ, says we are like a man applying a measure to Christ, who always finds him sticking out all around the edges.[51] It is the same with an individual vocation. The individual person's call from God has elements that stick out over the edges of general rules. And Christ is an individual person with his own individual human nature. Perhaps in another era he might have been a university professor lecturing on the history of courtesy, instead of being a carpenter building chairs and tables in Nazareth; and in that university context he might have pondered his mission to the world. But his vocation was to be a carpenter and then, putting his carpentry behind him, to proceed directly to the main concern of life, without ever denying the value of carpentry in God's scheme.

So we have to exercise the ordinary rules of good judgment when we examine his life and doctrine for his views on cultural values. We look in vain for nuggets of wisdom on the value of an education, on the exercise of the franchise, on the beauties of music and painting, on the importance of mathematics, on experimental farms and fish hatcheries for the improvement of basic industries, on the need and value of football for growing boys, on the precious gems of the Latin and Greek classics, and so on through an interminable list of the items we might draw up to classify the set of values of our own or of a bygone age. His silence, I would say, is the silence of disinterest without being the silence of condemnation. We are not faced with a choice of black or white. To make poetry your career, to love poetry, to have undeveloped power of appreciation of poetry, to condemn poetry—these are four of many possibilities and we may not say that, if Jesus is not in the first category, he must be in the fourth. His disinterest, I suggest, was not programmatic, but just tactical or maybe involuntary and an accident of history.

It may seem harder to explain his disinterest in starting schools and

---

51. Ernest C. Colwell, *New or Old? The Christian Struggle with Change and Tradition* (Philadelphia: Westminster, 1970), p. 104.

hospitals, campaigning against slavery or for the development of underprivileged peoples and the emancipation of women. For here there is question of justice and charity. But a moment's reflection may show these ideas too to be anachronisms. The idea of a hospital is a slow growth in itself; even when you have the idea, its practicability is a function of the availability of ways and means. Progress and the improvement of the human lot in general are still more remote and even slower to emerge. To make a very long story a little bit shorter, human thinking has a history of thousands of years; it needs thousands of years just because of the material substratum involved, just to give impressions time to form, images time to reach schematization, questions time to emerge, ideas time to ramify, etc. To expect all this to happen in a moment or even in a lifetime of thirty years, just because a man has the vision of God, is really nonsense.

I began this paper with a reference to Jesus as our lord and savior, as the way, the truth, and the life, our model. I return to that idea now and ask what, at the end of this study, can be said of the ideas and values of Jesus as guides for our minds and hearts. I hope that at least I have helped you eliminate a mistaken conception of the traditional doctrine on the vision of God. I hope we are now ready to talk of his encountering the world as fresh and new, of his learning day by day the values his people cherished, of revising them and moving beyond them in the creation of new values. I hope we are ready to grant the time-conditioned character of his mind and heart in regard to finite objects and even in regard to his language about the infinite and his choice of ways and means to orient ourselves toward the infinite. And therefore we may not simply attempt to quote him when there is question of the development of the third world, or condemnation of Fidel Castro, or dialogue with hippies and "Jesus freaks." These are *our* questions, to be solved by *our own* intelligence working in the light of faith.

But I have been just as concerned to eliminate mistaken views at the other end of the doctrinal spectrum. I have come down on the side of the traditional doctrine of the vision of God in Jesus; I thereby make him once again our teacher, and take a stand against radical secularity. What he teaches us is transcendent. He saw God, he knew God, he loved God. He also loved God's creation and by that fact is at one with the best in modern secularity. But our notion of creation is expanded through him; he himself is the first creation of God and what he experienced in himself he knew to be God's ultimate purpose in creation. That is what makes nonsense of radical secularity. The good of man is to be divine, but humanity is not divinity. Man is not made for bread alone but for every word that proceeds from God, and this word is more than bread for the hungry, music for the musical, culture for the masses, the whole range of what we regard as the human and civilized and cultural good. It is more, not quantitatively, but with an infinite qualitative difference. And this is what we learn daily from Jesus as from one who knows and needed not that any man should tell him or even that the word of the Lord should come to him to reveal it.

In my world then of subways and movie houses and ringing telephones and electric typewriters I do not ask the gospel record how the Lord Jesus handled it all; that is my own problem. But what I learn from the Lord Jesus is that I must handle it because he has relativized it.[52] It is not the all; there is always more. When I have learned from him that there is "more," the "less" can never again be the same. The "more" becomes my goal, not just as the distant end of a journey but as a fullness of mind and heart that accompanies me on the way. And Jesus is the way, not by reason of dress or state in life or particular vocation or prayer-language, but by reason of his life and passion and death, and the relationship to God which gave him his fullness of mind and heart, relativized all things earthly, and kept him united to God even as he went through the dark exit.

My last word is that what he means to me seems to come out most plainly in my experience of my own deficiencies and differences from him rather than in my positive approach to his state of mind and heart and his way. I mean, for example, that as I struggled to write this paper amid the ringing of phones, and the piling up of correspondence to be attended to, and the working out of the thousand and one little crises that find their way in a steady stream to the doors of administrators, I came to realize far better the calm strength of mind that was his through his vision of God. I could understand a little how his vision remained even when the crowds pressed upon him and neurotic heirs urged him to settle their lawsuits—remained and enabled him to concentrate on the purpose of life and the urgency of the *kairos*, while still relativizing the finite elements in which the *kairos* found its context. Similarly, it is in the weakness of seeking distractions from boredom and in the cheapness of so many of my heart's choices and the triviality of so much of my pastime, that I discern and dimly appreciate the heart of him who belonged to his Father, was one with his Father, and did always the things that were acceptable to his Father.

Of putting words on paper and making books there is no end. The fathers of the Church distinguished theology, or the science of God, and economy, or the science of his work on earth for our salvation. Then, tired of all their endless words, they developed the notion of

---

52. Historians relativize one period of history by measuring it against the indefinitely great possibilities revealed by other periods, but Jesus relativizes radically and ultimately by measuring all history against the eternal.

negative theology, an approach to God through what we do not know and cannot say about him. Maybe, after all these words on Jesus, we need a "negative economy" to bring us closer to his mind and heart through recognizing how he is different, and discovering in the fickleness and instability of our minds and hearts the horizon beyond which our leader beckons us.

13

Dialectic and the Ignatian *Spiritual Exercises**

This week of study has been advertised as a Lonergan Workshop, so my first step might be to work out an approach to such a workshop and to see how my paper can be located in the project. This is not just a simple exercise in thought, for there has been developing in regard to Fr. Lonergan's ideas a certain polarization from which I for one wish to separate myself. It seems to me that a sober approach would be to apply the first four functional specialties of *Method* to the study of Lonergan himself and to determine, each of us for himself, which of the four tasks he is trying to perform. If one objects that this is begging the question, that we are endorsing the program of *Method*[1] in order to study it, we could reduce the approach to simpler terms: assembling the data, determining their meaning, proceeding from meaning to what is going forward in the history of thought, and investigating the conflicts uncovered in this history with a view to taking a position of one's own. Surely no one will object to procedures described in these terms, or to our choosing any one of them as our interest at the moment. On that basis I would locate my own paper in the second area; it is an exercise in understanding, an attempt to discover what Lonergan means by "dialectic." My plan is to put the notion to work as a tool of analysis in the *Spiritual Exercises* of St. Ignatius Loyola.[2] In outward form, then, my paper is a study of the *Exercises,* not of dialectic; but I hope that in

---

*A paper presented at the third annual Lonergan Workshop, Boston College, 14–18 June 1976, where the general theme was "Theology as Public Discourse." Previously published in *Science et esprit* 30 (1978), pp. 111–27, and *Lonergan Workshop* 1 (1978), pp. 1–26.

1. Bernard Lonergan, *Method in Theology*; see ch. 5, "Functional Specialties." In Lonergan's own view, "the eight specialties. . . . would be relevant to any human studies that investigated a cultural past to guide its future" (*Foundations of Theology,* ed. P. McShane [Dublin: Gill & Macmillan, 1971], p. 233). By a simple extension the specialties, especially the first four of them, may be applied to the study of any thinker in the cultural field.

2. By the phrase "spiritual exercise" Ignatius refers to examination of one's conscience, praying, preparing one's soul to find the divine will, etc. He arranged his set of exercises in four weeks, in which the object of reflection is successively: sin and its consequences, the public life of Christ, the passion of Christ, the resurrection and ascension of Christ. The four weeks are enclosed by a kind of prologue (Principle and Foundation) and a kind of epilogue (Contemplation to Gain Love). Certain key exercises are regarded as

this application to a concrete case an idea of the nature and function of dialectic will appear. Insofar, of course, as the notion of dialectic is found helpful for an understanding of the *Exercises*, we will be providing an element for judging and evaluating Lonergan's *Method*, but that is a tentative by-product and not my direct purpose. The paper is a study of dialectic as an idea, not an exercise in dialectic itself.[3]

The subtitle of the workshop is "Theology as Public Discourse"; I have to relate my paper to that heading as well. Two difficulties occur at once in proposing the Ignatian *Exercises* as a term of comparison with the public discourse of theology. First, the *Exercises* are a very private affair between the exercitant and God; their results may be manifest, but the dialectic of their process is not, and does not therefore seem to offer a good analogy for dialectic as public discourse. Secondly, theology is a highly specialized academic pursuit, and the *Exercises* are not academic at all; there is certainly a cognitional element involved in making them, and it is surely related to theology, but the two forms of knowledge are as remote from one another as the realms of common sense and theory.

I hope the paper will itself be an answer to these difficulties. In fact, one of my aims is to distinguish more clearly public and private factors in the *Exercises*, and I think this distinction will be clarifying also for the study of theology as public discourse. Again, it is true that the *Exercises* are not theology, much less the highly specialized form of theology supposed by the functional specialties of *Method*. But there are striking similarities all the same. The *Exercises* head for a choice in life, as dialectic heads for a choice in theology. The choice they head for is a rather fundamental option involving a new religious horizon, much in the way that dialectic may involve a new horizon for the theologian. Both dialectic and the *Exercises* are initiated by an encounter with the past in the form of a person with a message. Both employ a technique in which self-searching is a central and crucial exercise. Both suppose the two phases of hearing and responding. We do seem to have at least a *prima facie* case for beginning our study; but, of course, to move our metaphor from lawcourt to kitchen, the proof of the pudding will be in the eating.

Ignatian specialties: those on the Kingdom of Christ, on the Two Standards, etc. The book also contains a great deal of ascetic advice, rules for the conduct of life, etc.
Editions of this little work are legion; a recent and authoritative one is found in *Monumenta historica Societatis Iesu*, vol. 100 (Rome: Institutum historicum Societatis Iesu, 1969). This gives four of the most ancient texts (including the autograph) in parallel columns, and adds the paragraph numbers that have become standard. I will use a manual edition with Fr. Roothaan's translation (*Versio litteralis*—from the autograph, Bruges, 1932), but will add the numbers found in the 1969 *Monumenta* edition.

3. One can complicate this issue as much as one pleases, according to his capacity for doing so; I shall return to it at the end of my paper.

My plan is simple. I will make an analysis of the *Exercises* from a Thomist viewpoint, using the analytic tools of the Thomist organon; I will show how the notion of dialectic may be used to carry the analysis further; I will conclude with some suggestions on further avenues of investigation.

It is natural enough to begin an analysis of the *Exercises* from a Thomist viewpoint, for it was after his studies at the University of Paris, and to some extent under the influence of his Thomist studies there, that Ignatius made the final version of his little book.[4] To come to specifics, the election of the *Exercises,* which is so central to their purpose and structure,[5] is conceived in Thomist terms, as, for example, when Ignatius exhorts the exercitant not to adapt the end to the means but rather to make the means appropriate to the end.[6] This is clearly the language of St. Thomas, who analyzes the election or act of choice in terms of willing an end, deliberating on means to that end, and choosing the means accordingly. His stock example is that of a sick person who wants to get well,—the end therefore is the restoration of health— takes counsel on how he may do so, and decides to call in the doctor.[7] The example is not very thrilling to us; maybe calling in a doctor was a bigger deal in the Middle Ages than it is now; or maybe St. Thomas considers that the stark simplicity of this example will serve better to outline the structure of the process.

What are the characteristics of the Thomist election? St. Thomas regularly describes it from the analogy of a syllogism. The end, he says, functions in matters of conduct the way a premise does in matters of understanding.[8] Again, the object of choice is conceived in syllogistic terms, for election of the object follows the practical judgment which is like the conclusion of a syllogism.[9] Further, one can arrange a chain of syllogisms in a hierarchical order descending from the more universal premise to the less universal, and you can do the same for a series of

---

4. The history of the book's emergence has been studied by H. Pinard de la Boullaye, *Les étapes de rédaction des Exercises de S. Ignace* (Paris: Beauchesne, 1950). The influence of St. Thomas may be estimated in a general way from the fact that Ignatius wrote it into his Constitutions (*Quarta pars,* c. xiv, n. 1) that "in theologia legetur Vetus et Novum Testamentum, et doctrina scholastica divi Thomae." See also n. 6 below.

5. The centrality of the election, sometimes neglected in the past, is now accepted; see Gaston Fessard, *La dialectique des Exercices Spirituels de saint Ignace de Loyola* (Paris: Aubier, 1956, pp. 32–33; and Karl Rahner, *The Dynamic Element in the Church* (Freiburg: Herder, 1964), p. 89.

6. No. 169. Direct reference to St. Thomas appears in the Rules for the Discernment of Spirits (no. 330), where Ignatius added a note to an early Latin version, invoking the *Prima secundae* of St. Thomas, 9, 1 & 6, and 10, 4 (see Fessard, p. 261).

7. *Summa theologiae,* I-II, 8, 3; 9, 4; and passim.

8. Ibid., 9, 3.   9. Ibid., 13, 3.

ends, with one person taking as an end in life what someone else, seeking a higher end, will reduce to a means. Thus, the patient's health is an end for the doctor; he takes this for granted, and does not deliberate about it at all. But health is subordinate to the good of the soul, so the patient himself may deliberate about health, whether he ought to seek a cure or be content to remain ill, in effect turning it from an end into a means.[10] You can go back to higher and higher ends, but you cannot do this forever,—"non est procedere in infinitum," St. Thomas was fond of saying—so where do you stop? What is the ultimate end? It is *bonum in communi*, the good in general, which is the very object of the faculty of will.[11] Then the highest good becomes identified with the ultimate end,[12] and, within the all-encompassing range of this orientation, you can choose freely from the list of particular goods. Here too the analogy with intellect is carried through: as there are first principles which are the source of all syllogizing, so there is the fundamental orientation of the will to good, which is the source of all choice and human action.[13]

With this set of concepts functioning as an organon, one can conduct a helpful analysis of the Ignatian *Exercises*. What is the motive power under which the exercitant is led through two weeks of exercises and brought to the point of making his election, his choice of a state in life? It is the end set forth at the beginning of the *Exercises* in the Principle and Foundation, and repeated again when the time comes to make an election: to praise, reverence, and serve God, and by this means to save his soul.[14] The same paragraphs reduce everything else on earth to the level of means, to be chosen so far as they lead to the desired end. With this orientation restored and made operative by divine grace, the First Week of the *Exercises* enters into their structure as a realization that the process to the goal has been frustrated by sin; the exercitant is therefore brought back from his wandering path in the triple step of shame, repentance, and purpose of amendment.[15] The Second Week functions positively as a pursuit of the end through a study of the means, or, in biblical language, through a search for the way which is Christ. That corresponds very closely to the structure of the Thomist *Summa theologiae*: "primo tractabimus de deo; secundo, de motu rationalis creaturae in deum; tertio, de Christo, qui, secundum quod homo, via est

---

10. Ibid.   11. Ibid., 9, 1.

12. Ibid., 1, 4 ad 1m.

13. Ibid., 90, 2; 94, 2. It is true that Thomas is more directly concerned with moral principles than with the will's orientation to good.

14. No. 23.

15. No. 48: "petere pudorem et confusionem"; no. 55: "petere magnum et intensum dolorem"; no. 61: "proponendo . . . emendationem," and no. 65: "poscere intimum sensum poenae . . . ne in peccatum deveniam."

nobis tendendi in deum."[16] There is no need here to accuse St. Thomas of reducing Christ to a mere means for men to use with a view to their salvation;[17] for present purposes, at least, we can take his language as merely translating what the scriptures say, for example, in the terms in which Luke reports Peter's sermon: "There is no salvation in anyone else at all, for there is no other name under heaven granted to men, by which we may receive salvation" (Acts 4:12).

So far we are solidary with a tradition that goes back to the *Didache* and its two ways of life and death, and before the *Didache* to the Old Testament. But Ignatius takes over a refinement that had grown up in the tradition—a division even within the way of life—and introduces it into the Second Week in his own quite characteristic way. It appears first, on the very threshold of this week, in the Kingdom meditation; under the figure of soldiery, so dear to St. Ignatius, we may say that the followers of Christ are divided into those who volunteer for the frontlines of battle, and those who are content to enlist and contribute their reasonable service.[18] But the option is brought out more sharply later when Ignatius puts in sequence for meditation these two topics: Christ obedient to his parents at home, and Christ leaving his parents at the age of twelve to be about his Father's work. This dialectically related pair of meditations has a clearly symbolic value for Ignatius, as is seen not only in what he expressly says about them, but in the liberty he takes with scripture, inverting the order found in Luke in order to bring home his point.[19]

Two Ignatian masterpieces must now be fitted into this pattern: the exercise on the Two Standards, and that on the Three Pairs of Men. From the Thomist viewpoint that we are adopting, the Two Standards[20] can be taken as a special exercise in deliberation on means to the end. Specifically the exercitant is made to study the love of riches and is led to see how such a love may turn him away from the goal of life as proposed in the Principle and Foundation. We are dealing therefore with an exercise in knowledge, where the objective is to get behind facades and discover the real effect of love of riches, to get a sense of where we may be led unawares by means that seem innocent on the

16. *Summa theologiae,* I, 2, prologus.

17. The Christology of St. Thomas, especially its place in an integral theology, has come under attack in various manners which do not concern us here, and something analogous has happened to the Christ of Ignatius as presented by Fessard. So, at least, G. Martelet believes; see his view of Fessard, *Nouvelle revue théologique* 78 (1956), pp. 1049–55, where he makes the case that Christ has been reduced to a result of sin.

18. *Spiritual Exercises,* nos. 96–97.

19. Ibid., nos. 134, 135; see nos. 271–72.

20. Ibid., nos. 135–48. The Two Standards are those of Christ and Satan. It is not that the exercitant is to choose between the two as such, but between the apparently neutral first steps by which each would lead us his way.

surface. Ignatius says in effect what the rat might say in the laboratory maze: things are not always what they seem; the immediate direction of a path is no real clue to where it leads in the end. But the rat can have as many chances as he likes, and we cannot; hence the crucial importance of finding out in good time where riches and honors may take us.

The Three Pairs of Men,[21] in contrast, is more an exercise in decision. The route has been clarified, but I am not ready to follow it. I remain like a signpost, pointing in the right direction, but not taking a single step toward the goal. Or I cast about for an alternative route that will be less demanding than the one taught me by the Two Standards. If there is a knowledge involved in the exercise of the Three Pairs, it is not a knowledge of the objective routes laid out before us; rather, it is the self-knowledge that lays bare the dodges to which I resort in order to remain deaf to a clear call.

It is this bare skeleton of the first two parts of the *Exercises* to which I will presently apply the notion of dialectic. At the moment, however, there remains the question of the Third and Fourth Weeks. It would be a very truncated form of the *Exercises* which omitted these last two parts and their epilogue, the Contemplation to Gain Love. Nevertheless, it is clear that they represent a distinct new phase of the *Exercises*, as different from the First and Second Weeks as the farewell discourse in John's Gospel is from the controversies of his chapters 7 to 10. The Thomist end/means structure no longer applies to these two weeks, and neither will Lonergan's notion of dialectic. However, the contrast itself will be enlightening, so let us see how these final weeks relate to the earlier. I would say that, on Thomist analysis, they stand to the first two weeks as a good to be shared stands to a good to be acquired. That is, as long as we think in terms of means to an end, we are concerned with what we may do, or achieve, or acquire; we are concerned, in other words, with a *bonum acquirendum*. What we wish to acquire is, or may be, extremely precious and noble: the conquest of sin, a place in the frontlines of Christ's army, ultimately salvation; still, it is something we strive to acquire for ourselves. However, that is not the whole story. The Christian way offers possibilities of a different order. Ignatius presents them in the last two weeks of the *Exercises*, and Aquinas provides (rather marginally, it is true) a further tool for their analysis. The further tool is the concept of the good to be shared and communicated,

---

21. Ibid., nos. 149–57. Each of the Three Pairs is uneasy about a sum of money acquired, not dishonestly but not purely for the love of God either; they all want to set things straight; the differences lie in their readiness to take the means. (There is no agreed explanation why Ignatius chose pairs instead of individual persons to represent the three types.)

the *bonum communicandum*.[22] This is not something we reach out to grasp at; rather, it is a spontaneous overflow, a necessity that love has for sharing whatever we possess with those we love and for entering into their state to share with them what they experience or endure. And this notion naturally has its application among friends.[23]

Now it is precisely this sharing, this union in condition and state and destiny with those we love, that is characteristic of the last two weeks of the *Exercises*.[24] From this viewpoint it does not matter in the least that in the Third Week we share the passion of Christ the Lord and in the Fourth Week we share his resurrection. The determining factor in each week is that we *share*. We are with Christ, wherever he be: in suffering and sorrow, if he happens to be in suffering and sorrow; in peace and happiness, if he happens to be in peace and happiness. The end/means structure has given way to a friendship/sharing structure. One may think of the mother who sits with closed eyes by the cradle of her child. She does not open them to satisfy her curiosity on who is passing; she does not look in alarm when brakes squeal down the street. Why? Because she is sharing the state of her child that was born blind. What good is she doing? What is she achieving? What purpose does she serve? The questions are all out of place, they belong in another context; the context now is that of the need which love has to share with the one who is loved.[25]

Let us return to the first two weeks and the exercises that lead up to the election, for it is here especially that we find a term for comparison with dialectic. Has the Thomist organon proved adequate for the analysis of this part of the *Exercises*? In the light of ideas available today, I have to say it has not. Briefly, and with a sweeping generalization to be corrected presently, I would say that Thomas puts the emphasis on the cognitional factor in decision, even to the extent of conceiving the process on the analogy of logic, where modern thought puts the emphasis on self-involvement in which logic is quite inadequate either as a tool for analysis or as an existential influence. The *Spiritual Exercises*

22. *Summa theologiae*, I-II, 1, 4 ad 1m; 28, 4 ad 2m; III, 1, 1.

23. Ibid., I-II, 65, 5; II-II, 25, 3; 26, 2.

24. *Spiritual Exercises*, esp. nos. 193, 195, 206, in the Third Week, and nos. 221, 224, 229, in the Fourth Week. See also the appendix of my *Old Things and New: A Strategy for Education* (Atlanta: Scholars Press, 1985).

25. On this analysis, the exercise on the Three Degrees of Humility (nos. 162–68) belongs with the Third and Fourth Weeks, for it clearly focuses on being with Christ with no "purpose" being served, no *bonum* to be acquired. Why then does it direct us to be with Christ suffering, instead of with Christ in glory, and why is it inserted here in the Second Week (before the election, Ignatius says, no. 164)? My surmise is that, whereas we will have eternity to rejoice with Christ, we have only a short life on earth to be with him in his sorrow and pain; the election should be made in accordance with this limitation.

show up this inadequacy. You do not go smoothly and directly from *bonum in communi* to the particular way of life to which you may be called at a crucial time of decision, not even if the orientation to good is a concrete and resourceful dynamism instead of an abstract conception and general willing of the end. Neither do you go smoothly and directly from the end as operative in the Principle and Foundation to the standard of Christ as presented in the Second Week of the *Exercises*. You might as well set a ship on its course and expect it to reach harbor two weeks later without further attention to the rudder. This surely is the lesson of history, and you can verify it for yourselves in personal experience as you grow older.

But I have to correct my too sweeping generalization on St. Thomas, whose honest realism resists the straitjacket of logic and provides many points of contact with more recent thought. I am not referring to his own use of the term "dialectic." There has been some effort to establish a link here,[26] but I think the effort is wasted: Thomist dialectic is just too exclusively a cognitional category. The place to look is rather on the periphery of his thought where Thomas continually breaks out of the confines of his own system. For example, there is the Aristotelian syllogism of four propositions which describes the person struggling with temptation. There are two majors: one, sin is to be avoided; the other, a pleasant thing is to be enjoyed. Each would have its own minor: this is sin; alternatively, this is pleasant. But in fact there can be only one minor and only one conclusion; which is it to be?[27] Though cast in logical terms, this exposition clearly breaks out of logic toward the sort of dialectic we are going to deal with. Again, there is the knowledge that seems to lie outside the ordinary process of the mind, a knowledge that is gained through the affective connaturality of the knower with the object.[28] This is very close to what we might describe as an apprehension of values leading to a corresponding judgment. Thirdly, there is the substitution of a higher end for a lower, a substitution effected by divine grace.[29] This corresponds to the shift in horizons that is the goal of dialectic. And finally, to close this paragraph, there is the Thomist recognition that conduct does not follow premises with the click-

26. J. Isaac, "La notion de dialectique chez saint Thomas," *Revue des sciences philosophiques et théologiques* 34 (1950), pp. 481–506; see pp. 505–506. Also, Gaston Fessard, *De l'actualité historique*, tome 1 (Paris: Desclée De Brouwer, 1960), pp. 14–15.

27. *Summa theologiae*, I-II, 77, 2 ad 4m; *In VII Eth.*, lect. 3, nos. 1345–47; *De malo*, 3, 9 ad 7m.

28. *Summa theologiae*, I, 1, 6 ad 3m; II-II, 45, 2; see also I-II, 23, 4; 24, 1-2; II-II, 97, 2 ad 2m; 162, 3 ad 1m. A classic expositor of St. Thomas on this question was Jacques Maritain; see his *The Range of Reason* (New York: Scribner's, 1952), ch. 3. A more recent one is John W. Glaser in *Theological Studies* 29 (1968); see pp. 746–51.

29. *Summa theologiae*, I-II, 9, 6 ad 3m; III, 2.

ing sequence of a logic-machine; we are dealing with contingent courses of action, Thomas says, and so reason has options, as it does in dialectical syllogisms or in rhetorical efforts to persuade another.[30] Though Thomas still speaks here in his habitual cognitional terms, he is not far from the remark Kierkegaard made apropos of Hamlet's shilly-shallying: "reflection can be halted only by means of a resolve."[31]

St. Thomas then breaks out of his system in various ways. But to say that is to suggest that we look elsewhere to bring into focus elements that were peripheral to his thought, so I turn to the notion of dialectic as set forth in Lonergan's *Method*. Here, at the outset, let me introduce two limitations. First, I am going to talk about the process from lower levels of human intentionality to higher, rather than about the reverse process. Fr. Lonergan has recently emphasized that "human development is of two quite different kinds." There is "development from below upwards," and this will be my concern; it proceeds "from experience to growing understanding, from growing understanding to balanced judgement, from balanced judgement to fruitful courses of action." The other kind is "from above downwards," the result of "the transformation of falling in love."[32] This would provide a term of comparison for the love of Christ which is a factor throughout the *Exercises* and especially in the last two weeks. I leave it aside, however, in this paper, well aware that in so doing I may seem to commit the folly of those who build just half a ship.[33]

Secondly, there is a distinction we may introduce within the context of the *Exercises*. The dialectical process in which the exercitant becomes engaged involves two moments or phases. There is the moment that regards the way of Christ as a set of truths and values to be adopted by anyone who chooses, and there is the moment that regards the exercitant's quite individual choice of a state of life in his own quite individual situation. I call them "moments or phases." It is important to find the right notion here, for we are probably not dealing with two stages of conversion undergone in a time sequence. I suspect that in the concrete decision of the exercitant the two moments are inseparably

---

30. Ibid., I, 83, 1. In his commentary on Aristotle Thomas tends to speak of action following necessarily on the practical syllogism (*In VII Eth.*, lect. 3, nos. 1345–46); in his independent work he is more cautious (*Summa theologiae*, I-II, 10, 2).

31. *Concluding Unscientific Postscript*, tr. D. F. Swenson & W. Lowrie (Princeton, NJ: Princeton Univ., 1944 [1846]), p. 105.

32. *Bernard Lonergan: 3 Lectures*, ed. R. E. O'Connor (Montreal: Thomas More Institute, 1975), p. 63. Also see ch. 20 below.

33. I am thinking of Lonergan's remark in *Insight*, p. xiii: "In constructing a ship or a philosophy one has to go the whole way." Surely the same principle holds when one proceeds in the opposite direction to perform an analysis. But the situation may be saved by an accurate anticipation of the omitted part; in any case, as Ignatius says in the *Exercises* (no. 18), "We just haven't time to do everything."

intertwined. But in thought we have to distinguish them, just as in psychological effect they differ and in the temporal sequence of the *Exercises* Ignatius has to propose them one after the other. At any rate I see the first as a matter for public discourse and therefore an appropriate topic for this workshop, and the second as quite private, a matter entirely between the soul and God.

The first moment, then, is the encounter of the exercitant with the way of Christ as discovered in a series of meditations on his public life, but notably and decisively as discovered in the meditation on the Two Standards, to which I shall return. In this moment the dialectic of the *Exercises* has a clear objective reference. The way of Christ can be studied from public documents—the gospels, the reflections of a hundred saints, and the studies of a thousand masters of the spiritual life. It contains a doctrine which can be explained, and a set of values which can be exemplified and presented by one person to another. Further, this explanation and this presentation can be made before an actual or potential multitude, from the pulpit of a church, or from the pages of a printed book. All of which amounts to saying that it is a general, if not a universal, way; it is communicable; it belongs in the realm of public discourse.

Not so the second moment in the dialectic. This is rather a wrestling of the soul with God in the particular choice of a state in life. Ignatius clearly hopes that the choice will be made in accordance with the way of Christ presented in the Two Standards. But clearly also the election is utterly individual, not general or communicable, not a matter for public discourse. We are in the area of my own freedom and much more of the sovereign freedom of God, and there is just no way either to push God around or to learn from public sources what his particular will is for me. Ignatius therefore develops his elaborate set of variables: I am to lengthen or shorten the different weeks, I am to fast or not fast, to use light or darkness, to adopt this or that posture in prayer, to try in a score of ways to tune into the message God is transmitting to me along private lines of communication. Above all, there are rules for the discernment of spirits; they are *my* spirits, the movements of *my* soul; they are not someone else's, not even the director's; they are not some general *Zeitgeist*. They are individual. The Spirit breathes where he wills when he wills, with what message he wills. One may emerge from the *Exercises* with a decision to be a hermit, to join an apostolic order, to enter politics—in every case the call lies in the mysterious depths of God's particular will for that person, even though the decision be to join others with a similar call.

It is clear then that my paper has to study directly only the moment of dialectic involved in encountering the way of Christ along with others in a general invitation, and not the moment involved in wrestling with the divine angel in the here and now of a personal decision.

We are turning from Thomist tools of analysis to those provided by Lonergan's dialectic, and the simplest way to effect the transition is through the concepts of horizontal and vertical liberty. What Thomas deals with in his end/means structure is horizontal liberty; what Lonergan deals with in his dialectic is vertical liberty. The latter could be described in Thomist terms as the substitution of one end for another. In the language of *Method*, however, it is a shift in horizons, a dismantling of the old and the establishing of a new, with a sequence that is not just genetic but dialectical; that is, it is not just a matter of successive stages of development, but a matter of the radical transformation we call conversion.[34]

To effect this shift in horizons is going to take time and effort; Ignatius certainly thought so, for he spread the *Exercises* over thirty days.[35] But to analyze the shift in cool detachment is easier, and we can be as long or as brief as we have time for. I propose to start with three rather general headings. First, the motive power. In Thomist analysis this is supplied by the dynamism of spirit open to the intelligible, to the true, to the good; and we are not to forget that the openness is that of spirit graced by God. Dialectical analysis uses the same dynamism and follows its unfolding through experience, understanding, and judgment, leading to affective response. While the first three specialties of *Method* are out of place here, there is something analogous to them in the contemplation of scenes from the life of Christ (experience), the effort to realize what they mean (understanding), and the sense of what has taken place in salvific history and my own life (judgment). So far we are close enough to St. Thomas. But dialectic adds not only response to the good but the element of personal encounter. In the fourth specialty of theology this means "meeting persons, appreciating the values they represent, criticizing their defects, and allowing one's living to be challenged at its very roots by their words and by their deeds."[36] This list, with the exception of the third item, is verified *par excellence* in the encounter with Christ which we experience in the *Exercises*. From both sides, whether we start with God and his goodness, or from myself and my relation to God, the accent falls on the interpersonal. This is true even in the First Week where I ponder what the savior has done for me and ask what I should do for my savior.[37] The element of challenge to something better is already present here, and it becomes channeled more effectively throughout the Second Week; thus, ten times in the

---

34. *Method*, pp. 235–37; and see p. 106. 35. *Spiritual Exercises*, no. 4.
36. *Method*, p. 247. 37. *Spiritual Exercises*, no. 53.

three exercises beginning with that on the incarnation Ignatius tells me I am to reflect on the Savior and draw some fruitful application to my own life.[38]

A second heading is the structure of the dialectic. Here there is a remarkable parallel between dialectic as a theological task and the structured process of the Ignatian exercise on the Two Standards. For to this exercise we certainly bring an assembly of materials from the life of Christ; there is certainly the completion of experience, understanding, and judgment by the factor of evaluation, though the four are not distinct tasks in the *Exercises* as they are in the specialties of theology. But there is more: the exercise on the Two Standards can be taken as the counterpart in prayer of *Method*'s comparison, reduction, classification, and selection of positions. Christ and Satan are set in contrast; their ways of operating are reduced to fundamental patterns; the two conflicting patterns offer alternative horizons to enable me to locate myself accurately in regard to the horizon of Christ. And, of course, in subsequent exercises I will develop the position I am expected to choose, the way of Christ, and will reverse the counterpositions through discovery and rejection of all that is incompatible with the position.

A third and very tentative heading is dialectic as method. Here Fr. Lonergan seems to distinguish encounter with the past and encounter with contemporaries who are engaged with us in study of the same past. Since method requires a collaborative effort, it is on the second member that the emphasis falls, and he writes: "it is only through the movement towards cognitional and moral self-transcendence, in which the theologian overcomes his own conflicts, that he can hope to discern the ambivalence at work in others and the measure in which they resolved their problems." In a reciprocal action, "it is through knowledge and appreciation of others that we come to know ourselves and to fill out and refine our apprehension of values."[39] Is there a counterpart to this collaborative effort of contemporaries in the making of the *Exercises*? The question could be made specific by asking about the value of making the *Exercises* in common with others and adding spiritual socializing to one's private prayer; as far as I know, Ignatius never envisaged such a practice, but development in that direction might take place, and then the notion of dialectic might prove a useful tool to render the practice methodical. Remaining closer to the Ignatian idea we could look on the saints as our collaborators, and in some sense contemporary with us, since we all study the same message from the past; then surely our encounter with them is illuminating for our self-knowledge, and per-

38. Ibid., nos. 106–108, 114–16, 122–25.   39. *Method*, pp. 252–53.

haps we would also speak cautiously of discerning the ambivalence at work in them. With regard to the study of Christ himself, it is clear that this is our chief means of discovering our own inauthenticity and resolving our conflicts; we would not speak of inauthenticity in him, but a theological question might be raised on the relation of his understanding to intellectual conversion, and the theological question might have repercussions in prayer. We are far from the beaten path here, but these vague possibilities also serve to suggest the latent force of dialectic.

Now I wish to focus on a point of the highest interest for theology as public discourse: the question of doctrines. It seems to me that here the *Exercises* provide a concrete instance of dialectic at work, that the dialectical process is very similar in theology and in the *Exercises,* and that there is reciprocal illumination, the theological notion enabling us to analyze better what happens in the *Exercises,* and the concrete case-study of the *Exercises* enabling us to understand better the nature and role of dialectic.

Begin with dialectic as it operates in theology. In Lonergan's presentation there is not only a clear path from dialectic through foundations to doctrines; there seems to be even a kind of natural unity in these three tasks. At any rate he links them in the following way: "There are theological doctrines reached by the application of a method that distinguishes functional specialties and uses the functional specialty, foundations, to select doctrines from among the multiple choices presented by the functional specialty, dialectic."[40]

Now the Two Standards (I return always to that exercise which is so central to my study) is directly concerned with doctrines, if we take doctrines in the broad sense of judgments of fact and of value, judgments of human ways, of Christ's example, of God's guidance, etc. The grace the exercitant asks for in this exercise is knowledge of the deceits of the evil one, and knowledge of the true life which the supreme and truthful leader makes visible.[41] This is a petition for doctrine, and the doctrine turns out to be a rather remarkable one: that love of wealth leads to desire for honors, which in turn leads to pride and so to the whole gamut of sin, but that Christ's way follows the exactly opposite course, from love of poverty to desire for humble position and so to humility and the whole range of virtues.[42]

It is the very strangeness and unexpectedness of this doctrine that makes it so useful as a case-study for grasping what dialectic is and does. For the question arises: How on earth does one ever arrive at such a doctrine and make it his own? It is certainly not an element in

---

40. Ibid., p. 298. See also p. 349: "to use foundations as a criterion for deciding between the alternatives offered by dialectic."

41. *Spiritual Exercises,* no. 139. 42. Ibid., nos. 142, 146.

the patrimony of wisdom handed down in our schools. It is not a doctrine operative in our everyday world of striving to make a living and get ahead a little, much less in the world of industry, commerce, and finance, not even in that of the professions, or of the arts and sciences. Of course, we know the answer, through either a real or a notional apprehension: we arrive at this doctrine in a dialectical process that simply dismantles one's old horizon, the one founded on the mentality of Horatio Alger stories, and establishes a new one that is learned from Christ with the help of the interpreting saints. I spoke of real or notional apprehension of this process, using Newman's terms. The apprehension is real if we have experienced the extraordinary light this exercise of the Two Standards throws on our past, revealing it, perhaps in its personal inauthenticity, but certainly in its profound conflict with the way of Christ. It is notional if we notice that it is the sort of thing the saints keep saying, and if, in our Catholic piety toward them, we recognize that they have got hold of something worthwhile.

I called this doctrine of the Two Standards a case-study. I had thought of calling it a paradigm. I hesitate over both words. The difficulty, very simply stated, is that, however public the case or paradigm, the efficacy with which it works depends entirely on the subject. We are moving inevitably, once we start using cases or paradigms, toward a dialectical involvement in which you and I as persons encounter one another face to face; that is, you and I here and now in this workshop, I with my values and my degrees of authenticity and inauthenticity, you with yours. There is no way we can engage in theology, deploy the full potential of the first four steps of *Method* and avoid this kind of encounter; the only alternative is to retreat to the safe and guarded area of the first three tasks as practiced in religious studies.

If we understand dialectic as I have explained it (and so far my purpose has been simple exposition), a host of possibilities rises, first as questions, and then, given certain answers, as proposals and policies in theology and the Church. For example, the question of pluralism: there are many schools of spirituality, each fully dedicated to the study of the way of Christ, each, nevertheless, discovering its own distinctive understanding of that way. Will theology, even as fully public discourse, likewise admit of a number of schools of doctrine corresponding to different apprehensions of value? Which is a way of asking whether there will be a number of denominations each with its own grace from God given and accepted according to its own situation, psychological, social, cultural, etc. Again, there is the question of Christian conversion. We hear complaints that *Method* does not deal with it. This perhaps is a complaint that *Method* is not two books instead of one, but it nevertheless raises the question: How would Christian conversion be understood in the context and terms of *Method*? Intellectual conversion is such a self-appropriation as allows us to relate common sense and theory in a philosophy of knowing what knowing is; moral conversion is such a self-appropriation as allows us to relate satisfactions and values in a moral self-transcendence that evaluates our faultiness; religious conversion is first God's taking possession of us and then our taking possession of the whole self and the whole natural world and orienting it to God. What is left under the heading of conversion? An orientation does not automatically provide a way; is it the way that is left? So that Christian conversion is a conversion to a way? In the Lucan message, Christianity is very much a "way" (*hodos*, Acts 9:2; 19:9; and passim); in both Thomist theology and Ignatian spirituality the way of Christ is a key notion and a key factor; would this also correspond to our view of Christian conversion as it affects a method? To put the question in other words: Does Christian conversion involve a new realm of transcendence, or, instead, a link between the everyday realm and that of transcendence? Finally, would "horizon" become analogous in another way if applied both to the transcendent and the way to the transcendent?

Questions multiply on the side of theology, but others are raised on the side of the subject. Take one example. Doctrines are truly objective when they proceed from an authentic subject involving himself existentially; subjectivity is methodically involved when there is self-appropriation by the subject; such appropriation is achieved by practice: "One has to produce in oneself the corresponding operation. One has to keep producing it until one gets beyond the object intended to the consciously operating subject."[43] But just here the fourth level of consciousness, on which dialectic is operative, presents a real problem. We can quite easily practice experiencing; we have only to open and close our eyes repeatedly. We can practice understanding, though not so easily; we have to make up problems and puzzles, or find them in a book. To practice judgment is still more difficult; in the nature of the case the judgmental process has to be slow and thorough, concerned with the real world instead of the fictitious one of artificial problems, and so cases for practice do not come readily to hand. But when we turn to decision it seems that cases for practice are excluded on principle. If it is a real decision, it involves me existentially, and then it is no mere "practice"; if it is a mere exercise, an example chosen for the practice, then it is no real decision, for it does not involve me existentially. The paradox: The practice of decision, by the very fact that it is merely practice, is no practice at all.

43. *Method*, p. 15.

Of course, the situation is not desperate. I believe that in group dynamics they cook up artificial situations and give you a role to play which more or less successfully simulates an existential involvement. Besides, as a student to whom I explained this paradox said to me, we involve ourselves every day in every real decision we make, even the small ones. And one can advert to those decisions later for purposes of self-appropriation. But I believe my paradox remains to block any formal exercises in dialectic, and I think it is worth pondering, for it brings home to us the demands that the fourth level is going to make on us, if ever we start doing theology on that level. As Philip McShane said apropos of some essays he edited: "What then is Lonergan getting at? The uncomfortable answer is that Lonergan is getting at you and me."[44] The discomfort can be acute in dialectic. Another way of putting it: Lonergan's *Method* can be conceived as an organon in the generic style of Aristotle's organon or Bacon's. But it is an organon with a difference. Those of Aristotle and Bacon are comparatively tame affairs, as impersonal almost as a slide-rule or a table of logarithms; Lonergan's, carried to the level of encounter, and it is integral only if you carry it to that level, becomes automatically a personal involvement with others.

I have been led to speak of using *Method* as an organon in doing theology, but now I wish to leave theology proper aside, to return to my starting-point, and speak again of the study of *Method* itself and, more generally, of the area of Lonergan studies. In my introduction I first suggested that a good way to approach these studies was to apply to Lonergan the first four specialties of his method, and I then stated that my own paper was to be an exercise in interpretation. I would like to repeat my suggestion of a general approach through the four tasks, insisting that I am raising a serious academic question, not just having a cosy chat with those who may form an in-group, or exercising diplomacy toward those who may feel like outsiders. For example, this year, as every year, hundreds of students will begin graduate dissertations in philosophy or theology; would it bring a much-needed clarity to their work if they got hold of the four specialties and determined for themselves with the help of this set of concepts just what they are doing, and indeed what they are competent to do in their situation?

As for my own paper, I suspect that it is going to seem to you, because of the enthusiasm with which I applied the notion of dialectic to the *Exercises,* that I have gone considerably beyond interpretation, even beyond dialectic, and have been advancing a personal position. It is true that ideas tend to exercise their own persuasion, but then we

---

44. *Introducing the Thought of Bernard Lonergan* (three papers reprinted from *Collection* with an introduction by Philip McShane, London: Darton, Longman & Todd, 1973), p. 7.

have to reflect all the more carefully to assign them their proper roles. We must make haste slowly. A danger I see in Lonergan studies at the moment, whether you are sympathetic or unsympathetic, is that of trying to move too fast, and I wish to reserve my inalienable right to lag behind. Let us reflect a little, therefore, on what I have done; it may indeed help us get a firmer grasp of what the four tasks really are. I do not deny that I made judgments, but they were judgments of the kind that belong to interpretation: that this is what Lonergan's dialectic means, and that this is the way it appears in the *Exercises*. I do not deny my enthusiasm for the notion of dialectic or even my opinion that it is where the action will be in theology. It is part of getting hold of an idea that it be a moving experience, but surely we know by now what is needed to add committed judgment and evaluation to the exhilaration of an idea or of an opinion. One could go on with this list of specifications, but it is simpler just to say that research, interpretation, and history in the field of Lonergan studies are really just beginning, and we are far from ready to begin dialectic here. For my own part I am still trying to clarify what dialectic is. My analysis of the Ignatian *Exercises* gives some clues to its nature and to its application in one area, but I have not tested my work in the cross-light from other analyses,[45] or studied the modifications the notion might undergo in application to an Ireneus, a Tertullian, or a modern Christian thinker. The more I realize the magnitude of the task before us, the more willing I become to limit my contribution to one small increment; that is all this paper is intended to be.[46]

45. There are many of these which I have not had space or time to discuss. Among the most relevant would surely be those of Fessard and Rahner (see n. 5 above). Fessard's work, however, differs from mine as much (at least) as Hegel's dialectic differs from Lonergan's, and that difference seems to produce results that leave us poles apart. Rahner's work, on the contrary (it is the third chapter in *The Dynamic Element* . . .: "The Logic of Concrete Individual Knowledge in Ignatius Loyola"), is much more directly related to what I have tried to do; except that I studied what I called the "public" moment in the dialectic of the *Exercises,* where Rahner studied the strictly individual element.

46. These paragraphs refine a bit my position at the Lonergan Workshop of 1974, but I would like to repeat one idea expressed there: that it is part of a study of Lonergan's *Method* to test it in action. When are we going to begin that implementation in theology?

14

Theology and the Past: Changing Views on the Sources*

The principle by which I divide into two talks what I have to say to you on theology, and relate those talks to one another, is extremely simple. We are just entering the month of Janus, who faced both the past and the future, so in the spirit of Janus I will devote my first talk to the views theology has taken of its sources in the past, and my second to the task theology must assume of constructing a future for itself and for the people of God whom it serves.

This principle of division, I say, is extremely simple. And so it is in itself. Still, it coincides with a polarization that is seriously dividing both the people of God and Christian theologians today. There are those on the one hand who rely with total trust on the past and emphatically reject any creative role for theology—in their most intransigent position they assert quite stubbornly that we have all the answers already. And on the other side there are those who adopt such a critical attitude toward the past and so extol the freedom of the theologian to construct his own independent doctrine that one wonders why they bother to call themselves Christian. Between these two poles there are more moderate positions all along the length of the magnet. And there is the "extreme center" where I at least like to locate myself. Evidently, our apparently simple division unlocks quite a Pandora's box of problems. And I can hope only to touch on some of them in these two talks.

My first topic falls under the general heading of theology's relation to its sources in the past. The purpose here is primarily historical. I propose to examine a series of positions that theologians have taken over the years since we first heard the Christian word one April morning

*The first of two papers read at the thirteenth annual conference of the Irish Theological Association, Killeshandra, County Cavan, 3–5 January 1978, where the general theme was "What is Theology?" (This first paper is largely a synopsis of my book, *Theology of the Christian Word* [New York: Paulist Press, 1978].) For the second, see below, ch. 15. Previously published in *Science et esprit* 31 (1979), pp. 21–32.

long ago, the first day of the week, around the year 30 AD. We will find, I think, a developing understanding of our relationship to the past as questions are raised in a genetic series and in some measure answered. And the understanding achieved at the term of this development may help us formulate a position today in 1978 that will respect the past yet release the creativity needed to move responsibly into the future.

The proposal to cover more than nineteen centuries of complex history in half an hour will cause historians either to smile tolerantly or to bristle with anger. And yet some overview of history is needed, if we accept as a fact the cultural difference between ourselves and our ancestors in the faith, and still wish to move back and forth between that ancient world and our present responsibilities. Further, I believe that theologians must make their own contribution to that overview, not indeed through the detailed knowledge that only historical scholarship can provide, but through a second-order reflection on the issues that have successively engaged the thinking of the Church, a reflection that may structure those issues into an intelligible sequence, and so join the past to the present in a genetic unity.

Now I have five key transitions in my structuring of history, and I locate them, with all sorts of cautions and qualifications, around the year 90 with the writings of St. Luke, the year 325 with the Council of Nicea, the year 1517 with Luther's 95 theses, the year 1843 with Newman's sermon "The Theory of Developments in Religious Doctrine," and the recent past with the proposal that revelation is history and history is revelation.

The exact pinpointing of the years 90, 325, and so on is highly arbitrary, and I offer it more as a mental convenience than as a set of crucial turning-points. The transitions are not neat and rapid; in all cases there are earlier stages in which what was later thematized existed as *vécu* in the Church and was even anticipated in efforts to bring the issue to conceptual clarity. There are then periods of slow growth and even of reversal of direction; they make our progress more like that from time zone to time zone as we circle the earth—the sun does not pause at Greenwich to endow that place with special importance; still there *is* a real progress and it *is* a mental convenience to take Greenwich as a transition point. Something like that is my structure of history.

I

If we take St. Luke's writings as marking the first transition, we have to assume a prior stage as given and make it the basis of all subsequent development. What is that prior stage? It is the Christian message as we first meet it in the documents, the message epitomized in chapter 15 of 1 Corinthians around the year 56 AD:

And now, my brothers, I must remind you of the gospel that I preached to you. . . .

First and foremost, I handed on to you the facts which had been imparted to me: that Christ died for our sins, in accordance with the scriptures; that he was buried; that he was raised to life on the third day, according to the scriptures; and that he appeared to Cephas, and afterwards to the Twelve (1 Cor 15:1, 3–5).

When I take this as given and make it a starting-point, I do not deny that this prior stage also emerged and represents a transition from a still earlier phase. Not only was there the explosion of faith at the time of the paschal and pentecostal events; there was even an immediate and considerable work of theologizing. But that first period of twenty years or so is dark and obscure and lacking in documentation; it does not provide us with the clarity we need for our point of departure. We could only work backwards from St. Paul and the gospels, and I must leave that kind of delicate work to the scholars.

What I do need to do, however, is to set our basic stage in contrast with the second in my list, the one I am going to characterize by transition to the Christian sources recognized as the word of God. At this basic stage then the message is not habitually known as the word of God. There is no focus on that aspect. It is known as the gospel, or as the kerygma, or, more simply still, in the words of the late C. H. Dodd, as the "message":

The term "message" has been chosen as the most comprehensive term available for the whole range of that which it is the business of the Christian ministry to convey to the faithful and to the world in general so far as it will hear.[1]

Dodd is choosing a modern English term, but there is a corresponding Greek term in the New Testament: *ho logos*. Only it is important not to translate *ho logos* as "the word," for "the word" by inevitable association of ideas is bound to be thought of as "the word of God," and that, in many New Testament passages, would be anachronistic. Consequently, The New English Bible will translate *ho logos* in a variety of ways to indicate its vaguer and more general meaning, not only as "message" (1 Th 1:6), but as "faith" (Gal 6:6), or as "preaching" (Col 4:3).

Now, somewhere along the line, gradually it may be, but surely under some determinate influence and in certain definite circumstances, this message, commonly known up to that time as the gospel or the ke-

---

1. C. H. Dodd, "The 'Message' in the Gospels and Epistles," in *The Ministry of the Word,* ed. P. Milner (London: Burns and Oates, 1967), p. 45.

rygma, came to be known and recognized and accepted as the very word of God himself. I postulate this transition rather than prove it. Still, the fact might be conjectured in advance of the evidence, from the very reverence in which the Jewish people, and so the first Christians, held the reality and the name of "the word of God." One did not lightly apply this sacred title to any word whatever, spoken by this or that person, even by those with authority in religious matters. The fact might also be surmised in comparing the narrative of the holy women on Easter Sunday with the usage of St. Luke many years later in the Acts of the Apostles. As far as we can judge from the gospel narratives, the women who went to the tomb on Easter gave the young Church the basic material elements of the apostolic message. But none of the disciples who heard the holy women would dream at that time of saying, "This is the very word of God"—not even if they thought the women had spoken the truth. Yet, sixty years afterwards, St. Luke regularly and almost systematically equates this message with the word of the Lord or the word of God.

That transition seems to me to cry for explanation. To say they were "only women" who first brought the message, but men and apostles who preached it round the world, is not to explain the transition but to shift the same question to another setting: How did the good news preached by the apostles come to be known as the word of God? In the context of the total overview of history that I wish to achieve, this is a transition comparable in importance to that by which Jesus the proclaimer became Jesus the proclaimed. But, whereas that latter question has received the attention of scores of scholars, my question seems to be regarded as a non-question by those competent to study it, and I am left with my surmises and half-educated guesses.

My guess, then, is that St. Paul may have begun the transition. For, first of all, the phrase does occur in his letters and indeed in the very first letter of his that we possess, 1 Thessalonians: "[W]hen we handed on God's message, you received it, not as the word of men, but as what it truly is, the very word of God at work in you who hold the faith" (2:13). But the phrase is not domiciled in St. Paul the way it is in St. Luke, and "gospel" and "kerygma" continue to be Paul's regular and favorite terms for the message. Further, I have no way of knowing that St. Paul was the first to take the step I postulate. But, if he was, and if the first documented use in 1 Thessalonians was the very first actual occurrence too, then the occasion for this creative step may be in the context of the passage. There seems to be a kind of challenge to Paul, as much as to say, "Why should we take your word for all this?" Which could have led Paul to the sudden realization: "It's not my word, it's not the word of men at all, it's the very word of God at work in you."

At any rate the concept is domiciled in the Church by the time of St. Luke; you can see this already in his gospel if you compare his accounts of the word of Jesus with those of Mark and Matthew; Mark speaks of the word, and Matthew of the word of the Kingdom, but Luke says simply that "the people crowded upon (Jesus) to listen to the word of God" (5:1). However, it is Acts that justifies our calling Luke the theologian of the word of God: some thirty-six times in that work we meet the concept, as "the word," or as "the word of the Lord," or as "the word of God"—three phrases used interchangeably to refer to the Christian message preached after Pentecost.

This development will have the most fateful consequences for theology. For the effect will be to shift emphasis away from the human speaker or writer, and from the time-conditioned elements in the word, to the eternal author of an eternal word. The style of the human author, for one thing, is of no consequence; what difference if Luke's style is so different from Mark's, when God is the real author of both gospels? Differences of content also lose their importance, and so does the idea of development within the New Testament; what difference if Mark does not mention the virgin birth and Matthew does? God, who wrote both accounts, knew what he was doing. The hierarchy of truths disappears; the Word was made flesh—that is part of the message; but so is the fact that Paul left his cloak at Troas; and, the two being equally the word of God, the two are to be equally reverenced. I am exaggerating, of course, to make a point; but the point is valid: that a one-sided attention to the divine author deprived us for centuries of the human side of the scriptures.

One could make a subheading here and trace the history by which the apostolic writings as writings came to be put on a par with the "scriptures"—with the "other" scriptures, 2 Peter will significantly say—and so come to be called the New Testament, and to be regarded as the word of God in the same way that Luke calls the apostolic preaching the word of God. But I have to limit my survey to the major theological steps, and, though there was a difficult psychological step involved here for those who taught that the "scriptures" ended with Malachi or maybe with Machabees, the theological difficulty had been overcome when Luke wrote his two-volume work.

II

We turn to our second major transition in our unfolding history. I see this step in the focus on the word of God as true, so that the sequence thus far is: in the beginning was the message, and the message came to be known as the word of God, and the word of God was thematized as true. I ask you to note my use of the word "thematize" which becomes especially significant with this step. I am talking of a transition from the *vécu* to the *thématique*, from a living reality to its cognitive appropriation. I am not therefore saying that the word of God was not true from the beginning, or that, earlier, the truth-element in the word was not important; I am only saying that the truth-element was not at first clearly differentiated. What we had was something "alive and active," cutting "more keenly than any two-edged sword," sifting "the purposes and thoughts of the heart" (Heb 4:12). But what we have now is a singling out of the truth that enables us to put it in the form of creeds and articles of faith.

At what point in space and time and under what circumstances did the transition to the word of God as true take place? I would locate it in the conciliar period, beginning with Nicea, when doctrine was distinctly and emphatically the issue, when the result of a council was formulated in a set of propositions, with anathemas attached to any denial of their truth. But this refers to full thematization. So we certainly have a concern for the truth in the New Testament writers, from Paul to John and 2 Peter; we have a concern for the truth in the apologists, in the formation of the creeds, in the great refutations of heresy that we find in Ireneus and Tertullian. But I think there is a degree of concentration in the conciliar period that entitles us to say: at this time thematization is complete—it is a matter of the focus finally becoming sharp. From this point of view we can relate our present step to Walter Bauer's work on heresy and orthodoxy.[2] Bauer thought our fathers had got it all wrong; they held that orthodoxy was first on the scene and heresy came along as a usurper. Not so, said Bauer; in many cases what we call heresy was first on the scene, and orthodoxy—so-called because it won out in the end—came along to displace it. From my point of view, however, it is possible that neither truth nor falsity was explicit at first; it is possible that both emerged at once and in opposition to one another, since truth is to a large degree undifferentiated and to some degree only latent in the original message.

Now this step too will have its fateful consequences in the history of doctrine and theology. There will be that progressive separation of truth from the living praxis of our religion which we have had continually to overcome. A distinction became a separation, and we had to join the two together again. For one example, Contenson's *Theologia mentis et cordis,* so I'm told, consisted in explaining the *Summa theologiae* of St. Thomas, section by section, and adding after each section some

2. W. Bauer, *Orthodoxy and Heresy in Earliest Christianity,* tr. a team from the Philadelphia Seminar on Christian Origins (Philadelphia: Fortress Press, 1971).

pious ascetical reflections. For a simpler example, there is the need we felt for adding to our older catechetical instructions some moralizing or application to life. The very need of such additions, and the artificiality they involved, underline the degree to which theology, in the process of differentiating the truth, had come to compartmentalize it, and to separate it from feeling and affectivity and practice. And so it seemed a new departure when the Second Vatican Council declared its orientation to be simply pastoral. Not as if previous councils had lacked a pastoral concern, but they were not remembered for that. What they were remembered for, what had accumulated in the tradition, what was codified in our manuals, what was studied in our schools, was the cognitive side. We had come to be oriented by the so-called Denzinger theology.

III

The theology of the future will overcome this isolation of the cognitive, I believe, and I will say something on that in my second talk. For the moment I simply wish to follow the course of the cognitive development and I have to say now that the insufficiency of conciliar truth simply as cognitive would in due time become manifest. This occurred in the next two steps of our history. When the focus had been for some time on the truth, the question arose of the sources of the truth. The sequence was quite natural: assume a position on any issue at all, and the perfectly normal question will be, "How do you know? What is your authority? On what basis do you say that?" And so our series is lengthened: in the beginning was the message, and the message became known as the word of God, and the word of God was thematized as true, and the truth had to be found in valid sources.

I locate this step at the time of the Reformation and Counter-Reformation. Again, what I am trying to pinpoint is the time of sharp focusing, of full thematization, of the clear and distinct question separated out from other concerns. Obviously so, for there is certainly attention to the sources very soon in our history. The Church of the early New Testament had its own special source: the scriptures, that is to say, what we call the Old Testament. There were the saving facts of the life, death, and resurrection of Jesus, as we found them epitomized in 1 Corinthians 15, but there was also the guarantee of their correct interpretation: the scriptures. Christ died for our sins, in accordance with the scriptures. . . ; he was raised to life on the third day, according to the scriptures.

As time went on, however, there was the most fascinating development in this question of assigning the authority for our belief. First, we notice that the Old Testament scriptures were not enough: the agents of the Christian word had to be added, and indeed to be specified and respecified; so they came to be known as the twelve, then as the apostles, then as witnesses in that special sense which emerges in Luke's Acts of the Apostles. Incidentally, I would like to see more general attention paid to the development within the New Testament of that concept; so often "witness" is put side by side with herald, evangelizer, and so on, as if their sequence was of no moment, when even the material frequency of the term in Luke and John might suggest that something is happening to the concept.

But this series of developments was only a beginning. With the death of the apostles, the apostolic writings took on new significance: they too became recognized as "scripture" on a par with the Old Testament, and were so accepted pretty much from the time of Ireneus. Then controversy forced a further refinement. Already with Ireneus and more clearly still in Tertullian it was seen that the scriptures would not suffice when both sides of a conflict appealed to them as their authority. Another criterion must be assigned, and they found it in the succession of bishops, especially those in the see of Rome, reaching from apostles down to their time. Trace that succession, Tertullian says, and then you will know who really owns the scriptures and has the right to their use. A century and a half later, with Athanasius, a further refinement is needed: with the succession prolonged through so many names, and with the churches themselves so many and so much at odds with one another, the criterion of Tertullian proves unwieldy; and so the concept of the "great" Church, the *oikoumene*, emerges and we are on the way to the concept of the living magisterium.

It is at this point that Luther enters our history, to recall the Church to the sources of all her doctrine. In a letter written January, 1519, barely a year after the 95 theses (they were dated 31 October 1517), Luther said: "[I]n our day . . . people everywhere in the world begin to ask not what but why this and that was said," and he applies this to the recent decretal of Pope Leo and his, Luther's, refusal to recant: "For what it [the decretal] says without any basis would not be established by my recantation."[3] There are two little phrases there that catch my eye: people are asking not "what" but "why" a thing is said, and what Pope Leo said was said "without any basis." We are at the point, I should say, where the question of the sources of doctrine has come into focus. Incidentally, in the same letter Luther adds the remark that Leo's decretal was not based on a single sentence from scripture or the fathers

3. That letter is found in R. H. Fife, *The Revolt of Martin Luther* (New York: Columbia University Press, 1957), pp. 315–16.

or canon law—a curious trio of sources, but that is beside the point now, when it is the principle itself of requiring an authoritative source that is our concern and interest. Again incidentally, it was perhaps only later with the Formula of Concord in 1570 that the Protestant *sola scriptura* came strongly to the fore, and only after Trent that the Catholic *scriptura et traditio* likewise emerged as a slogan; this particular difference does not interest me; what was clear from now on was that you could not just state your position: people everywhere in the world would ask not what you said but on what basis you said it.

IV

We come to our fourth major transition. What the sources controversy had underlined, though it was obvious enough, was that the original word lay in the distant past. This did not bother either side as long as a sense of history was lacking: the ancient word could easily leap across space and time and be valid in the modern age. But with the rise of critical history and a sense of human historicity the magnitude of the chasm appeared. You could no longer assume that a word of the year 30, though it be a word of God, was automatically applicable in the year 1530 or 1830. Neither the Reformers nor the Counter-Reformers had understood this. If the Reformers had understood it, they would not have based themselves exclusively on the written word; if the Counter-Reformers had understood it, they would not have taken refuge in an unwritten tradition. Both sides had to discover the historicity of the human race and apply it to the very word of God, acknowledging that it is also a word of man and consequently time-conditioned, subject to the historicity of all human utterance.

The two sides had to discover it, but they proceeded from different assumptions along different paths to reach different results. What gave them a profound community was the common need that gave impetus to the search. The Catholic way is best illustrated in one aspect of the Modernist program: to make an ancient word relevant in a modern situation. But the operative idea in this program was derived from Newman's work on the development of Christian doctrine. Not that Newman had the Modernist program in mind; so far as I know his purpose was *ad hoc* and limited: to meet a difficulty and answer a charge. The charge was that there were differences between earlier and later doctrines in the Church, and Newman, admitting the fact, would account for it through the latent potentialities of a great idea. But his solution could be appropriated for the purposes of Modernism: if a development had occurred in the past, it did so presumably to meet a need; what had happened once could happen again, and could continue to happen in the future. It seemed to many, it seemed to me at one time, that here, in Newman's idea of development, we had the adequate answer to the problem of the great chasm between ancient past and modern present.

The Protestant way was different. Not concerned as Newman was to defend unbroken continuity, indeed committed by their origins to claim a break in continuity, they would be slower to trust the notion of development. Their approach could more aptly be illustrated through a pair of biblical phrases: "Today if you hear his voice. . . ." is one, and another is Nathan's devastating word to David, "You are that man." In other words God still speaks to us in our individual situations through his original word; that is the assumption. But how explain this fact? One way is to base yourself on the early Heidegger, downplay the content of the message, and stress the existential side of the word as a call to me personally to bring me to self-understanding and so to decision. Or you could take a way based more on the later Heidegger, personify language itself, and think of the word as an event mysteriously operative through the preacher in a situation in which the hearer does not interrogate the word but the word interrogates him.

I keep insisting that my transition periods only bring into focus ideas that had been struggling already toward articulation. So, again, let me say that our newly formulated problem had an ancient history. Thus, in Old Testament times there had been a continual rewriting of the sacred text to make it relevant to a new age, but hardly with open admission of what was going on. With the fixing of the canon this procedure became unthinkable: no longer could we change one iota of the sacred scriptures. But other means were found to achieve the purpose: allegorization became the device of the early fathers, especially the Alexandrians. When allegory fell into disrepute, Catholics created the notion of a *sensus plenior,* to which there corresponded among some Protestants a *sensus pneumaticus.* But both of these seem in recent years to have died a natural death.

V

So the stage is set for the last major transition in my account of history, one taking place in our own day. Everyone seems to agree that the ancient word has a surplus of meaning which gives it a capacity for translation and application in far differing times and places; but how to pin down that surplus of meaning, by what hermeneutic to exploit it, with what exegetical or theological controls to tap its hidden wealth—that is the problem. Newman's idea may be valid up to a point, but it does not account for all the data; besides the linear developments he traced, there are dialectical factors at work, apparently independent beginnings, and even quite disconcerting reversals. Modernists might be more open to the dialectic of history, but they have no acceptable answer to the charge that they introduce new revelation. The Protestants have their own difficulties; existentialist approaches, besides dispensing with much of the word's content, seem to neglect what is called the strangeness of the ancient word, while the theology of the language-event seems to invest language with a mythology that most theologians are trying to overcome.

We have gone through a number of stages: from the original message to the message as word of God, from the word of God as alive and active to the word as truth, from truth as doctrine taught and handed on to truth as needing a basis in the sources, only to find now that the sources belong to far distant times and places with no automatic application to us today. Is there a way forward from this impasse? Is there anything we have overlooked in the ancient word? It seems that there is. There does indeed seem to be an oversight in all our previous stages: the word in question, even though it be the word of God, is expressed in human language. It is the word that comes to us from prophet or sacred chronicler, from apostle or evangelist, or from Jesus himself. But suppose that linguistic word is not primary or basic. Suppose that the basic word is not the one spoken or written by Moses, Isaiah, Mark, John, and the others, but the realities themselves about which Moses, Isaiah, Mark, John, and the others spoke or wrote. This could account for the surplus of meaning that we believe the word of God to contain, and perhaps also it will be possible to find adequate controls as we try to explore that surplus.

The first point at least is simple: every statement of prophet or chronicler, of apostle or evangelist, even of Jesus himself, is in the modern approach regarded as an interpretation. But an interpretation of what? Not just of some prior statement, for then we have a *processus in infinitum*. It is an interpretation of events, of historical realities, of the historical process. Now the suggestion is that this very history itself, history itself in its totality but especially as centered in Jesus of Nazareth, is God's primary word of which every other word is just a partial and imperfect interpretation. Then indeed we have a surplus of meaning, in fact, an inexhaustible source of further and further interpretation. Neither Mark nor Matthew, neither Luke nor John, gave us the definitive meaning of Jesus Christ; each gave us his partial, true, and ever so precious interpretation. But God said infinitely more in the Christ-event than any of them, or all of them together, could express; more even than the Lord Jesus himself, even if he gave much thought to his own meaning, could express in human language.

The point is not only easy to grasp; it has also a basis in our tradition. If we look, as we always do with our conservative eyes, for anticipations of this view in the past, they are not hard to find. In the scriptures we have Paul, and the author of the Letter to the Hebrews, and others, speaking of Old Testament events as types of corresponding realities in the New Testament—which is a way of saying that those Old Testament types, in their very own reality, as they happened in history, and not just as they were interpreted, were a word from God. Further, St. Thomas Aquinas provided a simple theological explanation. For him, God is active in all created activity: "Deus . . . est prima causa movens et naturales causas et voluntarias"[4] or, in the standard form of the axiom: "Deus operatur in omni operatione naturæ et voluntatis." It was easy then for Aquinas to take the further step, to say that, since God moves historical agents as easily as human author moves pen across paper, he may endow certain historical events with meaning; that is, God may, if he so chooses, not only operate as cause within their ontological reality, but speak in and through them, and thus express his infinite mind and meaning. What was not easy for St. Thomas was to generalize this principle, to say that God spoke not only in certain Old Testament types but in the whole of history. But, of course, St. Thomas was under no pressure so to generalize, the scriptures and the Church being, it seemed, quite adequate for the times; and, more fundamentally, he could not generalize the principle: he had no means of control over the meaning of such a primary word. The meaning of certain types was given by the New Testament, but what do you do with the whole sweep of history, if suddenly you are told that this is God's word and revelation?

So we come to the real problem of this stage: how do you control your interpretation of history? Even Pannenberg, who is probably the best-known exponent of history as revelation, has to concede, "Revelation is not comprehended completely in the beginning, but at the end of the revealing history."[5] Yet I think the situation is full of hope. We have one principle of control that St. Thomas lacked almost completely; that is, we have developed a theory or theories of history, a philosophy of history, a theology of history. And this supplies the *a priori* which is needed in every venture of thought, to guide it, control it, call it back when it strays. Such an *a priori* is itself subject to revision, certainly so; but even in its imperfect and revisable position it can be immensely helpful. We have another and more important principle of control: the ever neglected Holy Spirit, the forgotten Paraclete, the Cinderella of

4. St. Thomas Aquinas, *Summa theologiae*, I, 83, 1, ad 3m.
5. Wolfhart Pannenberg, "Dogmatic Theses on the Doctrine of Revelation," in *Revelation as History*, ed. W. Pannenberg (New York: Macmillan, 1968), p. 135.

theology. St. Thomas surely did not lack the Spirit, he did not fail to take account of the Spirit in his personal search for wisdom. And yet I think we have to say, without necessarily reviving Joachim of Fiore, that we are learning in our time to communicate with the Holy Spirit, not privately and individually, but publicly as a Church. And why not as theologians?

This then is the situation into which the centuries of thought on our sources have brought us: we do not seek new revelation, revelation is indeed complete, but not in the apostolic word, rather in the word that Jesus himself is and in the meaning he gives to all of history. The meaning of revelation, in other words, is enormously expanded. And, correspondingly, there is an enormous enlargement of the role of the Holy Spirit, when we do not confine him to a veto power at councils but allow him, in John's words, to lead us into all truth. With such a view we are not independent of the past, but we are surely freed for a new and creative future.

15

Theology and the Future:
Responsible Innovation*

If there is some truth in the historical analysis of my first talk, and in the new understanding of the sources that I think the centuries have contributed, then we have fulfilled one very important condition for a theology that is truly creative. That is, we have made room for a relation to the future and to a new theology that was certainly not easy and maybe not even possible when we thought of the word of God mainly as an eternal word in human language that would echo through the ages. If, however, the great and primary and all-sufficient word of God has indeed been spoken, but not in human language, if human language must strive forever to bring that word to expression, and one expression is achieved only to give way to another, then we have thrown back the horizons of theological thought till it is bounded only by the fullness of the knowledge God meant to express when he uttered his Son into the world. It becomes quite plain now that there is room for novelty; the categories and doctrines of the past are not the only categories and doctrines. The forty-two names of Jesus that the New Testament provides, rich and diversified as they are, are not the only names we may conceive; and, by the same token, terms like the hypostatic union of two natures, or the transsubstantiation of bread and wine, or the infallibility of the magisterium, are not the end of the matter, though maybe they are the end of the beginning.

We experience then a great release of creative energy, an immense expansion of our possibilities. There is, in the area of doctrine and theology, something like the freedom from the law which the gospel accords to the children of God. For in each case it is the interior operation of the Holy Spirit which is at work. He is at work with regard to the law: "To prove that you are sons, God has sent into our hearts

*The second of two papers read at the thirteenth annual conference of the Irish Theological Association, Killeshandra, County Cavan, 3–5 January 1978, where the general theme was "What is Theology?" For the first, see above, ch. 14. Previously published in *Science et esprit* 31 (1979) pp. 147–57.

265

the Spirit of his Son, crying 'Abba! Father!' You are therefore no longer a slave but a son" (Gal 4:6–7). And it is the same Spirit who is at work with regard to doctrines; he is the One who "will guide you into all the truth" (Jn 16:13).

Still that very analogy, bold as it may seem, serves as a salutary warning. For the New Testament freedom of the sons of God was not to be an excuse for licence: "Live as free men (Peter says); not however as though your freedom were there to provide a screen for wrongdoing, but as slaves in God's service" (1 Pet 2:16). Similarly, the release we experience in exploring the expanded meaning of the word of God will not lead us to scorn the past or to plunge wildly into any novelty whatever just for the sake of the novelty. As we turn then to the future, we will not forget the Janus figure which, while moving into a new era, managed also to keep an eye on the past. With that caution, I offer some reflections on the creative responsibility of theology for the future.

Since in presenting these reflections I will be following mainly the ideas of Bernard Lonergan, I need to mention at once two temptations we may experience in dealing with his thought: one is that of attacking his position without understanding it, and the other is that of defending his position without understanding it. From which you may conclude not only that understanding is the basic step, but also that it presents a great and ongoing difficulty. I speak with a certain conviction here, because for half my life I have been trying to understand Lonergan, and after thirty-one years understanding remains for me the basic step. And yet one does not give so many years to study of an idea without some *prima facie* evidence of its validity, just as one does not attack it without finding it *prima facie* disturbing, not to say radical. So this paper will be mainly expository, with that measure, however, of defense that may be needed to gain a hearing for my exposition. With that preface let me outline my headings: (i) the need of new categories in theology, (ii) the relation of the old categories to our new times, (iii) the foundations for the new categories, (iv) the precedent in our tradition for assigning these foundations, (v) the subjectivity of this approach to doctrines and theology, and (vi) the role of the community and of intersubjectivity in the process to counteract individualism.

I

Why do we need new categories, and how do we know we need them? We need new categories because of human historicity, and we know now that we need them because we have recently discovered human historicity. What is this human historicity that we all talk of? Let me quote one of Lonergan's simpler explanations:

[A]ll human doing, saying, thinking occurs within the context of a culture. . . . But cultures . . . have histories. It is the culture as it is historically available that provides the matrix within which persons develop and that supplies the meanings and values that inform their lives. People cannot help being people of their age, and that mark of time upon them is their historicity.[1]

When human historicity is not understood, doctrines can be freely imported across all boundaries of time and space; there is no tariff to pay. And so St. Thomas could import the words of scripture directly into his scholastic theology, and the theology manuals we studied a few years ago could adduce proof texts as premises that led directly to the desired conclusions. With human historicity firmly established, however, this does not work quite so easily; there is a heavy tariff to pay on imports from another culture, and the imports do not serve quite as readily as premises for a deductive theology.

II

My second question: What do we do with the old categories now that we propose to create new ones? Let me offer two clues. The first is an image, which I think will be instructive in regard to those doctrines of the past that may now seem less meaningful than when first enunciated. Suppose I am with my parents on the day of their golden wedding anniversary, and suppose, as we sit talking, I glance above their heads to the photograph taken on their wedding day fifty years before. The difference between then and now will be starkly evident, and several questions may arise: Is that a true picture of my parents? Are they the same persons now that they were then? Would another photo taken today try to reproduce that of fifty years ago, or would it try to relate to them as they now are?

The last question is, of course, tendentious, but it may make us think. My parents are the same but different. They are the same persons in their ontological identity: each a *subsistens individuum in natura rationali*. But our lives, so we have learned since hermeneutics became a favorite word, are the expression of what we are; not only our photos, but our very faces are a language to be exegeted (a person is responsible for his face by the time he is forty, I read once). So the photo does not correspond to what my parents now are; indeed, we have always to be

1. "Revolution in Catholic Theology," in *A Second Collection: Papers by Bernard J. F. Lonergan, S.J.,* p. 233.

critical enough to ask how closely it corresponded to what they were then, to wonder whether the photo was touched up, or whether the camera was an imperfect instrument or the cameraman a bungling artisan. More than that, their very faces fifty years ago, let alone the photograph, would no longer express the reality that they now are.

Apply this to the question of doctrines coming down to us from the past, remembering always the rule that you use an image as far as it serves your purpose but drop it when it begins to get you into trouble. The doctrines of any age are an expression corresponding to the needs of that age, which may or may not be the needs of another age. They are part of our patrimony, nevertheless; they are ours in so far as we are one community with our fathers in the faith, whether they met at Nicea in 325, at Chalcedon in 451, or at the Vatican in 1962. We have not only a sentimental attachment toward them, but a real need of them; and a need not only because they are in the line of development, and show us how we got where we are, but a need in many cases because of their continuing positive input. And yet, when all that is said and acknowledged, we need doctrines of our own for our own times to respond to our own needs.

Turn now to a clue of a quite different kind, one that I find in Lonergan's *Insight*. He is talking of the way fire has been conceived by scientifically minded persons across the centuries: "Fire was conceived by Aristotle as an element, by Lavoisier's predecessors as a manifestation of phlogiston, and by later chemists as a type of oxydization."[2] Here we have a series of quite new and indeed radically differing explanations of what fire is. But they are all explanations of the same continuing reality. We know that; no one reasonably doubts that Aristotle's fire and our fire, apart from accidental and irrelevant differences in color, intensity, and so on, are the same fire. But how do we know that? What binds the series of explanations together cognitionally? It is description, as opposed to explanation; we describe fire the way Aristotle did: It's hot! It burns you! Etc. "[D]escription supplies, as it were, the tweezers by which we hold things while explanations are being discovered or verified, applied or revised."[3]

Now that is a clue to how it is or may be with the realities of history. There is a narrative of the facts—let them be the saving facts of the life, death, and resurrection of Jesus—and that narrative, which conveys the facts to us in descriptive form, serves as the tweezers by which we retain contact with the reality, as we ponder its meaning and try one explanation after another. And the anchorage from which we start

2. *Insight: A Study of Human Understanding*, p. 737.
3. Ibid., p. 291.

again, when one explanation has run its course and served its purpose, lies in the descriptive account which remains relatively constant and allows us to reconsider our explanation, or radically revise it, or start all over again.

With these two clues we can, I think, handle two different sets of phenomena in our history. There is the sort of development you have from Tertullian to Thomas Aquinas in trinitarian doctrine, and I would consider that a linear development like a series of photographs of the same people. But there is the phenomenon of a change from thinking of the eucharist in terms of transsubstantiation to thinking of it in terms of transsignification; and this, I venture to say, is more like the series which starts always from the same descriptive account to work out quite different explanations.

If we leave mere clues behind for the more rigorous approach of Lonergan's *Method in Theology,* we find the relevant ideas in his first phase of theology, the mediating phase, in which we hear the word of our fathers in the faith, theology *in oratione obliqua,* and its four functional specialties of research, interpretation, history, and dialectic. These four are a powerful array of carefully distinguished procedures, each with its own purpose and technique: research to assemble the data, interpretation to tell us what they mean, history to follow the sequence of interpretations, and dialectic to submit the history to the crucible of criticism and choice. It is dialectic surely that will trouble our conservative minds and hearts, yet the other three lead inevitably to the fourth. One cannot stop with the assembled data, one has to ponder their meaning. But after a few centuries you observe that different interpretations have been given over the years, so you try to trace their sequence and find out what was going on; and this leads inevitably toward your own commitment to one side or another when views differ, and so you try to get to the root of differences, retain what is good, and purify the tradition of what was not authentic.

A brief note here, before passing to my third point. I distinguished between the linear development of trinitarian theology and the more dialectical development that eucharistic theology may be undergoing at the moment. In fairness to Lonergan I have to say that I have not based this distinction on his position. He would perhaps include both developments, insofar as they are valid and true, under the general form of a transposition of doctrines, which is one of his favorite terms. And in such transposition meaning is permanent, as he insists very strongly. As a result, he would find an assurance and safeguard for methodical theology, not only in the twofold interiority of the Holy Spirit and the dynamism of the human spirit (more on this later), but also in the permanence of the meaning of dogma.

III

Thirdly, there is the need, not only of new categories for new doctrines, but of new foundations for the new categories. Let me quote again from Lonergan, this time from a paper he read five years before *Method* appeared:

One type of foundation suits a theology that aims at being deductive, static, abstract, universal, equally applicable to all places and to all times. A quite different foundation is needed when theology turns from deductivism to an empirical approach, from the static to the dynamic, from the abstract to the concrete, from the universal to the historical totality of particulars, from invariable rules to intelligent adjustment and adaptation.[4]

If I have understood Lonergan in this passage, he is not denying logic its role in theology or any other science, but he is severely limiting that role. Logic works within a system, when certain truths are established to serve as premises; it does not suffice for the creative emergence of the system's principles. Logic, in other words, is helpless before the evolution of genera and species; it will never provide the creative insight into phantasm which understanding is; it cannot account for the particular in its particularity. And so all the logic in the world will not take you from the Palestinian way of thinking about Jesus to the Greco-Roman way of thinking about him, though each is not only valid in itself, but might serve (especially the Greco-Roman) as a basis for developing theological conclusions.

What then is the foundation for the new theology, the source of its new categories? Lonergan places it in interiority, interiority under the double aspect of transcendental method for general categories and religious conversion for special theological categories. Thus, he speaks of categories derived from "interiorly and religiously differentiated consciousness."[5] Again, he writes: "For general categories the base is the authentic or unauthentic man. . . . For special categories the base is the authentic or unauthentic Christian."[6] There is a shift here from the static product to the dynamic producing subject. Think of a train pausing at various stations along its route, but never reaching a terminal, continuing always its journey into the unknown. Which corresponds better to the human condition, the settlements at various points along the line, or the train itself journeying on forever? If we take seriously our title of pilgrim people, the answer will not be difficult. It is the moving train itself. The settlements look attractive, no doubt, but that

---

4. "Theology in Its New Context," in *Second Collection,* pp. 63–64.

5. *Method in Theology,* p. 282.

6. Ibid., p. 292. See pp. 327–28: "categories derived from contemporary interiority and its real correlatives."

is part of our permanent temptation. On the other hand, we need some reassurance that the train is going somewhere and doing so under some control. And that is the point of Lonergan's gigantic labor to find the irreducible structure of human consciousness, and of his continuing insistence on the gift of God's love as the reality to be objectified in the creation of new theological categories. Of course, we do not abandon or despise the safeguard of the outer word of doctrine.

IV

Is this approach of Lonergan utterly radical? I am going to propose, unexpectedly perhaps, that our own tradition supports the notion of a foundation for theology in interiority. It is possible to suppose, within the limits of the tradition, that all faith, and so all theology, had its originating moment in just such a way as we are postulating for a methodical theology. For one thing, we cannot be simply deductivist. For, if one doctrine derives deductively from another, and that other derives deductively from a third, we have to find a starting-point that is not itself a deduction, under pain of proceeding *ad infinitum*. The old way was to stop the backward process with God revealing truths; but that is regarded today as rather too simple. And even when we admit that God does reveal truths, we have still to ask by what process he revealed them, and are led quite reasonably to think of a religious conversion and internal experience in the agent that God chose for the revelation.

Take Genesis as an example. Does anyone suppose now that God spoke to some nameless author, or even to the great Moses, and said: "Pick up your quill and write, 'In the beginning God created heaven and earth'"? Do we not rather suppose that this author was first religiously oriented by the gift of God, then reflected on his experience, formed his view on the origin of the world, and expressed it in the way recorded in the opening chapters of Genesis? This is not deriving religious categories directly from interiority the way Lonergan proposes to do. But it is, or could be, a case of being carried by the dynamism of interior religious orientation to express a religious interpretation in objective categories. That is, we may ask whether the author of Genesis experienced in his own way "the feeling of absolute dependence" which Schleiermacher found as a co-element with the sense of freedom in immediate self-consciousness;[7] we may ask, and we may grant this as a possibility, even though we cannot prove it. We may ask similarly

7. Martin Redeker, *Schleiermacher: Life and Thought*, tr. J. Wallhauser (Philadelphia: Fortress, 1973), p. 115.

whether the experience resembled Otto's sense of the uncanny, and we may similarly grant the possibility. We may also accept Lonergan's view: "So it is by associating religious experience with its outward occasion that the experience becomes expressed and thereby something determinate and distinct for human consciousness."[8] And we may again grant the possibility that all this applies to the author of Genesis.

Of course, you will tell me—so let me tell you first—that I have proved simply nothing at all about the facts of the composition of Genesis. Indeed, I have not; I leave that to those who are Old Testament scholars. But the theologian has often to deal with what might be in the realm of theory, with a possible explanation of such facts as we have; and then it is within his province to say, "Yes, that is a possible explanation and a legitimate one within the boundaries of our doctrines and our theology." And to be able to say that much puts us already on the borders of tradition, looking hopefully across and anticipating a welcome from the community of the faith.

And is not some similar hypothesis tenable and even probable in regard to the source of the doctrine that Jesus taught? If we take seriously the synoptic accounts of his way of acting, we become increasingly uncomfortable with a view of his mind as a storehouse of all truth fully objectified and only waiting to be drawn upon when he wished to give it utterance. Whatever the beatific vision was, it does not seem to have involved that kind of encyclopedic knowledge. Rather, we suppose Jesus to have received some actuation, for example on the occasion of his baptism, through which his mission became objectified and articulated in his mind for the first time, or at least conceived with a determinacy that it lacked before. So again, we are back with the possibility—I think we may say this time, with the probability—of the kind of originating revelation that makes Lonergan's view less radical than it may at first have seemed.

V

I come to my fifth heading, the subjectivity of the approach to theology through interiority, and I begin by saying that theology now is much more a matter of personal involvement than it was in the past. Let us be clear on this: we have long believed there was a link between saintliness and theology, but we tended to regard the link as somewhat external. God would reward the saintly theologian with the right ideas, much as he would reward a pilgrimage with a miraculous cure. The saintliness was a condition of good theology; but it was not the very

---

8. *Method,* p. 108.

vein in which theology could be quarried. Today it is just that, though we prefer to speak of authenticity rather than of saintliness. Once more I quote Lonergan's *Method*: "Genuine objectivity is the fruit of authentic subjectivity";[9] again, the truth or falsity of value-judgments supporting doctrines "has its criterion in the authenticity or the lack of authenticity of the subject's being."[10]

The great catalyst here is Kierkegaard. His *Concluding Unscientific Postscript* has as its second subtitle (Kierkegaard was great on multiplying subtitles): "An Existential Contribution." The two divisions of the volume are "The Objective Problem concerning the Truth of Christianity" (less than one-tenth of the work) and "The Subjective Problem." This latter part has as its first subtitle: "The Relation of the Subject to the Truth of Christianity." At one point he gives four examples of what he calls "thinking directed towards becoming subjective."[11] One of these is "the problem of *what it means to die.*"[12] We can become immensely erudite on death without ever gaining the least existential understanding of what it means to die. We think about death as a universal, as something that happens to everyone. But, when death is not just a universal concept, not just an academic topic, when it is "something to be related to the entire life of the subject," then, Kierkegaard confesses, "I am very far indeed from having understood it, even if it were to cost me my life to make this confession. Still less have I realized the task existentially. And yet I have thought about this subject again and again; I have sought for guidance in books—and I have found none."[13]

Kierkegaard's work ridicules the great system-makers who cannot manage their own lives or even understand the great problems of life and death existentially. He does not take us to the point of deriving doctrine from existential involvement. For this I turn to the *Spiritual Exercises* of St. Ignatius Loyola. These are exercises *par excellence* in the self-involvement that Kierkegaard desiderates in the system-makers. It is not death in general that the exercitant studies, it is his own death; this he tries to understand in "thinking directed towards becoming subjective." But this thinking results sometimes in something very like a doctrine. Take the exercise on Two Standards, the standard of Satan and that of Jesus Christ. This is not a simple opposition of good and evil, but of two legitimate attitudes toward riches that end up in the diametric opposition of good and evil. The way of Satan, Ignatius says,

---

9. Ibid., p. 292.   10. Ibid., p. 37.

11. Soren Kierkegaard, *Concluding Unscientific Postscript*, tr. D. F. Swenson & W. Lowrie (Princeton: Princeton University, 1944 [1846]); see the table of contents for these examples.

12. Ibid., p. 147 (his italics).   13. Ibid., p. 152.

is to get us to start with a love of riches. And what's wrong with that? It's every poor boy's ambition to grow rich. But with a love of riches, Ignatius goes on, comes a love of honors. And now the road is turning, for with love of honors comes pride, and with pride every other evil. Whereas the way of Christ is to instill a love of poetry, from which comes a willingness—even perhaps a desire—for humiliations, and so one is led to humility and all the virtues.

Now we are dealing here with what looks like a clear case of doctrine: the Ignatian position on the relation of riches and honors to pride, or at least of the love of riches and honors to pride, is a doctrinal position. Further, it is not a doctrinal position to which we are likely to give a real assent, in Newman's use of the word, without personal involvement in the consequences. And further still, it's a doctrinal position that academics avoid when they are talking about the matter in the way that Kierkegaard deplored. It's easy to avoid self-involvement; one just reports what Ignatius said, analyzes his meaning, inserts him into the sequence of history, and so on. It's what Lonergan calls theology *in oratione obliqua*. But then we have heard only half the message, and that the lesser half. And yet academics are almost obliged to omit the other half, in deference to good manners.

So let me now become very ill-mannered, hypothetically. Suppose I began to add the other half of the message. Suppose I began to talk to you about these two standards the way Ignatius talked to his fellow-students at the University of Paris. Suppose I stood here in this academic institution and preached to you on the way of Christ. As, of course, I very well could. As I might well start to do this very moment. Let me ask now, growing more ill-mannered by the minute, "Are you beginning to feel uncomfortable?" "What is the man doing," you think, "standing up there and talking of preaching the *Spiritual Exercises* at us?" As the English say, in one of their fine phrases, "It isn't done." Let us end our little experiment, and revert to the academic. But am I right in guessing that you felt a certain discomfort at the way I threatened you with a sermon? If so, then we are at the very heart of the message of Kierkegaard (though we prescind from the problem he had with direct communication), we are at the very heart of a theology that claims genuine objectivity to be the fruit of authentic subjectivity, and we are also on the way to my sixth and final heading.

VI

My final point deals with the role of community and of encounter with others in formulating our theology. This is complementary to the individualist approach of my previous point, and corrective of its one-sidedness. For theology is a work requiring collaboration on a vast scale, and collaboration not only among theologians themselves, but also between theologians and the rest of the believing community.

A preliminary point is that the community extends over space and time to include our forefathers in the faith. There is encounter with the past to challenge us to faith and to theology. We know the power of the scriptures from the experience of reading them; most of us have had a similar experience from reading in Augustine's *Confessions* the story of his conversion. Naturally we think of such experience in terms of loving and believing and following. The Lord's message was, "[R]epent, and believe the Gospel" (Mk 1:15). Augustine's was, "The unlearned arise and take heaven by force, and here we are with all our learning, stuck fast in flesh and blood."[14] But the cognitive element soon emerges distinctly; the experience gives rise to wonder: "Who can this be whom even the wind and the sea obey?" (Mk 4:42); and wonder leads to theology, as the sequence of New Testament writings, in their effort to understand who Jesus is, makes clear. So far there is nothing very novel in this position: not only does faith seek understanding, faith in the sense of beliefs, but also love seeks faith, love wishes to know, it seeks a cognitive complement. However, in Lonergan's position there is a link between love and knowledge not only with regard to motivation but also with regard to content. There is an apprehension of value that not only powers our thinking but guides it. This position can surely be related to the Thomist knowledge by connaturality, though the links have not been studied, so far as I know. At any rate our beliefs on who and what Jesus is derive directly from the love of him that results from meeting him in the gospels.

There is also encounter with the present, with our contemporaries. It is a key element in Lonergan's fourth functional specialty, dialectic; so let me quote a couple of passages from chapter 10 of his *Method*: "Encounter is . . . meeting persons, appreciating the values they represent, criticizing their defects, and allowing one's living to be challenged at its very roots by their words and by their deeds."[15] Again, "it is only through the movement towards cognitional and moral self-transcendence, in which the theologian overcomes his own conflicts, that he can hope to discern the ambivalence at work in others and the measure in which they resolved their problems"; reciprocally, "it is through knowledge and appreciation of others that we come to know ourselves and to fill out and refine our apprehension of values."[16]

Of course, this works two ways, to revise our view of the past as well

14. *The Confessions of St. Augustine*, tr. F. J. Sheed (London and New York: Sheed & Ward, 1944), VIII, viii.

15. *Method*, p. 247.   16. Ibid., pp. 252–53.

as to help create our future. How much more efficaciously the gospel works upon us when we meet someone who genuinely lives it; and not only works upon our conduct but gives us new understanding: to encounter one who is genuinely just, genuinely charitable, genuinely other-worldly, is bound to give us new ideas of what Jesus may have been, and new ideas of what we ourselves are not, as well as an impetus to become other than we are. Everyone knows Tyrrell's description of the liberal's Jesus: he has looked down the shaft of a deep well and seen his own face reflected in the still water. Encounter with others challenges us to see the face of Jesus as quite different from our own.

And that seems to me to round off what I had to say to you, and so to provide a natural stopping-place. For if God's real word to us is Jesus Christ and all the history that centers on him, and if theology's task is to grasp and understand that word in its total meaning, then all of us, the liberal theologians and the Modernists along with ourselves, are engaged in the same task; we are searching like the Greeks who came to Philip and said, "Sir, we should like to see Jesus" (Jn 12:21). And what Tyrrell said of the Jesus of the liberals was only an application of a principle Thomas Aquinas, and long before him Aristotle, had enunciated: "Qualis unusquisque est, talis et finis videtur ei." It is what we are that determines our values; our values determine how we will see Jesus. So the task becomes one of self-knowledge and self-transcendence in the continual dialectic of intersubjectivity, of trying to find out who and what we are by a twofold encounter with the Lord and with our own contemporaries, in which we learn progressively who and what they are, of trying to become what we are not yet through that twofold encounter, and so of achieving the authentic subjectivity that Kierkegaard identified with truth and that Lonergan posits as the ground of genuine objectivity of doctrine.

16

The Janus Problematic:
Tradition versus Innovation*

Janus was the old Roman god of beginnings, and as well the god of gates, for in ancient times important events in life began at the city gates. So we have January, named from Janus, as the first month of each new year; it is the gate through which we enter a new unit of history, moving forward not without apprehension into the unknown future. A passage from M. Louise Haskins is pertinent here. "I said to the man who stood at the gate of the year: Give me a light that I may tread safely into the unknown. And he replied: Go out into the darkness and put thine hand into the Hand of God. That shall be to thee better than light and safer than a known way." No doubt most of us recognize these oft-quoted lines, and some of us remember how effectively King George VI used them in a Christmas message during the darkest days of the war.

But it is an obvious feature of a gate that you can go through it in either of two directions. For one person the new beginning is entering the city, for another it is leaving the city to seek a new life in the wider world. So Janus had two faces, looking in opposite directions. This duality applies *par excellence* to the two directions of time, the past and the future. We cannot reverse our direction in time, the way we can in space, but we can turn back in memory, recall the past, and bring it forward into the present; equally we can look ahead with anticipation, projecting, planning, preparing.

Thus the turn of the year is marked by a combination of backward and forward views. An old religious practice on 31 December was to sing the *Miserere* in repentance for past sins, and follow it with the *Te deum* in thanksgiving for divine blessings and the granting of a new year of grace. In private life there is a similar survey of the past and list

*Previously published in *Tradition and Innovation: Faith and Consent. Essays by Jesuits from a Canadian Perspective,* ed. J. B. Gavin (Regina: Campion College, 1983), pp. 13–36. Substantially the same material formed the content of The Aquinas Lecture for 1980, St. Thomas University, Fredericton, New Brunswick, given on 20 January 1980 under the title "The Modern Balancing Act: Tradition vs. Innovation."

of good resolutions for the future. The media abound in analyses of the year ended and forecasts of the year to come: in sports, in finance, in international affairs and so on.

Is anything more universally a part of human experience than this need to look in the two directions of past and future? By the same token, one may ask, is anything more banal, more trivial? What may give us pause before we answer no to the second question, is the way this feature of life has been made a theme by some of our poets, people wise in the science of humanity, philosophers without philosophical pedigree. Thus, Shakespeare has Hamlet ponder the never-answered question, "What is a man . . . ," and then go on to say:

> Sure, he that made us with such large discourse,
> Looking before and after, gave us not
> That capability and god-like reason
> To fust in us unus'd.
>
> (*Hamlet*, IV:4)

Now that phrase, "Looking before and after," has a history. Burns echoes the idea two centuries later.

> Still thou art blest, compared wi' me!
> The present only toucheth thee;
> But och! I backward cast my e'e,
>   On prospects drear!
> An' forward, tho' I canna see,
>   I guess an' fear!
>   ("To a Mouse")

Shelley repeats the very words with a slight grammatical variation.

> We look before and after,
> And pine for what is not.
> ("To a Skylark")

It may be, then, that the Janus attitude of the human race, as we look before and after, is not quite the trivial phenomenon we tend, on first thought, to pronounce it to be. Maybe we should say of it what St. Augustine said of time in Book XI of his *Confessions*: "What, then, is time: If no one asks me, I know; but, if I have to explain it to someone who does ask, I do not know." Indeed, a remark on time *should* on principle apply also to past and future, for they *are* time, they constitute it, they are time dissolved by a kind of grammatical chemistry into its elements. We can, if we will, add the present; but the present, if it is not to be a mere point without significance, includes the immediate past and the immediate future. The present situation is the one we experienced a moment ago; and the present agendum is the action we are just about to take. This simple pair of past and future are, then, the elements of time, as impenetrable as the compound; like a sacrament to that extent, they conceal a great mystery.

Let us, against the background of these reflections, turn more directly to our topic, which has a two-part structure in the way time has. There is tradition, that which is handed down to us from the past, which we do not create but receive as an inheritance, and there is innovation, that which is not handed down from the past, but is our own creation and input to the future. I believe it is enlightening and therapeutic to see this pair of terms from the perspective of past and future, to locate them in the setting of the perennial Janus problematic[1] of the human race.

I speak of therapy, because we are in a time of troubles, and the sharpest focus of my paper is not so much the two terms themselves, tradition and innovation, as it is the *conflict* between them, which seems to have reached a new degree of intensity in our age. I do not doubt that the conflict, like the problematic, is perennial. I do not doubt either that every generation finds the conflict especially acute, each in its own present, just because it has experience of its own conflict and has only history of other times. But surely there are ups and downs in this experience as in others, and there is good reason to think that, if we were to plot the graph over the centuries of conflict between tradition and innovation, there would be an extremely sharp peak in our time. I take "our time" broadly here, meaning not just this decade or generation or even this century in relation to previous ones, but this era of history extending over a number of centuries and all seen in relation to the long millennia of our more distant past.

I will study the topic under three headings. First, a bit of history that may help us understand the situation in context, and grasp why the conflict is so acute today. Then I will describe the resulting polarization, doing so in terms of the theological mind-sets that characterize the one side and the other. Finally, I will say something toward the resolution of the conflict.

---

1. "Problematic" is used as a noun in the sense now current among the philosophers, namely, that of a complex nest of questions out of which particular "problems" emerge and in which they have their contextual meaning determined. As for the phrase "looking before and after," I have just learned that its history not only goes forward from Shakespeare but also (and very appropriately too) far back across the centuries. Yves Congar quotes St. Bernard of Clairvaux as writing "ante et retro oculata' (*New Blackfriars* 62 [1981], p. 407), and the Rev. Lawrence C. Braceland, S.J., has assured me that Bernard's source is biblical. In fact, the *Nova vulgata bibliorum sacrorum editio* (Rome: Libreria editrice vaticana, 1979) has chosen, for Philippians 3:13, the reading, "quae quidem *retro* sunt, obliviscens, ad ea vero, quae *ante* sunt, extendens me . . ." (the emphasis, of course, is added).

1. The Shift from a Past-Oriented Culture to a Future-Oriented

I wish here to provide a historical setting for the present acute form of the conflict between tradition and innovation, and to do so in terms of a changed emphasis in our orientation toward past and future. I do not write with the scholarship of a professional historian. But we cannot get along without some history if we wish to understand ourselves; as Aristotle said somewhere long ago, we understand a thing best when we know its origins. So if we are not historians ourselves, we must read those who are and try to form some overall view of what has been going on and how we came to be where we are.

The thesis, then, is this. One of the great cultural changes of our time is a turning from a domination by the past to a freedom for the future. Once, and for a long age of history, there was a reverence for the "ancients" that made tradition sacred; but then, beginning in the seventeenth, eighteenth or nineteenth century (one can debate the key point in the transition), we abandoned that attitude to take a stand on our own creativity and face the future with an openness to innovation that often includes a degree of contempt for our ancestors. Symptomatic of the earlier attitude is a remark of Plato that in the good old days, people were better than we are and dwelt nearer to the gods, or the remark attributed to Bernard of Chartres, in the Early Middle Ages, that we are pygmies standing on the shoulders of giants. Symptomatic of the newer attitude is the demand for a complete break with what are called the "frozen cataracts" of the past,[2] and the ridicule poured on those who, it is said, go through life with their backs to the future.

An obvious source and carrier of the earlier attitude was the Judeo-Christian religious tradition. Creation began with a Paradise, an idyllic state, one on the basis of which Christian thinkers would not only build a core doctrine of the fall and the redemption but also elaborate some remarkable oddities of speculation on the original state of Adam and Eve. Then in the Hebrew religion the patriarchs were dominating figures. The Hebrew God was the "God of our fathers." Their heroes were the patriarchs and Moses. Repeatedly this shows up even in John's Gospel: "Are you a greater man than Jacob our ancestor . . . ?" (4:12); "Your accuser is Moses, the very Moses on whom you have set your

---

2. R. Wittram, as quoted by Jürgen Moltmann, *Theology of Hope*, tr. J. Leitch (London: SCM, 1965), p. 266: "To me the great historic events of the past always seem like frozen cataracts—pictures that have stiffened in the cold of vanished life and keep us at a distance." Plato's remark is put in the mouth of Socrates in the *Philebus* 16c–17a. John of Salisbury is our source for the remark attributed to Bernard of Chartres; see his *Metalogicon*, lib. III, c. 4 (*Patrologia latina*, 199, col. 900).

hope" (5:45); "We are Abraham's descendants . . ."(8:33). In a similar way the scriptures, coming to them out of the past, acquired an irrefutable authority (10:35).

Christians took over this attitude, and even accentuated it, though the situation is far more complex than that simple statement would indicate. The complexity is introduced by the *novum* that so emphatically characterizes early Christianity: Paul's new creation, John's born again doctrine, and so forth; this in logic should have had the effect of reducing reverence for what was older. Again, there was in Christianity a great heightening of the eschatological expectation that already marked the Jewish religion, and this too should have turned the Christian face definitely, even one-sidedly, to the future. Add that the return of the Lord Jesus was expected at any moment, literally so, and we would seem to have all the factors needed to turn Christian backs on the past and Christian faces to the future.

The remarkable thing is that the orientation to the past continued. The Christian scriptures, for one thing, were the Hebrew scriptures, what we now call the Old Testament; it was only slowly, with some hesitancy on the principle itself, that the New Testament writings came to command the reverence shown to those of the Old. Further, the Christians searched the Old Testament for the meaning of what had occurred in Jesus, and for prophecies that would show how God's eternal purpose was not frustrated by what seemed so discreditable; it was important to them to know that all had happened "by the deliberate will and plan of God" (Acts 2:23), "all the things which, under thy hand and by thy decree, were foreordained" (Acts 4:28). Even the return of Christ was to be, not simply a new age, but the restoration of all things to an original state (Mt 17:11; Mk 9:12; Acts 1:6; 3:21).

They not only took over the Jewish orientation to the past; they added their own backward reference. Paul may have focussed on the risen Lord in glory, but he had a firm anchor too in the events of the Lord's life and death on earth. He could even speak, almost reminiscently, of the early days of the gospel (Phil 4:15). In any case, as time went on and the return of the Lord was delayed, attention turned back more and more to the days when he was on earth. Gospels came into being. When Luke was writing, some two generations after Jesus, it had become important to establish the credentials of those who had handed down what had happened, and so the category of "witness" crystallized, someone "who bore us company all the while we had the Lord Jesus with us, coming and going, from John's ministry of baptism until the day when he was taken up from us" (Acts 1:21–22).

Thus tradition came into its place of prominence. To return to Paul again, even he, at an early date, could end an argument with the flat assertion that things are not done that way among us: "However, if you insist on arguing, let me tell you, there is no such custom among us, or in any of the congregations of God's people" (1 Cor 11:16). By the time of the Pastoral Letters this attitude had become sharply defined in a way that would furnish a pattern for centuries. Timothy is repeatedly charged to guard and hold fast the treasure entrusted to him (1 Tim 6:20; 2 Tim 1:13–14; 3:14–16; 4:1–5). Tertullian, that great phrasemaker, will formulate the principle in lapidary language against Marcion:

On the whole, then, if that is evidently more true which is earlier, if that is earlier which is from the very beginning, if that is from the beginning which has the apostles for its authors, then it will certainly be quite as evident, that that comes down from the apostles, which has been kept as sacred deposit in the churches of the apostles.[3]

The principle becomes established. There is direct continuity from the Pastorals through Tertullian to the way the Church of the fourth and fifth centuries looked back to the Council of Nicea and what the fathers had defined on that occasion; no question but that it was forever valid. Later councils, speaking on new questions for new times, would be held in equal reverence as they faded into the past: Trent in post-Reformation centuries, Vatican I in our century.

The Judeo-Christian religion was, then, a source and carrier of a backward-looking attitude, a reverence for the past, an almost unquestioning acceptance of tradition. But it would be a mistake to think it was the only carrier, or that this attitude was only a religious one. The orientation was general. Thus, in the great Renaissance period of the fifteenth century, there was a parallel and similar reverence for the pagan past, for its art, its literature, its law, its government. The Renaissance began, it seems, when the Christian rulers of Europe asserted their independence from religious authority and needed another authority to support their position; they found it in the pagan writings of antiquity.

Let us sketch this development. From the days of Canossa (1077) when Emperor Henry IV humbled himself before Pope Gregory VII, and still more from the time of the *Unam Sanctam* (1302), Pope Boniface's bull against Philip IV of France, the rulers of Europe were out to affirm their independence. But they could not legitimate their new position (the old had been legitimated by the Church, but that was exactly what they now objected to) without some authority. Now where did one find authority except in the past? For a thousand years the

---

3. *Against Marcion; Ante-Nicene Christian Library*, tr. P. Holmes (Edinburgh: T. & T. Clark, 1868), VII, Book IV, Ch. 5.

Church had appealed to *her* authorities, which were of course of ancient pedigree: scripture, the fathers, the councils. The rulers needed something parallel to that, and turned in their search to the old Roman law. Here was an ancient authority, one moreover that knew nothing of Christian revelation and the power of bishops, but one that was well worked out and solidly grounded in human reason and human right. It was made to order for their purpose. The scholars of the secular powers revived it, therefore, brought it forward into their times, and made it the foundation of the emerging state authority.

Such, it seems, was the beginning of that revival of the past which we have come to know as the Renaissance.[4] It was soon extended from a study of Roman law to a study of the ancient classics. It developed into a kind of adulation of the classics, making them masters to be imitated for all time in literature and art and culture in general. This extravagance may have been foreign to the original intention of the revival, but it is very germane to our topic, as showing how easily respect for a tradition can become uncritical acceptance.

When did the turn to the future occur? One is chary of pin-pointing the transition too definitely, the more so if one regards the Janus duality as a permanent feature of humanity. Forward-looking thinkers may occur at various times, and sometimes out of due time. Thus, Friedrich Heer, in his study of the Middle Ages, has a chapter on "The Twelfth Century Awakening," and speaks of that period as "an open age." He finds John of Salisbury typical of this open century in his "free, unprejudiced attitude towards even the greatest authorities of the past. . . ." But this movement does not seem to mark a transition, for the attitude typified by John did not endure; it would be impossible, Heer tells us, "even one or two generations later."[5] Again, when the Reformation came, its protagonists were, indeed, referred to by the Roman Catholics as innovators, but they themselves intended rather a return to the past than an openness to the future.

Probably we should look, for the significant turning-point, to the century immediately following the Reformation or to succeeding ones. Then we might think of the father of modern philosophy and mark the turn with the death of Descartes in 1650. Or we might think of the Enlightenment, generally regarded as a movement of the eighteenth century but equivalently present in the period between 1680 and 1715. Or of the scientific revolution that was roughly simultaneous with the Enlightenment. Or of the German Historical School that a century later

---

4. I have based this account on Walter Ullmann, *Medieval Foundations of Renaissance Humanism* (London: P. Elek, 1977).

5. Friedrich Heer, *The Medieval World: Europe 1100–1350*, tr. J. Sondheimer (London: Readers Union, 1962), pp. 76, 89, 92.

began to write finis to the anachronisms of earlier history. Or of Nietzsche and his smashing of the moral values and codes of the past to go beyond good and evil with his Superman. Or of Dadaism that carried the irrational into the world of art with its negation of the classical laws of beauty, around the time of the First World War. One has a number of choices for the important transitional events.

But it is probably a fruitless enterprise to try to pinpoint *the* moment of transition; it is much more important to know something of the factors involved. There was the new confidence in reason that followed on a repudiation of God-given truth. There was a new dominion over nature and the phenomenal expansion of technology that came with a new understanding of nature's laws. There was a new concept of the historicity of man, and not just a better technique for handling old documents, that resulted from a more accurate study of the past. There was the sense that not only does man develop in understanding but also he is creator of his own values. There was the debunking of the classical forms of art, to exploit human creativity in other areas than the technological and in ways quite as phenomenal.

A neat linguistic sign of the changed mentality is this: before the end of the seventeenth century "revolution" meant a return to the old, as in the "revolution of the stars"; now it means a new beginning.[6] Another weathervane showing the new turn is the notion of progress.[7] For example, Hegel plotted the progress of freedom in the movement of history from oriental despot through privileged Greco-Roman citizens to the infinite value and freedom of every individual person in the German world. This does not locate the break exclusively in our "modern" times but it does glorify the present in relation to the past. It is then a simple addition to take the further step from present to future, and this has been done by contemporaries like the late Ernst Bloch who has put quite a new emphasis on the future, is indeed a kind of geographer of the unmapped continent of the future. So we now have a futurology alongside all the other -ologies, and the summer of 1980 saw the First Global Conference on the Future held in Toronto with over five thousand delegates. The shift of focus from one Janus face to the other is remarkably clear.

What is one to say of this phenomenon? There are the familiar value-judgments, especially the extreme exaggerations on each side: the sar-

6. Michel de Certeau, "La révolution fondatrice, ou le risque d'exister," *Etudes* 329 (1968), pp. 80–101; see pp. 87–88.

7. I cannot, and need not, discuss here the extensive literature on the idea of progress. But I may say that I found a salutary caution against too simplistic a view of its history in Ludwig Edelstein, *The Idea of Progress in Classical Antiquity* (Baltimore: Johns Hopkins, 1967).

castic criticism of the past on the part of some enlighteners, notably in France; the scorn directed at futurist pretensions by some traditionalists.

Let me put it this way. When I studied history in high school over fifty years ago, the subject was divided into three great periods for the three-year course: Ancient, Medieval and Modern. It was a neat division, and the idea formed quite naturally that we were dealing with three equally determinate entities: the Ancient period ran its course, came to an end, was superseded by another; so did the Medieval; and the Modern period was equally well identified, even if it had not yet completed its course in the march of time. Is this not far too neat? My reading of sober and reliable historians leads me to think that the so-called Modern period does not constitute an era at all. It is not something constituted *in facto esse,* as the Scholastics might say, something with its own identity already determined. Rather it is a *fieri,* simply a transition to something else as yet unborn. Then we would say that the last three centuries are not an era, a period, an entity in time, an identity in history but a three-hundred-year January in the ages of mankind.

Let me cite here in evidence a remark of Karl Jaspers, the German thinker who was forced by Nazism to leave his post at Heidelberg and migrate to Basel: "For more than a hundred years," he wrote "it has been gradually realized that the history of scores of centuries is drawing to a close."[8] The idea is simply staggering in its implications. It is not just the era of European kings that has ended, or that of colonial expansion, or that of the Pax Britannica, or of the Pax Americana but the history of *scores of centuries.* If Jaspers is right, this "modern" era of ours is not at all an established *period,* it is merely transitional to something just dawning upon the world, something still in the future, in the womb of history. Then none of the elements I listed earlier constitutes the Janus-gate of the new beginning: not Descartes, or the Enlightenment, or the scientific revolution, or the German Historical School, or Nietzsche or any of the other factors that might be named; they are all simply single elements, or maybe only symptoms of something greater than any of them.

There is some support in everyday life for this view of the magnitude of the present transition in human history. I am thinking of the inability of the older generations to deal with the younger, to tell them anything clearly supportive and orienting. The new generations arrive on the scene experiencing unparalleled freedom from external constraint and an unparalleled potential for a creative life. But they are at a loss what

---

8. Karl Jaspers, *Philosophy and the World: Selected Essays and Lectures,* tr. E. B. Ashton (Chicago: Henry Regnery, 1963), p. 22. I have not tried to relate this notion to Jaspers' better known ideas on the axial period in ancient times.

to do with their freedom and their potential. They turn to various forms of experimentation, sometimes ruining their lives in the process. The only ones who seem to have something definite to tell them are the extremists at each pole: those who hold that all we need has been given us and we have only to hold fast to what was handed down, and those who have so cut themselves loose from the past that everything is permitted. If we really were in a Modern era, a well defined unit of history, surely we would have clearer ideas on what to hand on to succeeding generations. But we seem to be in the situation described by Rainer Maria Rilke:

> Each torpid turn of the world has
> such disinherited children
> to whom no longer what's been and
> not yet what's coming belongs.[9]

Rilke may have thought the turn of the world a more frequent occurrence; with Jaspers, I tend to think of it as occurring at intervals measured in scores of centuries.

One begins to understand how radical the opposition is between the two poles of tradition-oriented and future-oriented people, and why it has reached such a pitch of intensity today. It is at any time a fearful act to question our secure moorings in the past; it is equally fearful to assume responsibility for creating our own future. But the alternative is a refusal of responsibility in a blind adherence to what has come down to us. If the perennial Janus problematic is such as I have described it, there is bound to be confusion over tradition and innovation, with a certain polarization developing. If the present transitional movement is of the magnitude Jaspers attributed to it, the polarization is bound to reach an unheard of intensity and issue in the violent conflict that we are at present experiencing.[10]

11. Doctrinal Polarization

My business is not really cultural history; it is theology and in particular, theological doctrines. But theology has to read the signs of the times, and this means grasping what is going forward now in relation to what has gone before. I believe that the present doctrinal conflict in

---

9. Rainer Maria Rilke, as quoted by Hans Fantel, *William Penn: Apostle of Dissent* (New York: Basic Books, 1974), p. 83.

10. There is an odd contrast here between the human race and the individual human being: the race with advancing age seems to have changed its orientation from past to future, where we seem individually to change it in the other direction and become in our older years *laudatores temporis acti*. But then, the human race does not regard itself as having grown old, but as having just come of age.

the Church is illuminated by the history of what I have called the Janus problematic, the double orientation of the human race which results in some of us emphasizing one and some of us the other. It remains, however, for one whose business is theology, to analyze the doctrinal differences that result in the Church from this distressing division in society as a whole. I propose to do that, not so much by a detailed study of doctrines as by a study of contrasting mind-sets. Of course, the mind-sets have to be illustrated, and illustrated by the doctrines or nuances of doctrine that are held by this side or the other; but the illustrations can only be sketchy. An image of what I am trying to do may help. There is a point west of Banff, on the Trans-Canada Highway, which is almost an obligatory stop for tourists: The Great Divide, the height of land on the pass through the Rocky Mountains. At this spot, a little stream bubbles out from the wall of the pass, runs down to the roadway, and divides; and as the roadside sign tells us, some of the water turns west to follow its tortuous course to the Pacific Ocean, and some turns east to start its long and meandering journey to the Atlantic. This is a rather good image of the division in the Church as I propose to study it. Both sides belong to the Church; they read the same scriptures; they recite the same creed. But an accident of nature (biological, neural, psychic differences) or of history (parental influence, education, reading, friendships) turns one group this way and the other that. They face in opposite directions, and end up continents apart.

So, though they read the same scriptures, they have different sets of favorite texts and passages, as well as favorite gospels. Though they recite the same creed, they have favorite councils. Readers may test this by asking themselves: Do I prefer Mark or John as source of my Christology? Does Vatican I or Vatican II seem to me more of a benefit to the Church? The starting point, then, may be the same. Differences of doctrine may be almost insensible in the beginning. They may remain unnoticed if we leave them in isolation. But if we add them up they reveal two quite distinct patterns over a whole range of familiar doctrines: on God and creation, on Christ and the Church, on the Holy Spirit and Christian life. It is this polarization of mind-sets that I wish to study.

I begin with the past-oriented believer and his doctrine of God. His stress, then, will be on the omniscience and almighty power of God. God knows all, plans all, wills all, governs all. There is likely to be added here a particular view of eternity, according to which God exists in an endless duration; then he is conceived as having his plan ready from all eternity, an eternity that extends indefinitely into the past; and he is conceived as having knowledge of all that will be as eternity extends indefinitely into the future; of course, there is a providence that guides the whole course of history with divine efficacy throughout this endless duration. But with or without this view of eternity, God's plan is regarded as chosen in advance, with even Adam's fall integrated into it; it is a *felix culpa* providing a happy occasion for God's great redemptive act. There is, one might say, a divine blueprint for creation and for unfolding history.

The theology of creation corresponds to the forming pattern. Creation is already given as a unitary whole in the divine blueprint, where it manifests that order and harmony which only the divine artist can conceive and execute. The consequences are consistent with the ruling idea: things should remain what they were created to be. The plan admits a certain orderly evolution; this we are forced to admit, at least now, a hundred and twenty-five years after Darwin. But it is a controlled evolution: the universe is unfolding just as it should, within limits carefully drawn by nature. There is a tendency to think of evolution as belonging mainly to the past, indeed to the distant past of dinosaurs and some hypothetical missing link between man and his prehuman ancestors. In our age natural history has reached a plateau; a period of at least relative stability has set in.

Christology likewise corresponds to the pattern. First of all, the course of Jesus's life is part of the blueprint; so the second person of the blessed Trinity became man in order to carry out the divine plan, with the intention already formed of dying on the cross. But also the human mind of Jesus participates in the divine knowledge; through his beatific vision he saw the whole plan of God, and moved through history in conscious obedience to the known will of his Father. Again, his universal mission extended over the whole of time, so that he spoke and acted for later generations, providing them with a legacy of doctrine and conduct. Understandably, the Gospel of John is especially congenial to this Christology, for John repeatedly shows Jesus as knowing in advance what would happen.

Finally, the theology of the Holy Spirit and the Church corresponds to a pattern that has now become clear. In general, this orientation looks more to the Son than to the Holy Spirit; but it is Christian and Catholic and omission of the Spirit from the revealed mysteries would be unthinkable.

The role of the Spirit tends, however, to be determined by the Johannine passage which speaks of his recalling to the disciples what Jesus had already told them; thus his role in ecumenical councils was conceived as that of a "negative assistance": he has a kind of veto power to keep the councils from erroneous definitions of doctrine. There is no intention, of course, of subordinating the Spirit to the Son, but simply of taking seriously the once-for-all character of the revelation given in Jesus. Correspondingly, the Church has as her primary task to guard and hand on this deposit of faith, using the hierarchical and sacramental system given her from the beginning.

I have given only the headlines of a set of doctrines, but the headlines show a pattern, a way of thinking, a certain mind-set that makes the doctrines cohere in a kind of system. The pattern is that of continuity, an enduring sameness, a given stability, all reaching back to and deriving from a primordial plan of defined essences, natural operations, fixed precepts, stable institutions, ordered arrangements and a destined unfolding of history. Whether we think of the divine knowledge and will active from all eternity, or of the laws of the universe valid for all time, or of the clear vision Jesus had of our needs in every age and the clear formulas he provided to meet them, or the Church with her given structure and doctrines and the Holy Spirit to keep her on course, in every case we find the pattern of invariance, of a plan that is eternal, of a word that endures for ever.

Let us turn to the future-oriented believer and his or her doctrines. We will once more, I think, find a pattern; but the pattern here is quite different. First, God is conceived now with a stress on his continuing sovereign freedom. His eternity does not project into either past or future; rather, it is an eternal now. *Now*, at *this* moment, he is making his judgments, planning his world, issuing his decrees; and he is doing so in freedom, with multiple options remaining open to him in every decision. There is no denial of his omniscience, or of his sovereign power, for these believers too intend to be Christian and Catholic; but his mind and will are conceived through another model than that of a blueprint settled in advance.

Corresponding to the emphasis on the freedom of a God who is acting now, there is an emphasis also on the openness of creation rather than on its laws. It may be that the universe is still unfolding as it should, but it could unfold in so many ways; what has happened could have happened otherwise, and future happenings are still undetermined; there is a range of alternative possibilities, any one of which may be realized. And evolution continues. It did not stop because we arrived on the scene, as if it had come to a term with us; on the contrary, we might even expect it to accelerate under our guidance and semi-control.

History, even the life-history of Jesus, is no exception to the rule of an open development. When Mary uttered her *Fiat*, it was the signal for a divine entry into history that might have occurred elsewhere, or at another time or not at all. When Jesus struggled in Gethsemane on that April night, it was not yet fixed that he should die on the morrow; that was an option he made or accepted in prayer to his Father. Further, his human mind was not an infinite library of knowledge with instant retrieval of any item at any moment; rather, he is seen as thinking things out, of forming his message as time went on and of learning what he could communicate. Again, while his universal mission is not forgotten, there is a stress on his particular mission, which was only to the lost sheep of the house of Israel; and so he spoke to the audience before him, with their needs in mind, solving their problems with that generality which their situation required. Undoubtedly his more than human wisdom would have wide application; but he did not, as he spoke, envisage, say, a suburban parish of a North American city in the year 1980. Once more, there is a favorite gospel; but this time it is not the Gospel of John but that of Mark, for Mark shows Jesus as not knowing certain future events, as being surprised by what happens.

Finally, when we come to the Church, her tradition and the guidance of the Holy Spirit, we find the same freedom for creativity and adaptation. In general it is the view of future-oriented believers that the Holy Spirit has suffered some neglect, and they would correct this imbalance. He is seen therefore not only as recalling the past but also as the Creator Spirit leading us into the unknown future. The Church responds to the Creator Spirit, freely inventing the means that will, under divine initiative and with divine help, provide for needs as they arise. Tradition is still a perennial wisdom setting boundaries to our doctrines and decisions; but the wisdom is orienting rather than limiting and the boundaries are very wide indeed.

Again the nuances and emphases, when gathered together, form a distinct pattern in obvious contrast to the previous one. The direction is forward-looking; the impulse is one of freedom and creativity. The dominant ideas are those of possibilities to be realized; of inventiveness in realizing them; of a self-determination, deriving from and sharing in God's sovereign freedom, in deciding what we are to be, what we are to do, what we are to make of ourselves and our world. Whether we think of the divine freedom, or of the manifold possibilities of ongoing creation, or of the religious genius of Jesus of Nazareth, or of human dominion over the universe of nature and history or of the infinite resources of the Holy Spirit, the pattern is one of liberty, creativity, of a search for, and cooperation with God in forming, truth and value in a world that is our responsibility.

Let me close this sketch of polarizing mind-sets in the Church with a pair of images that, limping comparisons though they be, may still bring out the contrast. They are to be images of divine truth; both sides would regard this as a great mystery of which we know something infinitesimally small, and that through a glass darkly. But the two sides would image this situation quite differently. One might think of it under the familiar simile of the iceberg; only the tip is visible, but the rest is there, solid and firm. Similarly with divine truth: only a fragment is known to us, but the rest is there, securely stored in the divine mind, awaiting the moment of full revelation to us. Those with the alternative mind-set will need, however, a quite different image. They may think of an author who types at the head of the page the title of the essay he is to write. The topic is chosen, the general lines of his idea are determined, the boundaries are fixed beyond which he may not stray, if he is to remain true to his topic. But the rest of the page is still blank. A great creative work remains to be done. This too is a possible image of divine truth. Again, only a fragment is known; but now the rest is not yet there, it awaits the divine decision. So far as we are co-workers with our God, it is a possible image too of the task that is ours. God has typed out the title of his work of creation; with him we are to write the text, or a large part of it.

III. Toward a Resolution of the Conflict

The historical currents of the last few centuries have brought about a quite new orientation in wide areas of culture and among multitudes of thinkers and observers. It has resulted in a polarization between those who adhere to the new ways and those who resist them; and this polarization shows up, as one manifestation, in two quite diametrically opposed attitudes in the formulation of theological doctrines. I did not in my first section try to evaluate the historical currents. Did they represent progress? Or decline? Or partly one and partly the other? For the moment I was concerned only with the actual trend. Similarly, in presenting the polarized doctrinal tendencies in the second section I did not discuss them from the viewpoint of orthodoxy and heresy. Are they compatible with Church doctrines? Or incompatible? The question was left open. One may ask too: Does anyone really hold either set, or do they represent what are called "ideal types"? Again, to what extent are the two patterns complementary instead of contradictory to one another? Many such questions remain.

We can hardly leave the matter there. But at the same time one may find the problem much too big to handle. Hence the title of this third section, which will ring familiar to many readers because of the tentative character of "toward." Nowadays some of us are chary of providing solutions, but not wishing to be altogether silent, either because of the conviction that our ideas can make a contribution or because of the real responsibility to stand up and be counted, we write, instead of "solutions," certain "reflections" that move "toward a solution."

My first observation will be a platitude. We cannot repudiate either of the Janus faces that I have described, neither that which looks back to the past to learn from tradition, nor that which looks ahead to provide our own innovative solutions to the new problems that continually emerge in history.

For we are committed to a God who spoke in varied fashion through the prophets and then in the final age and in some final sense spoke to us in the Son. The faith *was* delivered to the saints once and for all, as the Letter of Jude states, and Christ *did* die once and for all, as the Letter to the Hebrews insists. Moreover, besides progress there is decline; besides enlightenment there is darkening and murkiness. So it is just not true that every day in every way things are getting better and better. But at the same time we are committed to a God who gave us dominion over the world. It is, however, a dominion in right which has to be achieved in fact. The Lord who is the once-and-for-all origin of our faith also forbade us to wrap our treasure in a handkerchief or bury it in the ground. Woe to me, St. Paul said, if I do not preach the gospel. And woe likewise to us if we stow the gospel away to keep it in safe storage, immobile and unproductive.

In the area of theology this means a respect for tradition, a loyalty to Church and creed; but it also means a commitment to the pursuit of truth, a critical judgment on past endeavors, and an involvement in modernity. Thus we are pulled two ways. There results the kind of polarization occurring repeatedly in the Church, as in the reaction of Vincent of Lerins to St. Augustine, in the Medieval opposition to St. Thomas Aquinas, or more recently, in the conflict over biblical studies at the turn of the century.

So much for a first observation. An innocuous one, surely, for who would deny the need of progress along with tradition? Not even Vincent of Lerins. But by the same token, not exceptionally helpful either toward a positive solution. Still, it is a useful caution, a pair of boundaries marked out, to keep us from the worst extremes. A second observation is directed to the traditionalists. It does not take sides, and is not *against* them, but it insists that they are not responding to the new need of the Church. The new need, if we are to achieve peace and a Janus-like balance of our two orientations, is to bring into play the future-oriented, the forward-looking mind. One may assert this as a permanent need, and do so on *a priori* grounds; but I believe one has to assert it as the specific need of our time, and *a posteriori*. It is the need that the signs of the times are pointing to, the need the Holy Spirit is bringing to our attention. It is not met simply by repeating traditional doctrines, however true those doctrines may be.

There is an illustration in the quite basic matter of creeds. The last fifteen years have seen scores of new creeds flooding the religious journals. Not only Churches and groups have produced statements of their beliefs, but various individual believers have done so as well, including some of our front-ranking theologians: Karl Rahner, Bernard Häring, René Marlé and others. From this abundance I choose two statements which, in the stark contrast they reveal, will illustrate my point better than pages of exposition.

The first is the *Credo of the People of God* written by Pope Paul VI in 1968. Readers may be familiar with it. In any case the content is so traditional as to require little exposition here. It begins with profession of faith in the one and triune God, the creator; it continues with his attributes, with separate statements of belief in each of the three divine persons; it goes on to the blessed virgin, the Church, the mass, the eucharist and so forth; it concludes with the last things and the communion of saints. It is a succint statement of apostolic belief along with the doctrines that have since been added to the Church's profession. For over a century we have had a useful collection of articles of faith, known simply as "Denzinger" from the circumstance that it was first edited by Henry Denzinger; the *Credo of the People of God,* one could say, is a "Denzinger" in miniature.

One would hardly ask for a clearer statement of what we are calling the traditional viewpoint. Few, I hope, would deny the value of such statements as distilling the sometimes prolix language of ancient documents. But the question remains, indeed it acquires a special urgency from the fact that this *Credo* appeared in the flood tide of recent creeds: Is it enough?

I believe it will be illuminating for this question to consider a quite different composition that appeared four years later, one developed by students of the Indian National Urban Industrial Mission Course at Dungapur, India. Let me quote the opening lines:

> I believe in one world, full of riches meant for
>   everyone to enjoy;
> I believe in one race, the family of mankind, learning
>   how to live together by the hard way of
>   self-sacrifice.
> I believe in one life, exciting and positive;
>   which enjoys all beauty, integrity and science;
>   uses the discipline of work to enrich society;
>   harmonizes with the life of Jesus,
>   and develops into a total joy.[11]

The creed continues with professions of faith in a morality of love,

11. See *The Expository Times* 83 (1971–72), p. 377. The *Credo* of Pope Paul VI can easily be located in the Catholic periodicals of the time, e.g., *The Pope Speaks* 13 (1968), pp. 276–82.

under the Spirit's control; in the life, death and resurrection of Jesus as proof of God's love; of God's purpose to unite everything in Christ. But enough has been quoted to show the quite different style, approach and content, and the sharp contrast between this and the creed of Pope Paul.

Now I am not arguing the superiority of this creed nor urging its substitution for that of Pope Paul or defending its adequacy as a Christian profession. The one feature I wish to point out is its creative and innovative character, the attempt it makes to speak to the real needs of a people for a faith to live by, not just one to repeat in formulas inherited from the past. It was written for India, one of the poorest nations of the world, and begins with a profession of faith in the world's riches; it was written by people who know what it is to suffer from racism, and it professes faith in one race, the family of mankind; it was written for a land where infant mortality is very high, where life expectancy even for adults is low, and it professes faith in life, the good life, a life of joy, a Christian life.

This is exactly the way the ancient creeds were formed: in response to the needs of the situation. The Apostle Paul wrote lines on the resurrection of Christ (1 Cor 15) that were destined to enter into the early creeds; he did so because there was question of the resurrection, and the question had to be answered. That was the pattern in the beginning; it continued to be the pattern for almost every article of faith that has been added to our patrimony. It is the sort of thing that the students of Dungapur were trying, however inadequately, to do in our time. If we condemn the inadequacy, the proper next step is not to complain about the failures of others but to try ourselves to do better what we may feel they did not do well enough.

My third observation is directed to those oriented toward the future and creative innovation. I make it, however, in the form of a cascade of questions. What attitude, I would ask them, would you have us take to the past? Given the historicity of our race, given the historicity of all our expressions of faith, be they scripture, creed, or conciliar definition, what are we to do with these expressions now? Do they come forward in any way into our time? Do they relate to us? Are they part of our faith in any way? If not, how justify the repudiation? But if they are, other questions press upon us. How do we deal with them? Our position cannot be merely that of observers who report on the faith of our ancestors, or of interpreters who explain it to us, or of historians who trace doctrinal developments, or of critics who evaluate an ancient author in terms of his horizon; in short, it cannot be the neutral position of people who stand aside from the community of our ancestors.

So the question remains and will not go away; how, after all our scholarship is exhausted, do we bring the past forward and make it our own?

I do not propose to spell this out any further. I have made the present point by way of questions, but its positive import will not be lost on my readers: namely, that much "historical-critical" work, while very effective in the destruction of lumber from the past, is considerably less so in saving what is valuable.

Not that the work of innovating theologians is to be suppressed. It is utterly essential that such work continue in the sense that inquiry, critique, search for relevance are part of the theologian's very purpose, his responsibility to the Church; for the Church to suppress this activity would be to tell the theologian to bury his treasure in the ground and thus merit the gospel condemnation of such sterility. Nor is it very helpful to instruct the theologian to make sure of the orthodoxy of his ideas before he sets them before the public. It amounts to suppression of *all* ideas to say that only good ideas, the correct ideas, will be allowed to circulate. It is the very nature of the cognitional process that ideas must occur by the dozen, or by the hundred or thousand, and be tested in their consequences, before one true judgment will emerge. Just as a million seeds fall to the ground for one tree to be added to the forest. Maybe theologians ought to be more acutely aware of the conditional character of their ideas and profess it more openly (as maybe I should do more expressly with regard to this essay), but we cannot expect them either to abandon the role of judgment (for they do not publish what they do not judge to be true) or to be the final judges in their own case (for ideas are the work of the individual theologian, but definitive judgment belongs to the whole people of God).

My concluding observation is more positive though it only points in a general way toward the solution of our Janus problematic in theology and doctrines. It would respond to the question "What are we to do?" and would respond in terms that first appeared, as far as I know, one hundred and ten years ago. John Henry Newman had sent a copy of his *Grammar of Assent* to a friend, Robert William Dale, who wrote at once, before even reading the book:

No one, as far as I know, has ever done for Theology what Bacon did for physical science, and since I saw the announcement of your Essay I have been looking for its appearance with great curiosity and interest, for there are many passages in your writings which indicate that you had given very much thought to many of the questions which would be illustrated in a Theological *Novum Organum. . . .*

Newman replied within three days:

You have truly said that we need a Novum Organum for theology—and I shall be truly glad if I shall be found to have made any suggestions which will aid the formation of such a calculus—but it must be the strong conception and the one work of a great genius, not the obiter attempt of a person like myself, who has already attempted many things, and is at the end of his days.[12]

The general idea is clear enough. Aristotle had created (though he did not know it, actually) a logic which functioned as an organon, an instrument of mind; and for millennia it served to systematize deductive thought and reduce the leeway for error. Francis Bacon saw the need for a new organon that would be inductive, and would do for experimental science what Aristotle had done for demonstrative thinking. Now Dale and Newman, two centuries after Bacon, saw the need for an analogous organon in the field of theology.

There is no room here, in an essay which has already gone beyond the editor's stipulation as to length, to study the history of this idea, to investigate Newman's own contribution to it, to detail the kind of organon needed for theology and how it would differ from both logic and the methods of experimental science, and to ask finally whether such an organon is presently extant and available for new and creative work in theology.[13]

But if these pages have any positive contribution to make, beyond analysis of the situation, it will be in the suggestion that our real search must be for long-range solutions, that we therefore look not so much to the theologies that abound in our time (however much we need them for immediate remedy, to tide us over our time of troubles), as to an organon that will be sufficiently "delicate, versatile, and elastic" (in Newman's words)[14] for the great work that we are called to do.

12. *The Letters and Diaries of John Henry Newman*, ed. C. Dessain & T. Gornall (Oxford: Oxford University, 1973), XXV, pp. 56–57.

13. I have gone into this question on some of these points in *The Lonergan Enterprise* (Cambridge, MA: Cowley, 1980).

14. *An Essay in Aid of a Grammar of Assent* (London: Longmans, Green, 1930 [1870]), p. 271.

17

Son and Spirit: Tension in the Divine Missions?*

A remark of George Tyrrell, in the work he completed just weeks before he died, will serve to introduce my topic. It has to do with the quest of the historical Jesus, as it came to be called, and specifically with what Harnack found as he joined in that quest: "The Christ that Harnack sees, looking back through nineteen centuries of Catholic darkness, is only the reflection of a Liberal Protestant face, seen at the bottom of a deep well."[1] Nearly three-quarters of a century have passed since Tyrrell's time, to make us a sadder and a wiser race. We no longer quote his remark with the smugness we might once have felt. We know far too well by now that the general principle latent in this particular case could be directed against any one of us. Not only Harnack, not only Loisy whose Christ-figure seemed to Tyrrell more Catholic than that of Harnack, but all of us throughout our history, from the four evangelists down to the latest liberation theologian to claim Christ as a revolutionary, we have all tended to conceive a Jesus, if not after our own image and likeness, at least after the model we feel our times demand, the figure of one who will symbolize our deepest aspirations, illumine our self-understanding, inform our world view, guide our deliberations, and in every way be our leader in the flux and chaos of our universe and our history.

With that introduction I proceed to develop my topic in three parts. First, I will briefly illustrate and analyze the tendency Tyrrell so unerringly disclosed in Harnack; then, I will describe the factors that at present call for and in some measure provide a new approach; finally, I will indicate the kind of systematic theology that might structure that new approach, and I will sketch the revised history that might be writ-

*A paper presented at the tenth annual Lonergan Workshop, Boston College, 20–24 June 1983, where the general theme was "The Redemptive Tension." Previously published in *Science et esprit* 35 (1983), pp. 153–69, and *Lonergan Workshop* 5 (1985), pp. 1–21.

1. George Tyrrell, *Christianity at the Cross-Roads* (London: George Allen & Unwin, 1953), p. 49.

ten in the light of that theology. For those who are wondering what this has to do with the Spirit who joins the Son in the title of my paper, or with the redemptive tension which is the theme of this workshop, I may say in advance that neglect of the Spirit has been partly responsible for the distorted Christ-figures I have referred to, that this has resulted in a tension for us between the role of Son and that of Spirit, and that I hope in this paper to help overcome that tension through a better view of the unity in the two divine missions.

I

This first part of my paper is not so much a thesis as it is a simple list of samples to illustrate a thesis that is now a commonplace. To begin at the beginning, there is the commonplace that the New Testament itself reveals a considerable variety of Christologies. Scholars trace early forms in the sermons of Acts, and the Christ of Paul can be delineated from his letters. But my first samples will be the more familiar Christ-figures of the four evangelists, where we find the rather stern and Jewish Jesus of Matthew, the strong Son of God battling demonic powers in Mark, the more humanist Jesus of the apologist Luke, and the only Son of John's Gospel, the one who came from above and moves with divine foreknowledge throughout his stay on earth. Are we dealing here with four writers who construct a Jesus somewhat according to the presuppositions of the author? We are not asking whether the picture drawn is false, but simply whether it is slanted by selection, or emphasis, or some such means. To answer an empirical yes or no to the question, we would need some independent source on the mind and religious situation of each writer, with which we might compare his Christ-figure. But I notice that scholars move readily in the reverse direction, that is, they construct the evangelist's character and situation out of his gospel, thereby granting implicitly and in principle the very link I am exemplifying.

More illuminating even than the gospels is the Letter to the Hebrews, for here the creative work of the theologian-writer is very much in evidence as he shows us a Christ who is high priest according to the order of Melchisedech. The evangelists based their Christ-figures more or less firmly on a narrative of the words and deeds of Jesus, but the Letter to the Hebrews cannot do that for the priesthood of Christ. Of course, the thesis is tied in a general way to the death on the cross and to certain facts in the life of Jesus; but it cannot be validated in the life of Jesus as a whole, for he did not belong to the Levitical tribe, nor did the early tradition coming down to our author make a theme of his priesthood. Hence the need, if one would have Christ be a priest, to make him a different kind of priest, and give his priesthood a different basis, through recourse to the figure of Melchisedech.[2]

Leaving the New Testament now, I propose to add a few soundings from later history, or, if "soundings" is pretentious, then a few headings that may recall a history you already know. There is, first, a group of Franciscans in Ockham's time who were deeply moved by the ideal of poverty set by their founder (as who is not?), but carried their enthusiasm to such an extreme as to assert that Christ, along with his apostles, exemplified the pinnacle of perfection by giving up "all dominion or ownership of property both 'singly and in common.'"[3] Four centuries later we find a quite different Christ in a quite different setting, but those very differences bring out the uniformity of approach. We read that for the philosopher Immanuel Kant, "The only true and sanctifying religion is that moral creed of which Christ was but the most eloquent preacher and most convincing witness."[4] Nearer our own times, I remember reading of some liberal theologian of a century ago, for whom Christ was "an enthusiast for humanity." I think also of the many books on spirituality of Archbishop Alban Goodier, whose Christ is such a lonely figure, opposed by his own people and those to whom he would bring his Father's word. Then there is Bonhoeffer's Christ, the man for others, and the Teilhardian Christ, who is the omega point, the fulfillment of natural evolution.

Enough of random samples. One may find a much longer and better documented list in Küng's *On Being a Christian*,[5] but I have quite enough for a general picture. It is more important to examine the credentials of the various authors in question, and to that end I add two samples that are poles apart. At one pole we find Juan Mateos and his radical, not to say revolutionary, Christ, who "rejected all the Israelite institutions: temple, monarchy, and priesthood."[6] Mateos is a biblical scholar of some note and, as we would expect, documents his study rather carefully. At the other pole there is Thomas à Kempis and a Christ (I owe this idea to a lecture by Juan Luis Segundo) who is very much a Medieval monk. And, of course, à Kempis, despite the scriptural text with which he starts *The Following of Christ*, provides nothing remotely resembling a documented case for his view.

2. J. W. Bowman, *Hebrews, James, I & II Peter*, The Layman's Bible Commentaries (London: SCM, 1963), pp. 17–18.

3. Terry J. Tekippe, "History: The Medieval Period," in *Papal Infallibility: An Application of Lonergan's Theological Method*, ed. T. J. Tekippe (Lanham, MD: University Press of America, 1983), pp. 142–48; see p. 147.

4. Léonce de Grandmaison, *Jesus Christ: His Person—His Message—His Credentials*, tr. (Book IV) A. Lane, vol. II (London: Sheed & Ward, 1932), p. 283.

5. Hans Küng, *On Being a Christian*, tr. E. Quinn (London: Collins, 1977), pp. 126–44.

6. Juan Mateos, "The Message of Jesus," *Sojourners*, 6/7 (July, 1977), pp. 8–16; see p. 12.

Are we, then, to say that there was indeed a problem with the Christ-figure of earlier times but that now, with the advent of biblical scholarship, we may hope for the real Christ, described with greater objectivity? We may indeed so hope, and we may certainly not dispense with scholarship, but just as certainly scholarship is not enough. The simple fact appears from the contradictory conclusions reached by scholarship, as when one author devotes his talent and diligence to proving that Jesus was married, and another devotes equal talent and diligence to showing Jesus as the model for celibate religious orders. The general explanation of the fact is found in the current view that praxis is complementary to learning in determining religious doctrine, so that a Medieval monk just *might* see what is hidden from the eyes of an exegete. More specifically, research, interpretation, and history—all, however objective their methods and techniques—are conducted by a subject with a particular horizon, and the results obtained by the researcher, interpreter, or historian will correspond to that horizon. There is needed, then, a dialectic of horizons that goes beyond scholarship, and a foundation for one's position that lies deeper than the technical rules of the discipline in question. Further analysis may be found in a work familiar to those attending this workshop, Fr. Lonergan's *Method in Theology*, so I conclude here the first section of my paper.

II

If I say now that the times demand and present thinking makes possible a new approach, I wish also to be moderate in my claims. It was not from a perverse motivation that Christians of all times described such personal Christ-figures, but from a deeply felt need. We remember Bonhoeffer's question, "What is bothering me incessantly is the question what Christianity really is, or indeed who Christ really is, for us today,"[7] and that phrase "for us today" brings home to us the need *we* have in Toronto or Boston *today*, for God among us, a need that is not satisfied by God in Palestine in biblical times. Nor is it an altogether perverse theology that makes of Jesus a chameleon to appear in various forms to suit the diversity of human cultures, for scripture proclaims his infinite resources, "all things are held together in him" (Col 1:17), and in him we are "brought to completion" (Col 2:9). Do not such resources argue an equally infinite adaptability, so that, wherever and whenever we live, under whatever conditions, we are to find in him "the way . . . the truth and . . . life" (Jn 14:6)?

7. Dietrich Bonhoeffer, *Letters and Papers from Prison*, enlarged edition, ed. E. Bethge (London: SCM, 1971), p. 279—from the letter of 30 April 1944.

I am not a radical, setting out in a new enlightenment to overturn the wisdom of centuries. But neither do I wish to be a reactionary, going through life with my back to the future. Our loyalty to the past involves understanding, testing, and evaluation, as well as acceptance; and, over and above that, we have a duty to the future, to add in the twentieth century our little increment to the wisdom of the previous nineteen. One thing this century has made clear is the pluralism and extreme variety of human meaning, human value, human ways and cultures. We have to ask how this affects our relation to Jesus of Nazareth, to whom we are drawn by the Father, but in whom we find much that is strange to us; we have to distinguish in his words and deeds what was particular to his situation and what is valid for everyone, always and everywhere. Further, if his life on earth does not provide the detailed blueprint we think we need to lead our own, we must ask what other resources our religion provides to have God-with-us in our pilgrimage. These two headings will structure the second section of my paper.

The general thesis of the multiplicity of cultures, each with its own legitimacy, is well established, and it will be enough to quote a thematic statement of Fr. Lonergan on the matter. The thesis was not, of course, his discovery, but he contributes, in the way that is characteristic of his work, to its clarity, its generalization, its integration into a comprehensive view of what it is to be human. There is the further advantage of putting the case in terms that will be familiar to participants in this workshop. He tells us, then, in a paper entitled "The Transition from a Classicist World-View to Historical-Mindedness," that it is quite possible to view man as such, "and man as such, precisely because he is an abstraction, also is unchanging."[8] This is the "classicist" view, which has had so long a reign in our tradition. The reign, however, has come to an end, yielding now to another view.

On the other hand, one can apprehend mankind as a concrete aggregate developing over time, where the locus of development and, so to speak, the synthetic bond is the emergence, expansion, differentiation, dialectic of meaning and of meaningful performance. On this view intentionality, meaning, is a constitutive component of human living; moreover, this component is not fixed, static, immutable, but shifting, developing, going astray, capable of redemption; on this view there is in the historicity, which results from human nature, an exigence for changing forms, structures, methods; and it is on this level and through this medium of changing meaning that divine revelation has entered the world and that the Church's witness is given to it.[9]

What we have in this passage is a sketch of a conceptual system for

8. *A Second Collection: Papers by Bernard J. F. Lonergan, S.J.*, pp. 1–9; see p. 5.
9. Ibid., pp. 5–6.

handling the phenomena of cultural change and for understanding how such change affects our relation to Jesus of Nazareth and to the scriptures that mediate him to us. Within this conceptual framework, then, let me insert a thesis from a famous essay of Rudolf Bultmann, on demythologizing the New Testament. His opening statement is: "The cosmology of the New Testament is essentially mythical in character,"[10] and his first thematic question: "whether, when we preach the Gospel to-day, we expect our converts to accept not only the Gospel message, but also the mythical view of the world in which it is set."[11] His own answer is clear: "We no longer believe in the three-storied universe which the creeds take for granted."[12]

The critical part of Bultmann's essay was followed by his own constructive effort to maintain the New Testament kerygma: his highly controversial existential interpretation. That does not concern me here. I wish merely to note that his critical thesis, the program of demythologizing, in its general lines, has been so universally accepted today that the younger theologians in my audience would likely be puzzled by all the fuss made over this essay forty years ago. I spoke, however, of acceptance of the thesis in its general lines, for many have felt a deep reluctance to accept it in the particular case of our Lord Jesus Christ. It is all very well to make the New Testament authors captives of their times and culture: but, as Matthew Arnold said of Shakespeare and we, with far greater conviction, may say of Christ, "Others abide our question. Thou art free." Nevertheless, the corresponding point had been made, a generation before Bultmann, about Jesus too. Again, I find it useful to take a sample of that earlier writing, and so turn to *The Quest of the Historical Jesus,* a work produced thirty-five years before Bultmann's essay.

The study of the Life of Jesus has had a curious history. It set out in quest of the historical Jesus, believing that when it had found Him it could bring Him straight into our time as a Teacher and Saviour. It loosed the bands by which He had been riveted for centuries to the stony rocks of ecclesiastical doctrine, and rejoiced to see life and movement coming into the figure once more, and the historical Jesus advancing, as it seemed, to meet it. But He does not stay: He passes by our time and returns to His own.[13]

The thesis, then, is the historicity of all things human, the multiplicity of human cultures, the strangeness of one culture for another, the

10. Rudolf Bultmann, "New Testament and Mythology," in *Kerygma and Myth: A Theological Debate,* ed. H. W. Bartsch, tr. R. H. Fuller (London: SPCK, 1953), pp. 1–44; see p. 1.

11. Ibid., p. 3.   12. Ibid., p. 4.

13. Albert Schweitzer, *The Quest of the Historical Jesus: A Critical Study of Its Progress from Reimarus to Wrede,* tr. W. Montgomery (London: Adam and Charles Black, 1910), p. 397.

strangeness for us of the culture Jesus knew, and, consequently, the difficulty of moving from his world into ours and the need of some mediating agent to effect the transition. It is not enough to say that he is God, the infinite source and therefore the exemplar of all that has been, is, or will be. It is not to the divinity but to the humanity of Jesus that we look when we search for our way and our truth. Shall we then distinguish in the human Jesus what is permanent and what is time-conditioned? By all means. But what will be the criterion for the distinction? And what the principle for adapting his message from the conditions of his time to those of ours?

The tendency has been to find in Jesus himself whatever we need to effect the transition. Would I be a Medieval monk? Then I will make Jesus a Medieval monk, and perhaps quote scripture now and again to support my position. Or would I be an agent of social change? Then I will make Jesus an agent of social change, and perhaps do a rather careful study of the scriptures in support of the thesis. But that, I maintain, is to neglect half the resources God has given us for living in this world, and at the same time to overload and strain the other half. The images from mechanics are crude, so let me put it more directly: there are two divine missions, that of the Son with his role and function, and that of the Spirit with his role and function. The roles are not the same, and neither one is superfluous. If, therefore, we try to legitimate our monastic rule or our social involvement by a too exclusive recourse to the Son, we commit a double distortion: we demand of the Son more than one human life on earth, even the human life of the Son of God, can contribute; and all the while we have a principle of the monastic and every other rule, of social and all other involvement, namely, the Holy Spirit of God, whom we leave, or would be willing to leave, standing by—a third of the trinitarian work force unemployed. So I come to the second heading of the second section of my paper: the resources of God-with-us that we have in the Holy Spirit, and the means our times provide for discerning and receiving guidance from his presence in and among us.

We are dealing here with the correction of an imbalance, as may be seen from the following geometric image. Our religion began, in the only way probably it could begin, as a Christocentric religion. Now, if the center goes, in religious as in planetary systems, what principle will hold things together? That kind of fearful question gave Copernicus some trouble when he would displace the center of our cosmos. It gave Kant trouble too, in the philosophical counterpart of the Copernican move, when he would shift the center of our cognitional universe away from the object to the subject. There were really two questions involved here: the basic legitimacy of that turn to the subject, and the adequacy of Kant's conception of the new subject-center. But the questions were not always clearly distinguished and so Scholasticism, unhappy in regard to the second, fought its long and losing battle in regard to the first.

Something a bit like that is happening in theology. Our religion cannot be Christocentric in quite the same way it was in the past, but we are troubled by the various efforts to conceive a new center. May I suggest that we discard the image itself of a center, and think rather of an ellipse with two foci? A circle, you know, is a special form of an ellipse, one in which the two foci coincide. Does that provide an image of our previous history in regard to Son and Spirit? I think so. The Spirit, instead of being allowed to be himself, functioning as a focus in Christian life, was brought into coincidence with the Son and so into a measure of oblivion (I remember a book called *The Forgotten Paraclete*). In the image of an ellipse the two foci of Son and Spirit are distinct and complementary. Of course, our God is triune, and eventually we must find a place for the Father, but at least we have a first approximation on the way to a complete integration of the three persons in the work of our redemption.

Further, the *kairos* has come for a shift from the Christocentric to the elliptical with the two foci of Son and Spirit. Once again, I repudiate any radical departure from our tradition. I am not saying that the Holy Spirit has only now come upon the scene, just in time to repair the damage done in the quest for the historical Jesus: the Holy Spirit was on the scene from the beginning—the real beginning, that of our first parents. I am not saying that the Holy Spirit is only now known to be on the scene; his presence was known to us from the early days of the gospel. But I am saying that our ancestors did not have a philosophy that would enable them to relate the roles of Son and Spirit in the fundamental way that is possible to us. Paul, Luke, and John each contributed something to the solution of the problem. Augustine and Thomas Aquinas organized things a bit with their doctrine of the visible and invisible missions. But it is only with the turn to the subject, with the emergence of a philosophy of interiority, with the replacement of causality by meaning as a basic category, that we have the conceptual system we need for an integrated theology of the roles of Son and Spirit in the world.

The philosophy of interiority is fundamental. But it has been a long time forming, and the measure of the difficulty in conceiving it is the continuing resistance among some philosophers to putting the data of consciousness on an equal footing with the data of sense, and so of developing a generalized empirical method. Then, over and above this initial difficulty, there is that of the full extension of interiority. For the full structure of knowing must be found. Then, affectivity has to be added to knowledge, and the two intelligibly related; thus, while St. Thomas could be said to have written a *theologia mentis,* his fellow-Dominican, Contenson, felt constrained four centuries later to write a *theologia mentis et cordis.*[14] Again, I suppose there have been mystics from the beginning; but only with writers like St. Teresa of Avila did we have the descriptive accounts that a theology of mystical interiority requires. So now, with our philosophy worked out, with the relevant religious phenomena described and catalogued, we are at last in a position to form a comprehensive theory of interiority.

If a philosophy of interiority is basic to a new theology of Son and Spirit, it is also true that the emergence of meaning to replace causality as a leading category provides an answer to a difficulty arising out of a more metaphysical way of thought. In this latter the Spirit, having no nature but the divine, can exercise no activity in the world that is proper to himself but only that which is common to the three persons. As the Council of Florence said, "Pater et filius et spiritus sanctus non tria principia creaturae, sed unum principium."[15] But this principle of metaphysical theology becomes secondary, even marginal, in a universe of discourse in which meaning, value, intentionality analysis, are basic. Now the Spirit has his distinct meaning, else he would not be himself. He brings his own meaning into the world with him, and meaning is constitutive of human and transcendent reality, so the world is affected by his presence. Finally, meaning is as much a source in intentionality analysis as efficient causality is in metaphysical thinking, so the Spirit can be a distinct source for theology without prejudice to the metaphysics of the divine operation. There should be no insuperable difficulty, then, in conceiving him as the principle of the indefinite adaptability which the historicity of man requires and the particularity of the God-man does not readily furnish.

III

It is one thing to suggest the need and possibility of a new theology, as I have been doing, and quite another to make that theology actual. I cannot undertake that latter task here, but I feel I owe it to my audience to give some hints on how I think it might be formulated. Most of you will be familiar with the notion of theology as the unity of eight functional specialties, so you will realize how little I am at-

---

14. C. Lozier, "Contenson, Guillaume Vincent de," *New Catholic Encyclopedia,* vol. 4 (1967), p. 264.

15. *Enchiridion symbolorum, definitionum et declarationum...,* ed. H. Denzinger & A. Schönmetzer, 33rd ed. (Barcelona: Herder, 1965), no. 1331.

tempting to do, when I touch on only two of them: I will sketch some parts of a new systematics, and, since a different systematics raises new questions and discloses new transitions in history, I will conclude my third section with some headings of a rewritten history.

The two objective poles of our theology are obviously God and humanity. God is a community of three persons. Though the one divinity determines what all three are absolutely (eternal, omnipotent, etc.), their relationships to one another determine what each is as a person, an individual self. What each is in his eternal being, he also is in his temporal being, in his role and function in the created family of God. The New Testament most often related the first two as Father and Son, but this had two drawbacks: it did not provide for the Spirit (the fathers of the Church had to deny that the Spirit was a grandson!), and the mode of human generation had to be utterly denied in thinking of God. Today there is a third drawback: "father" and "son" are male terms, the use of which is now seen as offensive to half our race. Happily, however, theologians came to think of the Son as the divine Word of truth and value, and of the Spirit as the Love that follows on that Word. Trinitarian theology, in this respect, was considerably in advance of other theology, using the categories of intentionality analysis, meaning and value, long before they became general in theology.

Our view of humanity will not have as ancient a pedigree as our rather traditional view of God. We may, however, lay an acceptable basis by saying with St. Thomas that "homo maxime est mens hominis."[16] Supposing, then, and omitting, the physics, chemistry, and biology of the human, we turn at once to human consciousness. Here, Lonergan's philosophy of the human includes two main areas that must be sharply distinguished yet closely related to one another, the more so since, in our enthusiasm for the first, we tend to be vague about the second. There is the structure of consciousness, and there is the history of consciousness, and these relate to one another as the permanent and the variable factors in the human. Structurally, there are the four levels familiar to those attending this workshop, each level with its outer orientation and its inner experience. But historically, there is the development and/or aberration of consciousness, with its uncountable brands of common sense, with the differentiations that make one person an artist and another a theologian, with the stages of meaning and value that follow one another in something like a pattern through time, with the various conversions that locate us within a horizon of knowledge and interest, and finally—the most neglected area of all—the interaction of the two paths of development, the upward path of

16. Thomas Aquinas, *Summa theologiae,* I–II, 29, 4c.

achievement from experience through understanding and judgment to values, and the downward path of tradition handed on in values and beliefs that are accepted in trust till developing understanding and widening experience give them meaningful embodiment.

Against this background of what God is and what it is to be human is to be sketched now the economy of Son and Spirit in the world. If, then, God is to communicate himself in a way that corresponds to his own being and to human orientation to the outer and the objective, the one to be sent for this purpose will be the one who is already God's objectified understanding and so can become, in a "natural" prolongation, the outer Word the human race needs. And if God is also to communicate himself in a way that corresponds to human subjectivity, the one to be sent for this purpose will be the one who is divine subjectivity surging up in the infinite Love that responds to the infinite Word. We may still speak of visible and invisible missions, and always of the biblical Son and Spirit, but we will have a new understanding of the one as sent into the world we meet through outer, objective data, and the other as sent into the world of interior, subjective data.

Further, to speak of those sent is to acknowledge a sender, from whose viewpoint we must try to understand both missions. Fr. Lonergan's basic analogy for such understanding seems to be the love of man and woman for each other.

When a man and a woman love each other but do not avow their love, they are not yet in love. Their very silence means that their love has not reached the point of self-surrender and self-donation. It is the love that each freely and fully reveals to the other that brings about the radically new situation of being in love and that begins the unfolding of its life-long implications.[17]

I hope all of us are able, in some way and in some degree, to appreciate the profound truth of this passage, whether through experience of a love avowed and fully bestowed, or through experience of a love that cannot be avowed and so must remain something less than a full self-surrender, or, if neither of these, then through the notional apprehension[18] that gives an indirect and imperfect appreciation. In any case, if I understand Lonergan, this analogy "explains" the ways of God in sending his Son and his Spirit. For, on this conceptual basis, he would "interpret the religions of mankind, in their positive moment, as the fruit of the gift of the Spirit."[19] It is God's love not yet fully avowed, for "there is a notable anonymity to this gift of the Spirit. . . .

17. *Method in Theology,* pp. 112–13.

18. John Henry Newman, *An Essay in Aid of a Grammar of Assent* (London: Longmans, Green, 1930 [1870]), chs. 1–4.

19. "The Response of the Jesuit as Priest and Apostle in the Modern World," in *Second Collection,* pp. 165–87; see p. 174.

What removes this obscurity and anonymity is the fact that the Father has spoken to us of old through the prophets and in this final age through the Son."[20]

And this is God's full avowal of his love: as St. Paul says, "Christ died for us while we were yet sinners, and that is God's own proof of his love towards us" (Rom 5:8); and St. John, "For God is love; and his love was disclosed to us in this, that he sent his only Son into the world to bring us life" (1 Jn 4:8–9). Our view, then, is linked with the New Testament and traditional theology, but does give us a new perspective, from which the members of the great world religions are not so much anonymous Christians as they are anonymous Spiritans.

Again, if the one sent as outer Word is not to communicate merely through an it (a burning bush, etc.), but as a thou and a self, and if that self is not to be the self of an angel or prophet but a self of God, then the person sent will become flesh and dwell among us. That means he will be made man in a particular time and place, under the particular conditions that human historicity makes inevitable. He will indeed be the center of history; he will be a focal point for our orientation, not only toward God, but also toward community in the human world. But the very historicity to which, in the completeness of his *kenôsis*, he has subjected himself, will automatically prevent his becoming an immediate model for the whole human race in all its variety. But the person who does not take flesh and dwell in our outer world, the one who is sent into our hearts, sent also as a divine thou and self, but only as divine, untrammeled by the *kenôsis* of human historicity, the one moreover who floods our hearts with the love that makes us spiritual and so able to "judge the worth of everything" (1 Cor 2:15), he will be the interior focal point for the creation of all conceivable human-divine meaning and all possible human-divine value, the one who will enable us to adapt to every changing condition while remaining true to the outer center of our history—a little like Wordsworth's skylark, "True to the kindred points of Heaven and Home!"[21]

In this view the economy of Son and Spirit in the world is set up in unity. Any tension that develops will be due, not to the Father's purpose, but to our failure to keep the two foci as clearly distinct as the Son and the Spirit are themselves distinct, and as clearly related in equality and complementarity as they are themselves related to one another in their divine being and their temporal mission. Such failure

20. Ibid., pp. 174–75.

21. During the long reign of Scholasticism the *kenôsis* was understood mainly in ontological terms. Bernard Lonergan set forth the corresponding psychological *kenôsis, De constitutione Christi ontologica et psychologica* (Rome: Gregorian University, 1956), p. 115. Now a third aspect emerges with the acknowledgment of the Son's historicity.

is, no doubt, part of the human condition, giving rise to apparent tensions, as one or other of the two foci is made into a single center. But that only means that we have a permanent task of maintaining in our theology the two-in-oneness of the Father's redemptive idea, a task then of continually re-reading our past to guide our future.

So we come to the second heading of our third section: the re-reading of history. The need for such a re-reading will be clear to those who agree with Lonergan that the history of a science cannot be written by one who does not know the science itself.

One would ever tend to overlook significant events and to set great store by minor matters. One's language would be inaccurate or out of date, one's emphases mistaken, one's perspectives distorted, one's omissions intolerable. . . . It is a commonplace today that to understand a doctrine one had best study its history. It is no less true that to write the history one has to understand the doctrine.[22]

It follows that, when the science takes a forward step, the history has to be rewritten. Thus, with every new understanding of the roles of Son and Spirit in the world, we will need a new history, both of their complementarity in the redemptive economy and of the church's understanding at different times of those roles. I have to confine my brief remarks to the latter: how, from the present perspective, I see the history of the Church's thinking on the relation of Son and Spirit in the economy.

The divine rationale, God's fundamental idea for the redemptive economy, the "secret kept in silence for long ages," is now disclosed, St. Paul says (Rom 16:26). But we will not expect it to be disclosed in the order in which God conceived it before those long ages; on the contrary, according to the principle that what is first in itself will not be first for us, we will expect our learning to be the inverse of God's planning. That is, God, "falling in love" with the human race, will also be drawn to "avow" his love. The "falling" is the gift of the Spirit, actually given from the beginning; the "avowal" took place at a particular time and place, when "the angel Gabriel was sent . . . with a message for a girl. . . . the girl's name was Mary" (Lk 1:26–27). But it is the avowal that we come to know first, just as it is the Son who is proclaimed and not the Spirit. Only slowly do we come to realize that the Spirit was long before given incognito, and continues to be given, even to those who have never heard of the Son or the gospel.[23]

---

22. *Method*, pp. 143–44.

23. In this view the self-communication of God follows an order that is the reverse of the order of processions. In the divine being the Father is the "first" person, the Son and Spirit "second" and "third"; but the Spirit is communicated *to us* first, the Son second, and the Father last of all.

Further, the New Testament writers, understanding the relevance of Jesus to themselves, but rather innocent of the cultural pluralism of God's creation, will naturally tend to attribute to the words and deeds of Jesus, and to every detail of those words and deeds, a permanent validity and immediate relevance to all times and all places. There will be no sharp distinction between the universal aspect and the particular, between the permanent and the passing; on the contrary, there will be a stress on Jesus as "the same yesterday, today, and for ever" (Heb 13:8).

But let us not exaggerate; in fact, already in New Testament times, adaptation is taking place in the presentation of the gospel. Thus, we find St. Luke relating a variety of approaches, depending on whether St. Paul is talking to fellow-Jews at Pisidian Antioch (Acts 13:16–41), to simple pagans at Lystra (Acts 14:15–17), or to sophisticated pagans at Athens (Acts 17:22–31). Moreover, our own question of the relation between the roles of Son and Spirit is on the verge of being articulated in St. Paul's letters. It is surely a marginal topic in one who could write: "I resolved that while I was with you I would think of nothing but Jesus Christ—Christ nailed to the cross" (1 Cor 2:2). But it does begin to emerge when St. Paul writes that God sent his Son, as it were, to make it right and proper for him to adopt us, to receive as sons those whom his own Son took as his brothers; and then God sent his Spirit that we might know experientially our new status, aware of the ability we now have through the indwelling Spirit to call God our Father, Papa, the way a child does (Gal 4:4–6).

St. Luke considered the matter more directly, and made it almost thematic, as the very structure of his two-volumed work suggests: one volume is a gospel of the Son and the other has been called a gospel of the Spirit. So the first volume ends, as the second begins, with instructions to the apostles to stay in Jerusalem till they receive the promised power: "I am sending upon you my Father's promised gift; so stay here in this city until you are armed with the power from above" (Lk 24:49; see Acts 1:4, 8). But it is St. John who has given the matter the most thematic and concentrated treatment. True to his established pattern, he has a sign and its expository discourse, with the difference that here the discourse precedes the sign.[24] The exposition is found in the farewell discourses, and the sign in the whole narrative of the death and resurrection. But there may be a special correlation—Dodd is not sure[25]—between Jesus' breathing his last on the cross (Jn 19:30) and his breathing "holy spirit" on the disciples after his resurrection (Jn 20:22). In any case, five great passages in the farewell discourses promise

24. C. H. Dodd, *The Interpretation of the Fourth Gospel,* paperback edition (Cambridge, University Press, 1968), pp. 290–91.
25. Ibid., p. 428; see also pp. 223, 442.

the Holy Spirit and describe in some detail the relation of his work to that of the Son.

Paul introduced our question almost in passing, while busy with his own question of law and freedom. Luke's concern is much more direct and closer to being thematic, but perhaps he has not yet posed the question in stark clarity: What is the relation of Son and Spirit? John, I venture to suggest, has done just that. Again, Paul's "explanation" is in terms of our sonship through the Son and our knowledge, through the Spirit, of our sonship. Luke's is in terms of what happened in the Son, and the power we have through the Spirit to witness to what happened (Acts 1:8; see Lk 24:48–49). But John's explanation is directly in terms of the relation between Son and Spirit. There is close unity, and there is even dependence of the Spirit's role on that of the Son (Jn 16:12–15). But it is clear also that the Spirit is sent in some sense to *replace* the Son: the disciples are not to be left orphans, they will receive *another* Advocate (Jn 14:15–18). Indeed, the new Advocate will be in some way better for them: "it is for your good that I am leaving you. If I do not go, your Advocate will not come, whereas if I go, I will send him to you" (Jn 16:7).

One can, then, trace a trajectory from Paul through Luke to John. The unifying factor is the emerging question of the relation of Son and Spirit. The differences are found in the obscurity/clarity with which the question is thematized, and in the variety of the proposed solutions. Now those very differences suggest the possibility of further understanding, and so of prolonging the trajectory into post-biblical times. But the work of prolongation, I would say, still awaits the worker. The next nineteen centuries show, in fact, a persistent reluctance to accept responsibility for the work; worse, they show a sort of suppression of the religious experience that fills the New Testament. I think of the difference between the direct guidance the Spirit gave the Church in the years covered by the Acts of the Apostles and the merely "negative assistance" that theologians would allow him to exercise at ecumenical councils. More fundamentally, I think of the way we tacitly downgrade the reality of his presence among us. It is as if we took over and gratefully applied the behaviorism of positivist psychology: the Son is really real, the Spirit not quite so really real: the Son was really sent into the world and was really here—after all, he took flesh and dwelt among us—the Spirit was not quite so really sent and is not quite so really present—after all, his presence is wholly interior, and the data that manifest his presence are only data of consciousness. The "only" is the operative and revealing word.[26]

26. It is worth noting how impoverished in themselves are the notions of an "invisible"

IV

I wish, in these concluding paragraphs, to say something on the tasks we now face if the preceding analysis and history have any validity. Let us first review the situation. It shows a twofold distortion. There is the stubborn effort I described earlier to find in Jesus himself, in his words and deeds, a sanction for our own way in the world, a model for every vocation under the sun, a guide in every situation. Suppose we have to take an attitude toward the government of El Salvador, or to judge when a baby is a baby in the womb of its mother, or to decide whether we should sell our stocks in Nestlé, or to find ways for a priest to relate to his parishioners—what do we do as if by instinct? We turn to the scriptures to see what Jesus did in parallel situations. Rightly enough too, but we are too ready to find parallels, too dependent on those we do find, too little concerned that we ask of Jesus what, in the Father's total plan, is not his to give. And there is the second distortion: not only do we require of Jesus what the *kenôsis* of human historicity leaves him unable to provide, but we at the same time fail to draw on those resources which the Father gave us for precisely the need we experience, namely, the real, the really real, presence of the Holy Spirit within us. We allow the focus which should be distinctly his in the ellipse of the divine missions to vanish, to merge with that of the Son in a Christo-centric religion, and so lose its proper identity. Of course, it *is* difficult to determine what the Spirit is saying. Diggings in Palestine, dictio-naries of Aramaic, the comforting feel of a holy book—all the data that make the mission of the Son so really real—they tell us nothing of what the Spirit is saying to us here and now. It is our interior life in the Spirit that assures our authenticity, and it is only through study of that interior life, shared with others in whom also the Spirit is present, that we can discern what he is saying.

The twofold distortion sets a twofold task for us: a reassessment of the roles of both Son and Spirit. The latter is going forward in the now well established discipline of the discernment of spirits and of *the* Spirit; it will make its way, if only slowly against stubborn resistance, and its progress is not likely to need, or be much helped by, anything I may say here. But we have hardly begun the former task, which involves a study of the horizons of Jesus, of the differentiations of consciousness

---

sending and a "negative" assistance, when compared with the rich potential of a Spirit present as source of an "inner word" in the world of the data of consciousness. But it should also be noted that this is said of those notions taken in themselves. In fact, St. Augustine on the *donum dei*, and St. Thomas on the new law which is the grace of the Holy Spirit, go far beyond the negativity of "invisible." As for "negative" assistance, it appears in the theologians, but I have not noticed the phrase in any formal declaration of the Church.

that apply to him, even of the role of conversion in his life, and so finally of what in his words and deeds is permanently and universally valid, and what is particular and time-conditioned.

True, we are more familiar now, thanks to biblical scholarship, with the particular coloring of Jesus' thought and speech and action, as it was influenced by his upbringing twenty centuries ago in Palestine— what Lonergan would call his brand of common sense which differed from the Roman, say, and certainly from ours. But what I am calling for goes beyond such a study. Brands of common sense all pertain to undifferentiated consciousness, and what we must add are the differentiations: most obviously, religious differentiation, but others too, like the differentiation of a word-artist. We would ask about his horizon in the sense of Lonergan's dialectic, which means asking about his conversions—intellectual, moral, religious—asking with appropriate care to distinguish the reversal of direction in a normal conversion from the positive forward momentum it supplies, but asking nevertheless. We would ask too about his interiority, and so about the distinction between his *praxis*—more directly a function of interiority and more likely to reveal the universal—and his *poiêsis,* which is more a function of external conduct and more likely to pertain to a particular time and place and people.

I conclude my paper with more diffidence than I have so far shown. There are evident dangers to the thesis I propose, and I fear them. I fear disloyalty to him "who loved me and sacrificed himself for me" (Gal 2:20). I fear diminishing the power of that meditation on the words and deeds of Jesus which has nourished thousands of saints and millions of sinners, notably through the *Spiritual Exercises* of my own Ignatius of Loyola. I fear belittling the present role of Jesus, as he reigns in heaven, "able to save absolutely those who approach God through him . . . always living to plead on their behalf " (Heb 7:25). I fear doing injustice to the institutional Church, whose authorities are sinful human beings like me but *do* represent the mother who gave me my Catholic parents, the mass, the sacraments, the scriptures, my tradition, the saints whom I admire from far off. I fear these things all the more because I think the changes rocking the Church these twenty years are not the aftershocks of a cultural earthquake that has occurred but the foreshocks of one that is still to come; that is, the changes are only beginning, and if there is to be any effect of an effort like mine to provide a rationale for change, it will be to accelerate the process.

Nevertheless, there is one danger that is also a temptation, and in that sense greater than any of these: to close our eyes to what is going on, to bury our heads in the well-known sands of irresponsibility. And there is a hope that is greater by far than any danger which will ever threaten us, the hope "that we shall enter upon our heritage, when God has redeemed what is his own" (Eph 1:14), that through Christ we "have access to the Father in the one Spirit" (Eph 2:18); in this hope we have assurance, not only that the Spirit will guide us but also that having recognized the strangeness of a Jesus who "passes by our time and returns to His own," we may follow and see where he is staying (Jn 1:39), and thereby discover "who Christ really is, for us today."

18

A Threefold *Kenôsis* of the Son of God*

The word *kenôsis* came into Christian theology from St. Paul's Letter to the Philippians, where it is asserted of Christ Jesus that he "emptied" himself. In Greek: *heauton ekenôsen;* in Latin: *semet ipsum exinanivit*, rendered in *The New English Bible*: "he . . . made himself nothing" (Phil 2:7). Exegetes are divided on whether Paul asserts this of the preexistent Son of God, in which case the *kenôsis*, the emptying, occurs in the event itself of the incarnation, or of the Son of God on earth, in which case the poverty of the Son's human condition is seen as a kenotic state in comparison with his being in the form of God. Whatever the correct exegesis of St. Paul, both of these aspects belong to the Catholic understanding of Christ: there is a poverty in his human state as compared with the divine, and this poverty was accepted by the eternal Son in the event of the incarnation.

In this article I simply assume the Catholic understanding of the incarnation and earthly life of the Son of God, and I ask what sort of *kenôsis* is involved. It is a question that must be asked over and over, without ever being settled once and for all, for with every advance in our understanding of the human condition we can answer the question with greater depth and new precision. I will speak therefore of a *threefold kenôsis* of the Son of God. True, there was one act of incarnation, one human nature assumed into union with the Word, one human life lived on earth; but various aspects of our humanity, and hence various aspects of the incarnation, are disclosed to us as we advance through history. From that viewpoint, of course, we might speak of the *manifold kenôsis* of the Son, for we do not know what further aspects will emerge in later centuries, but up to now human reflection has brought to light three aspects with a special claim to distinct consideration. I will call them the "ontological," the "psychological," the "historical" *kenôsis*; but I use the indefinite article in my title: "*A* Threefold *Kenôsis* . . . ," not "*The* Threefold . . . ," as if human reflection were coming to a halt after these three steps.

*Previously published in *The Papin Gedenkschrift, Dimensions in the Human Religious Quest. Essays in Memory of Joseph Papin, Vol. I: Theological Dimensions*, ed. J. Armenti (Ann Arbor: University Microfilms International, 1986), pp. 54–64.

315

1. The Ontological *Kenôsis*

The ontological aspect of the *kenôsis* is the one most familiar to traditional Catholic thought. Not that it occupied theologians to any great extent in the early centuries. On the contrary, there were no kenotic "theories" among either the fathers or the Scholastics. They simply made the preexistent Son the subject of the phrase I quoted from Philippians, and explained the *kenôsis* in such a way that there was no ontological change in either of the two natures of Christ. It was only later among Lutheran theologians that kenotic "theories" arose. For Luther had understood the *communicatio idiomatum*, the "communion of properties," not simply as a matter of true cross-predication (e.g., "God suffered," and "Jesus of Nazareth is God"), but of a physical communication of the divine attributes to the human nature of Christ. Then, of course, the question would arise of some real *kenôsis* which those attributes would suffer in being transferred to the humanity.[1]

Catholic theologians, however, still remained strongly attached to the doctrine of the Council of Chalcedon, which had affirmed two natures in Christ, each keeping its properties without change or intermingling. So they continued to understand the incarnation (and, of course, the text of Philippians) in such a way as to reject any real intrinsic change—which they held to be metaphysically impossible in any case—in the divine nature and attributes.

That had been the position of St. Thomas Aquinas before them, and it will be useful to go back to him, as showing both the traditional explanation of the *kenôsis* and, at the same time, the marginal character the whole question had in the tradition. A convenient way to demonstrate this is to consult the manual edition of indices to the two *summae* which has been issued by the Leonine Commission on the works of St. Thomas.[2] Here we find a list of twenty-two passages in which St. Thomas either quotes or refers to Philippians 2:7, but in passage after passage it is not the "exinanivit" that is the focal concern but rather some other phrase, often "in similitudinem hominum factus" as proving the true humanity.

Two of the more relevant loca are in the *Summa contra gentiles*. In one the adversary is Valentinus, and the focal text is John 3:13, on the Son of Man from heaven. Valentinus is reported as claiming that Christ brought a heavenly body with him, but the exposition St. Thomas gives

1. Yves Congar, "Kénose . . . II. Théologie," *Catholicisme hier, aujourd'hui, demain*, vol. 6 (Paris: Letouzey, 1967), cols. 1402–1403.

2. *Indices auctoritatum omniumque rerum notabilium occurrentium in Summa theologiae et in Summa contra gentiles S. Thomae de Aquino.* Editio leonina manualis: extractum ex tomo XVI editionis leoninae (Romae: apud sedem commissionis leoninae, 1948), p. 120.

is this: "Dicitur igitur filius dei descendisse secundum hoc quod terrenam substantiam sibi copulavit." Then he quotes St. Paul on the *exinanitio,* adding in explanation: "inquantum formam servi accepit, ita tamen quod divinitatis naturam non perdidit."[3]

In the other the adversaries are Theodore of Mopsuestia and especially Nestorius. The text of Philippians cannot be explained if we divide Christ in two, St. Thomas says. For it could not be understood of the "man" Nestorius posits, for this man was not at first in the form of God, then later to suffer an emptying; on the contrary, from being man he would have been given a share in the divine nature, and so exalted rather than emptied. Hence it would have to be understood of the Word; not, however, of the Word as inhabiting the man, for the Word inhabits all the saints and does so without being emptied. The proper understanding therefore of the union of the Word to human nature is this, that the Word of God truly became man. Only thus can we speak of an "exinanitio": the Word is emptied, that is, made small, "non amissione propriae magnitudinis, sed assumptione humanae parvitatis."[4]

There are rather meager pickings, then, in St. Thomas on the question of the *kenôsis.*[5] Still, the basic point is made and explained with sufficient clarity. Further, the sketch may be filled out by reference to the defects that St. Thomas acknowledges in Christ, more obviously those of the body,[6] but also certain defects that belong to the human soul.[7] There is a consensus, however, in later theology that ontology is not enough, that we must go considerably further in study of the *kenôsis* than St. Thomas did, so we may bring our brief discussion of the ontological *kenôsis* to a close with him.

11. The Psychological *Kenôsis*

The question of a psychological *kenôsis* in Christ is a new question, arising in Christology only as the new science of psychology made its way throughout the world of academe, and so finally extended its influence in this century into theology as well. My discussion of the question will be based entirely on the work of Bernard Lonergan, who

---

3. Liber IV, cap. 30, ad finem.

4. Ibid., cap. 34, ad finem, in the paragraph, "Adhuc. Apostolus dicit. . . ."

5. There is, of course, the commentary on Philippians, but we have only the *reportatio* of his students to show the views of St. Thomas; on ch. 2, verse 7, he says: "Hoc est intelligendum secundum assumptionem eius quod non habuit, sed non secundum evacuationem eius quod habuit . . . se exinanivit non deponendo divinam naturam, sed assumendo naturam humanam" (quoted by Adhemar d'Alès, *De verbo incarnato* [Paris: Beauchesne, 1930], p. 170).

6. *Summa theologiae,* III, 14.   7. Ibid., 15.

asks whether in Christ there is a psychological *kenôsis* (writing in Latin, he uses "exinanitio"), and answers that there is, proceeding to explain it in close parallel with the *kenôsis* he calls, by contrast, "ontological."[8]

The basic explanation remains fully Thomist, that is, the *kenôsis* consists in what we may call an addition rather than in a subtraction: the Son of God emptied himself, not by laying aside the divine but by adding the human.

Lonergan's distinctive contribution, however, lies in thematizing, conceiving, and explaining the psychological *kenôsis* as a new aspect of the question. The explanation is given in terms of consciousness, a notion that had occupied him through long pages of his book, *Insight*.[9] For present purposes, let us simply say that consciousness is a perfection belonging to a certain grade of being; hence, if it belongs to the human race, it belongs also to angels, and to God: as there is a human nature with a human consciousness, so there is a divine nature with a divine consciousness. But in Christ, since there are two natures, there are also two consciousnesses, one divine and the other human. Further, as the natures are not changed or intermingled, each retaining its own properties (Chalcedon), so also the two consciousnesses remain distinct, each with its own properties, without change or intermingling.[10]

So far the parallel with Chalcedon is exact, and the theological step taken by Lonergan would be much like that taken centuries earlier in regard to the two wills in Christ. That is, once it had been established that there are two natures in Christ, and determined that will belongs to the higher natures, it followed that in Christ there would be both divine and human will. Now, when we have determined that consciousness belongs to the higher natures, it likewise follows that in Christ there will be both divine and human consciousness.

But a special feature of the "exinanitio" now comes to light. For in consciousness we are conscious of the self as well as of our activities, and in Christ the self is divine. Hence, the Son of God, through his divine consciousness, is conscious of himself according to his infinite perfection; but also, through his human consciousness, he is conscious of the same self according to the poverty (*inopiam*) of his human nature. Concretely, Christ not only *is* man in the ontological *kenôsis* of the Word, but also *experiences* himself humanly in the psychological *kenôsis* of the Word.[11]

---

8. *De constitutione Christi ontologica et psychologica* (Rome: Gregorian University, 1956), p. 115, no. 90.

9. *Insight: A Study of Human Understanding;* consult the index, but see especially ch. 11, sections 1–4.

10. *De constitutione Christi*, p. 115.

11. In Lonergan's Latin (ibid.): "per conscientiam suam humanam est sui conscius

How can that be? My answer, I am afraid, must be a compromise, and a choice of too brief an explanation rather than none at all; so here is my compromise. For Lonergan, human knowing is a dynamic structure, self-assembling on the three levels of experience, understanding, and judgment, so that neither experience nor understanding is knowing in the full sense, but only an element in the compound activity that knowing is; not even judgment of itself is fully human knowing, though we can equate it with knowing insofar as it includes the elements of experience and understanding and adds the crowning element of affirmation.[12] That is, even though there is one object concretely, that object is attained cognitionally according to the level of the activity involved. We may see another person, but the seeing does not of itself include understanding or judgment, and so does not attain the other as either intelligible or existing; rather, it attains the other simply as seen, and this without the word, seeing, and still more without the concept of seeing; in Lonergan's Latin, the object is attained "sub ratione experti." Similarly, in understanding we attain the object "sub ratione intelligibilis," and in judgment "sub ratione entis."[13]

Now consciousness is experience in the strict sense, as distinguished therefore from understanding and judgment; but it is inner, not outer experience; that is, it is experience of one's self and of one's activities. Next, what holds for experience in general, in regard to attaining its object, holds also for inner experience or consciousness. That is, to experience oneself is not to understand oneself or to know oneself. An infant that suffers pain experiences the suffering and experiences the self, but can hardly be said to understand or to know the self. Such understanding and knowledge, in fact, are the achievement of years and years of effort.

To apply this now to Christology, we may say that Jesus experienced the self he was from infancy through childhood and adult life right to Calvary. He did so through his human consciousness. But that does not of itself mean that he understood that self or affirmed it as what in fact it was, the divine self; such further steps, in Lonergan's theology, are attributed to the beatific vision which gives understanding and judgment on matters divine. In the very precise Latin formulation, Jesus experienced the self he was simply "sub ratione experti." Nor is there any real difficulty in that position; the possibility is shown very clearly

---

secundum quod homo est," and again, "non solum est homo sed etiam se ut hominem experitur." The phrase "ut hominem" should not be taken as indicating the formal object of experience, for experience attains its object simply "sub ratione experti"—see the reference in n. 13 below.

12. See *Insight,* ch. 9.

13. *De constitutione Christi,* pp. 85–88, no. 76.

in an obvious fact: the birds and beasts of the Holy Land saw and heard someone who was a man, someone who was Son of God, but they did not see and hear him as man, or as Son of God, but simply as the object of sensitive experience, "sub ratione experti." If sensitive experience may attain the divine in that way, and if consciousness is inner experience, on that level it may be said that Christ through his human consciousness experienced the self he was.

III. The Historical *Kenôsis*

The ontological *kenôsis* is an idea familiar in Christology. The psychological *kenôsis*, though it may not be familiar, has at least been set forth in clear relation to the ontological, and the explanation has been available for nearly thirty years in Lonergan's Christology. But the historical *kenôsis*, so far as I know, has not yet been brought into focus as such; the elements of the idea are explicit in a thousand discussions, but they have not been collected, thematized under this heading, brought into relation with the ontological *kenôsis* and the psychological, and seen from one perspective as forming a unitary pattern with them.[14]

I call it the historical *kenôsis*, but it could as well be called the cultural, or the *kenôsis* according to the particularities of space and time—from all of which the reader will easily grasp the idea: the Son of God not only *is* human in the ontological *kenôsis*, not only *experiences* humanly in the psychological *kenôsis* the self he is, but also lives in a particular sociocultural situation, with the accompanying limitations that constitute the historical *kenôsis*.

To put it concretely, the one who has dominion over the nations (Ps 22:28) became a member of an ethnic group despised by the nations. The Lord of all history entered history at a particular time and place, and by that very fact was not, and humanly could not be, at other times and places. The eternal Word, who expresses the fullness of divinity, has to learn the Aramaic language to communicate with his people, and by that very fact is less well understood in myriad other languages. The creator, who conceives a million imaginary worlds in the divine thesaurus of possibilities, has to think in the images of one culture (falling stars, seven spirits taking possession of a man, etc.), and by that very fact will seem strange to those of a different culture. The one who is God and therefore spirit (Jn 4:24), will use human spittle for healing (Mt 7:33, 8:23) in the way of a people with certain standards of hygiene, and by that very fact will repel those with a different standard. In short,

---

14. I merely touched on the question in n. 21 of my article "Son and Spirit: Tension in the Divine Missions?"—see ch. 17 above. This paper can be regarded as an expansion of that footnote.

the Son of God, becoming one of us, submits to the social conditions, the cultural conditions, the limitations imposed by the particularities of time and place—and this, I suggest, can be conveniently conveyed by the term, historical *kenôsis*.

The history of the emergence of this idea is too complex to be written here. It will be enough to say that the gospels themselves recognize a particularity in the mission of Jesus: "I was sent to the lost sheep of the house of Israel, and to them alone" (Mt 15:24). This is still a long way indeed from the idea of a historical *kenôsis*; still, if one studies the three sermons of St. Paul narrated in the sequence of Acts 13:16-41, 14:15-17, and 17:22-31, and notices the remarkable adaptations of the gospel message that Paul effects in bringing the word to three quite different audiences, one will not need much more to conceive the time-conditioned character of the way the gospel was expressed in the early preaching, and so to conceive the historical *kenôsis* of the Son of God himself. It was, however, the universal aspect of the gospel that first became thematic—very properly so, if the apostles were to go forth and make all nations disciples (Mt 28:19). This universal aspect remains valid even in our day; nevertheless, we have come to understand better than our ancestors did the historicity of all things human (and of things divine as channeled through human agents), the validity of cultural diversity, the time-conditioned character of our language, our thinking, our mores. And this is now being applied to Jesus himself, as we recognize more and more clearly the "Jewishness" of Jesus.

More important at the moment than factual history is analysis of what is going on, and here I draw again on the work of Bernard Lonergan. A paper whose very title is revealing, "The Transition from a Classicist World-View to Historical-Mindedness," shows that he makes his own the ideas of modern thinkers on the historicity of things human and on cultural diversity.[15] But he does a great deal more than merely adopt what is becoming a commonplace in our time; he provides as well a depth of analysis and a range of application that are his distinctive contributions. Let us take as just one example among the elements of his analysis what he has to say elsewhere about common sense: "Common sense is common, not to all men of all places and times, but to the members of a community successfully in communication with one another."[16] A little later this is made more precise:

As a style of developing intelligence, common sense is common to mankind. But as a content, as a determinate understanding of man and his world, common sense is common not to mankind but to the members of each village, so that strangers appear strange and, the more distant their native land, the more strangely they appear to speak and act.[17]

Now this has immediate and wide-ranging consequences for the preaching of the gospel:

to preach to [the majority of the faithful] and to teach it one must use its own language, its own procedures, its own resources. Unfortunately these are not uniform. There are as many brands of common sense as there are languages, social or cultural differences, almost differences of place and time. So it is that to preach the gospel to all men calls for at least as many preachers as there are differing places and times, and it requires each of them to get to know the people to whom he or she is sent, their ways of thought, their manners, their style of speech. There follows a manifold pluralism.[18]

Analysis does not end with the study of common sense; in fact, it is only beginning with that study. Common sense is the realm of undifferentiated consciousness and besides this realm, with its various brands, there are the more generic differentiations of consciousness itself: the artistic, the theoretic, the religious, etc. Besides these differentiations, there are the stages of meaning that succeed one another. Besides stages of meaning, there are the various forms of conversion, and the differences due to members of a society being converted or unconverted. The diversity of common sense is therefore just an example of the many factors that divide communities from one another, that differentiate members within a community, that result in the pluralism of cultures, and thus ensure a particular character in all our endeavors, be they ever so universal in purpose and fundamental efficacy.

IV. New Tasks for Theology

The historical *kenôsis* I describe raises the very fundamental question of the extent to which the word of Jesus in his time is still a word for us today. As a much-quoted remark of Bonhoeffer put it: "What is bothering me incessantly is the question what Christianity really is, or indeed who Christ really is, for us today."[19] We cannot simply discard our tradition that Christ is the way, the truth, and the life, but if we admit the historical aspect of the *kenôsis*—a step that scholarship imposes, and the Pauline piety of Philippians sanctions—then we have to dig deeper than we once supposed to capture the meaning of Christ in our world. To that end I offer three reflections.

17. Ibid., pp. 272–73.   18. Ibid., p. 276.
19. Dietrich Bonhoeffer, *Letters and Papers from Prison*, enlarged edition, ed. E. Bethge (London: SCM, 1971), p. 279.

The first is that we have to be serious about distinguishing, in the words and deeds of the Lord, what is time-conditioned and therefore not directly relevant for us, and what is basic, pertaining to the universal human condition, and so relevant for everyone. It is clear that the call to discipleship will not apply in the same degree to Christ's using his spittle to heal the dumb and to his dying on the cross in obedience to the Father, but clear also that the question cannot be handled in a paragraph.

The second is that we have to undertake the analysis of the horizons of the New Testament writers. What were their suppositions, their interests and concerns, their views and values? How did those suppositions differ from ours? And, to come to the nub of the matter, what limits in their horizon might lead them to overlook the time-conditioned character of their message and so attribute universality and permanence to elements that were accidents of history?

The third is that we have to study again the relation between Son and Spirit in the world. If the Son underwent a historical *kenôsis*, the Spirit did not. If the Son had to speak in Aramaic, the Spirit speaks wordlessly in the universal language of interiority. If the Son lived only a few years in a small nation, the Spirit of the Lord fills the entire space-time universe. Have we demanded too much of the Son and by that very fact done irreverence to the Spirit the Father gave us?[20]

20. See n. 14 above. Later I came to realize that, though the Spirit does not suffer a *kenôsis*, we have to think of a self-limitation in the Spirit's exercise of the divine power—see ch. 19 below.

19

Son of God, Holy Spirit, and World Religions*

A year ago the Chancellor's Lecture at Regis College discussed the contemporary significance of Luther's theology.[1] The series began, then, appropriately enough for a college in the Toronto School of Theology, with an exercise in ecumenism. It was, however, ecumenism in the usual sense: dialogue and fellowship in the family of Christian churches, and it seemed natural to move on this year to the wider ecumenism: dialogue and fellowship in the family of world religions. It was a logical step, but not just logical; it would meet a religious need as well. The Toronto School of Theology was not primarily a business deal; it was a response to the gospel prayer that we might all be one. But it was a limited response, and the gospel prayer does not set any limits whatever to our search for unity. Is it not time then to hear the gospel again, to let it disturb our peace once more, time to transcend our own little world and think of the whole family of God, men and women "from every nation, of all tribes, peoples and languages" (Rev 7:9), to think of them in the variety of their religious beliefs and practices, and of our relation to them in the plan of God?

The area of world religions, then, is suggested by logic for this year's lecture; the topic is sanctioned by the call of the gospel. But there is for me a third and personal reason for the choice—it lies in the coincidence of President Monet's invitation with what I happened to be reading at the time. The invitation was to talk on some aspect of Bernard Lonergan's work, thus to honor him, as we then hoped, while he was still with us, and to celebrate his nearly eighty years in the service of the gospel and his long association with our College. The coincidence was that I happened just then to read the following claim: "Lonergan's insistence on the role of religious conversion . . . renders

*A lecture given at the annual convocation of Regis College, Toronto, on 26 November 1984. Previously published by Regis College in 1985.
    1. Carl E. Braaten, *Shadows of the Cross: On the Contemporary Significance of Luther's Theology,* Chancellor's Address I, Regis College, 21 November 1983 (Toronto: Regis College, 1984).

theological judgements undiscussable across the borders of the different world religions."[2] That coincidence proved decisive. It seemed to me that Lonergan's theology is made to order for discussions among world religions, that it is his doctrine of conversion, exactly that doctrine, that will foster such discussion. And so I find myself here this evening, paying tribute to this great theologian, and choosing, from a thousand possible topics, his contribution to the wider ecumenism of the world religions.

The topic is vast on both sides; can we do anything at all with it in half an hour? Only if we are ruthless in setting boundaries. A first limitation is to postpone dialogue with the world religions themselves; I will speak as a Christian to Christians, and will define an approach to the world religions from the Christian side. As for Bernard Lonergan, he has a specific and immediately pertinent contribution in his notion of conversions, but he has a more fundamental contribution, I think, in the background of his general ideas. Such ideas need long pondering rather than summary exposition, and how can we handle that problem in half an hour? The best tactic, it seems to me, is to state a position quite flatly, to lay down a thesis, and then give it such exposition as I have time for. With that procedure there will be clarity at least on what is central and what is marginal, and digressions will not be mistaken for the basic thesis itself.

Here, then, is the basic thesis. We have simply to reverse the order in which commonly we think of the Son and Spirit in the world. Commonly we think of God first sending the Son, and of the Spirit being sent in that context, to bring to completion the work of the Son. The thesis says that, on the contrary, God first sent the Spirit, and then sent the Son in the context of the Spirit's mission, to bring to completion— perhaps not precisely the work of the Spirit, but the work which God conceived as one work to be executed in the two steps of the twofold mission of first the Spirit and then the Son.[3] The corollary to this thesis

2. Brian L. Hebblethwaite, *The Problems of Theology* (Cambridge: Cambridge Univ., 1980), p. 19. I do not attempt to define the term "world religions" or catalogue those religions which qualify, for what I have to say will apply to any genuine religious movement. A curious thing: while some of Lonergan's critics find him too Christian to assist dialogue among the religions, others find him too generically religious to be helpful to Christians. It would be only an *ad hominem* retort to suggest that these critics on different sides get together on the question. Far more profitable is direct study of the complex and difficult thought of Lonergan himself, a task I only begin in this lecture.

3. The difficulty of Lonergan's thought insures a great diversity among his interpreters. I will not justify at any length the interpretation given here, or refer to other secondary literature, or even distinguish always between what Lonergan says and what I make him mean. But let me list a few pointers to further study.

One is that the thesis I lay down is the tacit supposition permeating all Lonergan's later work on Son and Spirit, and their created counterparts of outer and inner word, as will define a consequent approach to the world religions from the Christian side. It supposes that their positive moment is the fruit of the Spirit present among them, but that this partial moment calls for its completion: the need of the world religions to hear the gospel message is the same need still that the world had when God sent the only Son to be its way and truth and life (Jn 14:6). With that supposition in mind we will try to determine anew our relation, attitude, and approach to the world religions.

That is my thesis, briefly stated, setting forth the basis I find in Bernard Lonergan's theology for dialogue among religions in the wider ecumenism. It needs elaboration, of course; the meaning has to be

---

this pair is set forth in *Method in Theology*. Among several helpful papers to add to the message of *Method*, I mention two: "The Response of the Jesuit as Priest and Apostle in the Modern World," in *A Second Collection: Papers by Bernard J. F. Lonergan, S.J.*, pp. 165–87; and "Mission and the Spirit," in *A Third Collection: Papers by Bernard J. F. Lonergan, S.J.*, pp. 23–34.

Another pointer is that Lonergan's thinking goes beyond tacit supposition in the analogy (to be quoted presently) of a man and a woman in love; here it is all but explicit that God first gives the Spirit and then sends the Son. One might also refer to the passage that speaks of "the threefold giving that is the gift of the Holy Spirit . . ., the gift of the divine Word . . . , the final gift of union with the Father," *Third Collection*, p. 53 (in the paper, "Aquinas Today: Tradition and Innovation," pp. 35–54).

(That last quotation reminds us that, even with a unified doctrine of the divine missions, we have still incorporated only "two-thirds" of the divine gift. We must be ready, then, to correct our theology of the gift of the Spirit and the Son by the addition of the Father's self-giving; otherwise the picture will be distorted. As Newman said of the omission in a university of a significant part of knowledge, we suffer much more than the omission: we suffer also the mutilation of the whole and the distortion of the remaining parts. While recognizing the inadequacy of a language of "thirds" and "parts" for the Trinity, we can see an analogy here with Newman's point: there is not only a real lack but a serious distortion in a theology that does not incorporate the third and final step in God's self-giving. This is all the graver in our time of vanishing hope, when the younger generations despair of a future for themselves and the human race; it is just such a hope that the theology I call for would support. In the old Latin terms, we have a long tradition for the treatise, *De verbo incarnato*; we have hardly any for one to be called *De spiritu dato*; and, even when we have added that, we have still to integrate with these two a third treatise, *De patre sperato*.)

I seem to have digressed from the pointers I was giving to Lonergan's wider theological outlook. But the digression was not totally irrelevant, for more important than any particular pointers, it seems to me, is an understanding of what Lonergan was pursuing throughout his life, and of the way he went about his task. It was a matter always of digging to the very foundations, and therefore of indicating only sketchily, or not at all, what kind of building would be erected. Or, in a useful metaphor he himself borrowed from David Hume, "one does not conquer a territory by taking here an outpost and there a town or village but by marching directly upon the capital and assaulting its citadel" (*Insight: A Study of Human Understanding*, p. xxx). I would add still another metaphor, that of the American forces in the Pacific, leap-frogging over islands held by the enemy in order to strike at the heart of the opposition. Of course there remains "a prolonged task of mopping up, of organization, and of consolidation" (*Insight:* p. xxx). In military campaigns one must be sure that one's resources are equal to that task, just as in the realm of ideas one must foresee the implications of one's position and have a like confidence in its potential to meet the demands of truth and orthodoxy.

explained, the implications drawn out. It also needs defense; it must be grounded in the sources of our faith (recall that I speak as a Christian among Christians). My interest this evening is almost entirely in the elaboration of the thesis. But I wish to say one word of defense before I begin. I am afraid you may see the thesis as an attack on the very foundations of Christianity; so let me spend a moment on the single point of the order of the divine missions, defending my reversal of the traditional order of Son and Spirit.

My defense is quite simple. First, what I propose is not so much a new doctrine as a rearranging of doctrines already widely held. And the rearranging, the reversal I speak of, is not really a novelty, but just another instance of a general pattern and principle also widely held. The principle is that what is first in our eyes is not first in itself; on the contrary, what is first in our eyes is last in itself, and what is last in our eyes is first in itself.[4]

The obvious instance is the order of the first Adam and the last Adam. We naturally think, first, of Adam's creation, then of his sin and God's anger, followed by a divine relenting and after long ages redemption in Christ. But surely that cannot be the order of things in themselves; it supposes divine afterthoughts and "[t]here are no divine afterthoughts."[5] So theologians commonly, with firm support from the New Testament, think of the Christ as the centre and crown of creation, and therefore first in the divine plan, with Adam's creation fitting into that larger purpose, and his sin and human history following. A second instance is the way the Son of God came to be known. For he was known first as the son of a carpenter, then as a rabbi, a prophet, the Messiah, and finally as God's own and only Son. But Christians soon realized that this could not possibly be the real order, the order of things in themselves. What the Son was later perceived to be was not something he could *become*, but what he was from the beginning when "the Word already was" (Jn 1:1). Only later did the Word become flesh and live among us, the son, as was thought, of the carpenter.

Is it therefore such a hard saying that, if we think of the ontological rather than of the cognitional order, we should reverse the sequence in

4. A good locus for study of Lonergan's views on the *quoad nos* and the *quoad se*, and the opposite orders they follow, is his article, "Theology and Understanding," in *Collection*, pp. 121–41 (see esp. pp. 127–30). He derived the general idea from Aristotle via Aquinas; see *In II Metaph.*, lect. 1, no. 278, where Aquinas writes of the "duplex via procedendi ad cognitionem veritatis . . . per modum resolutionis . . . a compositis ad simplicia," and the "via compositionis . . . a simplicibus ad composita" (the latter are "prius nobis nota"). This is a pair that belongs to the cognitional field, but it is clear the ontological order of things in themselves corresponds to the "via compositionis." Aquinas has a variety of pairs called "duplex ordo," mostly ontological; one that comes close to the present question is the twofold order of time (*quoad nos*) and nature (*quoad se*).

5. *Insight*, p. 695.

which commonly we think of the divine missions? We speak, with Augustine, Aquinas, and a whole tradition, of the visible mission of the Son and the invisible mission of the Spirit. Obviously, what is visible must be first in the cognitional order of discovery, that is, first for us, and what is invisible must be last for us. But is it altogether fantastic, is it not rather to be expected, that the real order is the exact opposite? I do not ask you to accept that as your position, but perhaps, if I have removed the scandal, you will be ready to consider it as a hypothesis and so allow me to go on and elaborate the meaning of my thesis, my thesis remaining your hypothesis only.

1. Son and Spirit in the World

Part One of my talk takes up our basic thesis on Son and Spirit in the world. I will consider first our position on the mission of the Spirit.

In Roman Catholic theology (and widely, I think, in the churches) the doctrine has slowly emerged that everyone receives sufficient grace for salvation, that is, receives the divine favor and its transforming power, receives the grace that the New Testament calls "God's gift, not a reward for work done" (Eph 2:8).[6] Now Aquinas has a doctrine, which he developed out of the rich Augustinian doctrine of the Spirit as *donum,* of the third divine person as God's first and foundational gift to us. The Spirit is the Love that proceeds from infinite and loving Understanding uttering its Word of loving Truth. As proceeding from God, the Spirit can be sent into the world and bestowed on us as gift: not only *amor* then, but *amor donabilis*. Further, that gift of Love is God's first and foundational gift. There is an analogy in the human family. From the moment we are born we receive from our parents, day by day and hour by hour, a steady flow of gifts: food, shelter, care—all the things we owe to them over the years of childhood and growth. But their very first gift, the source and ground and reason for all the others, is the gift of their love: they loved us and therefore they bestowed on us everything else. It is the same with God: every good and perfect gift coming down to us from the Father of lights (Jas 1:17) is simply the natural consequence of God's first gift to us; and that first gift is the gift of personal Love, Love as a person sent to us, the *amor donabilis* who is the Spirit.[7]

Lonergan did not, therefore, invent the idea of the Spirit as God's

6. For an overview of the Roman Catholic position see the relevant theological dictionaries, for example, Karl Rahner & Herbert Vorgrimler, *Dictionary of Theology* (New York: Crossroad 1981), *s.v.,* Salvific Will of God.

7. *Summa theologiae,* I, 38, 2. I have paraphrased and illustrated a principle that Aquinas sets forth in his usual succinct manner.

first gift. He found it in Aquinas who found it in Augustine. But it is possible to do now what Augustine and Aquinas did not do, and probably could not do in their time, that is, make the gift universally applicable throughout the world, and so come to a theology of the Spirit's worldwide presence among us, a presence from the beginning of human time and to the ends of human space. Such is Lonergan's theology, as I understand it, of God's first step in the divine self–communication; a step taken not in the fullness of time but at the very beginning of time; a word, but one spoken in its own way, not outwardly through seer and prophet, but inwardly in the heart, and so a word to all God's people, Jew and Gentile, Christian and non–Christian.

The second step is in continuity with the first. In the fullness of time God sent the Son, not in opposition but in unity, not in subordination but in complementarity. The unity of the divine missions is guaranteed by the unity of the divine purpose from the beginning: there are no divine afterthoughts. Likewise we have to maintain an equality of roles, if we affirm the real sending of both Son and Spirit and a real presence of each among us. There are two ways we can fail to meet this requirement: when we think of Son and Spirit in the order of their manifestation, we have always to beware of subordinating the Spirit to the Son; equally, when we think of them in the order of God's giving, we have to beware of subordinating the Son to the Spirit, as if being less spiritual he were less important.

Now unity and complementarity suppose some relationship and order. Here Lonergan has his own beautiful and, I think, quite distinctive analogy: that of a man and a woman in love and of the two stages by which they achieve the fullness of being in love.

When a man and a woman love each other but do not avow their love, they are not yet in love. Their very silence means that their love has not reached the point of self-surrender and self-donation. It is the love that each freely and fully reveals to the other that brings about the radically new situation of being in love and that begins the unfolding of its life-long implications.[8]

---

8. *Method*, pp. 112–13. This is not a unique statement of the analogy. See also the following: "God's gift of his love has its proper counterpart in the revelation events in which God discloses to a particular people or to all mankind the completeness of his love for them. For being-in-love is properly itself, not in the isolated individual, but only in a plurality of persons that disclose their love to one another." (Ibid., p. 283.)

The *Method* passages were preceded by an even longer exposition in the 1970 paper, "The Response of the Jesuit . . .": "If a man and woman were to love each other yet never avow their love, then they would have the beginnings of love but hardly the real thing. There would be lacking an interpersonal component, a mutual presence of self-donation, the opportunity and, indeed, the necessity of sustained development and growth. There would not be the steady increase of knowledge of each other. There would not be the constant flow of favors given and received, of privations endured together, of evils banished by common good will, to make love fully aware of its reality, its strength, its

An analogy is only an analogy. We will not transfer it to God in any wooden fashion, as if God followed the hesitant steps of man and woman. Still, analogy is the only ready means we have for thinking about God with any understanding, and on the present understanding God really and truly falls in love with us, where that "falling" is the gift of Love, the sending of the Spirit. But, for reasons we must ponder long and deeply, God does not declare this Love from the beginning. There is the prolonged silence of the ages when God loves secretly, when the Spirit is present among us incognito, when in an almost human manner God holds back from a declaration of Love. Then at last, in this the final age, and in the most eloquent manner possible, the avowal is made; God's Love is declared, and the one and only Son is sent to be our savior.

On that last point, at least, all Christians will agree, for we have it in so many words from Paul and John. "Christ died for us while we were yet sinners, and that is God's own proof of his love towards us" (Rom 5:8). Again, "God is love; and his love was disclosed to us in this, that he sent his only Son into the world to bring us life" (1 Jn 4:8–9). Our thesis could indeed be stated in the very terms of either Paul or John, but we would understand the love Paul says God has "towards us," the love John says is "disclosed" to us—we would understand this as the very Love that is a divine person, the *amor donabilis* of God, given to all of us since the world began.

So much for the divine side of the trinitarian missions: God, it seems, needs both Spirit and Son to achieve the fullness of the divine being–in–love with us. What of our side? Is our need also twofold? Are we such that we need to receive God, have God among us, in two different ways? Here I call on what Lonergan calls "generalized empirical method," the notion that the data of consciousness are available for study, just as the data of sense are. Because they are data, the study is empirical; because the study includes all the data, it grounds a generalized method.[9] The technical phrase of philosophy falls harshly, no doubt, on religious ears. The idea, however, is extremely important for our present topic. It means the total and emphatic rejection of the spurious claims of behaviorism, of the view that the only data, or the only data to consider, are the data out there before our eyes. It means the recognition that significant things happen within, that there is inner experience of them: the understanding, judgment, exercise of responsibility that set us apart from the animals.

---

durability, to make love aware that it could always be counted on." (*Second Collection*, pp. 173–74.)

Clearly, this is an idea Lonergan had pondered well before using it for the analogy of the two divine missions; for his sources, see *Method*, p. 113, n. 15.

9. *Insight*, pp. 72, 243, and passim in Lonergan's works.

That position has momentous consequences for religion and theology. It means that we can relate our human experience to both Son and Spirit. There is "the harvest of the Spirit," and it is experienced interiorly and personally as "love, joy, peace, patience, kindness, goodness, fidelity, gentleness, and self-control" (Gal 5:22); some of Paul's list look to external manifestations, but there is no doubt about the inner experience. Secondly, there is the life that "was made visible," to be experienced outwardly, so that John could say: "we have heard it; we have seen it with our own eyes; we looked upon it, and felt it with our own hands" (1 Jn 1:1); and that outward experience is ours too, though vicariously, through the witnesses of the gospel.

I said earlier that Bernard Lonergan's ideas need long pondering and have far-reaching ramifications. Maybe you see now what I mean by that, but let me illustrate it with two short notes before I go on to the second part of my talk.

The first note is historical and regards the past. It says that most of us are practical binitarians. Binitarians: acknowledging only two divine persons; practical binitarians: not denying the third person doctrinally, but acting as if we did. The reliable Congar said years ago that, for fifteen centuries, the piety of the Church had been monophysite, dissolving the humanity of the Christ into the divinity.[10] We were not heretics in this matter—creed, council and catechism all held and taught the truth, that Christ is true God and true man—but we acted in our pious exercises as if we were. I am simply making a parallel statement about our binitarian piety.

The reason is simple: we are all ingrained behaviorists, behaviorists by nature or by original sin. To put it another way, we are born extroverts, extroverts from the first moment we grope for mother's breast. So, years later, our philosophy is naturally behaviorist. So are the structures of society that reflect that philosophy. So too is the natural bent of our religion and our religious institutions: our institutions always seem far more substantial than our charisms, and so the institutional Church naturally inclines to behaviorism, and naturally distrusts any movements that claim to come from the Spirit. The saints and mystics continually rescue the organizational Church from her latent bias, but we need a philosophy like generalized empirical method to perform a similar salvage operation for her theologians.

Of course we must recognize the limits of a philosophy. We are not Montanists announcing an incarnation of the Spirit, as was the case eighteen centuries ago. We do not expect a new spiritual Church to

10. Yves Congar, *Le Christ, Marie et l'Eglise* (Bruges: Desclée De Brouwer, 1952), pp. 54–67. (English translation, *Christ, Our Lady, and the Church,* [Westminster, MD: Newman, 1957], pp. 45–54.)

succeed one characterized as the order of clerics, as was the case with Joachim of Fiore eight centuries ago. Much less do we preach a new Pentecost;[11] the one Pentecost is alive and well and ongoing throughout the world. No, what is offered here as a contribution to Christian theology and thereby to the wider ecumenism is simply a new tool for understanding an ancient faith, a philosophy that shows us a twofold human need, a human receptivity for a twofold sending from God, a philosophy that accepts internal data as well as external, that has no trouble seeing the Spirit as really real, just as really real as the Son, just as really sent by God as the Son, just as really present in the world as the Son, with just as real a purpose and function.

My other note regards the future. We need to develop a doctrine of the self-restraint of the Spirit, a doctrine of the limitation self-imposed on the Spirit's reign over our hearts. Let us call it the *epochê* of the Spirit, borrowing the word from philosophy, where it means, in particular, suspension of judgment, or, more generally, a check on one's natural activity. We might understand this *epochê* of the Spirit as the counterpart of the *kenôsis* of the Son. Paul writes, perhaps quoting a Christian hymn, that the Son, though he was in the form of God, emptied himself (Phil 2:7); so, from the Greek word for emptying, *kenôsis*, theologians have developed a whole kenotic theology. I myself would say there are many aspects of this one idea. Thus, we can speak of an ontological *kenôsis* in the assumption of a human nature by the Word; of a psychological *kenôsis* in his human consciousness of the self he was; of a historical *kenôsis* in his submission to the space-time conditions of living in a developing human world.[12] None of these three can be transferred without change to the Spirit. But some counterpart of the general idea of Paul must surely be affirmed. After all, the Spirit present in our hearts still allows us to form the most preposterous ideas, to commit the most abominable deeds; there surely is some self-restraint, some self-imposed limitation, on the Spirit's reign over our hearts. I would see this self-restraint as being exercised in different degrees, as being removed step by step in the stages of history. Thus, it would be at its greatest degree of severity when the Spirit dwelt anonymously for long ages in our hearts. There would be a great release from self-restraint at Pentecost, after God's avowal of the divine Love

11. Though both Pius XII and John XXIII were willing to use terms like that. See *Acta apostolicae sedis* 46 (1954), p. 772: "una nuova misteriosa effusione di Spirito Santo," and ibid., 51 (1959), p. 832: "per novam veluti Pentecostem." I owe these references to Michael Shields, S.J.

12. I have expanded this idea in "A Threefold *Kenôsis* of the Son of God": see ch. 18 above. The notion of the ontological and psychological *kenôsis* is found already in Lonergan's *De constitutione Christi ontologica et psychologica* (Rome: Gregorian Univ., 1956), p. 115.

in the only Son. There will be a complete release in our final state, when we will know as we are known (1 Cor 13:12) and enjoy the full reign of the Spirit over all our conduct.[13]

11. Christianity and World Religions

Our basic thesis had to do with the Holy Spirit and the Son, each sent by God, each with a specific role in the world they entered. The corollary now has to do with the consequent relation within the world between Christianity and other religions. We will continue to study the matter from the viewpoint of Christianity, asking only two questions out of the multitude that arise: How will our understanding of non-Christians as gifted with the Spirit affect our general attitude and relation to them? And how will it affect our particular task of evangelizing them, of preaching Jesus the Lord to all creation?

It will be good to begin with a reminder of our impotence. In God's giving of the Spirit to the peoples of the world, we have no active role: if all initiative belongs to God, and if the Spirit is the first of the divine gifts, then we have nothing to do with the giving. What we can do concerns ourselves and our own attitude; here, in virtue of our own gift of the Spirit, we do have an active role. And my corollary follows

13. Christian and especially Roman Catholic theologians may not wrap their talents in a handkerchief or bury them in the ground; a tradition running from Origen to Newman and beyond, as well as the sanction of the First Vatican Council, supports their efforts toward a developed understanding of the gospel. But neither are they free to propound as doctrine of the Church any idea that enters their heads. The point of this platitude is that, though I consider that the inverse orders of the *quoad nos* and the *quoad se* provide solid support for the basic idea of this lecture, I recognize also the need in due course to spell out the details. Again, therefore, I offer a few pointers to take us beyond what is possible in a short lecture.

For example, it might be maintained that the Spirit is not given to the non-baptized without their voluntary acceptance; if such a view can be upheld, then we postulate that voluntary acceptance, as must anyone who holds that view and also holds that sufficient grace for salvation is given to everyone.

Or, it might be urged that there is a progression from the Spirit moving us to the Spirit inhabiting our souls (Trent). But that position could easily be incorporated into the postulated process of voluntary acceptance of grace.

Again, it might be asked how our position accords with the tradition on trinitarian relations and processions, and the answer would be the Thomist answer that a divine person is sent into the world by virtue of the same relation and procession that belongs to that person within the Trinity: the Spirit given to all peoples is given therefore by the first and second persons of the Trinity.

A much more likely question would ask what, on the present position, happened at Pentecost. Something certainly happened then, and something of great significance in God's salvific work. But, again, this is a difficulty for anyone who holds that the Spirit was present in the world before Pentecost; and would anyone maintain that Mary and Joseph did not have the Spirit at Bethlehem and Nazareth? We would generally explain the matter, I think, through a distinction between presence and manifest presence. My suggestion of an *epoché* in the activity of the Spirit would fit easily into that explanation.

my basic thesis in requiring a radical change in that attitude and in our religious relationship to the peoples of the world.

If that statement seems a very tame conclusion to a rather assertive build-up, then I have not made it clear or revealed sufficiently its implications, so let me put the matter more plainly through reference to a historical counterpart. I take this from Paul's letter to the Romans, chapters 9 to 11. Here we have the most agonizing reappraisal I know of in the whole of literature or history, where Paul, a Hebrew of the Hebrews, has to face and accept and explain the fact that his own people, the chosen race, had stumbled and fallen from God's favor. His very own people, occupying a privileged position in history, as custodian of an ancient promise and bearer of a great new gift of God, had refused to accept the gift on God's conditions, and by that refusal had lost, not only the newly offered gift but also the position that was uniquely theirs in regard to the ancient privilege itself. Not all the promises of the almighty and faithful God were enough to prevent their failure.

Well, we Christians, who have our own promises from the almighty and the faithful one, have also our own unexamined position of privilege to study most searchingly, and perhaps our own agonizing reappraisal to make. It is not enough to thank God daily for the blessings bestowed on us in Christ the Lord, blessings that seem to make us a people set apart, unless we acknowledge also that the infinite generosity and kindness of God our savior has included all the peoples of the world in the divine family, has made them all vessels of the divine election, and has blessed them all with the first and foundational gift of God, the divine Love in the person of the Holy Spirit. We too have to beware lest, by refusing to acknowledge the breadth and depth and height of the divine mercy, we become unfaithful stewards of the very privilege that we do in fact possess, and turn into avatars of the people so broken-heartedly lamented in Romans 9–11.

Does my corollary still seem to you a rather tame conclusion, or at least one sufficiently remote from any immediate consequences in the practical realm? Then let me suggest a possibility that might make it a much more personal matter for anyone of us, and force the agonizing reappraisal upon us in the most inescapable way. Suppose you think of someone very near and dear to you, a daughter perhaps, who comes home to her Christian family to announce that she is going to marry one of the Hindu or Buddhist religion. What would your attitude have been in the past? What would your attitude have to be now, if you adopt the thesis I have presented? I began by suggesting that you might wish to make my thesis merely your hypothesis, till you had tested it for its antecedents in our tradition. Maybe you will have further reasons now for regarding it as merely a hypothesis, reasons grounded more in its practical consequences.

What I am affirming, then, is our religious community with the world religions in some true and basic sense of the word, community, if not in the full sense of a common confession of faith, a common worship, and a common expression of hope in the eschaton. This community is effected by our common religious conversion, which, in Lonergan's view, is our common orientation to the mystery of love and awe through the indwelling Holy Spirit who is given to us.[14] We do not, therefore, go to the world religions as to strangers, as to heathens, pagans, enemies of God. For we are one with them in the Spirit, and expect to find in them the fruits of the Spirit.[15] If these fruits seem too often to be lacking, we will reflect that they are far too often lacking in ourselves also, though we have the outer word of doctrine and the sacraments deriving from the Son.

A new sense of community, a new understanding of what is really an ancient community, requires a new name. It was in the early days at Antioch that the people of "the new way" (Acts 9:2) were first called Christians (Acts 11:26). This coining of a new name occurred as an event in history, but history has a way of moving on, and maybe we need a new and parallel development now: the coining of a name to express our common gifting with the Spirit, just as a common profession of faith in Christ resulted in the name, Christian. I suggest that, until we find a better term, we think of ourselves as Spiritans, perhaps as anonymous Spiritans (not to wrest this name from the religious congregation that has used it for a long time so honorably). The term "anonymous Christians" is already in use, but it seems to me more meaningful and more accurate to refer to those of other religions as anonymous Spiritans. They are not, after all, Christians; but they very truly are Spiritans in the sense I give this word, though anonymously so.

Can we go even further, adapting various titles given to Christians and understanding them analogously of the peoples of the world? We understand ourselves, with Peter, as "a chosen race, a royal priesthood, a dedicated nation, and a people claimed by God for his own"

14. To read Lonergan with understanding in these matters requires us to get hold of a nest of terms. I would recommend that one start with the section, "Realms of Meaning" (*Method*, pp. 81–85), proceed to "Religious Experience" (ibid., pp. 105–109), and study the passages on religiously differentiated consciousness (for example, ibid., pp. 273, 277–78). Worth keeping in mind: Lonergan nowhere, so far as I remember, uses the phrase "experience of God."

15. See *Second Collection*, p. 174 (in "The Role of the Jesuit . . ."): "I am inclined to interpret the religions of mankind, in their positive moment, as the fruit of the gift of the Spirit, though diversified by the many degrees of social and cultural development, and distorted by man's infidelity to the self-transcendence to which he aspires."

(1 Pet 2:9). Can we not understand these terms as applying in some transferred sense to the peoples united in the community of the Spirit? They too have been chosen, claimed by God. If we have a priesthood of believers in virtue of our baptism, they have their own spiritual priesthood exercised in the interior temple of the Spirit. If we are dedicated by water and the word, they are dedicated by the Spirit pleading in their inmost hearts for them. We should be able, I think, while maintaining respect for our tradition, to open our minds and hearts to what the Spirit is saying to us, and develop a language in which to express to ourselves our new relation to the world religions.

It is another matter, however, to develop a language in which to communicate across the borders of the religions. In all that I have been saying, I remind you again, I speak as a Christian to Christians, using Christian language. This language is not, or need not be, the language of dialogue with the world religions. As they repudiate the term "anonymous Christians" so they may repudiate the term "anonymous Spiritans." As they repudiate a triune God, so they may repudiate our doctrine of a Spirit sent by God and poured into their hearts as into ours. We need, then, a common language that perhaps is not specifically Christian, but not specifically Hindu or Buddhist either.[16] The problem is not ours alone; it is common to us all. If we must find non-Christian terms to communicate with Buddhists on our common experience, equally they must find non-Buddhist terms to communicate with us.

We are here at a difficult point in our program. Let us take our bearings. I suppose, then, in all religions a conversion, a new orientation, a differentiation of consciousness, that is the result of God's gift of love. I suppose further that there is in this religiously converted state some element common to us all. This is guaranteed in some generic way by there being one God who offers salvation to one human race and bestows the divine favor on everyone. But that common element is first of all a reality before it is thematized. I do not say an unexper-

16. The question of a language of communication in matters religious comes up, of course, in the last chapter of *Method,* which is entitled "Communications." If readers find the treatment skimpy there, I would refer them to earlier sections, "Pluralism in Expression" (pp. 271–76) and "Pluralism in Religious Language" (pp. 276–81). The most pointed application of Lonergan's ideas to dialogue with world religions is in his paper, "Prolegomena to the Study of the Emerging Religious Consciousness of Our Time," *Third Collection,* pp. 55–73. See especially pp. 70-71, where he distinguishes between long-range approaches and present possibilities. For the former he refers to Whitson and Panikkar as quoted earlier in the paper (but Lonergan himself offers possibilities which I will discuss later in my text). For the latter he believes that ". . . at the present time specific discussion of emerging religious consciousness has to proceed on the basis of some convention. If it is not to be merely generic, it has to adopt the formulation of some particular tradition at least as a temporary or momentary convention . . ." (p. 70.) Then, if it is agreed to use Christian terms, he would speak of God's love given to us through the Spirit.

ienced reality. In Lonergan's theology it is experienced, but experienced at the level of infrastructure, without the suprastructure of language or rites, without the knowledge and doctrines that go beyond experience, without anything at all of that sort.[17] Some understanding of such a pure experience on the level of infrastructure may be had from the analogy of Augustine's inner word; this goes beyond experience, it is true; still it is neither Greek nor Latin, nor any other language whatever that we construct in fantasy and speak.[18]

There is no way, of course, for Augustine to communicate this inner word except through outward language, be it the language of look or gesture, the language of Greeks or Latins, or whatever. Similarly, there is no way to talk about pure experience without some elements of the suprastructure. For most of us, even to advert to it is the result of being directed that way by the public language, traditions, religious rites and ways of a particular people. Such suprastructure reveals the pure experience to those who look behind the words, gestures, rites, expressions; but equally it conceals the experience from those who attend only to the words, gestures, rites, expressions. The immediate problem is to bring ourselves to attend to the experienced religious conversion that is given as a common basis; for then, contrary to what our critic says, exactly contrary, we have the possibility of dialogue among the world religions. But how do we bring ourselves to attend to the experience without a common language? That is the further and more basic problem.

Let us go back to Lonergan, not the Lonergan who is a Christian perpetually quoting Romans 5:5 on the gift of the Spirit, but the Lonergan who is a religious philosopher groping toward a common lan-

---

17. For Lonergan's distinction here between infrastructure (religious experience) and suprastructure (naming the data, and subsequent operations), see the paper referred to in the preceding note, "Prolegomena. . . ." The infrastructure "is pure experience, the experience underpinning and distinct from every suprastructure. As outer experience it is sensation as distinct from percepton. As inner experience it is consciousness as distinct from self-knowledge, consciousness as distinct from any introspective process in which one inquires about inquiring, and seeks to understand what happens when one understands, and endeavors to formulate what goes on when one is formulating . . ." (p. 57).

On the public and the private aspects of language, see *Method*, pp. 253–57: the ordinary meaningfulness of language is essentially public and only derivatively private, but the original meaningfulness of any language is first a mental act, is then expressed, "and attains ordinariness when the perfected communication is extended to a large enough number of individuals" (p. 256).

18. Augustine rings the changes on this idea here and there in his *De trinitate*, where he struggles to find a human analogy for the eternal Word of God: "Whoever is able to get hold of a word . . . not only before it is sounded, but even before the images of its sounds are revolved in fantasy . . . can see . . . in this dim reflection some likeness of that Word of whom it is said: In the beginning was the Word" (Bk. XV, ch. 10, no. 19). But then we have a word that is not found in dictionaries: "It is neither Greek nor Latin, nor any other language" (ibid.).

guage for dialogue among the religions. We find now a number of phrases that may be helpful. Thus, he says that this "orientation to transcendent mystery . . . provides the primary and fundamental meaning of the name, God."[19] That may seem somewhat forbidding, but he speaks also of "an experience of the holy."[20] He holds that "from an experience of love focused on mystery there wells forth a longing for knowledge."[21] Ordinarily, he tells us, "the experience of the mystery of love and awe is not objectified. It remains within subjectivity as a vector, an undertow, a fateful call to a dreaded holiness."[22] His phrases for the desired objectification speak of "a clouded revelation of absolute intelligence and intelligibility, absolute truth and reality, absolute goodness and holiness."[23] But he refers also, and recurringly, to descriptions by other authors: Otto's *mysterium fascinans et tremendum,* Tillich's being grasped by ultimate concern, Rahner's Ignation consolation that has no cause.[24] In groping efforts like these Lonergan tries to go behind the Christian terms that are his predilection, and describe the religious differentiation of consciousness that he supposes in all the world religions, the religious conversion that, so far from being an obstacle to dialogue, is the ontic basis of all dialogue, the common possession that justifies our "dialogue with all Christians, with non-Christians, and even with atheists who may love God in their hearts while not knowing him with their heads."[25]

We must leave a topic on which I would very much like to delay, and go on to our second question, evangelization. Many of you, perhaps, would put this question first and make it the starting point of a Christian approach to the world religions. If I put it in second place, I do not make it secondary. As we call the Word of God the second person in the Trinity but learned at Nicea not to make that Word secondary in the Godhead, so evangelization of the peoples is not a subordinate task; it has for us the very same importance that God attached to sending the only Son into the world for our salvation. That is not a secondary matter for God, and neither is it secondary whether the only Son is preached among the peoples, whether or not the "treasures of wisdom and knowledge" hidden in Christ (Col 2:3) are shared by us

19. *Method,* p. 341. In this and the following quotations, I believe Lonergan is struggling toward that common language and approach which would complement the positions he refers to of Whitson and Panikkar. Are his terms open to his own criticism of being "merely generic" (n. 16 above)? I would say they escape that criticism insofar as we take possession of our interiority and relate the terms to the infrastructure of pure experience.

20. *Method,* p. 106.   21. Ibid., p. 109.

22. Ibid., p. 113.   23. Ibid., p. 116.

24. Ibid., p. 106. See also *Second Collection,* p. 173.

25. *Method,* p. 278.

with all those whom God loves. But, as we think of God sending the Son in a second step following on the hidden gift of the Spirit, so we think of evangelization as a second step following on our own change of heart toward non-Christians. We cannot shirk that task—woe to us if we do not preach the gospel (1 Cor 9:16)—but our approach will be modified by our new understanding of the situation.[26]

We are dealing, then, with a major difference side by side with a major community. If the presence of the Spirit gives us a common element of divine proportions, nevertheless our confession of faith in Christ the Lord sets us apart with a difference likewise of divine proportions. We have a treasure that others do not possess; it is a treasure, however, given to be shared. As the divine nature was not for the Son a booty to be clutched tenaciously (Phil 2:6), neither is our Christian gifting to be kept smugly to ourselves. There is no question whatever about that. The one question that concerns us is how to go about our task, how to carry out the mandate we have received: "Go forth to every part of the world, and proclaim the Good News to the whole creation" (Mk 16:15).

26. In general our Christocentric mentality inclines us always to neglecting the role of the Spirit; one may read the very useful book of H. R. Schlette, *Towards a Theology of Religions* (New York: Herder & Herder, 1966), and ask whether it does not illustrate this neglect. But equally theologians of the Spirit will have to beware of neglecting the role of the Son. And, over and above this doctrinal problem, there is the difficulty of theological understanding, of seeing the two missions in relation to one another, in the coherence of one divine plan, and in their relevance to integral human need. (See n. 3 above.) Some hints of Lonergan's views on this question are scattered here and there in his writings. For example: "Though God's grace is given to all, still the experience of resting in God ordinarily needs a religious tradition for it to be encouraged, fostered, interpreted, guided, developed" (*Second Collection*, p. 146, in "Theology and Man's Future," pp. 135–48). See *Method*, p. 113, where, after referring to the gift of God's love and its development into mystic states, Lonergan goes on to speak more expressly of the word: "But then, as much as ever, one needs the word—the word of tradition that has accumulated religious wisdom, the word of fellowship that unites those that share the gift of God's love, the word of the gospel that announces that God has loved us first and, in the fulness of time, has revealed that love in Christ crucified, dead, and risen."

These passages deal more directly with the need in us of love and tradition, the inner and the outer word, but they suppose and are related to the Love of God and Word of God, the two divine persons sent into the world. Later in Lonergan we find the more explicit statement: "Without the visible mission of the Word, the gift of the Spirit is a being-in-love without a proper object; it remains simply an orientation to mystery that awaits its interpretation. Without the invisible mission of the Spirit, the Word enters into his own, but his own receive him not." (*Third Collection*, p. 32, in "Mission and the Spirit," with a correction of a misprint there: "visible mission of the Spirit.")

As an appendix to these matters I note the concern many missionaries feel about the doctrine of anonymous Christians: Are missions any longer necessary? But, when the peoples of the world are considered as "anonymous Spiritans," the question acquires a new context and receives a ready answer. It becomes a question for God: Is the sending of the Son any longer necessary? God obviously thought it was, and so the answer to the missionaries' question is simple: missions are necessary with the same necessity that the sending of the Son had for God.

At first blush the way to proceed may seem utterly simple: read the Acts of the Apostles and do as they did. I do not think matters are quite so simple. First of all, I read a little farther in Acts and find Paul taking three quite different approaches to three quite different audiences: he speaks one way to his fellow-Jews (Acts 13:16–41), another way to simple folk who depend on rain for their crops (Acts 14:15–17), and a third way to the cultured despisers of religion on the Areopagus (Acts 17:22–31). Very evidently the way of the apostles varied according to their understanding of the situation. A second point: the apostles thought the gospel was necessary to save the world from the wrath that then seemed imminent, so hurried round with the greatest urgency to the peoples they knew. I am sure God used this understanding of theirs to further the immediate divine purpose, but subsequent history makes it very doubtful that this was meant to be a permanent pattern. Thirdly, there is God's own way of proceeding, the long haul of the *praeparatio evangelica*. For me, that is fundamental and decisive, and I must take a little more time to discuss it.

There are, then, two attributes of God to which I would draw your attention. They seem opposed, as happens so often, but we must learn to see them in their complementarity. Paul had a similar problem in his reappraisal of history, when he had somehow to hold in union the mercy and the severity of God. But I speak of a quite different pair of attributes. There is the God who hurries, and the God who takes time, who is slow, methodical, and thorough. The God who falls in Love with all of us, and hastens to give the Holy Spirit, is the God who is in a hurry. But the same God is strangely slow to declare that Love for us, to send the Word in human form and manifest the divine Love. There is the enormously long *praeparatio evangelica*. I find this extremely significant. God speaks in the divine silence as well as in the uttered word, and the message of this long silence is the message of the slow and methodical God. No doubt there is a variety of divine gifts, and some of you may feel called to go straight into the marketplace and there preach Christ crucified without any preliminary process. I will not deny your call; who am I to limit the divine variety? But by the same token I maintain the validity of another kind of call, based directly on the slow and methodical way of divine proceeding that we find in the long ages of silence. This is certainly Lonergan's way, and it is his contribution to the wider ecumenism that we are studying this evening.

It is time at last to turn directly to the relevance Lonergan's ideas may have for evangelization of the peoples of the world. Unfortunately, things are growing more complex, as they do on moving farther and farther from their roots, and it is time also to conclude my lecture.

What I can do in these last few minutes is indicate one orienting idea in the early Lonergan, which you could easily miss if your attention centers too exclusively on his later work.[27] I take you, then, not to *Method in Theology,* with its theologically rich notions of love, community, crosscultural bonding, intersubjective ties and expressions, but to the earlier and more prosaic Lonergan of *Insight,* specifically, to chapter 20 of that book. You remember that chapter 19 is called "General Transcendent Knowledge" and deals with the notion and existence of God, while chapter 20 is called "Special Transcendent Knowledge." I would say, with the advantage of hindsight, that of these two chapters the former is addressed to philosophers of God, and the latter to the world religions. Chapter 20 has been little studied in comparison with chapter 19. It is a long chapter—we meet here the phrase that has caused so many to chuckle, or maybe to fume a little, "In the thirty-first place"—but I think I can indicate briefly what the strategy is.

The strategy is to begin with a problem that is common to the human race, as patent to the secular world as it is to the religious, the problem of evil. It is not *just* a problem, one to be acknowledged and accepted with such fatalism as we can muster. No, it is a problem to which we expect a solution, if we believe in a wise and beneficent God, and that is the supposition after chapter 19.

Because God is omniscient, he knows man's plight. Because he is omnipotent, he can remedy it. Because he is good, he wills to do so. The fact of evil is not the whole story. . . . Because God exists there is a further intelligibility to be grasped.

In other words, "if God is good, then there is not only a problem of evil, but also a solution."[28]

From this starting point the key step forward, as so often in Lonergan's work, is heuristic. It corresponds to a category beloved of Newman, antecedent probability. That is, it tries to anticipate the general form of the answer. It asks what sort of solution would meet the need, would correspond to the human condition, would fit harmoniously into world order. It may be that the need could be met in a multitude of different ways, but can we at least determine the general lines that any solution would have to follow? Within this general strategic approach Lonergan works out his expectations, even to the thirty-first place.

Let me anticipate at once an objection to the strategy. The reader may claim that there is no such common starting point as I suppose,

27. Any profound thinker will take fundamental positions early in life and, equally, any profound thinker will develop with the passing years, to provide us with a perplexing problem of continuity and change. There is no way I can take up here the problem as it affects Lonergan, but readers should be aware of it.

28. *Insight,* p. 694.

that the world religions are far from agreement on the problem of evil and its relation to God. In answer I would continue to maintain a *radical* starting point common to the one human race that the one God loves. But I would admit a great difference in *immediate* starting points which must always be set exactly where people are. But that only says that we are, all of us, already on the move and have reached different stages along the way. So I suggest here a device that Thomas Aquinas recommends in a similar situation. When there are differences among Christians, he says, you can appeal to the whole Bible to settle them; for argument with Jewish believers, you restrict your source to the Old Testament; and, in dealing with unbelievers, you have simply to fall back on reason.[29] The parallel today is clear, though our problem regards content, not sources. Do we all believe in a wise and beneficent God? If not, go back (if we are taking Lonergan's route) to chapter 19 or as much farther as the need may take us to overcome fatalism, atheism, and so on. But if we do believe, go on to the next step. Do we admit a problem of evil, and expect our God to be concerned with it? If not, go back and establish that; but if we do, we can begin to discuss possible solutions, from the first place to the thirty-first, or the hundred and thirty-first, as far again as need takes us.

The steps, I say, are heuristic only. They anticipate a solution in its general lines, they do not determine it in its individual identity. Nor is it Lonergan's business in a work that is mainly philosophical to identify the one true Church or even the one true religion, much less to construct an apologetic for either. So the last section of his chapter 20, called "The Identification of the Solution," is little more than one page long. It summarizes the thirty-one points made earlier, offers some pastoral advice and promises divine help to those who seek the solution, "for the realization of the solution and its development in each of us is principally the work of God."[30]

My own concluding remark will simply say that the thirty-one converging notions, the developing trend, the mounting probabilities, point not directly to Jesus of Nazareth, but more directly and immediately to the Church of Christ. As if to say, with the First Vatican Council, that it is the Church which is, or should be, the *signum levatum in nationes,* a sign raised up to the peoples of the world.[31] As if to say that the world religions may be justified, or at least show plausible

---

29. *Summa contra gentiles,* I, 2.

30. *Insight,* pp. 729–30. For some views of the "later" Lonergan on apologetics, see *Method,* pp. 123, 130. Those are very sketchy remarks but we have to set the whole question within his discussion of dialectic in ch. 10.

31. Denzinger-Schönmetzer, *Enchiridion symbolorum, definitionum et declarationum de rebus fidei et morum,* 33rd ed. (Barcelona: Herder, 1965), no. 3014.

grounds, in seeing no reason to investigate certain events said to have occurred long ago and far away from them,[32] but they might have every reason to investigate a Christian reality present in their midst, and from that be led back to the events of long ago and far away that Christians claim as their origin. If that is so, our immediate responsibility in evangelization is clear: it is to make the Church what Christ our Lord would have it be, and on that basis begin to talk to others about Jesus of Nazareth.[33]

So I end where I began, asking the Church and ourselves in the Toronto School of Theology, for we are the Church: is it not time to let the gospel disturb our peace once more, time to transcend our own little world, so much smaller than God's, to think of the whole great family of God united with us in the bond of the Spirit, that Spirit who will in God's good time enable them to say with us that Jesus is Lord (1 Cor 12:3)? I thank you for your kind attention.

32. The Christian apologetic must thus take account of what has been called the "scandal of particularity" in God's manner of sending the only Son. (I have not yet discovered the origin of this striking phrase—which leads me to suggest that we need a *Dictionary of Theological Quotations* to set alongside the many dictionaries we have of literary quotations. Any takers for this little project?)

33. Early in this lecture I insisted that here we could only begin discussion of Lonergan's contribution to the wider ecumenism. Let me just indicate, as I conclude, the direction I think further study of his ideas might take, in relation especially to the "scandal of particularity." First of all, his comprehensive sweep would not allow this problem to stand in isolation: beside the scandal of particularity he would set the complementary scandal of universality, God's universal love for the human race. To a people rejoicing in their election, the latter is as scandalous as the former. Next, with his passion for fundamental ideas that admit of generalization, he would set the problem in a wider pattern: there is a scandal of particularity in the way different biological roles and functions are assigned to man and woman (Why should one sex and not the other be oppressed with childbearing?), in the disease that strikes at random in the human race ("Why me?" is an everyday phrase in which we express our offense at this scandal), in the famine that afflicts one nation while another abounds in food, and so on through myriad instances. Thirdly, his solution to the problem would, I think, be given in terms of his very fundamental views on world order; hence, we would need to study his ideas on the random, on emergent probability, on schemes of recurrence, and the like; we would have to insert this into his ideas (perhaps not yet sufficiently developed) on interpersonal relations, cooperation, institutions, and so on; and this again into his theology of history: progress, decline, Christian redemption. But maybe my point is clear; we have only begun the study of his enormously difficult, deeply penetrating, and widely ramifying ideas.

20

An Expansion of Lonergan's Notion of Value[*]

Eleven years ago, during the first Lonergan Workshop held at Boston College, I gave a paper called "An Exploration of Lonergan's New Notion of Value."[1] If I move now from exploration to expansion, I am only following a course already mapped in a Boston College brochure, which describes this workshop as a "conference exploring and expanding the implications of Lonergan's work." Of course, it is not just the *implications* of the work that need this double attention, but the *work* itself too; and so, having explored to some extent Lonergan's work on the notion of value, I undertake now to expand it.

Not as if the task of exploring were completed. Even with the many studies now available—too many to take account of here—I would still maintain that we have only begun to explore Lonergan's work on values, while its expansion is as yet little more than an idea. But the two tasks should go forward together, with attempts at expansion enabling us to explore more intelligently, and the resulting deeper understanding of the original helping us to achieve a more genuinely creative development. How much more intelligently, for example, do we read chapter 17 of *Insight* and explore its meaning, when we have at hand Lonergan's own expansion of that chapter in the differentiated tasks of his later work on theological method.[2]

Maybe that example of development from *Insight* to *Method* will serve also as a model for what I hope to do in this paper. In contrast to urban developments as we know them today, where the first step is to bring in the wreckers and begin the work of demolition, I wish to develop Lonergan's work, as he did himself, by drawing out what is already there in the potency of the original idea. He once remarked of such a thinker as Aquinas, "what the span of mortal life or the limitations of his era force him to leave undone, that none the less already stands potentially within the framework of his thinking and the sugges-

*A paper presented at the twelfth annual Lonergan Workshop, Boston College, 17–21 June 1985, where the general theme was "The Crisis of the Human Good." Previously published in *Lonergan Workshop* 7 (1987), pp. 35–57.
1. See above, ch. 4.
2. *Method in Theology*, chs. 7–10; see p. 153, n. 1.

tiveness of his approach."[3] There are those who favor, in their approach to Lonergan, a large measure of demolition and, insofar as that contributes to the human-divine world we are all engaged in building, let their work prosper. Myself, I continue to find it far more profitable to attend to what stands potentially within the framework of Lonergan's thinking and the suggestiveness of his approach.

In this paper, then, I will attend to two notions that stand already within that framework. Both notions are general, but they suggest immediate applications in the field of values, with important consequences, I think, for that crisis of the human good which is the theme of this workshop. They are, first, the two ways of human development and, secondly, the historical as opposed to the structural aspect of human consciousness.

1. The Two Ways of Human Development

A brief, though rough, statement of my position under this heading is the following. During the years 1974 to 1977 there became fully explicit in Lonergan's thinking and writing two contrasting ways of human development, one upward and creative, the other downward and traditional. These two ways were operative, but not thematized, in chapters 5 to 14 of *Method*. They were neither thematized nor sufficiently operative in chapters 1 to 4 of that book. And the work of expansion that I propose would make them thematic in chapters 5 to 14, and introduce them as a fully operative factor in chapters 1 to 4. That roughly is the position I have now to set forth, qualify somewhat, and justify.

What are these two ways that have emerged, for me at least, as a key factor in understanding Lonergan? Let us look at one of his own formulations of the idea.

Human development occurs in two distinct modes. If I may use a spatial metaphor, it moves (1) from below upwards and (2) from above downwards.

It moves from below upwards inasmuch as it begins from one's personal experience, advances through ever fuller understanding and more balanced judgment, and so attains the responsible exercise of personal freedom.

It moves from above downwards inasmuch as one belongs to a hierarchy of groups and so owes allegiance to one's home, to one's country, to one's religion. Through the traditions of the group one is socialized, acculturated, educated.[4]

The first way will be fully familiar to students of Lonergan; from the 1940s to the 1980s it entered deeply into all his work. The second way

3. *Grace and Freedom: Operative Grace in the Thought of St. Thomas Aquinas,* p. 140.

4. "Questionnaire on Philosophy," *Method: Journal of Lonergan Studies* 2/2 (October 1984), p. 10—with the correction of a minor misprint.

is much less familiar, so let us see it again in a somewhat longer formulation.

The handing on of development . . . works from above downwards: it begins in the affectivity of the infant, the child, the son, the pupil, the follower. On affectivity rests the apprehension of values. On the apprehension of values rests belief. On belief follows the growth in understanding of one who has found a genuine teacher and has been initiated into the study of the masters of the past. Then to confirm one's growth in understanding comes experience made mature and perceptive by one's developed understanding.[5]

None of us, I trust, will give undue attention to the "spatial metaphor" of up and down movements: the type of image in use here is not the one that is the fertile source of insight; it is rather the type that is a handy mnemonic for an idea. Nor will we identify this pair of movements with the *via analytica* and *via synthetica* that figured prominently in Lonergan's Latin theology;[6] those are two ways of ordering ideas within the level of thought (with corresponding judgments, of course), but the present pair deals with the movement from one level of consciousness to another. Some of us, however, will wish for what is so often necessary for an understanding of Lonergan's ideas: the history of their development in his thinking; if not the history of the upward movement—which may be well enough known—at least the history of the downward movement, which, so far as I know, has not been studied at all.

I cannot set forth that history here, but I will give a few pointers to guide further investigation. There is the pairing found already in Thomas Aquinas, and noted by Lonergan early in his career, of the *origin* and the *use* of insight. The act of insight originates in dependence on phantasm; it is a development from below. But acquired and now habitual insight is used in the other direction to call up the appropriate phantasm; it is development from above in the application of one's understanding. Now this pairing is explicit in the *Verbum* articles of the late 1940s.[7] A second pointer is the symbiosis of knowledge and belief. Knowledge is developed from below; it is a third step after experience and understanding. But belief is communicated in tradition; it is a handing on, or development from above. And this pairing receives a good deal of attention in *Insight*,[8] with the downward path from the truth of faith to theological understanding being thoroughly studied

5. "Natural Right and Historical Mindedness," *A Third Collection: Papers by Bernard J. F. Lonergan, S.J.*, p. 181.

6. *Divinarum personarum conceptionem analogicam evolvit Bernardus Lonergan, S.J.*, pp. 23–28; *De deo trino*, vol. 2, pp. 33–41.

7. *Verbum: Word and Idea in Aquinas*, pp. 29, 156.

8. *Insight: A Study of Human Understanding*, pp. 427–29, 706, and passim.

in Lonergan's trinitarian writings.[9] A third pointer is the fact that conviction can follow on our being in love. Love is fourth-level or maybe fifth-level activity, while conviction is third-level; to derive one's convictions from one's love is therefore development from above. And this idea, we may be surprised to learn, is already explicit in the trinitarian treatise of 1957.[10]

So we come to 1972 and *Method in Theology,* where, I have claimed, the two ways are operative but not thematized in chapters 5 to 14. They are clearly operative in the two phases of mediating and mediated theology: the first of these proceeds from the level of experience (data provided by research) through the levels of understanding (interpretation of the data) and judgment (the history of what really happened, of what was going forward) to the fourth-level challenge of values impelling us to decision (dialectic); the second phase moves through the four levels in the reverse order.[11] Lonergan even speaks of the first phase as rising and of the second as descending.[12]

Nevertheless, that second phase, though following through the four levels the sequence of the downward movement, is not set forth in chapters 11 to 14 as resulting from a dynamism working from above. We shall see more on this presently, but my position may be tested at once in a preliminary way. Recall this passage from the essay "Cognitional Structure": "Human knowing is . . . formally dynamic. It is self-assembling, self-constituting. It puts itself together, one part summoning forth the next, till the whole is reached."[13] Here we have the dynamism of the upward movement affirmed as a general principle. That principle is central to Lonergan's lifetime work. It reappears in chapter 1 of *Method* and it structures chapters 6 to 10; if those five chapters advert to it only occasionally, no more is necessary, so clearly is the principle operative there.[14] But now consult the opening paragraphs of chapters 11 to 14, looking for a parallel dynamic to move one from foundations through doctrines and systematics to communications. One will not find it much in evidence. Nor should one expect to. If, as I believe, the first integral sketch of the dynamism at work occurs only in 1977 ("On affectivity rests the apprehension of values. On the

9. *Divinarum personarum,* p. 17; *De deo trino,* vol. 2, pp. 20–23.
10. *Divinarum personarum,* pp. 179–80.
11. *Method,* pp. 133–36.   12. Ibid., p. 142.
13. *Collection: Papers by Bernard Lonergan, S.J.,* p. 223.
14. It was made operative in advance through the general basis given in ch. 5 where the upward dynamism of development is applied directly to the four specialties of chs. 6 to 10: p. 133 and again on p. 134. Notice that neither of these passages mentions the corresponding downward movement; and, even on p. 142 where this movement is mentioned, there is no discussion of its dynamism.

For a sample of particular advertence to the dynamism of the upward movement, see p. 246 on the task of adding (fourth-level) dialectic to research, interpretation and history.

apprehension of values rests belief "—as quoted above), we are hardly likely to find explicit advertence to it in 1972.

In my opinion then it was only in the period from 1974 to 1977 that the two ways, as a general idea of human development, each with its own dynamism but each also complementary to the other, came sharply into focus. The first and rather groping effort to name the two ways in the present sense I would locate in "Mission and the Spirit," published only in 1976 but written, it seems, in 1974.[15] The idea develops notably in "Christology Today: Methodological Reflections"[16] and in "Healing and Creating in History"[17]—it's my surmise that this is the order of writing—to reach maximum clarity in two papers of 1977, one before the American Catholic Philosophical Association[18] and the other before the Catholic Theological Society of America[19] The emergence and repetition of a name that had not been used in this sense before, the clear progress in formulation from 1974 to 1977,[20] the appearance of the idea in almost every paper Lonergan delivered during this period—all this evidence points to the breakthrough of a new insight and the thematization of what had not up to that time been attentively considered.

Of course, there occurs here the old problem of continuity versus development. It occurs in regard to any thinker of stature, and has been raised repeatedly in regard to Lonergan, some of us insisting more on the development, others more on the continuity. Where we put the emphasis matters less than understanding what went forward and assessing its significance. I have characterized the change from *Method* to post-*Method* writings as a progress from the operative to the thematic. Is that a significant change? As a type of change, I believe it is and I would adduce what seems to me an outstanding instance. For thousands of years, most of us would hold, the four levels of human consciousness have been operative: people have in fact noticed the data, tried to understand, raised in some way the question of truth, and acted responsibly. Now, if we try to trace the emergence of this into thematic study, we might well take Plato as representing thematization of the

---

15. *Third Collection*, p. 32.
16. Ibid., pp. 76–77.
17. Ibid., p. 106.
18. Ibid., pp. 180–81.
19. Ibid., pp. 196–97.
20. What I take to be the first formulation, in "Mission and the Spirit" (*Third Collection*, p. 32) has the downward development move from God's gift of love through the three conversions; this is not the later formulation. Again, in "Christology Today" (*Third Collection*, p. 76) development is "ordinarily" from below upward; later formulations seem to put the two movements on an equal footing, so that both are "ordinary."

There is a parallel development in Lonergan's ordering of knowing and loving. Some passages of *Method* (pp. 122, 278, 283, 340) make it an exception when love precedes knowledge, as it does in God's gift of love. I would not say it is an exception in later writings.

intelligible, Aquinas as representing that of the existent, and Kierkegaard that of self-involving responsibility; and this in turn might incline
us to agree that the thematic does indeed mark a significant step beyond
the operative.[21]

But now, if there is any kernel of truth in my position, we have to
go back to *Method in Theology* and ask what this work would look like
had Lonergan at that time conceived the two ways explicitly and incorporated the idea into the structure of the volume. More to the point,
how would we ourselves now incorporate it into *Method*? Personally, I
would make little change in the Foreground chapters (i.e., 6 to 14) or
in chapter 5 that structures them; the two ways, I have claimed, are
already operative there and could be made thematic with the introduction of little more than brief statements in the opening paragraphs of
each chapter. Moreover, I have indicated the hints to be found already
in chapters 6 to 10, on the dynamism at work to carry us from research
through interpretation and history to dialectic. The problem is not so
simple for chapters 11 to 14, but, in the backward light cast by the 1977
statements on the two ways, we should be able to find at work the
dynamism that moves us from foundations through doctrines and systematics to communications. The Background chapters, however, where
the two ways are not as such operative, are another story; what then
would they look like if they were to incorporate the two ways?

My view is this. Chapter 1 is almost exclusively concerned with development from below, and so needs a complementary chapter (or
section) to deal with development from above. Chapter 4, on the contrary, is almost exclusively concerned with development from above,
and so needs its own complementary chapter or section to deal with
development from below. Chapters 2 and 3 are somewhat different, not
falling definitely into either pattern; both, however, would benefit from
the organizing power the two complementary ways would provide.

Chapter 1, then, is almost entirely concerned with development from
below. It deals with the basic pattern of operations, and that pattern
shows a movement from experience through understanding and judgment to responsible decision. There is no attention to the development
which begins in the affectivity of the infant, continues with apprehension of values, and goes on to belief and growth in understanding, to
culminate in experience made mature and perceptive. For that second
movement we need a whole new chapter; or, if we add a distinct part

21. Another way of putting this progression is to say that it goes from the universal
in the particular to the universal set apart as universal and thus made available for use in
myriad instances. Thus, the dynamism operative in foundations, doctrines, systematics
and communications is a universal in the particular (or at least a genus in the species);
but the universal set apart as a pattern is values, reflection, understanding and experience.

within the present chapter, the present treatment would be called, not "Method," but "Part One: Method in Development from Below," with the added section called "Part Two: Method in Development from Above."

One would base that second part on another and quite different dynamism. The dynamism of the upward movement is the eros of the human spirit:[22] it is the subject, the questioning subject, the subject as operator.[23] But in the new downward direction, the dynamism is not simply subjective; it is intersubjective, it is the intersubjective in its full range from spontaneous intersubjectivity to persons in community.[24] We are "we" before we are "you" and "I" and this makes operative a dynamism of love that is quite distinct and different from the eros of *Insight*.

With the basic element defined and made thematic, we may go on to notice the great difference in modes of operation as the two dynamisms move us in opposite directions from level to level. To start with an example at the top: it is one thing to move up from judgments of facts and values to a responsible decision (third level to fourth); it is quite another for a mother to ponder in love what is best for her child (fourth level to third). In the former we may well speak of duty, and think of it as the "Stern Daughter of the Voice of God," but surely not in the latter. Or, to go for another example to the bottom of the structure and the relation between image and insight: it is one thing to struggle for the upward emergence from the image of insight into the image (first level to second), and quite another to evoke images in illustration of an insight we already possess (second level to first). In the former case, as Lonergan said years ago, "we are at the mercy of fortune, the sub-conscious, or a teacher's skill . . . in a ferment of trying to grasp we know not what," but in the latter "we can operate on our own, marshalling images to a habitually known end."[25]

Let us turn to chapter 4 of *Method,* doubly fascinating now, for not only does it illustrate and confirm my general position, but also it ceases to be the puzzle it long has been in relation to chapter 19 of *Insight*. The main movement, then, in chapter 4 of *Method* follows a pattern exactly the opposite to that of chapter 1. Where the latter moves upward from experience to the existential self and needs the addition of the complementary downward movement, this chapter in the main follows

22. *Insight,* see the index, *s.v.,* Dynamism.

23. Ibid., see the index, *s.v.,* Operator.

24. I use the word "intersubjectivity" to refer here to the full range of relations between subjects; this is not, I think, the particular use Lonergan sometimes makes of the term, as when it refers to the intersubjectivity that is "vital and functional," an intersubjectivity of "action and feeling" (*Method,* pp. 57, 59).

25. *Verbum,* p. 29.

the line of development from above and needs the complement of development from below. For the key notion is certainly that of being in love with God. This is a dynamism that takes over the whole of life, a dynamism that dismantles old horizons to set up new ones, that appears in religious conversion, that is an inner word of love leading to faith, the eye of love, and eventually to the beliefs of a community which is formed and bound together through sharing in this love. And all this is the result of God's gift, not ultimately of our own doing. There can hardly be any doubt that the movement here is the religious form of the one described by Lonergan five years later as the development that begins in affectivity to move through values, judgments and understanding to mature and perceptive experience.

Is this chapter 4 simply a movement from above and no more? I think not. The short first section[26] deals with the question of God. It does so in terms of the unfolding structure of consciousness: inquiry, reflection, deliberation. It does not do so in terms of God's gift of love but rather in terms that a humanist could accept. Only later, neatly mediated by the notion of self-transcendence, do we move from the question of God to the gift of divine love: the upward movement of consciousness shows a *capacity* for self-transcendence but being in love with God is the *actuality* of self-transcendence.[27] If, then, this chapter were to be expanded in the balanced form suggested by the two ways of development, everything in section 2 and what follows could stand as it is, but the short first section would become a fuller treatment of the question of God and of a philosopher's answer to that question: it would be chapter 19 of *Insight* as Lonergan might have rewritten it in 1977.

Let me digress here for a moment to deal with a long-standing puzzle in Lonergan's writings. This developed as follows. When *Insight* appeared in 1957 a great deal of attention was given at once to chapter 19, "General Transcendent Knowledge," a chapter which works out a philosophical notion of God and affirms the existence of the God who is so conceived. The attention was by no means entirely favorable, and Lonergan himself eventually added his own critique of this famous chapter:

The main incongruity was that, while my cognitional theory was based on a long and methodical appeal to experience, in contrast my account of God's existence and attributes made no appeal to religious experience.[28]

26. *Method*, pp. 101–103.   27. Ibid., p. 105.

28. *Philosophy of God, and Theology: The Relationship between Philosophy of God and the Functional Specialty, Systematics*, p. 12. This particular admission was reinforced by the more general one Lonergan made on the last seven chapters and epilogue of *Insight*: "Some of the points made then I still like; others have been superseded in the light of further reading, conversing, reflecting" (*A Second Collection: Papers by Bernard J. F. Lonergan, S.J.*, p. 275).

This admission led to the widely held view (and very welcome it was, for it dispensed one from study of that diabolically difficult chapter 19) that Lonergan had abandoned the ill-fated attempt of *Insight* to prove the existence of God. In fact, as he expressly declared on that same occasion and more than once repeated, he had not abandoned the *Insight* position at all.[29] But then the puzzle ramifies into three questions: What really is the relation of chapter 19 to his later work, say— to *Method* or to *Philosophy of God, and Theology*? How is one to interpret his own statements on his earlier and later views? To which one adds the first question of all: How does one understand the demanding pages of chapter 19 itself?

I believe we can throw considerable light now on the first two questions, and put the third in a clearer perspective. The relation of chapter 19 to the later work is largely the relation to one another of the two ways we have been studying: chapter 19 is the upward movement from experience (our world) through understanding (contingency of that world and the need of explanation) to the judgment (once we admit the real is being and being is completely intelligible) that God exists. Chapter 4 of *Method*, on the other hand, is largely the downward movement from the love of God as divine gift, to the effort to conceive the Giver of that love and render some account of the strange attraction we feel. This downward movement is plain in *Method*[30] but is spelled out far more fully in *Philosophy of God, and Theology*. Here, after speaking of religious experience as God's gift, Lonergan continues:

I have argued that it is this gift that leads men to seek knowledge of God. God's gift of his love is God's free and gratuitous gift. It does not suppose that we know God. It does not proceed from our knowledge of God. On the contrary I have maintained that the gift occurs with indeed a determinate content but without an intellectually apprehended object. Religious experience at its root is experience of an unconditioned and unrestricted being in love. But what we are in love with, remains something that we have to find out. When we find it out in the context of a philosophy, there results a philosophy of God. When we find it out in the context of a functionally differentiated theology, there results a functional specialty, systematics. So it turns out that one and the same God has unknowingly been found and is differently being sought by both philosopher and theologian.[31]

What of our second question, Lonergan's own attitude toward his earlier and later work? I would say that all this time it was in process, that the last sentence of the passage just quoted represents his intermediate position of 1973, but that it would need the clarity of his 1977 principle

29. For an example of the repetition see workshop: *Question Sessions* (Chestnut Hill, Ma: Boston College, 1977, unpublished), "First Discussion," p. 21.

30. *Method*, pp. 109, 116, 340–41.   31. *Philosophy of God*, pp. 50–51.

of the two ways to get chapter 19 of *Insight* and chapter 4 of *Method* into a unified view. Finally, we can see chapter 19 itself in better perspective now. It was an answer to a question, but for the later Lonergan the question itself was more important than the answer: "In *Method* the question of God is considered more important than the precise manner in which an answer is formulated."[32] Not everyone will answer the question in the way chapter 19 does but, if they are not obscurantist, they will at least raise the question and do so under the influence, unknown perhaps to them, of God's gift of love.

Let us return now, though briefly, to the omitted chapters 2 and 3 of *Method*. The question occurs whether they too can be seen as dominated by the influence, either of the upward movement (with chapter 1) or of the downward (with chapter 4). They do not, I would say, show any very clear pattern one way or the other.[33] In any case both might gain in clarity from importing back into their structure the two ways of 1977. Then chapter 2 would speak first, as it does now, of values as a human creation, as determined by the person who is the originating value, as worked out intelligently and rationally and chosen responsibly by the human agent: of values in other words as terminal, as products of the upward movement of human development. But the chapter would deal also with values as handed on, as taught and communicated from generation to generation, of values as received, received with due criticism and openness to their revision, but still part of our heritage. Chapter 3 would be organized in a similar way, to study first the development of meaning from the ground up, in the slow learning process of the human race, but then to study also the communication of meaning, the handing on of meaning as a legacy and its reception as a heritage. In both chapters this second, downward movement would exploit Lonergan's later and repeated references to the process of socialization, acculturation and education,[34] a trio of terms to which I will presently return.

I have been suggesting possible ways of importing Lonergan's 1977 ideas backward into the chapters of *Method*, but I would wish my suggested ways to be taken only for what they are worth: granted that there is a task here, there may be several ways of going about it. One might, for example, divide the whole "Background" of *Method* into two parts, one beginning with the present chapter 1 and following the upward process through its series of steps, and the other beginning with chapter 4 and following the downward process through its parallel but

---

32. *Second Collection,* p. 277.
33. At the 1985 Lonergan Workshop I was quite incautious on this point, putting chs. 2 and 3 too categorically in the upward pattern with ch. 1.
34. "Questionnaire on Philosophy," p. 10; *Third Collection,* pp. 181, 197.

inverse series. The important thing for me is not the diverse structures that might be erected, but the structuring power itself of the two ways.

In this context a related question crops up with its own peculiar fascination. For it is noticeable that the ideas of chapter 2 are very much the ones that occur again in chapter 10, on dialectic; likewise, that the ideas of chapter 3 are very much the ones that occur again in chapter 7, on interpretation. So the question arises whether each of the first four functional specialties should not have its own Background chapter (with appropriate preparation also for specialties five to eight, once the two ways are introduced into the Background). The question has a special force when pointed at history: there is at present no Background chapter for this, and one wonders whether that is the reason why Lonergan needed two chapters (8 and 9) when he came to expound this functional specialty. Even research might well have its own Background chapter, preparing for a fuller explanation of that specialty and filling a lacuna which Lonergan himself acknowledged late in life.[35] We are here in the position perhaps of the followers of Mendeleev: Lonergan often spoke of him as setting forth the pattern of the atomic table, leaving gaps which later scientists filled in as they discovered this or that missing element; one could well maintain that, in a similar way, Lonergan has suggested a "periodic table" for the Background of *Method,* and that it is up to us to fill in the missing chapters.

I have not forgotten the theme of this workshop, which is the crisis of the human good, but the clear relevance of the two ways to that crisis enables me to be brief on their application. There is need then to take seriously the double task of the creation and the handing on of values: the attentive, intelligent, reasonable and responsible production of terminal values, and the love of and loyalty to a tradition that receives and guards and hands on the heritage of hard-won values. The crisis of the human good, as crisis, is a product of the present historical situation in regard to the relation between the two parts of the task. For in all stages of human development beyond the earliest, the creation of values and their handing on live in a symbiosis that is also a dialectic: the creation is not *ex nihilo* but out of a tradition that must be criticized, and the handing on is not a passive channeling but an effort also to improve, revise, build up. Then a major disruption of the relation brings on a crisis; that is the situation today, but more of that in the second part of my paper.

35. In a letter to me dated 3 March 1980: "I fear that my book did not emphasize enough the importance of research: my own work in that specialty was Gratia operans and Verbum, about eleven years of my life. It is from the mind set of research that one most easily learns what Method is about: surmounting differences in historicity."

One question remains before I turn to my second heading; it is a major question and I can but introduce it. That Lonergan's own thought might be expanded through the suggestive power of his two ways of development is, I hope, clear enough. How that expansion might affect the structuring of his *Method in Theology* is a topic, I also venture to hope, that from now on we will wish to ponder. But there is a far larger task whose magnitude we should not ignore: it is the creation of a climate of opinion and mores in which our task can be seen and accepted as a task, especially that part of the task which is the handing on and receiving of a tradition. How is the community at large to be made aware of, and respond to, the dynamism that is at work here and its mode of operating? Lonergan's trio of terms for the process by which any set of meanings and values is handed on is "socialization," "acculturation" and "education." How can we measure the labor involved in bringing his expanded notion of meanings and values, through socialization, acculturation and education, into the publicly received set of meanings and values?

There is a clue to the magnitude of the task in the labor to give a domicile in accepted ways of thought to the upward movement. Of that latter we might say that chapter 1 of *Method* is largely a distillation of *Insight,* and that huge book in turn was a distillation of years of study of the modes of common sense, the sciences, and philosophy. In my view something of parallel magnitude must be undertaken to bring the process of socialization, acculturation, and education, as it regards the meanings and values in question here, to methodical maturity. The materials at hand are abundant enough; they are there in the enormous wealth of our literature, our history, our laws, our sermons and hagiography, our music and dance, our ceremonies and pageantry, our political traditions, our educational systems. By this sketchy list I mean to suggest that the materials at hand include not only the content of a set of meanings and values, but also ways of handing on that content. To have the materials at hand with unexamined ways of handing them on is not, however, to meet the need, or to come anywhere near it. The very urgency of the present crisis of the human good brings out the crying need to attend to the dynamism of the downward movement of development, to study its modes of operation, to appropriate in corresponding terms the process of socialization, acculturation and education and make it methodically operative. The materials of common sense, of the sciences, of philosophy, were at hand in abundance when Lonergan undertook to write *Insight,* yet few of us would deny the magnitude of the task presented in writing that book. A task of something like similar magnitude must be envisaged if method is to enter and guide the path of development from above in the human situation.

11. Historical and Structural Aspects of Consciousness

The second part of my paper and my second heading for expansion of Lonergan's notion of value is just as important as the first, but it lies closer to the surface, at least in *Method,* so we can deal with it more rapidly. Once again, however, it will be a matter of setting forth a very general position before we can make applications; still, the applications are obvious and immediate, and will not delay us.

The expansion I call for now is the addition of the historical aspect of consciousness to the structural, where "addition" means merely bringing into focus what has been repeatedly touched on in Lonergan's writings, or means giving a distinct recognition and its own technical name to what has long been present. To borrow from other languages, it is making *thématique* what has been *vécu* or studying *in actu signato* what has existed *in actu exercito.*

First, then, the structural side of consciousness is clear enough: it is constituted by the four levels that are its invariant factor, enabling us to organize our conscious activity according to the categories of attention, intelligence, reasonableness, and responsibility. But the historical aspect is the variable factor: it refers to what happens on any level of the structure and happens in variety, now one way and now another; or, we might say it refers to what fills the structure, and fills it in a multitude of diverse combinations, with different degrees of emphasis, and so on. It seems to me we can appropriately call this the historical side of consciousness, but it should be distinguished from that differentiation of consciousness which is a part of modern culture and which is already familiar to Lonergan's readers under the name, historical consciousness. This "historical consciousness" is a recent acquisition of the human race, hardly existing two centuries ago; it runs through the four levels, but is oriented toward the object, attending to data in their changeable character, attempting to understand them in that regard, and so on. But the historical side of consciousness that I refer to is not a recent acquisition; it lies within consciousness as such; it is a permanent aspect of the subject, one that was there from the start.

Maybe it will be best, instead of trying to describe or define this aspect, simply to give a partial listing of the diverse states resulting from the various ways that consciousness unfolds. Many of these lie at hand, quite explicitly attended to in Lonergan's work. There are, for example, the literally innumerable brands of common sense, the variety of the differentiations of consciousness, the different forms of conversion and the several possible states consequent on the presence or absence of any particular conversion, the two ways of human development and the changing ratios of emphasis they receive at different times or among diverse peoples and cultures. This diversity, I say, is already at hand in Lonergan's writings; in fact, many of the items listed above can be found in a single paragraph of *Method*.[36] But, though listed, they are mingled indiscriminately with the structural elements. They need to be distinguished, separated out, brought under one generalized heading, seen as pertaining to one general historicality of consciousness itself and as set in contrast with the general structural side of consciousness. To be noted: though the states are many and diverse and no one can combine the totality of states in one consciousness, nevertheless the consciousness of everyone is marked with the underlying historicality that gives rise to the many states, to some states in this person and to others in that.—With this brief exposition we can proceed to the theme of our workshop, applying our general category first to the field of values and then directly to the crisis of the human good.

I would maintain, then, that under the present heading too there is the possibility of expanding Lonergan's notion of value. In fact, it is especially in the field of values, and rather strikingly here in contrast to the field of meaning, that the historical aspect of consciousness needs more thorough study, with corresponding attention to the developing character of values. This contrast can be seen, clearly with the aid of 1985 hindsight, in the early Lonergan of the *Verbum* articles, where the development of understanding is very much in evidence,[37] but there is no corresponding study of the development of values. Now the 1968 lecture, *The Subject,* did set in motion a new approach to value; but only slowly, so it seems, did the full implications of his new position dawn on Lonergan. Thus, we have in *Method* a very extensive study of the stages of meaning,[38] but no such study of the stages of value. Sebastian Moore has reported that the first thing Lonergan said to him was "Concepts have dates."[39] To one who knows Lonergan's cognitional theory those three little words speak volumes, but I would say we need to hear the parallel statement, "Values have dates." There are elements in *Method* that could be brought together to underpin such a statement, and the statement itself might yet be found in the legacy of Lonergan's papers, but his published writings do not seem to take up the question in any detail.—Here then is one instance of a need to add the historical to the structural, for the structural side of the good had been worked out as early as *Insight,* in relation to the structural aspect of consciousness.[40]

36. *Method*, pp. 286–87. 37. *Verbum*, pp. 51–59.

38. *Method*, pp. 85–99.

39. Sebastian Moore, "For Bernard Lonergan," *Compass: A Jesuit Journal,* special issue honouring Bernard Lonergan, S.J., 1904–1984 (March, 1985), p. 9.

40. *Insight*, pp. 596–98. See also *Method* (pp. 47–52) on "The Structure of the Human

That values have dates does not, however, account for the present crisis of the human good. It does mean that values have to be created, handed on, and learned; but in more stable times or in periods of more gradual change the learning may well keep pace with the changes. What underlies the crisis of the human good in our day is the extraordinary rapidity of the changes that have been introduced pell mell into our way of life. The upward way of development enjoys a luxurious growth, like that of vegetation in the rain forests of tropical lands, and takes on as many exotic forms. The downward way of development has not had time to adapt to the new situation or to bring the moderating influence of a valid tradition into union with the critical spirit of the times, so that together they might create a new and viable set of values. Time, of course, inexorably passes; or, if you prefer, is eventually given. More serious is the lack of a philosophy, in the broad sense that Newman would give the term, to provide the consolation we need in time of crisis and to forge the instrument of mind and heart, the new organon, that would enable us to deal with it. Meanwhile there is failure, chaos, catastrophe.

Let me put this in a parable, for a certain great Teacher, we are told, taught always in parables, and we do well at times to imitate, as best we can, that dominical practice. The present parable is about two lands and two peoples, each with its own problem. The problem of land one and people one is that they have no memory; they have phenomenal inventive power but remember nothing. Today they learn to spear fish with a stick, but they wake up tomorrow in complete forgetfulness of the day before, and must start all over again. Being geniuses for invention they are not especially bothered by this—until one day someone invents a nuclear bomb and, having no tradition to guide them in its use, they allow it to destroy them. The problem of land two and people two is not lack of memory; they have excellent memories. You might even say that this constitutes their problem: their memories are so good that they cannot get away from their past or do anything creative. Once by chance they captured a warrior from a neighboring nation that had the bow and arrow. Adopting this weapon as their own, they lived happily with it for many years—until one day their neighbors invaded their land with muskets and destroyed them.

There is little need to explain the parable. We ourselves, the human race, are those two peoples combined into one, with our double need for the winds of creative change and for the ballast of moderating memory. Not much need either, I think, to dwell on the significance,

---

Good." Not that the two accounts agree in every respect (a question too complex to take up here), but that in each case there is a concern for structure.

for the present crisis of the human good, of Bernard Lonergan's legacy of ideas, judgments and values. His analysis, twenty years ago, of the crisis in which we still labor ran as follows:

Classical culture cannot be jettisoned without being replaced; and what replaces it, cannot but run counter to classical expectations. There is bound to be formed a solid right that is determined to live in a world that no longer exists. There is bound to be formed a scattered left, captivated by now this, now that new development, exploring now this and now that new possibility. But what will count is a perhaps not numerous center, big enough to be at home in both the old and the new, painstaking enough to work out one by one the transitions to be made, strong enough to refuse half-measures and insist on complete solutions even though it has to wait.[41]

Lonergan's own period of waiting was not just passive but one of unremitting labor to work out the transitions that have to be effected. May those of us to whom it falls to carry on his work, to explore and expand its implications, may we too wait actively and energetically, exploring what the span of mortal life forced him to leave undone, expanding what stands potentially within the framework of his thinking.

41. *Collection,* pp. 266–67.

21

The Life of the Unborn: Notions from Bernard Lonergan*

The "termination" of so many young lives—in the United States alone, a million and a half each year—lives that would otherwise have issued in the birth of children, members of the human race, must be traumatic for those immediately involved: the lawyers and moralists who deal with the legal and ethical aspects; the pastors who help the troubled to form their consciences and to be true to their responsibilities; above all the persons who are co-creators with God of this young life, the ones on whom the decision, whichever it is, will weigh most heavily, the potential parents.

The decisions taken in this area are not just traumatic for those immediately involved; they raise a question of conscience for everyone, even for those who work in the remoter areas of academe, and we must all respond to that question. We must do so now, for those millions of lives are being terminated now, and we may not shirk our present responsibilities until such time as we have answers for all the questions that occur to us. It is not just the right to life that is at stake, but very great and fundamental values over a wide range, values formed in our history, handed on in our traditions, enshrined in our laws, shared by a community. In the breakdown of community, and the challenging of ancient values, in a situation where the understanding that might assure consensus is lacking, we must form our consciences as best we can on short-range and *ad hoc* criteria, and fall back on authority when intrinsic reasons and long-range principles fail us.

Those, however, who work in those remoter areas of academe that I mentioned have a further obligation: to work toward the long-term understanding that is essential to a peaceful solution of the issues. In this they have the paradigm of a principle laid down and a pattern traced centuries ago by Thomas Aquinas. Asked once whether we should settle disputes by authority or by reason, he answered that, when it is a question of truth in theology, one has recourse to authority. Not

*Previously unpublished. Dated May, 1986.

so when it is a question of understanding; then one must go to the heart of the matter, using our powers of reasoning. Otherwise, he says, students may subscribe to the truth being taught, but lacking understanding they will go away with empty minds.[1]

In the area under discussion the need for understanding is urgent. The need, of course, is always there, even in regard to the truth that is revealed by God, the most sacred articles of our faith. We can individually bow to authority, set aside the ideas that would question it, and suppress the views that would contradict it. But we cannot count on the human race as a whole to submit in this way. As Newman said on the most fundamental Catholic doctrine, that of the Trinity: "it was impossible to go on using words [those of the baptismal formula] without an insight into their meaning."[2] Now what applies to revealed truth applies also and *a fortiori* to the truth we must gain in struggle and achievement, and it applies *par excellence* and with great urgency to truth in the field of human conduct. There is a helpful witness to that in the decision Bernard Lonergan made in his last years, to devote his remaining time and energy to the study of economics—on the ground that our moral theology had been issuing in this field precepts based on a quite inadequate economic science. Moral theology, I think he would have said, can no more do without a valid economics than systematic theology can do without a valid philosophy.

All this is relevant to what I wish to attempt in this essay. My field of work is located in the remoter areas of academe, but I cannot be indifferent either to those millions of lives being terminated annually, or the other millions who must make decisions on the life of the unborn. Next, the influence of Thomas Aquinas and of his position on understanding and authority has given me a lifelong and basic orientation. Then, thirdly, there is the influence that has been most direct and potent, that of Lonergan; the example of his pastoral interest in economics validates for me the impulse to take up the present question, and to try to contribute something, not indeed to the whole range of issues involved, but to the one quite limited task of understanding the life of the unborn.

That does not mean at all that I will try to do here what Lonergan has done in economics. His efforts were deployed on two levels: that of an underlying philosophy of humankind and human history, with notions of human intentionality and human intersubjectivity, of human development and human institutions, etc.; and the level proper to eco-

---

1. *Quodlibetum IV*, q. 9, a. 3: "Utrum magister determinando quaestiones theologicas debeat uti ratione, vel auctoritate."

2. John Henry Newman, *Tracts Theological and Ecclesiastical* (London: Longmans, Green, 1924 [1874]), p. 152.

nomics, with its specific ideas and principles. My contribution in the field of the life sciences will be confined to the level of an underlying philosophy. It will not then by itself give an understanding of the life of the unborn, much less suffice for an ethics in regard to the unborn. But I would maintain that the life sciences and ethics need the level of philosophy for a perspective on what they are doing.

One more remark on the relation of this essay to Lonergan. It is not just method and procedures that I will owe to him, but the content of the essay as well. But, since the ideas to be adduced belong more to the class he would call heuristic, that is, directing investigation rather than defining results, I will follow his usage and speak of them as notions. As heuristic, they will not come to any conclusions about the life of the unborn in respect to its specific quality; nevertheless, I hope that those engaged in the life sciences will find them helpful, especially those familiar with Lonergan's work. To the latter I would say that my contribution is neither interpretation nor development of Lonergan. I simply bring together three loca in his writings that at present lie apart, that brought together in sequence and unity may throw a revealing light on the life of the unborn. They deal respectively (1) with soul as the intelligible component of living matter, (2) with finality as the immanent intelligibility of developing material reality, and (3) with self-mediation as the route taken by an organism to reach its developed state.

1. Soul as Intelligible

I turn first to work that Lonergan did forty years ago in the context of his theology. His particular question need not concern us here, but its elaboration took him deep into Thomist cognitional theory, where he dealt with the role of understanding in forming our concepts, and with the reality of that component of material beings which is grasped through understanding. In illustration he had recourse to an example of the keenest present interest: the intelligible component of living things—that which we call "soul."[3]

The word, of course, has taken on connotations that are many and various, and not all of them valid or happy. But we can leave most of them aside in dealing with the Aristotelian notion. Soul here is a perfectly straightforward object of scientific study. It is not, however, a distinct material element of reality; but neither is it a submerged meta-

---

3. Publication began in *Theological Studies* 7 (1946) and continued into 10 (1949). The articles were later collected and published in book form as *Verbum: Word and Idea in Aquinas* (Notre Dame: University of Notre Dame, 1967). Reference will be made to this volume.

physical element in the sense of something beyond apprehension, much less of a ghost in a machine. To look for the soul is not to search in a dark room for a black object that does not exist. It is rather to do what every scientist continually aims at doing, discovering the intelligibility of the material object being investigated. Now that intelligibility is the object of understanding, and soul is simply a special case of the intelligible, whether we deal with the intelligibility of vegetative life in the plant, of sensitive life in the animal, or of rational life in the human being. If the scientist discovers an intelligible element unifying the data provided by the material entity we call human, that scientist has discovered the human soul. I quote:

Aristotle's basic thesis was the objective reality of what is known by understanding. . . . When, then, Aristotle calls the soul a *logos*, he is stating his highly original position, not indeed with the full accuracy which his thought alone made possible, but in a generic fashion which suited his immediate purpose; and it is that generic issue that remains the capital issue, for the denial of soul today is really the denial of the intelligible, the denial that understanding, knowing a cause, is knowing anything real.[4]

The simple conclusion I would draw from this position is that the issue in regard to human soul does not regard something distinct and separate, but exactly the contrary: it regards a unity-identity-whole.[5] So

4. *Verbum*, pp. 20–21. Note that soul, or universally the formal cause, is the *directly* intelligible component; other components of material reality are intelligible in and through the form.

Some traditional scholastic distinctions will illuminate Lonergan's use of the word "component." As a first approximation, there are "parts" of matter, as when one divides a pie. There are the somewhat different material "parts" of a living body, as when one considers hands, feet, etc. And there are the logical "parts" of a definition, as when one defines "man" as a "rational [specific difference] animal [genus]." But when we speak of soul as form we are talking about the "components" that scholastic philosophy names "potency," "form," and "act." This is a use of the word "component" that is very different from that which equates it with a material "part" or even a logical "part." The components in question now are a unity corresponding to the unity of the process by which we know them. That is, just as there are three levels of cognitional activity—experiencing, understanding, and affirming—that make up a single knowing, so also the contents of the knowing make up a single known, and the reality known is a unity. We do not know a first being by experiencing, a second by understanding, and a third by affirming.

To come to the present application, we are speaking of a scientific explanation of living things. A scientific explanation is a theory verified in instances. As verified, it refers to the component called "act"; as theory, it refers to the component called "form"; as instantiated, it refers to the component called "potency." Thus a human being is a unity: as existing in act, as informed by soul, as "this" being at this point in space-time. What is important to grasp here is this: soul is not a submerged metaphysical entity in the sense of a black object in a dark room. It is the real component known in scientific explanation, the intelligible form of what we see, hear, touch, in this instance of flesh and bones. It is in this sense that "soul" is a component. (On all this, see *Insight: A Study of Human Understanding*, pp. 431–34.)

5. See *Insight*, esp. ch. 8, "Things"; e.g., p. 248: "Thus, the thing is the basic synthetic

that we would not establish the existence of a human soul by finding some distinct entity or element, but then neither do we falsify the affirmation of that existence by not finding some distinct entity or element. This much can be said, I think, without elaborating a cognitional theory or an epistemology or a metaphysics; no doubt all these are ultimately involved, but scientists may feel, justly enough, that these areas not only lie outside their terms of reference, but are not needed for valid science. I would agree that our spontaneously operative cognitional dynamism, our natural epistemology, and our latent metaphysics will serve us quite well in the field of science; but it can hardly harm our investigations to have a more accurate notion of what we are looking for, or not looking for.

11. Finality as the Intelligible Factor in Development

Our second locus is found in *Insight*, Lonergan's independent cognitional theory and philosophy, published some ten years after his work on Aquinas. The discussion still has to do with intelligibility, so this point is in series with the previous one, but specifically now with the intelligibility of development. The progress from the Thomist studies is therefore from the intelligibility of an entity that could be conceived somewhat statically to the intelligibility of a developing entity in its development, that is, we have moved to the law of growth of material things—in particular of that material thing which is a human body.

The key word here becomes "finality," but it should be noted at once, for the avoidance of much misunderstanding, that finality is not the final causality of the Scholastics; that was an extrinsic cause, but Lonergan's finality, denoting an immanent intelligibility, would pertain to an intrinsic cause, just as much as does the *logos* which Aristotle discovered in material reality. Nor is finality to be *imagined*, as though it were some very thin, very strong towline pulling the material reality

---

construct of scientific thought and development. It embraces in a concrete unity a totality of spatially and temporally distinct data." It is central form that grounds this unity; in the present case, the human soul. Perhaps it will help toward an understanding of these ideas to quote a paragraph from Lonergan's chapter, "Things":

"Now the notion of a thing is grounded in an insight that grasps, not relations between data, but a unity, identity, whole in data; and this unity is grasped, not by considering data from any abstractive viewpoint, but by taking them in their concrete individuality and in the totality of their aspects. For if the reader will turn his mind to any object he names a thing, he will find that object to be a unity to which belongs every aspect of every datum within the unity. Thus, the dog, Fido, is a unity and to Fido is ascribed a totality of data whether of colour or shape, sound or odour, feeling or movement. Moreover, from this grasp of unity in a concrete totality of data there follow the various characteristics of things" (*Insight*, p. 246).

into the future, or a jet engine somewhere within the body. Finality, then, does not pertain to fancy but to fact, to the present reality of this particular body, but to that reality as intelligible, and specifically to its development as intelligible.

What then is finality? It is the dynamic aspect of the real. It is not merely dynamism but directed dynamism. The direction does not, in the most general case, come from a determinate form toward which it is pointed, for generically the dynamism has the indeterminacy of Thomist prime matter, and is a feature of the whole material universe. Nevertheless, it is not nothing. Neither is it directionless; but the direction is that of the law of effective probability. Finality is "an immanent intelligibility operating through the effective probability of possibility."[6]

Thus far, finality as a dynamic aspect conceived with the generality of Thomist prime matter. But that is only the start of the story. With the realization of initial possibilities, the dynamic aspect does not vanish, the developing reality does not cease its onward and upward drive; on the contrary it is open to, and propelled toward, higher and higher integrations. But—and this point will become crucial for the life of the unborn—the higher the integration is, the less dependence there is on that substratum of potency (the "coincidental manifold") which is subject to the law of effective probability. Thus we find that in the organism, in the psyche, and in intelligence, there is an independence of those lower quantities that are so important for probabilities. So Lonergan remarks, in a kind of *reductio ad absurdum,* that "the meaning of one's dreams is not a function of one's weight, and one's ability in mathematics does not vary with one's height."[7]

What does all this mean for our topic? It was written around thirty-five years ago and, though it was illustrated through organic, as well as psychic and intellectual development, and has therefore a broad application, it was not meant specifically as a philosophy of developing life in the unborn. Nevertheless, as a study of genetic method at the most basic level, it will pertain to the development of embryo and fetus too, as it does to the development of child and adult. Its relevance, however, is rather that of a heuristic notion than that of a determinate idea. Hence Lonergan concludes his exposition with the remark: "It

6. *Insight,* p. 448. It is important to distinguish the probability that is effective in the physical world from the probability that is a quality of a judgment. The latter is an effort of the mind to reach truth, but unable to do so with certainty. The former is operational in the physical universe to bring about events—hence, *effective* probability. See *Insight,* pp. 67–68, 550.

7. Ibid., p. 463.

has all been, of course, very general. It is meant to be so. A heuristic structure is only the framework in which investigation is to introduce specific laws and particular facts."[8]

Methodologists, along with philosophers and theologians, would be out of their element in trying to determine those specific laws and particular facts. That does not mean they have nothing relevant to say; there is, in fact, a third and immensely important notion to be introduced now from the general area of method and philosophy.

III. Life as Self-Mediation

This third notion emerged a decade after Lonergan had finished writing *Insight,* when he became interested in the term "mediation" and worked out its meaning for lectures in the summer of 1963 at Gonzaga University in Spokane and Thomas More Institute in Montreal. At the latter institution the lecture was entitled "The Mediation of Christ in Prayer," and it was under this title that the Spokane and Montreal materials were recently collated and published.[9] But the philosophical part can be studied quite independently of its application to the prayer of Christ; it proceeds, in typical Lonergan fashion, through the notions of "Mediation in General" (pp. 1–4), "Mutual Mediation: The Functional Whole" (pp. 4–6), "Self-Mediation" (pp. 6–12), to come to "Mutual Self-Mediation" (pp. 12–14). Our interest is in "Self-Mediation," which divides into subsections on "Living" (pp. 6–8), "Consciousness" (pp. 8–9), and "Self-Consciousness" (pp. 9–12). Sooner or later Lonergan's views on consciousness should be applied to the data we have on consciousness in the unborn, but that would mean a whole new study, so for economy of presentation I restrict present discussion to the self-mediation we find generically in the living organism.

An obvious starting point is the distinction between machines and organisms: "Both . . . are functional wholes; but machines are made while organisms grow." Lonergan proceeds to the explanation of this growth: "The growth of an organism is a self-mediation. The organism originates itself by giving rise to physical parts within itself. Such growth is a process of division. . . ." Then, linking this notion with our second section above, he adds: "The process of division is governed by a finality."[10]

We shall presently notice the extent to which finality governs the division, and is operative in the developing life of the organism, but

8. Ibid., p. 478.
9. *Method: Journal of Lonergan Studies* 2/1 (March, 1984), pp. 1–20.
10. Ibid., p. 6.

meanwhile it will be worth our while to fill in some details in the description of self-mediation. Consider then the following lines:

At any stage of its growth the organism is alive at that stage and preparing later stages. As alive at that stage, it is a set of functional parts in a functional whole. There are different centers of immediacy, with the centers giving the whole all the properties of each of the centers. But as moving from one stage to another it will exhibit transitional developments, useful for a time but later disappearing. It is extremely useful for the infant, for example, to be able to feed at the breast, but it is just a transitional development. On the other hand, moving from one stage to another the organism will exhibit anticipatory developments that have no great utility at the given stage but are extremely useful or essential later on. For example, the size of the child's brain is out of proportion to the rest of its body, but the brain does not increase in bulk the way the rest of the body does. In other words, there is something more than mutual mediation to the organism. There is the structuring which regards both functioning at the moment *and* future functioning.[11]

Let us return to the finality that governs the division of cells. As the reader will expect, the resulting growth is much more than a matter of mere increase in size; there is a process of specialization or differentiation, and this process "involves the creation and exploitation of entirely new possibilities." But the finality of the developing organism is not exhausted even by the process of specialization. We come then to the notion that is the most immediately relevant one I have found in Lonergan to the life of the unborn.

The organism lives, it has a reality that is superior to the whole business of cells and their differentiation and specialization. This living is quite different in kind from the living of the single cells or the multitude of single cells. It is the living of the whole organism. A higher set of functions emerges on the renewable substratum and develops and sustains itself, as it were, on a higher level ... The *telos* is the self-developing and self-sustaining functional whole that develops through the development and functions through the functioning of its parts.[12]

In this passage we have an epitome of what Lonergan has added to Aristotle and Aquinas on the concept of the soul. Soul, they would agree, is the directly intelligible component of the living thing. But in this material universe things develop according to laws that neither Aristotle nor Aquinas would have been able to formulate in detail, laws which Lonergan was able to pin down through his notion of immanent finality. Finality, however, if Lonergan is right, operates quite differently in living and non-living things, and among living things quite differently in the lower and the higher forms of life. In the higher forms, self-mediation more and more replaces the indeterminacy of the merely

11. Ibid., pp. 6–7.   12. Ibid., p. 7.

potential and even the law of effective probability. The Aristotelian concept of the soul as *logos* is now found to have unsuspected possibilities; it not only unifies the data in their static reality but governs and unifies as well the whole process of development from the beginning.

We have to ask science to determine whether or not self-mediation operates in this way, as we have to ask science to determine "specific laws and particular facts" in every area of the life sciences. Nonetheless, we are entitled to explain, from the side of a philosophy, and to ask science to understand, just what the question is that is being asked. There is a parallel here with the point made earlier in regard to soul: if we are looking for a distinct material element, or for a submerged metaphysical entity, or maybe for a ghost in a machine, we will only conclude that soul does not exist; but if we grasp the role of understanding in apprehending reality, and arrive also at an understanding of a unity-identity-whole that centers all the correlations science studies in things, then we may well conclude to the existence of "soul," however unhappy we may consider the term itself. Similarly, if in our search for finality we look for that tow-rope leading reality into the future, we will regard it as a myth exploded long ago by methodical science; but if we look instead for the intelligibility of development, as a scientific account of phenomena that were treated in the infancy of the science as chance variation, then we are at least open to the possibility of discovering finality in the material universe. To come, then, to the present aspect of the question, if we think of self-mediation as the life-science equivalent of lifting oneself by one's bootstraps, we will hardly be bothered even to look for it; but if we understand it as the intelligibility of a structuring that is dynamic, that dynamically brings to realization what lies within the potency of the dynamism, then we may or may not find it, but at least we have not ruled it out of court in advance by a misunderstanding of the question.

There is an illuminating analogy here with the dynamism of human knowing. The latter operates consciously, and we are abstracting here from the conscious; nevertheless, it is in order to notice the self-assembling pattern in the more familiar field of human knowing, and through that analogy obtain some understanding of the less familiar organic field. Human knowing then involves many distinct activities, none of which by itself may be called human knowing. It is the combination, under the influence of a dynamic structure, that constitutes human knowing. But the combination is self-assembling.

Experience stimulates inquiry, and inquiry is intelligence bringing itself to act; it leads from experience through imagination to insight, and from insight to the concepts that combine in single objects both what has been grasped by insight and what in experience or imagination is relevant to the insight. In turn, concepts stimulate reflection, and reflection is the conscious exigence of rationality; it marshals the evidence and weighs it either to judge or else to doubt and so renew inquiry.[13]

Through this analogy, maybe, those of us who are not experts in the field can gain some understanding of the way an organism "develops through the development and functions through the functioning of its parts."

Nevertheless, it is not analogous but proper understanding that we seek, and such understanding is the province of those who collect and classify and study the data of the life sciences. Will they be helped by the foregoing notions? That is for them to say. I only hope that they will not speak prematurely on the matter, without considering the teamwork that a combination of heuristic notions with determinate data and concepts may make possible; without asking, in their quest for understanding, how understanding works and thereby come to some methodical and very fruitful insights into what they are doing.[14]

13. *Collection: Papers by Bernard Lonergan*, p. 223.

14. On the other side, I have to ask myself whether these ideas, so sketchily traced, will contribute anything to understanding the life of the unborn in its specific quality. I have no answer to that question, but the gravity of the situation leads me to offer my study for publication in the hope, or at least on the chance, that it may help; it is a situation in which we must all do what we can, however futile the effort may turn out to be.

In any case, I have to thank Edward Sheridan, Bela Somfai, and Michael Stogre, for reading my essay and providing very helpful critiques.

22

The Church as Learner: Two Crises, One *Kairos*[*]

There are two parts to this talk. The first part takes us up to the colon in the title: the Church as learner, therefore. After the colon, the second part, in which there will be subdivisions: two crises, one *kairos*.

1. The Church as Learner

The first part looks simple. It *is* simple, but not quite as simple as it looks. The complexity shows up if we ask—and press a little—the question: To which do we give priority in the Church, to teaching or to learning? My thesis will be that learning has the priority. At first glance that seems fairly commonplace. Certainly it is the unanimous position in regard to the divine source of our learning: everyone, from pope to peasant, would agree that we learn from God, and only when we have first learned are we able to teach. But even in regard to created sources of faith and knowledge, it seems evident enough that we are learners first and teachers only in second place. Again, everyone from pope to peasant must learn from sources, sources that are given us precisely that we may learn from them. What do we do when a question arises on faith or morals? We turn to tradition, scripture, creeds, councils, to learn the answer there first, and then—if it is our vocation—to teach it to others.

But now let us press the matter a little. Suppose we put our original question to the sources themselves, and ask in that context whether teaching or learning has the priority. Some will answer, teaching, and they will do so with unshakeable certitude. For a kind of fundamentalist mind, the buck stops there: there is an original teaching, and it has

[*]A lecture given at the opening of the Lonergan Center at Boston College on 23 October 1986 and, in revised form, at the fifth annual Lonergan Colloquium, Regis College, Toronto, on 4 December 1986. Previously published (in its earlier form) as " 'The Role of a Catholic University in the Modern World'—An Update," in *Communicating a Dangerous Memory: Soundings in Political Theology,* ed. F. Lawrence. Supplementary issue of *Lonergan Workshop* 6 (Atlanta: Scholars Press, 1987), pp. 1–16.

absolute priority. In that case, for the Church as a whole, it is not learning but teaching that has the priority. It may well be that for individual members of the Church learning always comes first, but that is only a limited and relative priority: limited to us, or some of us, and relative to an original situation where things are different. In that original situation, and therefore for the Church as a whole, teaching has priority, a priority attached primarily to sources given us by God, and secondarily to the magisterium also given us by God to interpret the sources.

Well, that is exactly where the question of this paper begins. Where the unquestioning mind comes to rest, that is just where we wish to raise a question. Early tradition is our teacher, granted; and that teaching has priority for us. But did early tradition first have to learn? If so, how? Scripture also is our teacher, as it has been through many centuries. But did scripture first have to learn? If so, how? Creeds and councils teach; do they also learn? Similarly, the magisterium interprets and teaches; does it first need to learn? And again, and always, if so, how?

It should be clear by now, but maybe it is better to be explicit on the matter, that by learning I do not mean simply accepting a doctrine from someone else on that someone's authority. Learning in this paper means following the ordinary cognitional processes, whether in the realm of nature or the realm of grace. It means asking questions on matters of which we are ignorant; forming an idea of a possible answer, indeed forming several ideas of different possible answers; weighing the pros and cons of the several alternative ideas; finally, coming to a judgment, and being able to say "I've learned something." It is in this sense that I ask whether tradition learned before it taught, whether scripture learned, whether councils, creeds, and magisterium learned. It is a meaning poles apart from the fundamentalist view of, say, inspiration, in which the inspired author is like a musical instrument, passive in the hands of the divine music-maker.

My thesis, it now appears, is not quite commonplace. To all the questions in my list, insofar as they are questions about fact, the answer is: yes, there is a learning first, always a learning first. Tradition learns, in this sense of course that those handing on tradition learn. Scripture also learns, in the sense that scriptural writers do. Creeds and councils learn, or their authors do, before they teach. And, finally, the magisterium learns; that is, those authorized to exercise the magisterium learn.

So my thesis affirms an absolute priority of learning over teaching in the Church, even with regard to the sources, divinely created and divinely given, of our faith. The sources are sources that have learned. I don't deny the divine prerogative of using the seer as musicians use their instruments, but I don't think God made us with human minds and human hearts in order to treat us like dumb materials. The ordinary course of events is different. Here, once you leave the omniscient God and divine wisdom you are in a learning universe, and dealing with a learning Church, where learning has the absolute priority. So I am not talking about a division of people in the present Church, a division between those who teach and those who learn. I am talking about a division of functions: the function of learning and the function of teaching. Further, the functions belong to the whole Church, so that the whole Church has to learn before it can teach. How Church members then divide into teachers and learners, that is a second question, with its own topicality, but it is not the question I am dealing with.

To illustrate my thesis, let me give you two examples; they will make my point better than a dozen explanations. Take first our Christian freedom from the Mosaic law. When teaching is assumed to have priority, we will say that scripture teaches this freedom: there it is in black and white in the New Testament. But when learning is assumed to have priority, we have to ask how scripture learned it, and we might study chapters 10 and 11 of Acts, where we read of the vision Peter had of the great sheet let down from heaven with all kinds of animals held in the Mosaic law to be unclean; there we would find some indication of the process Peter went through in learning this truth and so give a concrete meaning to the abstract phrase "scripture or at least tradition learns," and to the principle "scripture and tradition learn before they teach."

It is true Peter had more than ordinary help from God in his vision. But the point is, it was not help that set aside the ordinary learning process; it was the kind of help that on the contrary stimulated the learning process, providing an image in which the insight might occur to Peter. Still it may be that you are not yet ready to yield the point. You may wish to fall back on a prior teaching. Peter, you may say, did indeed learn before he taught in this matter, but that does not establish the absolute priority of learning in the Church, for the Church as a whole may have got it from others who did not have to learn the way Peter did: Paul, for example, got it by revelation in a simple acceptance from on high that did not involve learning in the present sense of the word. Maybe he did, but we notice that the first letter we have of Paul, 1 Thessalonians, says next to nothing about this great truth, while Romans, written five or six years later, is full of it. Unless we postulate a new revelation in the interval, hence repeated ready-made revelations given to Paul at need and out of the blue, revelations which make learning in our sense superfluous, we are forced again to ask how Paul learned it, and to face the question of principle more generally: Does learning have priority in the very sources of our Christian doctrine?

There is, of course, a great deal of obscurity in regard to Christian origins and the emergence of what we now call sources. Much clearer is the course of events when we turn to conciliar history. So let us take for a second example the divinity of the only-begotten, in the sense in which we proclaim that doctrine now in liturgy and catechism. When the question of an original learning is not raised, and teaching is tacitly assumed to have priority, we still say that we, or the present Church, learned this truth from the Council of Nicea. But when it is granted that the priority may belong to learning, we have to ask where Nicea learned it; then we find ourselves studying a two-hundred-year period of learning, from Theophilus of Antioch through Tertullian and Origen to Dionysius of Rome and Arius, a period culminating in the definition of Nicea, in which the 318 bishops gave expression to what the Church had spent two centuries learning.

Let us now take a third case, but third only in the sense that we study it in third place, not in the sense that it is another example in series with the two examples already seen. It is in fact the paradigm case, the one pattern for any example whatever that we may consider of Christian learning. Jesus, we know, advanced in wisdom and age. He learned obedience from the things he suffered. He strove to the very end to learn the divine will, ready always to do it, but asking whether there was not another way than the one the Father seemed to have chosen. Indeed, he asked questions of others too, not all of them rhetorical surely, some of them presumably in order to learn the answers. And we observe him learning with surprise matters that came to his attention during his public ministry.

To affirm then that we are a learning Church is simply to affirm our Christian discipleship, a pattern of life that in this as in other matters is modeled on Jesus of Nazareth. We do indeed belong to a learning Church, and our learning Church had a learning founder. There should be no more than a momentary hesitation in making so simple an affirmation.

But why should there be even a momentary hesitation? It is because we have laid so much stress on the teaching Church—and this not as a function related to and integrated with a learning function, but as an office belonging to certain people—that we have not attended to the learning function, though it is primary in regard to the Church as a whole and in relation to the totality of our cognitional procedures. Thus, we are like a bird that has one wing hugely overdeveloped, while the other, through lack of exercise, has been allowed to atrophy: we can hardly take flight on wings of eagles in that condition. Or we are like a biologist friend of mine who spent long hours squinting with one eye through a microscope—so I remember the story—with the result that he almost lost the use of his other eye. That, I submit, is the situation in the Church today. We have concentrated almost exclusively on the teaching office; we have not seen our learning function as a Church problem, or studied its implications, or developed its criteria, or assumed responsibly the tasks it imposes. We cannot correct that imbalance overnight, any more than we can restore atrophied muscles in a day's exercise, but there should not be more than that momentary hesitation I mentioned in accepting the basic orientation, beginning to attend to the data, and studying ways and means to perfect our learning role.

11. Two Crises, One *Kairos*

We come now to the second and longer part of my paper, and to a question that I earlier raised but did not pursue. The question I raised and did pursue, if only briefly, was one of fact: Is it a fact that learning is primary, so that even our teachers learn? Is it a fact that tradition learns, that scripture learns, that creeds and councils learn? I did not delay on that question. I think we have only to attend to our learning founder and to the long history of a Church that has been continually learning, and we will have little difficulty with the fact.

But besides the question of fact, there are the what and why and how questions for understanding: What is the learning process, why should there be a need of learning in the Church, how do we relate any new learning we achieve to what we received as handed down and so believed in advance? These are really just different ways of putting the one general question for understanding, and to them all we have to add the particular question of why the general question is raised in our time and does not seem to have troubled our ancestors so much.

There is an immense field here for study, and perhaps the simplest way to enter it in a brief lecture is to take that added particular question of what is going on in our time. That is, maybe in an analysis of what world and Church and theology have been up to in modern times, we can throw light on the underlying questions and reach the same goal to which speculative questions would lead us more directly. My analysis then of the present situation will be as follows: there have been two quite distinct crises in modern times, occasioned by two quite distinct learning experiences, but due more basically to our reluctance in each case to learn, so that, in a famous phrase from *Insight,* the Church arrives on the scene "always . . . a little breathlessly and a little late," in other words, in a state of crisis.[1]

The first crisis I will call the crisis of scholarship. It began some three centuries ago, it came to a peak about the turn of our century, and it has been slowly fading as we slowly learn the lesson that history has been slowly teaching us. The second crisis I will call the crisis of *aggiornamento*. It began about a hundred years ago, it emerged as a distinct problem in the sixties of this century, in my view it has not yet peaked, and it constitutes the really serious crisis today. Those are the headings of the analysis I will presently sketch, but I will propose also something of a solution and, since this event is billed as a Lonergan colloquium, you will not be surprised if I turn to him for help in our twofold crisis. I will suggest then that his two phases of theology meet the two crises quite directly in a one-to-one correspondence: the phase of mediating theology meeting the crisis of scholarship, and the phase of mediated theology meeting the crisis of *aggiornamento*.

1. The Crisis of Scholarship

A simple and convenient way to introduce the crisis of scholarship is to ask what happened in Catholic academe after the Middle Ages. (I'm dealing, you notice, with the Roman Catholic Church—not, I hope, in any partisan spirit, but just because it's the church I'm better acquainted with.) The Medieval universities, then, were thoroughly Catholic, and they were in the vanguard of intellectual progress. Today's Catholic universities, we are forced to admit, are condemned on either one or the other of these points: the university world regards them as intellectual laggards but, if they try to emerge into the twentieth century and reverse the judgment of the university world, then the Church condemns them for failing to be Catholic. It's a no-win situation. So what happened since the Middle Ages?

One thing that happened, very obviously, was the work of positive scholars, of people like Richard Simon, Leopold von Ranke, and John Henry Newman, where by Newman I mean the Newman of the essay on the development of doctrine. (I take these names out of the history books, without pretending to be an expert on any of them, not even on Newman; but their place in the history of ideas is clear enough, and I can safely rely on the common estimate of their work and role.) People like these then were a new vanguard, the vanguard of that area of learning which Lonergan characterizes as the area of scholarship: research to collect the materials, study of their meaning in interpretation,

1. *Insight: A Study of Human Understanding*, p. 733.

judgment of what was going forward to write the history of thought. We might think of Ranke as standing for archival research, of Simon as standing for scriptural interpretation, of Newman as standing for the history of ideas. But we do so only by appropriation, and for a convenient mnemonic; just as we appropriate creation to God the Father, though all three divine persons are active in creation, so the trinity of scholars in our example engage, all three, in research, as they engage, all three also, in interpretation and history.

Now their work occurred in the modern university, or at least in the context of the modern university, and could hardly have occurred outside that context. But it did not occur in the context of the Catholic university. Ranke was a professor in the University of Berlin; Newman wrote his essay as an Anglican, though one on the way to Rome; Simon was a Catholic and a member of the Oratory, but his work got him expelled from that body—he had denied that Moses wrote the five books that begin our Bible, the Pentateuch.

Simon provides a particularly good illustration of the way the crisis of scholarship arose. It was not a matter of faith that Moses had written the Pentateuch: it was simply an unexamined supposition. But unexamined suppositions were so interwoven with beliefs, and the conditions of scholarship were so little known, and so little distinguished from those of doctrine or those of systematic theology, that to deny Mosaic authorship of the Pentateuch seemed subversive of the faith at its very source. Here then is a first-class example of what I am calling the crisis of scholarship.

Another good illustration is provided by Newman's *Rambler* article of 1859. Newman had studied the role of the laity in the Arian crisis and found it a stabilizing factor in a time of considerable wavering. This got him into enormous trouble, gaining him the reputation in Rome, Coulson tells us, "of being the most dangerous man in England," resulting also in having "a formal accusation of heresy preferred against him by the Bishop of Newport."[2]

Today the crisis of scholarship is at least partly over, though partly it is with us still. It is over with regard to various particular items of erudition and the legitimacy of scholarly procedures in their regard: in these particular cases we have slowly learned our lesson. Thus, we no longer hold that Moses wrote the Pentateuch, and we know why we should take that position. We no longer defend the genuinity of the Johannine comma,[3] and we are able, on grounds of textual criticism,

2. John Coulson, p. 2 of his introduction to John Henry Newman, *On Consulting the Faithful in Matters of Doctrine* (New York: Sheed & Ward, 1961 [1859]).

3. The Johannine comma is a short passage on the three who give witness in heaven: the Father, the Word, and the Holy Spirit. It was interpolated into the text of 1 John (at 5:7) around the year 800.

to justify its exclusion from the New Testament: it was simply not part of John's letter. Likewise, we no longer claim that Athanasius wrote the creed which for centuries we called Athanasian, and we are able to show on acceptable historical grounds that it is to be located after Augustine.

But the crisis of scholarship will never be fully over, as long as we have no clear notion of what scholarship is, cannot relate it to the foundations of our faith, or distinguish it from doctrines, systematic theology, and communications. That is, as long as we lack an integral picture, one that distinguishes and relates research, interpretation, and history among themselves, as a mediating unit of theology, and locates them within the total academic enterprise in relation to the mediated phase which culminates in communications. Until that happens, we will fight an ongoing series of battles; we may win them all, but we will remain in a continual state of war.

This is where I believe Lonergan's view of theology is helpful. His first phase, the one he calls mediating, deals especially with the scholarly disciplines. His analysis enables us to set them in relation to the second phase where faith and doctrines and preaching are involved—of that in a moment—but it also helps us put some order in scholarship itself, to see research, interpretation, and history (or the work of Ranke, Simon, and Newman) as all of a piece, as integral parts of one whole area, that of what in the past was known as positive theology. Thus, insofar as scholars are doing research, they have the limited but legitimate objective of collecting data which will be submitted to further questions, but questions on another level. On that next level scholars ask the meaning of the data and, insofar as they do, they have the limited but legitimate objective of studying ideas and providing materials for a third level of questions. On this third level they ask what was going forward: they have the still limited but legitimate objective of writing history. Their history in turn prepares for the next step: a dialectic that studies the horizons within which the earlier Church worked and expressed its faith, that enables scholars therefore to relate earlier horizons to their own, and the faith of the earlier Church to theirs.

In this way the whole business of scholarship comes into perspective. We can call on Tischendorf[4] and his colleagues to determine what texts belong in the New Testament. We can call on the exegetes to tell us what a term like "Son of God" meant in Mark, what it meant in Matthew, what it meant in John, what it meant in Paul. We can call on historians to study what went forward from Paul to Mark, from Mark to Matthew and John, as we can learn from Newman what went on in

---

4. Constantin von Tischendorf (1815–1874) was a New Testament textual critic; among his achievements was the discovery of the Codex Sinaiticus.

laity and episcopacy during the Arian crisis of the fourth century. A great deal of this kind of activity and exercise of scholarship can be had without directly affecting our own faith, for it is theology in what Lonergan calls indirect discourse: what Mark, what Origen, what Nicea said. Of course, if Mark and Nicea were found to contradict one another, and scholars were to regard both as normative for their faith, then there would be a problem; but that kind of problem in the abstract is hypothetical, if made concrete it will often be a pseudoproblem, and a sense of development and history will keep scholars from creating pseudoproblems where there are no real ones.

2. The Crisis of Aggiornamento

The time comes when scholars, if they are also believers, must stand up and be counted, move from indirect to direct discourse, and declare what they themselves hold. Whether or not a certain text belongs in John, whether or not "Son of God" means the same in Mark and in Nicea, whether or not Eusebius of Cesarea kept the Catholic faith—all these questions are studied by scholars in indirect discourse. But what do the scholars themselves hold? If our responsibilities were fulfilled simply by repeating what scripture or the councils said—what Mark and Matthew said, or Luke and John, Nicea and Trent and Vatican I— then positive theology would be the end of the matter. Once scholarship had done its work and determined what the sources really taught, there would be no further problems, and no further work beyond reconciling any apparent contradictions in the sources. But our responsibilities are not fulfilled by simply repeating the sources, and further problems do arise—as the fellow learned who wrapped his talent carefully and cautiously in a package, and kept it ready to hand back on his master's return.

It is not enough then to keep the talent wrapped up, to guard the deposit carefully and faithfully. Not to develop the deposit is actually to fail to guard it carefully, to fail to be good and faithful stewards. And it is to precipitate another crisis, a crisis of a new kind which I will call that of *aggiornamento*. I settled on this word for lack of a better one, after groping through my vocabulary, trying several others, and discarding them for one reason or another: for example, the crisis of creativity or of the creative leap, the crisis of modernity, of relevance, of *actualité*.[5] That list will at least help explain what I'm getting at, and

---

5. In "'The Role of a Catholic University in the Modern World'—an Update," I spoke of this second crisis as the crisis of creativity. But that makes creativity pertain too exclusively to the second phase of theology (I am grateful to Robert M. Doran for pointing this out), whereas all understanding is creative, and understanding pertains to both phases.

a little history will add further clarity. There is the rather grudging recognition long ago by Vincent of Lerins that there must be some measure of development of doctrine. Newman made this a topic in theology, but attended more to past development than to ongoing and future phases. The latter idea becomes explicit with Leo XIII and *Aeterni patris;* he coined the phrase "vetera novis augere et perficere": cherish the old, yes, but also add to it and improve upon it. But Leo was not really pushing the *nova*—the context rather is a condemnation of innovators who abandon the old and run after the new, instead, Leo says, of saving the old and adding the new.[6]

A significant step, showing a new attitude toward the *nova* by a person in authority, was taken by the lovable and still not fully appreciated Pope John XXIII. We tend to think of him as rather absentmindedly one day deciding to call a council, whereas there is mounting evidence that this was a much more deliberate move, that John had a far shrewder sense of the needs of the times than he sometimes gets credit for. At any rate, as he set forth the purpose of the council he had called, he went considerably beyond Leo in approval of the *nova.* True, he spoke at length on fidelity to the tradition—no one will fault him for that—but then he went on to describe the specific purpose of the council. It had not been called, he said, to reiterate old dogmas—we don't need a council for that. No, we need a council because we need to move forward, to go beyond the past.[7] Pope John, it seems, had written his speech in his own Italian, but delivered it at the council in the Latin of his curial staff. Later that year, he had an opportunity to repeat his message, this time in his own words, and we discover that his call for forward progress is not well conveyed by the colorless Latin of "iter pergentes"; what he wants, he says in the more colorful Italian, is "un balzo innanzi"—a leap forward. This does not sound much like a mere rephrasing of past dogmas, or a simple use of resources already traditional. In fact, it is not anything so simple; the forward leap involves study, he says, of modern methods of research and of the literary forms of modern thought.[8]

Now, what Pope John pictured in his vivid metaphor of a leap forward, and sketched very rapidly in his reference to modernity, that is exactly what Lonergan tries to work out, methodically and in detail, in his second phase, that of mediated theology. "There are," he writes,

6. *Acta sanctae sedis* 12 (1879), pp. 97–115; see p. 111.

7. *Acta apostolicae sedis* 54 (1962), pp. 785–95; see pp. 791–92. English translation in *The Documents of Vatican II,* ed. W. Abbott & J. Gallagher (New York: Guild, 1966), pp. 710–19; see p. 715.

8. *Acta apostolicae sedis* 55 (1963), pp. 43–45; see p. 44. For the relation of this talk of Pope John to his speech at the opening of the council, see Joseph Komonchak, "What's Happening to Doctrine?" *Commonweal* 112 (1985), pp. 456–59, and his letter, p. 654.

"real problems of communication in the twentieth century, and they are not solved by preaching to ancient Antioch, Corinth, or Rome."[9] To speak to the people of Toronto today in 1986 instead of to the people of Corinth in the year 56, to dialogue with the universities we are part of here and now, instead of with the Areopagus philosophers of the first century, that is the task of theology today. For theology mediates between a religion and a culture,[10] cultures show an infinite variety, and any given culture undergoes transformations with time. The scholarship of research, interpretation, and history studies the various forms from Palestine to Vatican II in which our one religion was inculturated; the crucible of dialectic studies the horizons of each inculturation to get behind the formulations and reach their underlying intention; then, in relation to that intention, the second phase of theology takes a creative leap into our own times, our own places, our own cultures. We are no longer dealing simply with what Mark or Luke or Nicea said, though we will hold, and express in our way, the same faith they held and expressed in theirs; we are dealing rather with that creative formulation of the faith needed if we are to speak to our contemporaries, or indeed if we are to have clarity about our faith for ourselves, and make the ancient dogmas nourishing for our spirits.

So we come to the four specialties of the second phase: foundations, doctrines, systematics, and communications. You won't expect me to go through them one by one, but I wish to make two points to relate this second phase to the present crisis in the Church.

The first point regards the magnitude of the work before us. Lonergan had a clear grasp of this right from his student days to his maturity. Enormous tasks lie ahead, he kept telling us. And I think I would do both him and my audience a disservice, did I not draw attention to the massive character of the reconstruction needed in our time. But I cannot go into details now; what might be useful, if we are to seek help in Lonergan, is to clear away some misunderstandings of his approach. For one thing it is not isolationist; the interiority that is studied in foundations as the source of our categories in doctrines is a shared interiority, not the musings of a hermit theologian; we commit a serious oversight if we neglect the role of community in the second phase of theology, for it supplies the dynamism for this phase as the intentionality of human spirit supplies it for the first. For another thing, the coherence systematics aims at involves a relation to the whole universe, and to the whole network of sciences by which we try to dominate that universe and organize our contemporary experience; it is another se-

---

9 *Method in Theology*, p. 140.

10. Ibid., p. xi; more exactly, "A theology mediates between a cultural matrix and the significance and role of a religion in that matrix."

rious oversight to think that the theologian deals only with texts and monuments from the past, and to neglect present experience; Lonergan's way involves a massive engagement with the experience of modernity, at deeper levels perhaps than most people notice. For a third thing, the final specialty of communications is not a one-way street; it is another oversight to think of the theologian as pontificating; there is feedback, an important factor affecting the formulation of our doctrines and consequently of our systematics.

The other point I would make is more particular. It regards doctrines, and a question that reactionaries find especially sticky: What is the relation between the old dogmas and the new formulations? It is sticky, of course, for all of us who have a high esteem for the role of truth, but perhaps it is possible to put truth into a wider context than the reactionaries do, and see it in the integral intentionality of human spirit and the existential subject, as well as in the creative fidelity of a believing community. For even in that context the believer and theologian "still needs truth . . ." and "The truth he needs is still the truth attained in accord with the exigences of rational consciousness."[11] So how does truth fare in the *aggiornamento* of Lonergan's *Method*? What, if anything, happens to it in the second phase of theology?

The first thing to realize is that the answer is not simple. It is not simple, because the situation is not simple. The situation includes the eternal God at one pole and a changing human history at the other, a human history which changes so profoundly that a moral precept, say, against charging interest on money, can be right today and wrong tomorrow. Contingencies nearest to God will share the divine stability, like the three contingencies of what God has done in sending the only-begotten, what God is still doing in giving the Spirit, what God will do among us in the eschaton. But even here, though the realities are fixed in themselves, our conception of them is subject to change; thus, Thomas Aquinas did not add a single attribute to the divinity, or a single person to the Trinity, but he certainly left our conception of God different from what he found it when he began to do theology. Contingencies farthest from the stable center will of course be subject to change in both ways: in themselves, and in our conception of them.

Against that background we can attempt an answer to the question of truth and *aggiornamento*. First, there will be a purifying of the tradition: at one time certain Christians received baptism for their dead, and Paul doesn't seem to condemn it (1 Cor 15:29); but we regard it as a mistake, and purified our practice of this element before it became a tradition. Then there is the question of unexamined suppositions to be

11. Ibid., p. 242.

examined for acceptance or rejection: we have seen the Church examine what was previously unexamined in regard to the Mosaic authorship of the Pentateuch. Thirdly, there is the reversal of trends heading toward becoming a dogma: thus, there seems to have been an almost universal expectation in the young Church of an early return of the Lord, but this expectation was reversed by events, or—you might say in this case—by a non-event, as expectations of an immediate return were disappointed. Fourthly, there is the removal of barnacles or excrescences that become attached to valid belief, or get formulated with a dogma though they are not part of the dogma—as may have happened with many of Aristotle's categories when Medieval theology entered conciliar definitions.

There are dozens of other happenings in the cognitional world, but only now and then, tiny and unafraid, there emerges an element of truth. I borrow a phrase here from Chesterton, in some disregard of the setting in which he used it. In his poem about Lepanto, he saw Don John emerging from a European silence:

> In that enormous silence, tiny and unafraid,
>   Comes up along a winding road, the noise of the Crusade.

I would say, in my adaptation: in that enormous racket of what goes on in the Church's mind, tiny and unafraid, comes up along a winding road—the road remains winding—the still, small voice of truth. We ourselves individually walk about with heads full of a hodgepodge: dreams, images, affects, questions, opinions, assumptions, suspicions, guesses, beliefs, memories—a whole hodgepodge with here and there a truth which we hardly recognize as such. Well, the Church walks through history listening to an even greater internal bedlam, occasionally stopping to define a truth, and not always able to provide on demand a statement of what precisely pertains to the truth element and what to the hodgepodge.

And, nevertheless, there is truth, and in Lonergan's position it is sacred. So, again, what happens to it when we pass from first phase to second in theology? What does Pope John's creative leap forward do to it? What happens is that the truth is transposed. I suggest two approaches to the meaning of that word, "transposed." One is through music where, I'm told, a melody is transposed from key to key. Another approach, more familiar to me, is through mathematics; here the formula that locates a point in space is transposed from one set of coordinates to another, the point remaining in the same "absolute" location while the set of coordinates, and so the formula, becomes quite different.

More concrete than either of these approaches is the actual history of a doctrine and its transposition. Thus, the Palestinian way of thinking about Christ was in terms of the Son of Man found in the book of Daniel, and when they would elaborate a theology of Christ they did it in terms of their angelology. But this was transposed by Paul and others, when the Church moved into the Hellenic world, into a way of presenting Christ that would have more meaning for the Greeks. Then the formulas of Paul and John were transposed in their turn to give the Nicene formula of one who is *homoousios* with the Father. Now, in 1986, one of our most urgent tasks is a further transposition of our doctrine on Christ, one that will take the leap forward from Nicea in a creative restatement for our world of what God has done in sending the only-begotten.

3. *Conclusion: The One* Kairos

I have suggested the integral approach of Lonergan as a way to recognize, distinguish, relate, and deal with what seem to me two distinct and serious crises of our time. But to put those two crises into the wider history of our race, and see the present as one *kairos,* as a time of providential opportunity, I turn to Karl Jaspers and a remark of his that keeps haunting me. "For more than a hundred years," he says, "it has been gradually realized that the history of scores of centuries is drawing to a close."[12] It was Jaspers who located the axial period of history in that time, roughly from 800 to 200 before Christ, when all through the world civilizations there was a giant stirring that put human thinking, human self-understanding, and human history on a new course. Well, I believe Jaspers is saying now, in this brief remark I quoted, that we are going through another axial period: the history of scores of centuries is drawing to a close—and the history of new ways of being human, latent in the giant stirring of our times, is about to begin.

That says exactly the two things needed to unify my talk. First, that our distance from our origins is going to be immeasurably greater than it was, with a consequent urgency in the need to put our house of scholarship in order; and, secondly, that our need of a creative restatement of our faith is going to be immeasurably greater than it was, with a consequent urgency to take that leap forward which Leo XIII would rather hesitantly allow, which John XXIII expressly called for, which some theologians in the Church, twisting and turning in their resistance, keep striving to prevent, a leap forward that I think Lonergan would help us achieve through the method he labored to introduce into theology.

12. Karl Jaspers, *Philosophy and the World: Selected Essays and Lectures,* tr. E. B. Ashton (Chicago: Regnery, 1963), p. 22.

I speak of urgency, but it is not an urgency measured in terms of hours, days, or even years. When the history of scores of centuries draws to a close, it does not do so overnight. An axial period is not just a decade. Further, in the history of ideas there is no *Blitzkrieg:* it took centuries for the *Summa* of Thomas Aquinas to replace the *Sentences* of Peter Lombard in the schools; it will take time for theologians to rethink the specialty that is theirs, and take time for the Church to reformulate her faith, after the new axial period we live in. But by the same token, disaster in the world of ideas, as contrasted with the world of nuclear fission, cannot occur overnight. In other words, we have time—years, decades, centuries, if God gives continuance to human history—to work at our task.

No, the urgency I speak of is measured by the responsibility we have to speak. There are those, Lonergan says, who are determined to live in a world that no longer exists.[13] They speak with a dogmatism rarely equalled in our history, condemning change, distributing labels of heresy, scenting danger everywhere. In my view they are themselves the greatest danger in the Church today, and I feel the same responsibility to speak out against them that they feel in the task they have assumed of saving the Church. But, if I want to move forward with Pope Leo, with Pope John, in the direction in which I think the Church is being led by the Spirit, I want to do so with fidelity too to the past and to the truth that the same Spirit has guaranteed. Further I need to locate myself in the ongoing work, and I know very well that I need those with a vision that ranges more widely and penetrates more deeply than mine, to show me how to join fidelity and creativity; or, failing that, those with a wisdom that will help us meanwhile to weather the crisis, until someone with vision is given us. Whether or not Lonergan's vision will prove to be an enduring help is a question we must finally leave to history to decide, but meanwhile you may at least find it worth while to ponder a little what he has to offer.

13. *Collection: Papers by Bernard Lonergan, S.J.*, p. 267.

EPILOGUE

Homily at the Funeral of Bernard Lonergan*

Dear friends, my brothers and sisters in the family of God.

With this holy eucharist, and with these ceremonies, we take our leave of one who was with us throughout a long life, and was related to us in many ways. To some he was an older brother, an uncle or cousin. To others a fellow-religious in the family of Ignatius. To still others, a teacher among his students, or a colleague in the world of academe and in the Christian intellectual apostolate. In each of these capacities, and in the diverse ways they suggest, he was very dear to us.

With all of us, with all God's people, he was present in another way that lies at a deeper level: as one of the great human family, with its joys and its hopes, its griefs and its anxieties; as one who came forth, as we all did, from the hand of God, whose life on earth, as for each of us, was a pilgrimage; as one to whom the word has now come, as come it will to us all, that his pilgrimage is over, his days on earth completed, his time fulfilled, his life arrived at its term.

To speak in this way is to suppose that life has a unity. It is to suppose a plan, an ordered course, not just the aimless wandering between a chance beginning and a meaningless end. And so we ask, naturally and with human affection, as relatives and friends, but reverently too, as before God and the mystery of human life, we ask what made the unity in the life of Fr. Bernard Lonergan. We know that three times at least in his life he was very near to death, only to be saved, from a human viewpoint, by major surgery, but from a higher viewpoint, surely by the will of a mysterious providence. And so we wonder about that mysterious providence. Why did not God say, sixty-five or twenty or even two years ago: This life has reached its term? Why only now did God see it as whole and complete?

There is, of course, the familiar metaphor of the course of the day: the morning, noon and evening of life, as forming a natural unity.

*Given at Our Lady of Lourdes Church, Toronto, on 29 November 1984. Previously published in *Compass: A Jesuit Journal*, special issue honouring Bernard Lonergan, S.J., 1904–1984 (March, 1985), pp. 21–23, and by Regis College, Toronto, in 1985.

Personally I find a great appeal in that metaphor as applied to the life of Bernard Lonergan. I think of the morning of his life in the valley of the Lièvre. I remember Lampman's poem about morning on that river

> Like a vapor from the forge
> Of a giant somewhere hid,
> Out of hearing of the clang
> Of his hammer, skirts of mist
> Slowly up the woody gorge
> Lift and hang.

And I picture the boy Bernard, as his eyes dwell on those morning mists, and his young mind opens already to receive the wonder of the world. I think of the noontide of his life, when he was at the height of his power in Italy. I remember his own words on the work of Aquinas, that it "shines as unmistakably as the sun on the noonday summer hills of Italy."[1] And I think of his own magnificent intelligence, shedding new light during those years on old questions, uttering wisdom with the clarity of the Italian skies. I think finally of the evening of his life, spent at Regis College and Boston College, when his great masterpieces were done. And again I find a fitting description of this in his own lines on "the serenity of old age, when perforce the self becomes selfless as the field of enjoyment contracts to joy in the enjoyment of others, in the romping vitality of grandchildren."[2] His grandchildren, to be sure, were his students rather than flesh and blood descendants, and some of us are rather greyhaired to be grandchildren; but it is true that in his declining years he could rest more quietly, knowing that his work was going forward, carried on with boundless energy by a numerous spiritual progeny.

It is a pleasing picture, especially for one who has lived out his allotted fourscore years. And yet I know that it is too idyllic—too idyllic by far for a life that did not in fact run smoothly from morning mists through noonday sun to the shadows of evening. And what alone is important, such a life does not bear much resemblance to the life of him who is our way and our truth, of him whose way and truth Bernard strove throughout life to understand, so that, in the Ignatian prayer, he might love him more and follow him better.

Is it not then to that very source itself, to him who is our way and our truth, that we should turn for enlightenment on our question? He who was sent into the world to be our leader, who invited us to follow him and become his disciples, he seemed to provide, in his great prayer at the last supper, the perfect summation of what a human life on earth

---

1. *Verbum: Word and Idea in Aquinas,* p. 219.
2. *Collection: Papers by Bernard Lonergan, S.J.,* p. 37.

should be: "I have glorified thee on earth by completing the work which thou gavest me to do" (Jn 17:4). Have we here the clue we seek to the unity of life, of life for anyone? Is it not to be found in completing the work that God has given each of us to do? And must we not study the work that Bernard was given to do, and thus discover the unity of his life, and the mystery of the providence that spared him so long?

If so, we will look, first and most naturally, at his sixty-year career in seminary and university; for there, without a shadow of doubt, his particular vocation lay. We will examine his teaching and lecturing, his published and unpublished writings, the recorded consultations and interviews and responses to questions, his studies of his beloved Thomas Aquinas and his own independent philosophy and theology, the method he created to push forward the boundaries of knowledge in these and other fields—the whole great accumulation of half a century of unremitting labor and productivity, the products of his mind, and not just of his mind, but of his mind and heart, works of beauty too and not just of arid argument.

Is this the place to find the clue we seek? Certainly it is an area we would gladly explore, those of us who are convinced of the importance of that productivity for Church and world. But maybe this is not the time, nor this the place, for that exploration. In any case are we quite sure that the meaning and unity of life is to be discovered there? Is it the works we produce externally, be they works of hand or voice, of mind or heart, is it these products that reveal the mind of God on the work given each one of us to do?

At least, they do not seem to tell the whole story. Too often the great lord of life and death cuts short work half done or only started. Sometimes we are listening to a symphony on the radio, and a glorious piece of music is moving to achieve its incomparable unity, when a hand reaches out to switch off the radio, and the music comes to a sudden end, broken off in mid course. Does not God sometimes seem to act that way with us?

Bernard Lonergan was spared so shattering an interruption of his work. But even he had to round off one great book before it was really finished, complete another in shorter form, pressured by ill-health and an uncertain life-span, leave a third only partly ready at his death. And if we go back to the divine model himself, we find that his work too, considered as a product, was not so obviously completed: a few uncomprehending disciples, squabbling among themselves at the last supper itself, and running to escape at the first sign of danger—does this adequately describe the work that God gave the only Son to accomplish?

Maybe we have been somewhat hasty in determining what the prayer at the last supper means; maybe there is something more to be said.

Indeed there is another aspect to the task set the Son of God, and I find it in the Letter to the Hebrews: "It was clearly fitting that God for whom and through whom all things exist should, in bringing many sons to glory, make the leader who delivers them perfect through sufferings" (2:10). And, again, "Son though he was, he learned obedience in the school of suffering, and, once perfected, became the source of eternal salvation for all who obey him" (5:8–9).

Here surely is a new insight on the work that Jesus was given to do: not now the calling of disciples, not the teaching of a doctrine, not the founding of a church; rather, a work that directly concerned himself. He was to learn obedience, he was to perfect himself, he was to make of himself what God would have him be. To be sure, it was in and through achievement of the work which is a product, that he was to perfect himself, and make of himself what he was to be—through his calling of the disciples and the founding of a church—but in the order that Hebrews reveals, first to perfect himself and then to bring many children to glory.

And now maybe we can see a little more clearly, and in relation to the life of our lord and only master, what the work was which Bernard Lonergan was given to do, and how the years of his life form a unity. I would like, in order to make this clearer still, to use here a pair of ideas from his own writings. I know that some of you loved Bernard without always understanding what he wrote. But, just because you loved him, I know also you would like to hear how he would explain what I have been trying to say. He would use a pair of Greek words, *poiêsis* and *praxis*. *Poiêsis* refers to the work we produce, the product. When a carpenter builds a house, or a musician composes a sonata, or an author writes a book—all that refers to *poiêsis*. But *praxis* lies behind all such production; it refers to our own conduct: our own deliberations and choices and decisions, our own responsible actions. There is a unity in the two: a carpenter does not build a house without making a deliberate choice, and we have no responsible action unless we do something. But it is *praxis* that makes us what we are, in what Bernard would call our existential decision: the decision of what we are to make of our lives, that is, what we are to make of ourselves. And, as what we make of ourselves is more important than any house we build, or music we compose, so in the very Son of God, as Hebrews says, it was of first importance that, Son though he was, he should learn obedience. From that the *poiêsis* would follow: the doctrine, the disciples, the Church.

It is here too that we must look for the pattern of Fr. Bernard's life. More and more, as I discover in never-ending study of his writings, as I reflect on his manner of life, especially in these recent years, more and more, it seems to me, it was this realization that guided him as he moved from the noontide of life to its evening. I think of a line that in its simple profundity speaks volumes to me, as I think it will to you. Writing of the good choices and actions that make us what we are, he calls them "the work of the free and responsible agent producing the first and only edition of himself."[3]

The "first and only edition of himself"—that is a book I and each one of us must write alone as we go through life, producing day by day a new paragraph, to achieve the first and only edition of myself. The empire of an Alexander, the plays of a Shakespeare, the music of a Beethoven—all testify to the great potential of the human race. But God could raise up from the stones of this church those who would provide the empire or the plays or the music that God's people need, or indeed the great works of Bernard Lonergan. There is only one person who can toil throughout life, who must toil throughout life, under God's grace, of course, to accomplish the work given me at birth to do, and, turning it over to God at the end, say, with my lord and master, "It is finished."

This is the work that Bernard Lonergan was about all his life, whether coursing down the rapids of the Lièvre with brothers Greg and Mark, or lecturing in Latin to six hundred and fifty students in the Gregorian University, or listening indulgently to the papers of his disciples at a Boston College Workshop, or—not least—accepting and enduring these last two years the gradual fading of his mental powers.

The one and only work that really mattered was the work of which he wrote last Monday morning the final paragraph, and turned it over to his maker for censorship and—we have not the slightest doubt—for divine approval.

3. *A Second Collection: Papers by Bernard J. F. Lonergan, S.J.,* p. 83.

The Writings of Frederick E. Crowe

1. *Conflict and Unification in Man: The Data in the Writings of St. Thomas Aquinas*. Doctoral dissertation. Rome: Gregorian University, 1953. Excerpts published by Gregorian University Press, 1953.

2. "Convention of the Catholic Theological Society of America." *Sciences ecclésiastiques* [later *Science et esprit*] 6 (1954), pp. 262–65.

3. "Universal Norms and the Concrete *operabile* in St. Thomas Aquinas." *Sciences ecclésiastiques* 7 (1955), pp. 115–49, 257–91.

4. "Devotion to the Holy Eucharist." *The Canadian Messenger of the Sacred Heart* 66 (1956), pp. 685–90.

5. "Index." In *Insight: A Study of Human Understanding*, by Bernard Lonergan. London: Longmans, Green; New York: Philosophical Library, 1957, pp. 749–85.

6. "The Origin and Scope of Bernard Lonergan's *Insight*." *Sciences ecclésiastiques* 9 (1957), pp. 263–95.

6a. "The Origin and Scope of Bernard Lonergan's *Insight*." In *Appropriating the Lonergan Idea*, by Frederick E. Crowe. Washington, DC: The Catholic University of America, 1989, pp. 13–30. (Reprint of pp. 263–79 of no. 6.)

7. "Pastoral Care in Large Cities." *The Canadian Messenger of the Sacred Heart* 68 (1958), pp. 277–83.

8. "Complacency and Concern in the Thought of St. Thomas." *Theological Studies* 20 (1959), pp. 1–39, 198–230, 343–95.

9. "Complacency and Concern." *Cross and Crown* 11 (1959), pp. 180–90.

10. "Reign of the Sacred Heart." *The Canadian Messenger of the Sacred Heart* 69/6 (June, 1959), pp. 4–6, 43.

11. "Review: *Experimental Knowledge of the Indwelling Trinity: An Historical Study of the Doctrine of St. Thomas*, by J. Dedek." *Theological Studies* 21 (1960), pp. 687–88.

12. "St. Thomas and the Isomorphism of Human Knowing and Its Proper Object." *Sciences ecclésiastiques* 13 (1961), pp. 167–90.

13. "How Inflexible is Catholic Dogma?" *Crosslight* 2/4 (Summer, 1961), pp. 14–26.

13a. "Development of Doctrine and the Ecumenical Problem." *Theological Studies* 23 (1962), pp. 27–46. (Reprint, with minor changes, of no. 13.)

14. "Review: *Les missions divines selon saint Augustin*, by J.-L. Maier." *Theological Studies* 22 (1961), pp. 476–78.

15. *The Most Holy Trinity*. Mimeographed notes. Toronto: Loyola Institute of Sacred Studies, 1962.

15a. *Il Dogma Trinitario*, tr. J. Navone. Rome: Gregorian University, n.d. (Italian translation of no. 15.)

16. "Review: *Structures et méthode dans la Somme théologique de saint Thomas d'Aquin*, by G. Lafont." *Theological Studies* 23 (1962), pp. 314–16.

17. "On the Method of Theology." *Theological Studies* 23 (1962), pp. 637–42.

18. Editor, *Spirit as Inquiry: Studies in Honor of Bernard Lonergan. Continuum* 2 (1964), pp. 301–552.

18a. Editor, *Spirit as Inquiry: Studies in Honor of Bernard Lonergan*. Chicago: St. Xavier College, 1964. (Reprint of no. 18.)

19. "Introduction." In *Spirit as Inquiry: Studies in Honor of Bernard Lonergan*, pp. 306–307.

20. "The Exigent Mind: Bernard Lonergan's Intellectualism." In *Spirit as Inquiry: Studies in Honor of Bernard Lonergan*, pp. 316–33.

21. "Bibliography of the Writings of Bernard Lonergan." In *Spirit as Inquiry: Studies in Honor of Bernard Lonergan*, pp. 543–49.

22. "A Birthday to Notice." *America* 111 (July–December 1964), pp. 804–805.

23. "Neither Jew nor Greek, but One Human Nature and Operation in All." *Philippine Studies* 13 (1965), pp. 546–71.

23a. "Neither Jew nor Greek, but One Human Nature and Operation in All." In *Appropriating the Lonergan Idea*, pp. 31–50. (Reprint of no. 23.)

24. *The Doctrine of the Most Holy Trinity*. Mimeographed notes. Toronto: Regis College, 1965.

25. "Development of Doctrine: Aid or Barrier to Christian Unity?" *Catholic Theological Society of America Proceedings* 21 (1966), pp. 1–20.

25a. "Kyoogi no Hatten: Kirisuto kyoo Itchi no Tasuke to naru ka," tr. M. Kooitchi. *Shingaku Digesto*, Natsu, 1968, pp. 49–56. (Digest, in Japanese translation, of no. 25.)

26. "Review: *The Second Vatican Council and the New Catholicism*, by G. Berkouwer." *Canadian Journal of Theology* 12 (1966), pp. 142–43.

27. "Review: *Salut et rédemption chez saint Thomas d'Aquin: L'Acte sauveur du Christ*, by B. Catão." *Theological Studies* 27 (1966), pp. 282–84.

28. "Full Communion with the Separated East." *The Canadian Messenger of the Sacred Heart* 76 (November, 1966), pp. 6, 8–9.

29. "Insight." *New Catholic Encyclopedia*, vol. 7 (1967), p. 545.

30. "Intuition." *New Catholic Encyclopedia*, vol. 7 (1967), pp. 598–600.

31. "Theological Terminology." *New Catholic Encyclopedia*, vol. 14 (1967), pp. 37–38.

32. "Understanding." *New Catholic Encyclopedia*, vol. 14 (1967), pp. 389–91.

33. With David Burrell, "Index." In *Verbum: Word and Idea in Aquinas*, by Bernard Lonergan. Notre Dame: University of Notre Dame, 1967, pp. 221–300.

34. Editor, *Collection: Papers by Bernard Lonergan, S.J.* New York: Herder and Herder; London: Darton, Longman & Todd, 1967.

35. "Introduction." In *Collection: Papers by Bernard Lonergan, S.J.*, pp. vii–xxxv.

35a. "The Growing Idea." In *Appropriating the Lonergan Idea*, pp. 3–12. (Reprint, with minor changes, of pp. viii–xix of no. 35.)

36. "Index." In *Collection: Papers by Bernard Lonergan, S.J.*, pp. 269–80.

37. "*Aggiornamento*: Eternal Truth in a Changing World." *The Canadian Messenger of the Sacred Heart* 77/2 (February, 1967), pp. 8–12.

38. "*Aggiornamento*: Changing Forms of Life and Worship." *The Canadian Messenger of the Sacred Heart* 77/3 (March, 1967), pp. 10–14.

39. "*Aggiornamento*: Do Dogmas Change?" *The Canadian Messenger of the Sacred Heart* 77/4 (April, 1967), pp. 18–22.

40. "*Aggiornamento*: Is There a New Morality?" *The Canadian Messenger of the Sacred Heart* 77/5 (May, 1967), pp. 18–23.

41. "*Aggiornamento:* The Church in the Modern World." *The Canadian Messenger of the Sacred Heart* 77/6 (June, 1967), pp. 18–23.

42. "*Aggiornamento:* The Wide World My Parish." *The Canadian Messenger of the Sacred Heart* 77/7-8 (July–August, 1967), pp. 8–11.

43. "*Aggiornamento:* The Church and the Churches." *The Canadian Messenger of the Sacred Heart* 77/9 (September, 1967), pp. 16–19.

44. "Your Questions." [Comments on questions submitted by readers of nos. 37–43.] *The Canadian Messenger of the Sacred Heart* 77/10 (October, 1967), p. 15; 77/11 (November, 1967), p. 17; 78/1 (January, 1968), pp. 14–15; 78/4 (April, 1968), p. 9; 78/5 (May, 1968), p. 15; 78/7–8 (July–August, 1968), p. 16; 78/9 (September, 1968), p. 14; 78/10 (October, 1968), p. 8.

45. "A Jesuit Makes a Pilgrimage to Martin Luther's Shrine." *The Toronto Daily Star,* 28 October 1967, p. 16.

46. "Bernard Lonergan." In *Modern Theologians, Christians and Jews,* ed. T. E. Bird. Notre Dame: University of Notre Dame, 1967, pp. 126–51.

47. "Christology and Contemporary Philosophy." *Commonweal* 87 (October, 1967–March, 1968), pp. 242–47.

47a. "Christology and Contemporary Philosophy." In *God, Jesus, and Spirit,* ed. D. Callahan. New York: Herder and Herder, 1969, pp. 137–52. (Reprint of no. 47.)

48. "Review: *Newman on Tradition,* by G. Biemer." *Theological Studies* 28 (1967), pp. 590–92.

49. "Fear, Hate and Sin at the German Wall." *The United Church Observer* 29/22 (15 February 1968), pp. 26–27.

50. "Sorrow and Hope at Bonhoeffer's Death Camp." *The United Church Observer* 30/3 (1 April 1968), pp. 25–26.

51. *A Time of Change: Guidelines for the Perplexed Catholic.* Milwaukee: Bruce, 1968. (Chs. 1–7 are reprints of nos. 37–43 respectively.)

52. "Christologies: How Up-to-Date is Yours?" *Theological Studies* 29 (1968), pp. 87–101.

53. "Review: *Bible et tradition chez Newman: Aux origines de la théorie du développement,* by J. Stern." *Theological Studies* 29 (1968), pp. 777–79.

54. "Development of Doctrine." *American Ecclesiastical Review* 159 (1968), pp. 233–47.

55. "Review: *Revelation and Theology,* by E. Schillebeeckx." *Theological Studies* 29 (1968), pp. 339–40.

56. "Salvation as Wholeness: Theological Background for an Ecumenical Programme." *Canadian Journal of Theology* 14 (1968), pp. 228–37.

57. "Review: *Revelation and Theology 2,* by E. Schillebeeckx." *Theological Studies* 29 (1968), pp. 779–81.

58. "Pull of the Future and Link with the Past: On the Need for Theological Method." *Continuum* 7 (1969), pp. 39–49.

59. "What Can Join Us to the Love of Christ?" *The Canadian Messenger of the Sacred Heart* 79/6 (June, 1969), pp. 1, 13–15.

60. "But is There a Fault in the Very Foundations?" *Continuum* 7 (1969), pp. 323–31.

61. "Dogma versus the Self-Correcting Process of Learning." *Theological Studies* 31 (1970), pp. 605–24.

61a. "Dogma versus the Self-Correcting Process of Learning." In *Foundations of Theology: Papers from the International Lonergan Congress 1970,* ed. P. McShane. Dublin: Gill and Macmillan, 1971, pp. 22–40. (Reprint of no. 61.)

62. "First International Lonergan Congress: A Report." *America* 122 (January–June 1970), pp. 452–53.

63. "The Conscience of the Theologian with Reference to the Encyclical." In *Conscience: Its Freedom and Limitations*, ed. W. C. Bier. New York: Fordham University, 1971, pp. 312–32.

63a. "The Responsibility of the Theologian, and the Learning Church." In *Appropriating the Lonergan Idea*, pp. 172–92. (Reprint, with minor changes, of no. 63.)

64. "Introduction." In *Grace and Freedom: Operative Grace in the Thought of St. Thomas Aquinas*, by Bernard Lonergan. London: Darton, Longman & Todd; New York: Herder and Herder, 1971, pp. ix–xi.

65. "Jerusalem at the Heart of Athens: The Christian University." *The Maroon & White* 19/7 (June, 1971), pp. 1–3.

65a. "Jerusalem at the Heart of Athens: The Christian University." In *Appropriating the Lonergan Idea*, pp. 163–71. (Reprint of no. 65.)

66. "Early Jottings on Bernard Lonergan's *Method in Theology*." *Science et esprit* 25 (1973), pp. 121–38.

67. Editor, assisted by Conn O'Donovan & Giovanni Sala, *The Early Latin Works of Bernard J. F. Lonergan*. Typescript, Regis edition. 4 vols. Toronto: Regis College, 1973.

68. "General Introduction." In *The Early Latin Works of Bernard J. F. Lonergan*, each vol., pp. ii–vii.

69. "Editor's Introduction." In *The Early Latin Works of Bernard J. F. Lonergan*. Vol. 1: *De notione sacrificii*, pp. ix–x.

70. "Editor's Introduction." In *The Early Latin Works of Bernard J. F. Lonergan*. Vol. 2: *De ente supernaturali*, pp. ix–xiii.

71. "Editor's Introduction." In *The Early Latin Works of Bernard J. F. Lonergan*. Vol. 3: *De scientia atque voluntate dei*, pp. ix–xii.

72. "Editor's Introduction." In *The Early Latin Works of Bernard J. F. Lonergan*. Vol. 4: *Analysis fidei*, pp. ix–x.

73. "Dogmatic Theology." *New Catholic Encyclopedia*, vol. 16 (supplement, 1974), pp. 132–33.

74. With Philip & Fiona McShane, "Index of Subjects." In *A Second Collection: Papers by Bernard J. F. Lonergan, S.J.* London: Darton, Longman & Todd, 1974, pp. 284–300.

75. "Eschaton and Worldly Mission in the Mind and Heart of Jesus." In *The Eschaton: A Community of Love*, ed. J. Papin. Villanova, PA: Villanova University, 1974 [c. 1971], pp. 105–44.

75a. *Escatologia e missione terrene in Gesù di Nazareth*, tr. G. Sala. Catania: Edizioni Paoline, 1976. (Italian translation of no. 75.)

75b. "Eschaton and Worldly Mission in the Mind and Heart of Jesus." In *Appropriating the Lonergan Idea*, pp. 193–234. (Reprint of no. 75.)

76. "The Mind of Jesus." *Communio: International Catholic Review* 1 (1974), pp. 365–84.

76a. "The Mind of Jesus." In *Le Christ hier, aujourd'hui et demain*, ed. R. Laflamme & M. Gervais. Québec: Laval University, 1976, pp. 143–56. (Reprint of no. 76.)

77. "The Power of the Scriptures: Attempt at Analysis." In *Word and Spirit: Essays in Honor of David Michael Stanley*, ed. J. Plevnik. Toronto: Regis College, 1975, pp. 323–47.

78. "A People of Serene Joy: Memories of an African Congress." *Annals of the Propagation of the Faith* 33/1 (February–March, 1976), pp. 4–7.

79. "Doctrines and Historicity in the Context of Lonergan's *Method:* A Review-Article." *Theological Studies* 38 (1977), pp. 115–24.

80. "An Exploration of Lonergan's New Notion of Value." *Science et esprit* 29 (1977), pp. 123–43.

80a. "An Exploration of Lonergan's New Notion of Value." *Lonergan Workshop* 3 (1982), pp. 1–24. (Reprint of no. 80.)

80b. "An Exploration of Lonergan's New Notion of Value." In *Appropriating the Lonergan Idea,* pp. 31–50. (Reprint of no. 80.)

81. *Theology of the Christian Word: A Study in History.* New York: Paulist Press, 1978.

82. "Dialectic and the Ignatian Spiritual Exercises." *Science et esprit* 30 (1978), pp. 111–27.

82a. "Dialectic and the Ignatian Spiritual Exercises." *Lonergan Workshop* 1 (1978), pp. 1–26. (Reprint of no. 82.)

82b. "Dialectic and the Ignatian Spiritual Exercises." In *Appropriating the Lonergan Idea,* pp. 235–51. (Reprint of no. 82.)

83. With Sara Butler, Anne Carr, Margaret Farley, & Edward Kilmartin, *A Report on the Status of Women in Church and Society: Considered in Light of the Question of Women's Ordination.* New York: The Catholic Theological Society of America, 1978.

84. "Review: *Newman and His Theological Method: A Guide for the Theologian Today,* by T. Norris." *Doctrine and Life* 29 (1978), pp. 391–92.

85. "Foundational Theology." *New Catholic Encyclopedia,* vol. 17 (supplement, 1979), pp. 235–37.

86. "Theology and the Past: Changing Views on the Sources." *Science et esprit* 31 (1979), pp. 21–32.

86a. "Theology and the Past: Changing Views on the Sources." In *Appropriating the Lonergan Idea,* pp. 252–64. (Reprint of no. 86.)

87. "Theology and the Future: Responsible Innovation." *Science et esprit* 31 (1979), pp. 147–57.

87a. "Theology and the Future: Responsible Innovation." In *Appropriating the Lonergan Idea,* pp. 265–76. (Reprint of no. 87.)

88. *Method in Theology: An Organon for Our Time.* The Pere Marquette Theology Lecture. Milwaukee: Marquette University, 1980.

89. *The Lonergan Enterprise.* Cambridge, MA: Cowley, 1980. (Ch. 1 is a reprint of no. 88.)

90. "Report on the Regis College Lonergan Center." *Lonergan Studies Newsletter* 1/2 (April, 1980), pp. 6–8.

91. "Birthday Celebrations." *News Letter: Upper Canada Province* 55/4 (May–June, 1980), pp. 5–6.

92. "'Interiority' Going Forward?" In *Dialogues in Celebration,* ed. C. M. Going. Montreal: Thomas More Institute, 1980, pp. 260–85.

93. "Bernard Lonergan's Thought on Ultimate Reality and Meaning." *Ultimate Reality and Meaning* 4 (1981), pp. 58–89.

93a. "Bernard Lonergan's Thought on Ultimate Reality and Meaning." In *Appropriating the Lonergan Idea,* pp. 71–105. (Reprint of no. 93.)

94. "*Creativity and Method:* Index to a Movement. A Review Article." *Science et esprit* 34 (1982), pp. 107–13.

95. "The Present State of the Lonergan Movement." *Lonergan Studies Newsletter* 3 (1982), pp. 9–10.

96. "Lonergan's Early Use of Analogy: A Research Note, with Reflections." *Method: Journal of Lonergan Studies* 1/1 (Spring, 1983), pp. 31–46.

97. "The Janus Problematic: Tradition versus Innovation." In *Tradition and Innovation: Faith and Consent. Essays by Jesuits from a Canadian Perspective,* ed. J. B. Gavin. Regina: Campion College, 1983, pp. 13–36.

97a. "The Janus Problematic: Tradition versus Innovation." In *Appropriating the Lonergan Idea,* pp. 277–96. (Reprint of no. 97.)

98. "Son and Spirit: Tension in the Divine Missions?" *Science et esprit* 35 (1983), pp. 153–69.

98a. "Son and Spirit: Tension in the Divine Missions?" *Lonergan Workshop* 5 (1985), pp. 1–21. (Reprint of no. 98.)

98b. "Son and Spirit: Tension in the Divine Missions?" In *Appropriating the Lonergan Idea,* pp. 297–314. (Reprint of no. 98.)

99. "Lonergan's Search for Foundations: The Early Years, 1940–1959." In *Searching for Cultural Foundations,* ed. P. McShane. Lanham, MD: University Press of America, 1984, pp. 113–39.

100. "The Human Mind and Ultimate Reality: A Lonerganian Comment on Dr. Leahy." *Ultimate Reality and Meaning* 7 (1984), pp. 67–74.

100a. "The Human Mind and Ultimate Reality." In *Appropriating the Lonergan Idea,* pp. 106–15. (Reprint of no. 100.)

101. "Transcendental Deduction: A Lonerganian Meaning and Use." *Method: Journal of Lonergan Studies* 2/1 (March, 1984), pp. 21–40.

102. Editor. *A Third Collection: Papers by Bernard Lonergan, S.J.* New York: Paulist Press; London: Geoffrey Chapman, 1985.

103. "Editor's Introduction." In *A Third Collection,* pp. 1–2.

104. "Index." In *A Third Collection,* pp. 251–56.

105. "Lonergan's Last Year." *Lonergan Studies Newsletter,* special commemorative issue (February, 1985), pp. 5–6.

106. "Reflections on Fr. Lonergan's Funeral and Burial." *Lonergan Studies Newsletter,* special commemorative issue (February, 1985), p. 7.

107. Co-editor, with Robert M. Doran, *Compass: A Jesuit Journal,* special issue honouring Bernard Lonergan, S.J., 1904–1984 (March, 1985).

108. "Collège de l'Immaculée-Conception: Where It All Began." *Compass: A Jesuit Journal,* special issue honouring Bernard Lonergan, S.J., 1904–1984 (March, 1985), p. 9.

108a. "Le Collège de l'Immaculée-Conception: où tout a commencé," tr. E. Richer. *Nouvelles de la Province du Canada-français* 4/4 (Avril, 1985), no pagination. (French translation of no. 108.)

109. "Homily, Funeral of Father Bernard Lonergan, S.J." *Compass: A Jesuit Journal,* special issue honouring Bernard Lonergan, S.J., 1904–1984 (March, 1985), pp. 21–23.

109a. *Homily, Funeral of Father Bernard Lonergan, S.J.* Toronto: Regis College, 1985. (Reprint of no. 109.)

109b. "Homily at the Funeral of Bernard Lonergan." In *Appropriating the Lonergan Idea,* pp. 385–90. (Reprint of no. 109.)

110. *Old Things and New: A Strategy for Education.* Supplementary issue of *Lonergan Workshop* 5. Atlanta: Scholars Press, 1985.

111. "A Note on the Prefaces of *Insight.*" *Method: Journal of Lonergan Studies* 3/1 (March, 1985), pp. 1–3.

112. Editor, "The Original Preface," by Bernard Lonergan. *Method: Journal of Lonergan Studies* 3/1 (March, 1985), pp. 3–7.

113. "Bernard J. F. Lonergan, S.J., 1904–1984." *Canadian Theological Society Newsletter* 5/1 (March, 1985), pp. 6–8.

114. *Son of God, Holy Spirit, and World Religions: The Contribution of Bernard Lonergan to the Wider Ecumenism.* Toronto: Regis College, 1985.

114a. "Son of God, Holy Spirit, and World Religions." In *Appropriating the Lonergan Idea*, pp. 324–43. (Reprint of no. 114.)

115. "Father Bernard J. F. Lonergan, S.J." *News Letter: Upper Canada Province* 60/3 (May–June, 1985), pp. 15–18.

116. "A Note on Lonergan's Dissertation and Its Introductory Pages." *Method: Journal of Lonergan Studies* 3/2 (October, 1985), pp. 1–8.

117. Editor, "The *Gratia operans* Dissertation: Preface and Introduction," by Bernard Lonergan. *Method: Journal of Lonergan Studies* 3/2 (October, 1985), pp. 9–49.

118. "Bernard Lonergan and Liberation Theology." In *The Third World and Bernard Lonergan: A Tribute to a Concerned Thinker*, ed. W. Ysaac. Manila: Cardinal Bea Institute, 1986, pp. 1–15.

118a. "Bernard Lonergan y la teología de la liberación." *Humanidades Anuario* (Universidad Iberoamericana) 8 (1984–85), pp. 11–23. (Spanish translation of no. 118.)

118b. "Bernard Lonergan and Liberation Theology." In *Appropriating the Lonergan Idea*, pp. 116–26. (Reprint of no. 118.)

119. "A Threefold *Kenôsis* of the Son of God." In *The Papin Gedenkschrift, Dimensions in the Human Religious Quest. Essays in Memory of Joseph Papin, Vol. I: Theological Dimensions*, ed. J. Armenti. Ann Arbor: University Microfilms International, 1986, pp. 54–64.

119a. "A Threefold *Kenôsis* of the Son of God." In *Appropriating the Lonergan Idea*, pp. 315–23. (Reprint of no. 119.)

120. "Bernard Lonergan as Pastoral Theologian." *Gregorianum* 67 (1986), pp. 451–70.

120a. "Bernard Lonergan as Pastoral Theologian." In *Appropriating the Lonergan Idea*, pp. 127–44. (Reprint of no. 120.)

121. "Graduation: End or Beginning?" *Christ the King Seminary News* 50/3 (Summer, 1986), pp. 2–4.

122. "Lonergan, Bernard." *The Encyclopedia of Religion*, ed. Mircea Eliade (1987), vol. 9, pp. 19–20.

123. "The Task of Interpreting Lonergan: A Preliminary to the Symposium." In *Religion and Culture: Essays in Honor of Bernard Lonergan, S.J.*, ed. T. P. Fallon & P. B. Riley. Albany: State University of New York, 1987, pp. 3–16.

123a. "The Task of Interpreting Lonergan." In *Appropriating the Lonergan Idea*, pp. 145–49. (Reprint of no. 123.)

124. "'The Role of a Catholic University in the Modern World'—An Update." In *Communicating a Dangerous Memory: Soundings in Political Theology*, ed. F. Lawrence. Supplementary issue of *Lonergan Workshop* 6. Atlanta: Scholars Press, 1987, pp. 1–16.

124a. "The Church as Learner: Two Crises: One *Kairos*." In *Appropriating the Lonergan Idea*, pp. 370–84. (Reprint, with revisions, of no. 124.)

125. "An Expansion of Lonergan's Notion of Value." *Lonergan Workshop* 7 (1987), pp. 35–37.

125a. "An Expansion of Lonergan's Notion of Value." In *Appropriating the Lonergan Idea*, pp. 344–59. (Reprint of no. 125.)

126. "The Life of the Unborn: Notions from Bernard Lonergan." In *Appropriating the Lonergan Idea*, pp. 360–69.

127. Co-editor, with Robert M. Doran, *Collected Works of Bernard Lonergan*. 22 vols. anticipated. Toronto: University of Toronto, 1988–.

128. "Preface." In *Appropriating the Lonergan Idea,* pp. xi–xii.

129. *Appropriating the Lonergan Idea,* ed. M. Vertin. Washington, DC: The Catholic University of America, 1989. (Collection comprising nos. 6a, 23a, 35a, 63a, 65a, 75b, 80b, 82b, 86a, 87a, 93a, 97a, 98b, 100a, 109b, 114a, 118b, 119a, 120a, 123a, 124a, 125a, 126, & 128.)

130. "From Kerygma to Inculturation: The Odyssey of Gospel Meaning." *Lonergan Workshop* (to appear).

131. "*Insight:* Genesis and Ongoing Context." *Lonergan Workshop* (to appear).

132. "Rethinking the Religious State: Categories from Lonergan." *Science et esprit* 40 (1988).

133. "Rethinking Moral Judgments: Categories from Lonergan." *Science et esprit* (to appear).

134. "Rethinking the Divine Three Among Us: Categories from Lonergan." *Science et esprit* (to appear).

Index